NATHAN BEDFORD FORREST

A Biography

By Jack Hurst

Vintage Civil War Library

VINTAGE BOOKS

A DIVISION OF RANDOM HOUSE, INC.

NEW YORK

First Vintage Civil War Library Edition,
March 1994

Copyright © 1993 by Jack Hurst
Maps copyright © 1993 by William J. Clipson

All rights reserved under International and Pan-American
Copyright Conventions. Published in the United States by Vintage Books,
a division of Random House, Inc., New York, and simultaneously in
Canada by Random House of Canada Limited, Toronto.
Originally published in hardcover by Alfred A. Knopf, Inc.,
New York, in 1993.

#B10 7-10-07

Grateful acknowledgment is made to the Massachusetts Commandery Military
Order of the Loyal Legion and the U.S. Army Military History Institute
for permission to reprint the frontispiece photograph.

Library of Congress Cataloging-in-Publication Data
Hurst, Jack.
Nathan Bedford Forrest: a biography/by Jack Hurst.—
1st Vintage Civil War library ed.
p.   cm.—(Vintage Civil War library)
Includes bibliographical references and index.
ISBN: 0-679-74830-X
1. Forrest, Nathan Bedford, 1821–1877. 2. Generals—United States—Biography.
3. Confederate States of America. Army—Biography. I. Title. II. Series.
E467.1.F72H87 1994
973.73'092—dc20
[B] 93-42200
CIP

Book design by Robert C. Olsson

Manufactured in the United States of America
10 9 8 7 6 5 4 3 2 1

To the memory of
Charles McKinley Hurst,
who in his much more diplomatic way
was a fighter too

CONTENTS

MAP OF
NATHAN BEDFORD FORREST'S
CIVIL WAR

BATTLE

NATHAN BEDFORD FORREST

Prologue

A DOZEN YEARS after the Civil War, the South overturned its outcome. Representatives of Ohio governor and former Union general Rutherford B. Hayes surrendered to former Confederates who had become United States senators and congressmen, and Hayes's emissaries agreed to restore to the South the complete home rule Confederate armies had lost in the rebellion quelled in 1865. In return, Southerners provided the thin margin that defeated Democrat Samuel J. Tilden and elected Hayes president. Bending their conservative-Democratic principles, they certified questionable Republican ballots in Louisiana and South Carolina and handed those states to Hayes, thereby deciding a deadlocked race by a single electoral vote and averting a threatened resumption of formal hostilities. Once installed as the nation's nineteenth chief executive, Hayes withdrew from Louisiana, South Carolina, and Florida the last occupation troops of Reconstruction. The Confederate South was left free virtually to reenslave that third of its people whom Abraham Lincoln had declared emancipated in 1863.

The twelve-year struggle following Robert E. Lee's surrender at Appomattox, Virginia, was in some ways as ugly as the four years of war had been: a guerrilla affair in which bands of unreconstructed rebels made night attacks in ghostly shrouds symbolizing the Confederate dead. Their methods, however, were anything but ghostly. Beating, whipping, and murdering, they drove from ballot boxes blacks and whites seeking—some sincerely, some otherwise—to further the fragile concept of racial equality. Before Hayes's surrender, these night riders already had recaptured most of the old Confederacy piecemeal. The political power in Virginia and Tennessee had been reclaimed in 1869, North Carolina and Alabama the following year, Georgia the year after that, Texas in 1873, Arkansas in 1874, and Mississippi in 1875. The Hayes "bargain," as it became known, returned the final three secession states—Florida, Louisiana, and South Carolina—to neo-Confederate control that would last most of another century.

While the ex-Confederates were anointing Hayes in Washington, the brief but pivotal leader of their clandestine war for Rebeldom's restoration was dying in Memphis, Tennessee. Impoverished, old before his time, his magnificent frame reduced to a gaunt shell of hardly a hundred pounds, fifty-five-year-old Nathan Bedford Forrest—fiercest and arguably most brilliant icon in the Confederate military pantheon—had accepted at last the Christian faith of his family's women and begun to sound repentant. A fellow Confederate general who saw him during this twilight of his strength found the once-demonic warrior possessing "the gentleness of expression, the voice and manner of a woman."[1]

"I am not the same man you . . . knew," he told a former military aide who hadn't seen him in years.[2]

Hardly. The man the former subordinate had known was the South's storied "Wizard of the Saddle"—an epic figure who, having risen from log cabin privation to wealth as an antebellum slave trader, became the only soldier South or North to join the military as a private and rise to the rank of lieutenant general. He was also the intrepid combatant who killed thirty Union soldiers hand to hand, had twenty-nine horses shot from beneath him, and was so feared by even his most warlike opponents that one of them, William T. Sherman himself, pronounced him a "devil" who should be "hunted down and killed if it costs 10,000 lives and bankrupts the [national] treasury." Lee, Sherman, and other leaders on both sides ultimately were quoted as declaring him the most remarkable soldier the war produced.[3]

A cavalryman, Forrest was little given to the foolhardiness common to mounted soldiers in his era. He often conserved manpower by using his force as a lightning infantry whose horses were employed to reach critical points at which to dismount and fight behind cover. Whether he was mounted or afoot, however, his aim always was ultimately offensive: to find the most advantageous positions from which to attack—over and over, often from several directions at once. When the enemy turned to flee, he sometimes pursued for days, still attacking. Like the men of Stonewall Jackson, except more personally, Forrest's soldiers feared him more than the enemy, and with good reason. Assaulting or shooting them with his own hands when they tried to run from battles, he compelled them to run in the opposite direction. His favorite military tactic was the charge, which he so trusted that he employed it even on a charging enemy rather than simply await assault.

Symbolizing his approach to life, the charge also was usually the best means of achieving one of his primary military goals. That goal, and his postwar description of it, became one of history's more renowned formulas for the successful conduct of warfare. His aim, he said, was to get to the critical position "first with the most men." That, however, was merely prefatory to his overall objective. Whereas Sherman famously defined war simply as "hell," Forrest's definition of it was more specific, refining organized combat to its awful essence. "War," he said, "means fightin', and fightin' means killin'."[4]

Albert T. Goodloe, meeting Forrest after the war aboard a steamboat, asked how he managed to win nearly all his battles despite almost invariably being severely outnumbered. The answer was that of a man who not only fought but thought. He said that most men regarded a battlefield "with horror and consternation" and that he therefore tried to make its initial appearance "as shocking to the enemy as . . . possibl[e]," hurling "his entire force against them in the fiercest and most warlike manner possible. He would thus overawe and demoralize . . . at the very start" and, "with unabated fury," continue the demoralization "by a constant repetition of blows . . . killing, capturing, and driving them with but little difficulty."[5]

Forrest had a low opinion of West Point dogma, particularly the maxim that a third or so of a commander's force should be held in reserve. In the battle of Sand Mountain, he even sent forward the quarter of his force which normally held the horses of the others, ordering the animals to be tied to bushes. "If we are whipped," he explained tersely to a skeptical subordinate, "we'll not need any horses."[6]

His unfailing fury was matched by a canny single-mindedness. His decisions under fire were generally quick and brilliant, as if he anticipated every battle development. Subordinates attributed this apparent prescience to cerebral bouts of "planning," during which he sat motionless, chin on chest, or paced outdoors in methodical circles. His concentration was so rapt at such times that during one such outdoor walk, after being repeatedly interrupted by someone attempting to start a conversation, he knocked the man unconscious with a single blow of his fist and continued circling, stepping over the prostrate form each time his route brought him back to that place. Throughout it all, he said nothing.[7]

His cunning extended far beyond the mere mechanics of fighting. He was, for example, one of the Civil War's most industrious gatherers and conservers of every military resource, from rifles to hogs. He also possessed a genius for spreading fear of himself among his enemies. From his camps he dispatched carefully instructed "stragglers" to disseminate inflated reports of his troop strength. Sometimes he even made elaborate shows of such strength for the benefit of captives, then permitted them to escape and spread their own, more believable exaggerations.

He fought to win, shrinking from nothing the prospect of victory appeared to require. Several times his demand for surrender warned opposing officers-in-charge that if capitulation was not swift, he would put their entire units "to the sword." A less specific threat of annihilation— "I cannot be responsible for the fate of your command"—preceded what is regarded as the supreme flaw in his military record. He has never been cleared of perpetrating the Fort Pillow Massacre, an 1864 atrocity whose exact details remain cloudy, but in which many black Union soldiers and a lesser number of white ones plainly were killed after attempting to surrender. The Fort Pillow Massacre is notable not only for its intrinsic ugliness but because it can be viewed as a prelude to other horrors. Two years after Appomattox, Forrest was reincarnated as grand wizard of the Ku Klux Klan. As the Klan's first national leader, he became the Lost Cause's avenging angel, galvanizing a loose collection of boyish secret social clubs into a reactionary instrument of terror still feared today.[8]

What sort of man did all this? By most accounts, two different ones: a soft-spoken gentleman of marked placidity and an overbearing bully of homicidal wrath. When rage overcame him, which always occurred in the face of challenge, his normally quiet voice rose to a shrill roar and his face and eyes filled with blood. At such moments, he appears to have been capable of virtually anything.

Reared in an area and era in which law was a luxury, Forrest grew accustomed to enforcing it himself. In an antebellum fight with several men in which his aged uncle was killed, he faced the attackers down alone with a gun and a knife and won. After the war, he invaded a cabin in which a black man was threatening to beat his often-abused wife; when Forrest intervened unarmed and the man turned on him with a knife, he grabbed the bully's own ax and killed him with a single blow of its handle.

During the war, the four major wounds he received included one inflicted by a Confederate subordinate whom he killed with his own hands in retaliation. Contemptuous of formal military training, he brooked little interference from better-educated officers. In late 1862 at Fort Donelson, he refused to be surrendered by an irresolute triumvirate of Confederate generals and instead led an escape by the fort's 3,500 cavalrymen. At Shiloh, he ignored orders to guard a tranquil creek and charged into the thick of the fight. A year later, he angrily quit the army of General Braxton Bragg by informing Bragg to his face that if their paths crossed again, "it will be at the peril of your life." His vanity and testy impatience with failure, along with his superiors' apparent jealousy and stupidity, squandered an extraordinary human instrument who might have changed the war's course on its decisive western front.[9]

Almost gigantic by the standards of his time, he was six feet one and one-half inches tall and weighed 180 pounds, and in disputes with fellow officers the threat of physical violence was always at least implicit. His inclination toward personal combat, and the almost rueful control he sometimes exerted over it, are illustrated by a story Confederate general Earl Van Dorn once told a subordinate. Van Dorn had accused Forrest of prompting a staff officer to write a newspaper article claiming for Forrest some battle plaudits that were properly due Van Dorn. He thereupon suggested to Forrest that the two of them "settle our differences" in the direct, illegal manner to which many gentlemen in the hotheaded South resorted. Van Dorn then "stepped to where my sword was hanging against the wall, snatched it down, and turned to face him," causing Forrest to rise, advance a half-step, and begin drawing his sword. Then, Van Dorn said, "a wave of some kind seemed to pass over his countenance" and he "slowly returned his sword to its sheath" and said that, although Van Dorn knew he was "not afraid" of him, "I will not fight you," because "[i]t would never do for two officers of our rank to set such an example to the troops." Shamed, Van Dorn agreed and apologized, recalling afterward that "we parted to be somewhat better friends. . . . Whatever else he may be, the man certainly is no coward."[10]

This incident suggests several complex facets of Forrest's personality. Almost desperately, he assumed the role of gentleman. His civilian dress has been characterized by admirers as bordering on foppish, and his good name he regarded even more seriously than was normal on the brawling, chip-on-shoulder frontier along which he grew to manhood. Whether he took his reputation seriously enough to encourage military subordinates to write journalistic articles about him is difficult to ascertain now, but his wartime aides-de-camp did include at various times at least three prominent newspapermen.[11]

Van Dorn's phrase "whatever else he may be" suggests there were questions about that, and there were. Even in a South powered by slave labor, a slave trader was no man to be looked up to, especially in society's higher circles. That Forrest managed to overcome much of the stigma of this business owes probably not only to superior character, as admirers long have asserted, but to his location on the frontier, where class distinctions tended to blur. He also earned enough money to buy some respect that might not have been accorded him otherwise. Unquestionably, he commanded uncommon amounts of it for a slave trader. Years before donning the uniform in which he found fame, he was elected to responsible local political offices and formed valuable friendships among the power elite of what was then the Southwest. The wealth and influence he achieved selling slaves, in fact, elevated him to the level where ability and fearlessness could win him his unmatched military advancement.

Van Dorn's story also demonstrates how officers of his day rewrote reality into the higher-flown language they deemed worthy of leaving to posterity. Forrest rarely spoke in the carefully measured phrases and clauses of Van Dorn's account. His normal mode of talking can be inferred from the few of his handwritten letters that survive. The only elegance about them is a labored pretense. For example, he responded to onetime associate Minor Meriwether, with whom he had had a falling-out, that "all diferances between us air satisfactory setled and I asure you that thair is no unkind feling towards you from me. I have . . . never felt unkindly to wards your Self only when I felt you was using your influance against my Intrest."[12]

A note more typical of his manner, perhaps, was his wartime response to a soldier's third request for a furlough: "I told you twist Goddammit Know." By "twist" he meant "twicet," lower-class Southern for "twice." By "Know," he meant "no."[13]

His conversational inelegance is perhaps illustrated best of all by a newspaper account of a short speech he delivered late in the war to the army of General John B. Hood, after arriving from western Tennessee to lead Hood's advance columns out of northern Alabama on a last desperate attempt to recapture Nashville. The Montgomery *Daily Mail* reported that, after noting he had come there "to jine you . . . to show you the way into Tennessee," he added a homely but proud summary of his exploits in which he boasted that "in the streets of Memphis . . . the women run out in their nightclothes to see us, and they will do it again in Nashville."[14]

In several respects, he resembled fellow fiery Tennesseans Andrew Jackson, whose presidency spanned the years of his boyhood, and Andrew Johnson, who signed his postbellum pardon. They, too, were men of unsteady letters, boundless courage, and hot blood. Jackson, especially, possessed a similar talent for making difficult decisions swiftly and a willingness—almost eagerness—to participate in the violence that often passed for law in his day. Like both of these presidents, Forrest was not regarded by friends and neighbors as any sort of archfiend. Rather, most of them seem to have found him generally the opposite.

Possessed of a total of just six months' schooling, Forrest displayed a knack for emphatic sentence construction and an instinctive grasp of mathematics. The balance among his vices and virtues, as character traits were then tallied, leaned heavily toward the latter. The only personal characteristics of which he himself seems to have been ashamed were a fondness for gambling—large sums—and a strong tendency toward profane, although not vulgar, language. He neither drank nor used tobacco, his respect for women and clergymen was marked, and he delighted in children. He also loved horses and horse-racing and had a pointed sense of humor. At a dinner during the war, to a society woman who inquired why his hair had turned gray while his beard remained dark, he replied that it was possibly because he tended to work his brains more than his jaws.[15]

His leadership at Fort Pillow and of the Klan notwithstanding, Forrest was no sadistic racial bigot, although the extravagant claims of some of his apologists are unconvincing. Much, for instance, has been made of his reported reluctance to divide slave families, and of his habit of providing newly bought slaves with new clothes and hygienic care; but such practices can be attributed as easily to good business considerations as to humanitarian concern, since slaves treated kindly were less apt to run away. Apologists also note that he offered to free forty-five of his slaves if they would serve his troops as teamsters, and that the slaves acquiesced. Forrest's offer could have been no more than a shrewd military proposition that the slaves agreed to out of fear. There is proof, however, that he kept his promise and freed them before the war's close.[16]

Writers present at his death and funeral noted many blacks among the thousands of mourners who viewed his corpse and followed it to the cemetery. One suggested that there had been those—white and black, presumably—who had feared him. Some of the traits that inspired the fear also inspired his widespread veneration. "Desperate," a word often employed contemporaneously to describe his courage, also characterized not only his temperament but his times. It certainly characterized those during which he accepted leadership of the Klan.[17]

The last significant Confederate commander to stack arms in 1865, he dismissed his troops with one of the more eloquent and conciliatory farewell messages made by a rebel general. Rather than flee the country, as many of his peers did then, he went home to a world ajar with the advent of a new age. With all his former wealth now lost, he devoted most of the rest of his life to attempting to recoup it—and, for a time, to reestablishing an antebellum-style status quo. Accomplishing the latter, he failed miserably at the former. After cotton farming, he moved successively into insurance and then railroading. He was bankrupted by each in turn.

He did not follow the example of other Confederate generals and hire himself out to lead the reactionary Mexican armies of Emperor Maximilian, but he gave at least momentary thought to conquering Mexico himself. He told friends he could do it in six months with 30,000 men and 20,000 rifles—and afterward would confiscate mines and church properties, set himself up as ruler, and open the country to 200,000 Southerners he expected to flock there. The Mexican dream, however, remained merely that. Instead of conquering Mexico, he remained in Memphis and conspired for a while to reconquer the South. Furies he helped loose eventually defeated the Loyal Leagues, the Freedmen's Bureau, the Union League, various state militias, and other groups dedicated to the civil advancement of Southern blacks and non-Confederate whites.

Yet Nathan Bedford Forrest requires no apologists. Reality, not apology, reminds that his times were as extraordinary as his life. He did not institute slavery; born into a nation in which it had been a prominent feature of the status quo for more than two centuries, he simply sought— in a normal human reaction—to keep his world from disintegrating around him. The violence he employed to that end seemed almost as normal in its place and time as it seems barbarous today. Born and bred on a bloody frontier, he became bloodier in combat against Grants and Shermans, new-style soldiers reverting to ancient-style total war to win.

He could argue with considerable truth that most of those who professed to be outraged by slavery's inhumanity were as jealous of the economic advantage it accorded slaveholders as they were concerned about the plight of the slaves. After Appomattox, most of those supporting aid for the freedman appeared to favor it largely as punishment for the former master. There was considerable Northern interest in granting the land of Southern slave owners to their onetime slaves, but there was no Northern interest at all in giving freedmen Northern land and protecting their safety and civil rights by bringing significant numbers of them north; indeed, at that time few Northern states permitted blacks much more than the all-but-serfdom that postwar Southern legislatures instituted shortly following the surrender. The fears Forrest and his fellow Southerners long harbored of a racial Armageddon were no less real because the Armageddon never came; Nat Turner's rebellion in Virginia in 1831 and a bloody Haitian slave revolt of 1832 gave substance to the threat.

Forrest should not be condemned too quickly, too reflexively, or too self-righteously. Like Andrew Jackson, he was compelled by his times to make hard choices, and by today's standards some of his became some of history's worst. Jackson, arguably the greatest American of his epoch, might be remembered in much the same light as Forrest had more of the victims of his persecutions — the American Indians — survived to reproach his posterity. The wrongs committed by great men tend to be as large as the men themselves, and Forrest's were appropriately titanic. Yet even these were carried out with an indomitable, ruthless courage, and when his frenzied life permitted him time to reflect before acting, he usually did the moral thing, at least as he understood it. Although history to date has accorded him scant credit, he not only ordered the dissolution of the Ku Klux Klan but went on to disavow repeatedly its race hatred, to protest and decry racial discrimination, and, during his last two years of life, to publicly call for social as well as political advancement for blacks.

By the lights of his time and place, Nathan Bedford Forrest was a great man; for the modern era, he offers an example even greater. His story not only recounts the implacable struggles of an intelligent man of action against the longest kinds of odds. It traces an exceptional American's remarkable philosophical journey.

Part 1

FRONTIERSMAN

1

THE SAGA BEGINS with tallish tales, anecdotes told and retold until many of them take on qualities of myth. Southerners are widely considered America's best storytellers, and they outdo even themselves venerating their heroes. Still, the essence of Nathan Bedford Forrest rises from the worshipful press-agentry of his antebellum legend like that of some backwoods Lancelot: a man of hair triggers — quintessentially Tennessean, Jacksonian, frontier American.

None of the lore is more dramatic or prophetic than the tale of the fierce horseman who, one late-summer day in 1845, came to the aid of two marooned women and their black driver at a creek ford near Hernando, Mississippi. The driver was struggling to free their carriage from a mudhole, and two young men acquainted with the women had the misfortune to be also on hand. They sat on horseback beside the stream, leaving the slave to try to extricate the vehicle's wheels alone; it was the Sabbath, the story goes, so perhaps they wanted to avoid soiling their Sunday finery. The third horseman, when he arrived, exhibited no such fussiness.

He reined in at the creek's edge, hitched his horse to a fence, and waded out to the carriage. Asking the women's permission, he carried them one by one to dry ground, re-entered the water, set a shoulder against a carriage wheel, and helped the driver free the lightened vehicle. Then, before handing the women back up to their seats, he turned on the two onlookers and roundly castigated them for uselessness, threatening them with physical harm if they didn't leave at once. They did.

The women turned out to be the widow Elizabeth Montgomery and her eighteen-year-old daughter, Mary Ann, fairly new residents of Horn Lake, Mississippi. Horn Lake was a genteel community in which prosperous people from nearby Memphis were wont to spend time, and the women may have been a little chagrined at the stranger's high-handed treatment of their two young friends. Nevertheless, mother and daughter thanked him for his help and were about to drive off when he introduced himself. He was Bedford Forrest, a twenty-four-year-old mercantile dealer with an office on the public square of the seat of their mutual county, DeSoto. In keeping with the pushy directness that seemed to be his nature, he asked for permission to call at their home. Considering the service he had just rendered, it might have seemed rude to refuse, and they didn't.[1]

Driving away, the comparatively sophisticated Mary Ann Montgomery—she had attended the Nashville Female Academy—could hardly have been impervious to the young horseman's striking impression. Although she had never seen him before, she almost certainly had heard not only of him but of his spreading reputation for volatility. She may even have read about it in a Memphis-area newspaper the previous March 21. In a prominently displayed article, the *American Eagle* of that day announced that a "most bloody affray" had occurred in Hernando "between several men some eight or ten days since." The hazy account said a "T. J. Matlock, Esq., and his brother and overseer on one side . . . had a dispute with another person," when a "young Mr. Forrest made some interfering remarks; sometime after which he and the Matlocks met, . . . some exciting language rose" and "one of the Matlocks . . . raise[d] a stick to strike Forrest, who immediately drew a revolving pistol and set it to work as fast as possible, shooting both of the Matlocks through; the younger T. J., through the shoulder and the upper part of the breast, and the other through the arm, which has since been amputated; Mr. T. J. Matlock lies in a doubtful state; young Mr. Forrest also received a slight pistol wound in his arm." The *Eagle* went on to lament "the death of old Mr. Forrest, father of the other, who stood some yards off, during the affray, offering no interference; it is said he was deliberately shot down by Mr. Matlock's overseer, without the least provocation; other reports say the pistol was not aimed at him; the overseer is in jail. Mr. Forrest was a most worthy and estimable citizen."[2]

The accuracy of the *Eagle* account is at best approximate. The "old Mr. Forrest" killed that day was actually the younger Forrest's uncle and business partner, not his father. Later and more accepted accounts also have it that the precise date was March 10, that there were three Matlock brothers as well as the overseer, and that the "other person" the Matlocks' dispute was with was the uncle, Jonathan Forrest, who was killed by a shot intended for the nephew. These later accounts also have it that the fight began when a Matlock raised not a stick but a gun, that young Forrest interceded for his aged kinsman, and that, having only two balls in his pistol, he was thrown a knife by a bystander after emptying the handgun.[3]

The young merchant proved to be a man who didn't waste time. Within days after the meeting at the creek ford, he called on the Montgomerys in Horn Lake, again behaving as imperiously as at the ford. On the porch of the Montgomery home he found two other prospective callers: the same pair of young men who had sat their horses by the stream that day. With more physical threats, he ordered them away again, undeterred by the fact that one of them was studying for the ministry. Once more they left, and he was invited inside, where he proceeded to propose to Mary Ann. She hesitated—it was, after all, only the second time in her life she had spoken with him—and he went on to state his case. If she accepted any such suitor as the two he had dismissed twice from her presence, he asserted, she often would find herself as helpless as that day at the creek; whereas he and the business he operated could support her comfortably and securely. He was determined to marry her, he added, and would bring a marriage license on his next visit. On the third visit, she accepted his proposal, and in late September the Hernando newspaper noted that "[o]n Thursday evening, the 25th inst., by the Rev. S. M. Cowan, Mr. N. B. Forrest" had been married "to Miss Mary Ann Montgomery. The above," it added, "came to hand accompanied by a good sweet morsel of cake and a bottle of the best wine."[4]

The whirlwind courtship fits the pattern of the groom's lifelong behavior in situations of challenge, but there lately has come to light a possible explanation for some of his commanding demeanor the day he first met the Montgomerys. Hernando's three municipal officers in mid-1845 included Town Constable N. B. Forrest, a post to which he may well have been elected because of his performance in the Matlock fight. He was also elected county coroner. Perhaps in "rescuing" the Montgomery women and dismissing their idle friends, he felt he was assuming his civic role of policeman.[5]

His community credentials notwithstanding, procuring the minister for his wedding was no easy task. Although there is no proof the Montgomery women had heard of him before they met him, the Rev. Samuel Montgomery Cowan—the bride-to-be's uncle and guardian—apparently had. According to a classmate of Mary Ann's who was visiting the Montgomerys at the time, Rev. Cowan initially declined when Forrest asked for his niece's hand. "Why, Bedford, I couldn't consent," he replied. "You cuss and gamble, and Mary Ann is a Christian girl."

The insistent suitor's answer was not only clever but theologically unassailable. "I know it," he said, "and that's just why I want her."[6]

2

HE NEEDED HER, too. The Montgomerys were the kind of people an ambitious young mercantile dealer was well advised to cultivate.

With a pedigree said to include a General Richard Montgomery killed in Benedict Arnold's 1775 attack on Quebec (and now known to have boasted distant kinship to Tennessee-Texas hero Sam Houston), they had come from Pennsylvania by way of Virginia, settling in eastern Tennessee soon after the Revolution. Elizabeth Montgomery and her husband, War of 1812 veteran William H. Montgomery, were first cousins born in Blount County, Tennessee; by the time he died in 1829 at age thirty-seven, however, they owned 350 acres of land near the town of Cowan in Franklin County. Widowed at twenty-seven, Mrs. Montgomery was left with four small children (Mary Ann, the second, had just turned three), so her brother, Rev. Cowan, probably became their guardian at that time. Thirteen years later, in 1842, Mrs. Montgomery and the children moved with him when he accepted a pastorate in Horn Lake.[1]

By then, he was a prominent Presbyterian minister, and he and his sister moved among the region's slaveholding class. Evidence of their status includes not only Mrs. Montgomery's carriage driver at the ford but also a DeSoto County courthouse record showing that in 1845 Rev. Cowan was given permission to sell "a certain Negro girl named Margaret aged about twelve years, also a negro boy named Tom aged about fifteen years . . . to the highest bidder for cash at the courthouse door in Hernando" to satisfy a debt owed him by another county resident. Two other Co-wans, the minister's younger brother John and his brother-in-law Alfred, are mentioned in the document, and other records indicate that a number of other Montgomerys and Cowans, most hailing from the Tennessee counties of Blount and Franklin, were in DeSoto County by then, buying land, mortgaging property, paying off the mortgages, and lending modest amounts of money. Such connections could be useful to a young business-man.[2]

Young Forrest operated a struggling livery stable and farm-supply business dealing in everything from feed and seed to the equipment with which to produce them, meanwhile trading in horses, mules, and other livestock on the side. The most valuable livestock item at the time was the slave, and even this early in his career Forrest had begun to be associated with it. A glimpse inside his earliest business, and its nature, is afforded by a county deed book. The very day of the killing of Jonathan Forrest, a half year before his nephew married Mary Ann Montgomery, the late senior partner mortgaged the following property: "one Negro man named Bob aged about forty years, one Negro man named Bill aged about thirty years, one Negro woman named Eliza aged about twenty-five, one Negro girl named Ann aged about sixteen, one Negro girl named Phebe aged about nine years, all slaves for life; also all my stock of Horses, Cattle and Sheep consisting of five head of Horses, twenty head of Cattle and fifteen head of Sheep; also one waggon and one yoke of oxen and seventy-five barrels of Corn. . . ."[3]

Heirs to English, Scottish, and Irish yeomen, the Forrests had been primarily traders of cattle, horses, and mules. In less distinguished fashion than the Montgomerys, they had scrabbled along the advancing frontier for a century or so, but their circumstances hadn't always been so humble. The first of the family to achieve the notice of history, Shadrack Forrest, did so in western Virginia, moving from there around 1730 into what later became Orange County, North Carolina. The North Carolina census of 1790 shows in that area a Shadrack Forrest owning a slave and 787 acres of land, a holding larger than three-fourths of all the others listed in the record. In 1806, Shadrack was still alive and healthy enough to move with the family of his second son, Nathan, to Sumner County, Tennessee, thirty miles northeast of Nashville. No record indicates they bought property in Sumner, but four years later Nathan Forrest bought 150 acres on Caney Spring Creek in Bedford County, fifty miles southeast of Nashville, for $150. The next year, Shadrack Forrest bought 471 acres along the same creek, the deed being signed by Shadrack and Nathan.[4]

On July 13, 1821, in a primitive log cabin in this area, the wife of Nathan's eldest son gave birth to twins: Nathan Bedford, apparently named after his grandfather and the county in which he was born, and Fanny. A view of the Forrests and the way their neighbors regarded them is provided by an area resident who recalled long afterward that grandfather Nathan Forrest "had a small farm and nursery of fruit trees" and fathered five boys and three girls. "William, the oldest son . . . , was a blacksmith by trade. The other sons of Nathan Forrest were principally engaged as traders in live-stock; except one, who was a tailor." The rememberer added that the Forrests "were all energetic, high-minded, straightforward people. I have never heard of any of them being dissipated or connected with anything that was disreputable."[5]

Seeking a route out of deepening unprosperousness and obscurity, the Forrests tarried there for a quarter century. They put down thin roots near

the present town of Chapel Hill, a part of Bedford County later split off
to help form the newer county of Marshall. Here the family's most famous
member began building his legend on a junior scale. He first distinguished
himself by remaining alive, no mean feat in itself at that place and time;
two of his eight brothers and all three of his sisters died early of typhoid
fever. He didn't survive peacefully, though. A woman who lived nearby
during his childhood recalled that, whether at play or getting whipped by
his mother, he could yell louder than any other child in the neighborhood.[6]

A number of boyish exploits, varying in intrepidity, have been handed
down. On a blackberry-picking foray, young Nathan Bedford single-
handedly killed a large rattlesnake with a stick after failing to rally any of
his fellow children to help him. He dived a dozen times into a creek for
a smaller playmate's dropped pocketknife, refusing to stop until he retrieved it. Riding horses to water one day, he was thrown by an imper-
fectly broken colt into a pursuing pack of vicious dogs, only to gape
wonderingly as the dogs fled in fear of this object flung into their midst;
later, he would say this taught him the value of boldly attacking, even with
inferior strength. At the shop of his tailor uncle one day on the threshold
of his teens, he charged a crowd of loitering adult tipplers with a pair of
shears, goaded by their ridicule of his refusal to join in the merriment.
Community talk had it that if he hadn't been caught and restrained by his
uncle and some other men, he might have wounded some of the drinkers;
but while he was being held, they fled.[7]

He had just entered his teens when his family left Tennessee for
northern Mississippi. According to an 1868 biography to which he gave
his blessing, William Forrest's finances had "gone to wreck," but the
circumstances of the wreckage are unclear. Perhaps his health already was
failing; on the other hand, his financial acumen from the beginning never
seems to have been marked. The cabin in which his eldest son was born
was the home of his wife's family, and Bedford County records indicate
he owned no land at all until 1826, six years after he married. The first land
he did acquire, fifty acres on Spring Creek, was "sold" to him by Nathan
Forrest for $1. In 1830, William bought 181 more acres on Caney Spring
Creek for $588, meanwhile selling the other fifty acres for $400. Just three
years later, though, the family felt constrained to move to the wilds of
northwestern Tippah—now part of Benton—County, Mississippi,
where there is no record they ever purchased real estate at all. Rather,
William Forrest apparently leased a hill farm near land belonging to his

wife's relatives, the Becks. The names of several Becks—who also relo-cated there from Bedford County, Tennessee, around the same time—are to be found in Tippah and Benton County records.[8]

In 1837, when his eldest son was not quite sixteen, William Forrest died of causes lost to history, leaving young sons and a pregnant widow. The family's formal leadership passed to Mariam Beck Forrest, a gray-eyed woman who stood about five feet ten, weighed 180 pounds, was so religious that she kept the Sabbath by cooking Sunday's dinners on Saturday, and still thrashed at least one of her sons with peach-tree switches when he was eighteen years old.[9]

Of Scotch-Irish descent, the Becks had emigrated from South Carolina into the Bedford County area a few years before the Forrests. They owned considerable land there, and if Mariam Beck is a fair example of them, they were vigorous, tough-minded, and prolific. Mariam not only bore William Forrest eleven children, she bore a second husband four more.[10]

She seems to have prevailed over her environment through implacable refusal not to. Soon after William Forrest's death, she and her unmarried sister Fanny, who lived with the Forrests at the time (and probably was the namesake of her eldest son's twin), rode ten miles through the Missis-sippi wilderness to call on their nearest neighbor—by whom, in gratitude, they were presented a basket of baby chickens, a prize on the wild frontier. Toward dusk on their return journey, within a mile of home, the two sisters found themselves pursued by a panther. The sister begged Mrs. Forrest to drop the basket of chicks, which the panther apparently had scented, but she refused. When their horses had to slow to cross a high-banked creek within earshot of their home, the panther attacked. Mrs. Forrest's horse, bleeding profusely from the big cat's assault, reared and threw its assailant into the stream, then died, while the panther fled as the rest of the Forrest household came running with their dogs. Clawed severely on her neck and shoulders, Mrs. Forrest had her clothes torn from her back, but she held on to the chickens.

Another of her eldest son's youthful exploits immediately followed this incident. As soon as Mariam Forrest's wounds were dressed, he took a flintlock musket and some hounds into the night to wreak vengeance. In deep woods around midnight, the dogs treed the panther, and the youth waited below in the dark until dawn brought sufficient light for a shot. By 9 A.M. he returned home carrying the animal's scalp and ears. Legend quotes him as having grandly told the matriarch, "Mother, I am going to kill that beast if it stays on the earth." His actual words probably weren't that pretty, but their spirit was one he would live by most of his life: no creature, four-legged or otherwise, could harm him or his with impunity.[11]

His youth was spent in hard times that easily fostered such attitudes. He eventually recalled that most of his evenings during this period were spent before the fire making frontier clothing—buckskin leggings, coonskin caps, or shoes—for his younger brothers. To be in the fields by dawn, the family ate breakfast by candlelight, and few of the eldest son's days, no more than three months each in Mississippi and Tennessee, were spent in school; surviving was a higher priority than getting educated. He doesn't seem to have been too interested in formal education, anyhow. One of his teachers later described him as "an athlete" who would rather wrestle than study. The activities young Forrest loved best, though, the ones in which he invested the few idle moments he had, were those involving animals long prized by scrabbling, trading, Forrest menfolk: horses and dogs. Since hunting was as much a necessity as a pastime, his only real recreation appears to have been "an occasional horse-race."[12]

He and his younger brothers continued the land-clearing and cultivating begun by their father. Raising corn, wheat, oats, and cotton, they gradually accumulated cattle, horses, and mules. By 1840, three years after their father's death, Forrest is said to have so managed the small farm that the family enjoyed relative prosperity, although there is no indication the land ever became theirs.[13]

Tests of the man of this family continued. Newly divested of its prior Indian population, the neighborhood began filling up, and the Forrests soon had a neighbor much closer than ten miles away. When an adjacent farmer's ox began tearing down fences and consuming crops on Forrest-tended land, word went to its owner that the animal would be shot the next time it offended, and the neighbor replied that anybody who shot the ox would be shot himself. The animal soon trespassed again, and the eldest Forrest son shot it dead. When the neighbor appeared carrying a gun of his own and began climbing a fence between the two farms, he was met by a shot that put holes in his clothes. Falling off the fence, he rose and ran, and his neighborliness improved thereafter.[14]

By February of 1841, the younger Forrest brothers—John, William, Aaron, Jesse, and Jeffrey—were sufficiently grown that the eldest, now nearing twenty-one, felt able to hazard his first military experience. He enlisted in a Mississippi unit formed to aid the fledgling government of his eventual kinsman Sam Houston in Texas. The Lone Star Republic was facing threats of invasion by Mexico, whose lands it had appropriated, and in Holly Springs, Mississippi, these threats were considered grave enough that Captain Wallace Wilson raised a company of volunteers. Wilson's unit turned out to be its own worst enemy. After traveling to New Orleans, it was forced to disband after mismanagement of funds left it without the means to book steamer passage the rest of the way to Texas. Most of the rest of the aspiring soldiers returned home, but young Forrest and a few others went doggedly on to the fledgling city of Houston, only to find Texas in no need of their services; the Mexican War wouldn't begin for another five years. Out of money, the disappointed young Mississippian found a job splitting fence rails at a rate of fifty cents per hundred to acquire the resources to get home.[15]

He arrived back in northern Mississippi four and a half months after leaving, with a Texas fever that sent him to bed for weeks. Recuperating but still too weak for farm labor, he began to engage formally in the calling so favored among Forrests: cattle and horse trading. This first venture was with an uncle, but soon, probably after his health was restored, he returned to the heavy work of the farm.[16]

One day soon afterward his mother, summoned by one of her younger sons, found Forrest cursing and whipping a team of oxen mired in a rapidly swelling creek. Realizing that the whip and the curses were confusing the animals, she told him to get hold of himself and let the oxen calm down. There wasn't time, Forrest responded, handing her the whip. He then jumped off the ox cart and grabbed a pole to try to free a rear wheel, prying frantically at it while his mother cracked the whip. With the water becoming dangerously high and the cart still as mired as ever, he threw aside the pole, splashed his way to the front of the cart, and bit an inch of flesh out of an ear of one of the oxen. With a lunge of pain, the animal jerked the cart forward, and vehicle and team were freed before the flood could inundate them.[17]

The homestead was in comfortable circumstances, and Forrest became a steadily more active livestock trader. In the fall of 1842, he left home for good, probably for several reasons. His mother soon would remarry, becoming the wife of Joseph Luxton and thus relieving her eldest son of the responsibility of heading the family. Forrest, at the same time, was passing into his majority just as others in the family were drifting westward again, gathering in DeSoto County. The vehicle of his own departure was supplied by the astuteness of his livestock speculations; they had been so successful that his uncle Jonathan offered him a junior partnership in his Hernando mercantile, livestock trading, and livery stable business.[18]

The nephew was an excellent addition to the enterprise. He not only was adept at counting dollars; he was so single-mindedly industrious about earning them that he shunned both tobacco and liquor. His disdain for alcohol is said to have developed while he was still on the farm. Having noted that strong drink made some men weep and others angry, he decided to discover his own reaction to it in the woods, where, if it made him vicious, he could harm only tree trunks. What it caused him to do he later said he couldn't remember, but he returned from the forest with a fever so severe that he fell into prayer, promising the Almighty that if he survived he never would drink alcohol again.[19]

The need for clearheadedness had been well nigh perpetual in his life and trading in the backwoods anyway, to say nothing of surroundings more urban. The assault on his uncle Jonathan wasn't the only example of the lightning swiftness with which danger could arise on the streets and highways of the expanding frontier. A few months after the fight in the Hernando public square, he faced another attacker on the scene of another killing. Perhaps acting in the capacity of town constable, he was riding from Hernando to Holly Springs with a Hernando attorney named James K. Morse when Morse was waylaid, shot, and killed by a planter named Dyson. Forrest eventually testified in the prosecution of Dyson, but his action on the spot doubtless prompted lively public discussion in the region. When Dyson turned his double-barreled weapon toward the constable, he looked down the barrel of a pistol already drawn and cocked. The man behind it coolly informed the killer he had best shoot straight, that his was "now a game at which two could play."

Dyson lowered his weapon. He later explained that its second barrel was loaded only with buckshot, a charge he deemed insufficient to deal with Forrest.[20]

3

THE NEWLY WED FORRESTS set up housekeeping in a Hernando house hardly grand, but above average for America's southwestern frontier. Located near the center of town, it combined two log cabins constructed side by side, then covered with clapboards to form a single house with two chimneys. A low porch overlooking the nearby street shaded four windows. The door led into a central hall between the two foundation buildings, and there was a half-story attic above. No mansion, it was no simple homestead either. In Hernando at that time, it was middle-class.[1]

Forrest bought it two and a half weeks after his uncle was killed. Before that, he may have rented a room in town, perhaps along with the uncle. After becoming sole proprietor of the business, however, he paid $300 for Hernando Lot 231 on March 28, 1845. The acquisition wasn't necessarily reflective of sudden entry into wealth, for the death of his uncle probably burdened the young trader with heavy debts. The mortgage document Jonathan Forrest filed the day he died discloses not only the extent of his property but also a list of his liabilities and references to the ways in which some of them were incurred.[2]

Jonathan Forrest apparently owned no land—just the five slaves, five horses, twenty head of cattle, fifteen sheep, two oxen, one wagon and seventy-five barrels of corn cited in the mortgage agreement—but that document discloses that his debts were considerable. He owed Hernando pioneer Edward Orne (who had given area residents forty acres on which to build their town) and Benjamin Saunders $2,224.15 "on a judgment rendered in the circuit court of said County of Desoto in favor of said Sa[u]nders & Orne against me on the 28th of September, 1844 with interest on that sum since that time." He owed another $258.08, plus interest, to another firm of two partners, apparently named Biggs & Rier, "in judgment obtained by them against me in the said Circuit Court of said County of Desoto" on the same September 28, 1844.

He also was "indebted to the creditors and heirs of James W. Putman dec[ease]d in the sum of eighteen hundred dollars or thereabouts for that amount of money collected by me as administrator of the Goods & Chattels, rights and credits of said James W. Putman dec[ease]d belonging to said estate of James W. Putman and used by me and applied to my own private and individual business transactions. . . ." He also owed the Putman estate another $600, which Putman himself apparently had lent him. He acknowledged owing a Charles Foster $300, plus interest, for that sum apparently collected by him from another man in Foster's name "sometime in 1842 and applied to my own use and benefit." He even was unable to repay one of his own relatives, a Joseph Forrest, two separate $150 debts incurred in March and December of 1843. The document concludes that as he was "also indebted to divers other persons to an amount greater as I apprehend than I will be able to pay and being anxious to secure to my said creditors hereinbefore named and enumerated in the payment of their debts," DeSoto County tax assessor Samuel T. Cobb was authorized to dispose of his cited property by private or public sale if the debts weren't paid by December 26, 1846.[3]

Whether the violence which released Jonathan Forrest from further struggle with these obligations had to do with his none-too-meticulous financial dealings is impossible to establish now. It seems oddly coincidental that the uncle was killed on the day this humbling document was filed. His nephew's personally endorsed first biography, however, while seeming intentionally reticent, gives little indication that the mortgage document and the public-square violence had any relation to each other. It says only that "[w]ithout going into the details of the origin of the quarrel, it will be sufficient to mention that Jonathan Forrest . . . having been the 'security' on the bond of one Martin James . . . as the guardian of some orphan children, a misunderstanding and violent controversy arose. . . .'' The possibility that the "orphan children" were the Putman "heirs" mentioned in the mortgage seems considerable.[4]

It also seems clear that Jonathan Forrest's business was no prize when his sudden death conferred its sole proprietorship on his nephew. That, along with his Beck genes, may partially explain the energy with which the nephew began branching out into new enterprises. Other impetus may have been supplied by increasing family obligations. In 1846 Mary Ann Forrest gave birth to a son, William Montgomery Forrest, and in 1847 to a daughter, Frances A.—yet another "Fanny." By 1848 his eldest younger brother, John, would have returned from service in the Mexican War as a half-paralyzed cripple, shot through the lower spine, and Forrest, having headed the family so long, may have felt constrained to help support him. The 1850 census shows the Forrests as a family of four with three additions: a Mrs. Ann "Cowen," thirty-five, doubtless a relative of Mary Ann's; Joseph F. Forrest, twenty-five; and J. Patton Anderson, twenty-eight. The latter two were probably boarders, young Forrest doubtless a cousin; his occupation is listed as "Clerk C. Court," while Anderson—who later would become a Confederate general—was a lawyer. The head of this household, "Bedford Forrest," owned $1,000 worth of real estate, but his "profession, occupation or trade" was listed as "none."[5]

In addition to his mercantile and livery-stable business and his speculation in livestock and slaves, Forrest eventually opened a stage line connecting Hernando with Memphis, twenty miles to the northwest; then he started a brickyard. An ambitious undertaking of the latter got him into dire financial straits in the late 1840s. According to the characteristically vague authorized version of the story, Forrest had become contractor for the erection of "a large academy" in Hernando and sustained "a severe loss through the breach of trust of an agent empowered to draw money for him from a bank in Memphis."[6]

The only other mention of the contracting disaster, a reminiscence by longtime Hernando resident Henry Yates in 1879, partially corroborates the story. Yates recalled that the project prompted abortive violence between Forrest and Yates's great-grandfather, a comparatively wealthy Hernando-area planter named John Robertson. Forrest, Yates said, "was nothing but a brick mason" and "slave trader" who also "owned a livery stable" and "couldn't even write his own name." Robertson, on the other hand, "was on the board of trustees for the male academy" whose building Forrest had constructed. When Forrest attended a trustees' meeting, demanded to be paid, and "insulted my great-grandfather," Robertson "didn't like it, and . . . challenged him to a duel in the street. . . . Dr. Dockery [a Hernando alderman] and another man drew up the letter stating the time and everything, and when they took it to Forrest for his signature, he agreed to it." When the appointed hour arrived, however, Robertson "strapped his guns on his hips, and Forrest already had run off to Memphis. He was a chicken, but history has labeled him as a fighter."[7]

Yates's pride in his forebear's manliness is forgivable, but his assertion that Forrest was physically afraid of his great-grandfather is ridiculous. If Forrest "ran off" to Memphis to avoid the duel, it was not from any fear for his own life; he had risked it too many times before and would do so too many times again, in the face of greater odds, for such a motive even to be considered. In fact, it conforms to a pattern that recurred consistently throughout his life: his anger was quick and impetuous, but when it had time to cool he tended to opt for the more prudent course. Surely he already had thoughts of moving from Hernando's comparative backwater into the ever-more-bustling trading capital of Memphis, and he surely discerned that of all his varied enterprises, the one offering the best financial future was that of slave-trafficking. Yates recalls that his great-grandfather's father, General Julious [sic] Ceasar [sic] Nichols Robertson, was one of DeSoto County's largest slave owners; that, in fact, General Robertson had so many slaves on his plantation that it was called "slave town." A young trader desiring to expand a slave business would hardly wish to antagonize the area aristocracy by killing as influential a member of it as the son of the general.[8]

Forrest's modest slave business and such other endeavors as the academy-construction enterprise no doubt had given him occasional entree into the company of such people as the Robertsons, but probably on a strained basis, especially in early life. His lack of education and polish was something he appeared to feel painfully throughout his years, and he understandably feared and distrusted evidences of literacy and refinement; "I never see a pen but what I think of a snake," he later would say. In cultivated company he moved most comfortably outdoors, where conversation tended to be more colloquial and directed at his areas of greatest knowledge: horses, livestock, slaves, dogs, and guns. Having recovered control of his temper, such a man may have known no way to avoid the disastrous duel except to leave town on extended business.[9]

Whatever the truth of Yates's story and the explanation of Forrest's behavior in it, Forrest hardly can be faulted for wishing prompt payment for building an edifice as large as an academy, especially after the unscrupulous agent had indebted him to the bank in Memphis. Perhaps it was this crisis, as well as the arrogant attitude of the area's upper class toward him and his financial predicament, that determined him to renounce more respectable but less remunerative pursuits and cast his lot totally with slave-trading.

What Forrest had been doing up to this time, selling slaves while also trading in other farm supplies, was not only common but natural then. To sell the other farm supplies, the merchant had to get to know many farmers and planters who also needed to buy or sell slaves, and he was already engaged in the kind of rural sales excursions that slave trading demanded. There was a stigma attached to full-time slave trading, though. Uprooting one's human property from its home and releasing it to the whims of prospective buyers was viewed with such distaste that to have to sell slaves at all was a sign of financial trouble among the rich. Fancying itself humane, the aristocracy regarded slave trading as a way coarse pretenders could gain entry, if not wholehearted acceptance, into the planter class by trafficking in misery. Refined Mary Ann Forrest may have resisted the idea of full-time slave trading, but her husband wasn't the sort to quibble over appearances. He wanted a way to prosper quickly, and at that time and place there was probably no more profitable field than slave-dealing.[10]

Black humanity was becoming the agricultural South's single most valuable commodity. In Mississippi, restrictions against the importation of slaves across the state's boundaries by professional traders (nervously enacted in the wake of the Nat Turner rebellion in 1831) had been repealed in 1846, and the "gang" of blacks required to operate a plantation was soon to be worth more than not only the plantation itself but also all its other livestock, produce, and accessories combined. The route of the trade was such that its human "goods" naturally moved from the more settled, eastern South to the frontier wildernesses of Mississippi, Louisiana, Arkansas, and Texas, prompting "notoriously high" prices to be paid for slaves in the markets of Louisiana and Memphis.[11]

It is thus understandable that in early 1852, after a three- or four-year period possibly required for recovery from the academy calamity, the mathematically adept young trader moved his family twenty miles north-westward. He resettled them in a boomtown then on the way to becoming the inland slave-trading capital of the Southwest.[12]

Part II

SLAVE TRADER

4

THE FIRST COMMERCIAL mention of Forrest in Memphis property transaction records is as the partner of Hernando-based slave trader S. S. Jones. Prior to moving back to Tennessee—and perhaps in preparation to—he seems to have widened the scope of his slave-dealing significantly, so he probably was out of Hernando often during his last years there; in fact, one of his reasons for moving may have been to avail himself of the more extensive transportation and communication facilities Memphis offered. In the spring of 1852, the year and season in which he moved, Forrest is known to have gotten as far away as southern Texas.[1]

The evidence of the Texas trip is an incident on a steamboat bound for Galveston from Houston, the first leg of a journey back to Memphis. In a too-frequent occurrence then, the pilot of the craft got into a race with another vessel as a travel-weary Forrest tried to sleep on board. Roused by an incipient gunfight among card-playing gamblers and wary of being accidentally shot in his berth, he rose and, as the account goes, "by a few peremptory words, his resolute manner, and imperious will, quelled the disturbance just on the verge of a general melee." He then walked out onto the deck to get some air and found the steamboat's chimneys overheating from the rigors of the progressing race. After protesting to the captain, who was drunk and so committed to the contest that he vowed to win it or "blow the old tub with every soul on board to h—l," Forrest uncharacteristically retired to the boat's rearmost area to await the inevitable: a loud boiler explosion that soon followed. Some sixty people are reported to have died in the wreck, but thanks to rescue efforts by the other vessel involved, nearly that many were saved. Forrest, despite "a severe contusion of the shoulder" and loss of all his luggage, helped remove survivors to the other boat and then tried to "alleviate the suffering of the wounded" the rest of the way to Galveston.[2]

He had gone to Texas, the account evasively explains, to accomplish "the adjustment of some business affairs"—probably the delivery of some slaves to a Texas planter, since his other pursuits seem unlikely to have demanded trips of such distance. Slaves just bought or sold usually were marched overland by traders or owners, and the primary inland, western hub of these treks was Memphis. It was a major collection point for both raw cotton bound for the ports and manufacturing plants of the Northeast and slaves headed southwest to power relentlessly expanding plantations.[3]

Compared to Hernando, Memphis was a municipal colossus. The year after the Forrests moved there, its roster of businesses listed "19 groceries; four hat, cap, and boot stores; 37 dry-goods stores; 15 clothing merchants; four auction and commission merchants; two book stores, one musical instrument store, two dentists, five merchant tailors, three millinery establishments, three saddleries, 17 foundries, plumbers, etc.; one flouring-mill, five hardware stores, eight drug stores, two real estate agents, nine hotels . . . three factories, two daguerreotypists, three printing offices, six painters, 10 furniture stores . . . three banks, 40 law firms, 32 physicians, three livery stables, three jewelers, Memphis Medical College with eight professors, and four newspapers." The budding metropolis was not, however, beautiful. An antebellum steamboat traveler from St. Louis to New Orleans remembered it as "a dreary, dingy, muddy melancholy town," though "rich in bales of cotton."[4]

Sitting on bluffs fifty feet above the flood crest of America's primary river, Memphis had been founded thirty-three years earlier by four prominent land speculators. This quartet, which included Andrew Jackson, no doubt saw the immense future value in the place, which as early as 1736 had been the site of a fort and trading post established by the French explorer La Salle. It was the best location for a sizable town between the mouth of the Ohio River and Natchez, Mississippi; no other place on either side of the Mississippi River was sufficiently high, dry, extensive, and level to accommodate a full-fledged city.[5]

The town was laid out in 1820 and incorporated in 1826. By 1830, cotton had established itself as the dominant crop throughout western Tennessee, northern Mississippi, and eastern Arkansas, and it proliferated wildly. The thousand bales of it received by the Memphis market in 1830 increased fiftyfold by 1836 and tripled again by 1850. The city's white population in 1850 was 6,335 (along with some 2,500 blacks) and would double by 1854, swelling not only with native whites and their slaves but also with large numbers of Irish and German immigrants; by the end of the 1850s, census takers would count 22,623 Memphians. When the Forrests moved there, the city was linked by steamboat lines not only with New Orleans, to which a round-trip required two weeks, but with Cincinnati and Louisville to the north. A telegraph link with Nashville had been completed in the late 1840s, around the same time New York news dispatches became available to the interior of the country via Cincinnati; this permitted foreign economic reports to reach vitally interested Memphis cotton merchants in about three weeks.[6]

Memphis was a city in which the strong prevailed and prospered and the weak suffered and died. It was infested with gamblers at cards and dice, who became so numerous in the early 1840s and again in the 1850s that vigilante lynch mobs formed to drive them on up- or downriver. By contrast, other types of gamblers were the new community's pillars, for there were more respectable fortunes to be made by men willing to endure discomfort and risks. The discomfort included stifling summer heat and streets choked with dust or brimming with bottomless mud. The risks included dying of the place's pestilential fevers. In 1851, ninety-three people succumbed to cholera alone, and yellow fever—which later would rage more memorably—was noticeably active beginning in 1852.[7]

Forrest was likely out of his new city of residence about as often as he was in it. His business demanded scouring the rural countryside of several states for slaves who could be bought cheaply and brought into Memphis to be sold at a profit. At this stage of his slave-buying career, he must have handled a lot of sales for planters or more prosperous slave traders on the usual two and a half percent commission. On these excursions he doubtless moved his human goods the way most others of his profession did: on horseback, driving them along afoot in a column of twos. One contemporary Southerner had little praise for the average merchant of this sort, satirically portraying him as a "coarse, ill-bred person, provincial in speech and manners, with a cross-looking phiz, a whiskey-tinctured nose, cold hard-looking eyes, a dirty tobacco-stained mouth and shabby dress," a man who routinely separated family members of all ages and relations and often dealt in "vicious" slaves "sold for crimes or misdemeanors, or otherwise diseased ones sold because of their worthlessness as property." He arrayed these undesirables "in good clothes, makes them comb their kinky heads into some semblance of neatness, rubs oil on their faces to give them a sleek healthy color, gives them a dram occasionally to make them sprightly, and teaches each one the part he or she has to play. . . . At every village of importance he sojourns a day or two, each day ranging his 'gang' in a line on the most busy street."[8]

Forrest had his similarities and his differences with this stereotype, but the business itself, with its stretches of idle time away from home, probably accentuated an already noted appetite for gambling in a vigorous man who used neither whisky nor tobacco to help pass his time. Like that of most traveling businessmen, it was a life that involved a lot of waiting and consequent boredom. Operating on a small scale with limited funds, most slave traders "attended estate and execution sales and sought out private owners who wished to dispose of a slave or two" in such slave-exporting areas as Kentucky and the eastern, upper states of the South; they then fastened together their purchases and drove them southward and westward into the more thriving cotton- and sugar-raising areas. Forrest, who soon went into successive partnerships with other Memphis dealers, may have taken many of his slaves back to high-priced Memphis and let the buyers come to him.[9]

The earliest mention of the new merchant, late of Hernando, among Shelby County's property records is one detailing a transaction made November 27, 1852. In a neat, feminine-appearing hand, a clerk wrote the first of many such entries that would be ascribed to the newcomer in the next nine years:

> *Received of Finetty Bowen Seven hundred and Seventy five dollars*
> *for a Negro Man named Gerry aged about Thirty five years which*
> *Negro we warrant to be sound in body and Mind and a Slave for life*
> *and title good and free from all incumberance. Forrest & Jones*[10]

5

> FIVE HUNDRED NEGROES WANTED. — WE will pay the highest
> cash price for all good Negroes offered. We invite all those
> having Negroes for sale, to call on us, at our Mart, opposite
> Hill's old stand, on Adams Street. We will have a lot of
> Virginia Negroes on hand, for sale, in the fall. Negroes bought
> and sold on commission. HILL & FORREST.

FOLLOWING WHAT WOULD prove to be a lifelong pattern, Forrest restlessly changed professional associates. Forrest & Jones dissolved after barely a year, and he briefly became the junior partner of the well-established Memphis slave trader Byrd Hill. Although Memphis legend has it that no slave ever ran away from Forrest, the new partnership advertised in the local *Eagle & Enquirer* of July 27, 1853, for the return of a runaway named Nat Mayson.[1]

Forrest's initial purchase as an individual slave trader of which there remains a record—and apparently the only such transaction he ever made with a firm in which he was a principal—involved the new Hill & Forrest firm around this time. He bought from it "a Negrow [sic] woman named Catharine aged seventeen and her Child named Thomas aged four months boath of which we warrant sound in body + mind and Slaves for Life and the title fully guaranteed." The purpose of this seemingly special purchase appears impossible to ascertain now. The woman may have been bought to be a housekeeper or simply as an investment, since the value of slaves— particularly that of young, child-bearing females—was rapidly rising. There is also the possibility that this Catharine was, or became, something more. Years later, after her master's name had become unpopular with the Northern press, a highly sensational New York *Tribune* dispatch datelined Knoxville, Tenn., would claim that a slave named Catharine (and spelled that way) had been his mistress and had borne him two children. The partisan invective of the brief article might make it dismissable were it not intriguingly stressful of the name "Catharine" (while Mary Ann's goes unmentioned) and supported by several other Forrest family names and business activities whose accuracy is verifiable. The Shelby County Register's document, however, seems to be the sole indication still extant that the Catharine of the newspaper report may have existed.[2]

Less than three months after his purchase of the seventeen-year-old slave and her infant, Forrest began acquiring Memphis real estate. On February 1, 1854, "Nathan B. Forrest of Shelby County" bought from another county resident, John A. Allen, a downtown lot affording sixty-three feet, nine inches of frontage along commercial Adams Street between Second and Third. The price was $4,500—$1,000 down and two notes of $1,750, one due February 1, 1855, and the other twelve months later. Soon after this transaction was entered in the county deed book, another entry noted that the new owner of the Adams Street property also had bought a "Negro man named John aged 22," who was warranted to be "sound in body and mind and a slave for life and the title fully guaranteed."[3]

The Adams Street lot, located beside an establishment formerly known as both Manning's Tavern and the Union Inn, included a "brick tenement" that housed not only the Forrest family but probably also John, Catharine, and Thomas, at least until the latter three could be sold; the lot was the first part of what soon became a larger Forrest compound of living quarters and slave-trafficking facilities. The appearance and atmosphere of this compound were recalled in 1923 by Horatio J. Eden, a Memphis-born

Arkansas barber who in the 1850s—as a child of "four or five"—was sold with his mother at the Forrest establishment. Its "yard was a kind of square stockade of high boards with two room negro houses around, say, three sides of it and high board fence too high to be scaled on the other side or sides." The slaves "were all kept in these rooms, but when an auction was held or buyers came, we were brought out and paraded two by two around a circular brick walk in the center of the stockade. The buyers would stand near by and inspect us as we went by, stop us and examine us[:] [o]ur teeth and limbs and a Doctor generally [would examine] if there were sick negroes." Eden said his mother later explained to him that the buyers always examined them "to see if there were any scars on our body from a whip as it indicated a vicious temper or as they said a 'bad nigger.' "[4]

Southern Caucasian legend has it that the proprietor of these premises was emphatically good to his human stock in trade. Writer Lafcadio Hearn, who was visiting Memphis at the time of Forrest's funeral in 1877, reported that he was said to have been "kind to his negroes; that he never separated members of a family, and that he always told his slaves to go out in the city and choose their own masters." No slave took advantage of this freedom to run away, Hearn said, because "Forrest taught them that it was to their interest not to abuse the privilege; and, as he also taught them to fear him exceedingly, I can believe the story. There were some men in the town to whom he would never sell a slave, because they had the reputation of being cruel masters."[5]

Colonel George W. Adair, an Atlanta slave dealer and later newspaper executive "intimately associated with Forrest during this period of his career," has been quoted in particularly roseate terms, asserting that Forrest "was overwhelmed with applications from many of this class, who begged him to purchase them." Adair went on to say that when "a slave was purchased for him, his first act was to turn him over to his negro valet, Jerry, with instructions to wash him thoroughly and put clean clothes on him from head to foot," thus making the slave "proud of belonging to him." Adair said Forrest "was always very careful when he purchased a married slave to use every effort to secure also the husband or wife, as the case might be, and unite them, and in handling children he would not permit the separation of a family."[6]

He is reported to have been "kind" to his slaves, yet to have "taught them to fear him exceedingly"; was it possible to be the one while doing the other? Possibly so, because a little fear could go a long way. The inflammatory but in some ways accurate New York *Tribune* dispatch of

1864 would charge that his slave yard was "a perfect horror to all negroes far and near" and that his method of punishing a "refractory" slave was to require four others to hold the victim "stretched out in the air" while Forrest and his crippled brother John, whom the dispatch described as the establishment's "jailor and clerk," would stand "one on each side" and "cut up" the victim with bullwhips "until the blood trickled to the ground." The article went on to claim that slave women had been "stripped naked" and whipped with a "heavy leather thong dipped in a bucket of salt water," and that one male slave had been whipped to death with a "trace chain, doubled," and secretly buried.[7]

This dispatch's account of such whippings could well be expected to horrify Northern readers of 1864 almost as much as those of today, but whipping wasn't uncommon in the antebellum South. Interviews with freed slaves contain countless descriptions similar to those in the *Tribune* article, differing only in minor details. Sallie Carder, who lived as a slave in western Tennessee and was interviewed at age eighty-three in Burwin, Oklahoma, recalled that there "was a white post in front of my door with ropes to tie the slaves to whip dem." For the whippings, she said, owners or overseers commonly used "a plain strap, another one with holes in it, and one dey call de cat wid nine tails which was a number of straps plated [i.e., plaited] and de ends unplated." The slaves would be whipped with "a wide strap wid holes in it and de holes would make blisters. Den dey would take de cat wid nine tails and burst de blisters and en rub de sores wid turpentine and red pepper."[8]

Dealing with a large and constantly changing number of slaves on as temporary a basis as his salesmanship could render possible, Forrest—and his brother John, who was involved in the Memphis business by 1857, if not before—had to have stringent discipline, and whipping was the most common punishment to accomplish it. It perhaps was more "kind" and "humane" in the long run to make an occasional horrific example of some transgressor of a rule, thus rendering the large majority eager to obey every rule and making the whippings a rare occurrence. As horrible as whippings were, they seem to have been considered by both blacks and whites to be of less importance than the separation of families.[9]

As an "intimate" associate, Colonel Adair had to have known what Lafcadio Hearn and most others unfamiliar with the language and customs of slave dealing probably did not: that to be successful, a slave trader had to be known as humane, at least in the areas where he bought slaves. Few planters of any prominence would sell to a trader possessing any other kind of reputation, either because of their own sensitivity or out of sensitivity to the opinions of their peers. Selling in itself was to be avoided whenever possible. "Few persons of good standing and not traders ever admitted that they had sold slaves, except 'involuntarily'; virtually none admitted that they had divided families."[10]

Yet many, probably most, actually did divide families; they stood to gain more profit by doing it. Some even did so openly. "It seems almost incredible that any one should advertise willingness to separate husband from wife, and a mother from her little children, yet this was sometimes done. Without suiting the purchaser, the highest price could never be obtained." Even the arrangement of slaves in the sale-yard promenades — often in lines "according to sex and in descending order of height" — seems to have been "[f]or the convenience of purchasers and to eliminate family ties." That way, a buyer could feel less constrained to buy a whole family and less guilty about not doing so.[11]

The kind of treatment Adair says Forrest gave newly purchased slaves apparently wasn't unusual. At least, to try to make the human merchandise as attractive as possible was common among traders, some of whom went to considerable lengths. In the same year the Forrests moved to Memphis, an attorney commissioned by a planter client to sell a slave wrote that he "procured the services of a Broker whose business it is to do such things. He had his hair carded and his person washed and a supply of clothes was procured to set him off. . . . A few days training improved his air and manner much and a sale was effected." One former slave later recalled having the job of helping a none-too-scrupulous St. Louis trader prepare a shipment of blacks for the New Orleans market and being "ordered to have the old men's whiskers shaved off, and the gray hairs plucked out, where they were not too numerous, in which case we had a preparation of blacking to cover it, and with a blacking brush we would put it on. . . . These slaves were also taught how old they were . . . and after going through the blacking process, they looked ten or fifteen years younger."[12]

That Forrest's yard was no paradise is indicated by Eden's recollection of a day when he and the other blacks were being promenaded for buyers. A slave broke formation and "kicked over a chamber [pot] that was near and broke it. The guard — I do not know whether it was general Forrest or not, but I remember it well — picked up another chamber and broke it over the negro's head. I remember seeing an old negro woman washing his head at a pump." On the other hand, Eden's account indicates not only that Forrest was more considerate of mothers with small children than many other slave dealers but also perhaps that he was, as Hearn was told, choosy about the kind of masters to whom he sold. Eden recalled that his mother told him "they always tried to keep us together and sell us together; that some man wanted to buy her and another wanted me but the master held us together and we were sold finally to a Mr. —— Eden of Paducah, Ky. He was a good man and treated us kindly."[13]

The Forrest establishment does not seem, however, to have been always as uniformly humane and considerate of slave family units as Adair implied. Years later, onetime slave Louis Hughes wrote that his wife's mother and her seven children were sold in Forrest's slave yard and "none of this family were sold to the same person except my wife and one [of her] sister[s]." It isn't absolutely certain, though, that the Forrest firm itself was involved in these transactions; Hughes says his mother-in-law and the seven children were brought to Memphis from Kentucky by two other Negro-traders, so these slaves may just have been lodged in the Forrest facilities, which were open to such use for a fee.[14]

There were virtually no laws against division of slave families in any Southern state besides Louisiana. Louisiana forbade selling slave mothers away from children less than ten years of age as well as introducing into its borders slave children under ten without mothers if the mothers were alive. From Memphis, Forrest needed to worry about Louisiana law only when selling there (which he doubtless did many times), but if, as both the Eden memoir and 1854 Shelby County deed books indicate, he tried to comply with the idea of the Louisiana law in most of his Tennessee operations, he did so out of intelligence as much as humanity. A happy slave was one more likely to work well and less likely to run away; a slave mother sold away from her small children, on the other hand, was likely to be distraught and restless, while the children, like any other creatures removed too soon from their mothers, were likely to undergo trauma that could affect their growth, temperament, and, hence, future profitability.[15]

A man who always appreciated and took excellent care of horseflesh, Forrest probably did the same with his slaves when doing so didn't interfere with his profits—and for good reason. Reared in backwoods deprivation, he learned early to make maximum use of resources and to abhor waste. Treating a slave poorly, rendering him or her unable to fulfill the desired role at optimum efficiency, was foolish. He must have bought many slaves the way other shrewd traders have acquired livestock since time immemorial: purchasing them from unprosperous masters in poor condition, feeding them well, and selling them to richer masters in a state not only better but more profitable.

The sales recorded by him in Memphis during 1854 include one child under ten sold independently of a parent; they also disclose the formation of another partnership. In November, the new firm of N. B. Forrest & Josiah Maples sold to Lavinia and Lemuel Smith for $600 "the following slave to wit: Page a girl aged about nine years, sound in body and mind — to have and to hold said slave to the said Leml. Smith his executors etc forever. . . ."[16]

The year 1854, however, was not one of unmixed blessings. There was at least one wrenching domestic reverse. On June 26, according to an entry in the county death records, six-year-old Fanny Forrest died of "dysentery." The Memphis *Daily Appeal* of the following July 4 listed hers as one of seventeen Memphis deaths for the week ending July 1. It specified the cause of her death as "disease[,] Flux."

Her father, whose love of children was marked, could take little solace from remarks by W. J. Tuck, secretary of the town's board of health, appended to the death list: "We have no epidemic prevailing here, our city being unusually healthy for the season of the year. . . ."[17]

6

Forrest & Maples
SLAVE DEALERS
87 Adams Street
Between Second and Third,
Memphis, Tennessee,

Have constantly on hand the best selected assortment of FIELD HANDS, HOUSE SERVANTS & MECHANICS, at their Negro Mart, to be found in the city. They are daily receiving from Virginia, Kentucky and Missouri, fresh supplies of likely young Negroes. Negroes Sold On Commission and the highest market price is always paid for good stock. Their Jail is capable of containing Three Hundred, and for comfort, neatness and safety, is the best arrayed of any in the Union. Persons wishing to purchase, are invited to examine their stock before purchasing elsewhere. They have on hand at present, Fifty likely young Negroes, Comprising Field Hands, Mechanics, Home and body Servants, Etc.

THE MEMPHIS BUSINESS apparently blossomed quickly, for the whole of page 251 of the 1855 Memphis city directory is used for this advertisement of Forrest's partnership with Josiah Maples. The same directory indicates that Forrest was beginning to use his brothers in the operation and that the Adams Street compound was divided into the slave-dealing office and the family residence. The publication lists two Forrests: the proprietor's younger brother Aaron — "A.H., clerk, 87 Adams" — who boarded at 85 Adams, and "N.B., slave dealer, 87 Adams" residing at 85 Adams.[1]

The profits of the trade during this era, in which the prices of slaves in the burgeoning Southwest were rising quickly, are indicated by the return on a two-week investment Forrest & Maples made on three — "Ellick aged 30, Rhita aged 40 + her child Ellick 6 years" — purchased from Miss S. I. Stailey on October 16, 1854, for $1,450. On November 2 the firm sold what apparently was the same trio — listed this time in the Shelby County Register's records as "Ellick age 33, Ritter age 38, Ellick Jr. 5 years old" — to Sam Tate for $1,600. Such profit (more than 10 percent in seventeen days) was commonplace, made possible by the economic tenor of the time and place. Large-scale agricultural activity in newly settled Mississippi, Louisiana, Arkansas, and Texas was so frenzied that labor to power it was in short supply. The shortage was so pronounced that there was serious and continual Southern agitation for a reopening of the African slave trade, which had been closed by federal law in 1808. Owning blacks was becoming increasingly profitable, and most Southerners who could afford to do so bought as many of them as they could.[2]

Slaves were inexpensive to keep; according to "liberal estimates," the costs of maintaining a slave for a year "weren't more than $30" — partly, perhaps, because medical care for them was so neglected that its cost usually amounted to less than a dollar a year per slave. And they were "readily salable or hired out" by the time they were "6 or 8 years old," and the income from so doing was as favorable as, or even better than, that of selling. As early as 1832, a prominent slave owner noted that "the interest on money is 4 to 6 per cent. The hire of male slaves is about 15 per cent upon their value; in ten years or less, you have returned your principal with interest." In the 1850s the price of hiring "commonly ranged from 10 to 20 per cent of the market value of the slave, apparently averaging from 12 to 15 per cent...." Hiring prices were naturally highest in Mississippi, Louisiana, and Texas. The family of President James K. Polk sent from Tennessee to Mississippi a blacksmith more than sixty years old to be hired out for $487 a year.[3]

"Cotton and Negroes are the constant theme — the ever harped upon, never worn out subject of conversation among all classes," Mississippian

Joseph Holt Ingraham said of the Southwest as early as the 1830s. Of the two parts of this "theme," the lesser in importance was cotton. An observer's comment about Maryland and Virginia was true of much of the South: "[S]laves were seldom kept . . . for the sake of raising crops, but crops were often cultivated for the sake of raising slaves." A healthy black child barely past infancy was worth two or more workhorses, while a prime Southwestern field hand could sell for more than ten or fifteen horses, or for scores of cattle, sheep, and hogs.[4]

It is hardly surprising, then, that Southern slaveholders were keenly attentive to the "breeding" of slaves. Only small minorities of them seem to have conducted it in any systematic way, but virtually all appear to have encouraged their slaves to produce as many children as possible. One plantation mistress complained that slave women were pushed toward "reckless propagation" by offers of "less work and more food." She added that in "most" cases the resultant "increase is mere animal breeding, to which every encouragement is given, for it adds to the master's live-stock and the value of his estate."[5]

Many owners offered their slave women more than just additional food and premium working conditions. In addition to a cabin and a garden plot of ground, slave owner James H. Hammond of South Carolina gave an additional bounty of five dollars to first "marriages" among his slaves. For every baby satisfactorily cared for which reached the age of thirteen months in good health, he also gave the mother a muslin or calico frock. Some owners promised the slave women freedom after they had borne a certain number of children. As a result, there were startling reports of fecundity—and consequent profits. Another South Carolinian, Edmund Ruffin, estimated that a "gang" of slaves normally would multiply their numbers by four in thirty or forty years. Court reports documented such cases as a Nancy who bore seventeen children, a Hannah who bore fourteen or fifteen, and another, unnamed slave who bore thirteen. An antebellum physician recalled a single black couple who brought him an increase of $25,000 in forty years. Another remembered: "As soon as a man had the money he bought a girl, and before many years she had a family that was worth $10,000."[6]

For the master who could live from the labor of his slaves, wealth was inevitable. Ten young slaves, half of whom were girls, were worth less than $5,000 in 1840, but if they tripled in number in fifteen years, as they well might, the value of them and their children would be some $20,000— not counting the worth of their labor and that of any crops they tended. Gains far above that are reported to have been possible in Alabama,

Mississippi, and Louisiana "if one gave the closest attention to slave-rearing, raising crops, and buying more negroes to make new plantations out of cheap and fertile virgin soil; it was possible, but rare, only because enterprise and thrift were rare." Adept at figures, Forrest was nothing if not enterprising and thrifty. He had watched the progress of the slave economy through an ever-deepening association with it for twenty years and combined a profound understanding of its financial possibilities with the will and energy to extract its maximum profits. Sometime in the early 1850s, if not before, he seems to have decided to try to capitalize on all the ways one could profit from slave owning.[7]

In the process, he was forming acquaintances with the most prominent Memphians. Sam Tate, to whom he sold slaves in late 1854, was surely the attorney who was president of the Memphis & Charleston Railroad. The A. Wright to whom he sold four slaves around the same time as the Tate transaction was apparently Archibald Wright, noted jurist and ultimately Supreme Court justice of the state of Tennessee. R. B. Hawley, an 1855 customer, was a grocer and commission merchant, and Minor Meriwether was chief engineer of the Memphis & Tennessee Rail Road.

Forrest's penetration of his city's power elite was not without the occasional reverse. In 1855, banker and civic leader Isaac B. Kirtland—to whom Forrest & Maples had sold a fourteen-year-old slave named Dick on December 14, 1854—sued the partnership in chancery court, charging breach of promise and seeking damages of $2,000. He charged Forrest & Maples had warranted "said Slave to be sound, healthy, sensible and a Slave for life," but claimed that, instead, "the said Slave named Dick . . . at the time of the sale thereof was not sound and healthy but was unsound and unhealthy and was of no use or value to the said plaintiff and . . . this said plaintiff hath been put to charges and expense" to care for and keep "Said Slave Dick and for money expended in employing physicians and medicines." Kirtland added that he filed his suit after Forrest & Maples refused to return the $975 he paid for Dick, "although often requested. . . ." The verdict in the case is unknown. The only notation on the surviving copy of the lawsuit indicates that the defendants contended they weren't liable.[8]

Perhaps this lawsuit cooled Forrest's ardor for partnerships. The day of the last Forrest & Maples sales recorded in the Register's office, two younger Forrest brothers, William and Aaron, sold an eighteen-year-old slave named Bob for $1,050 to a Mary C. Temple. This transaction suggests the possibility that the eldest Forrest brother was already doing some business outside his partnership with Maples. For the next two years he apparently worked as head of his own business, splitting his profits with no partner while acquiring agricultural holdings that would make his slave dealings even more profitable.[9]

For $9,175 in cash, he purchased 797.5 acres on Big Creek in suburban Shelby County in early 1856. The same day, for $15,325, he also bought from the same person, John Harrison, "the following slaves to wit: Rodger aged 58, John aged 31, Sandy aged 30, Edwin aged 26, Rodger Jr. aged 24, Cuff aged 22, George aged 18, Cyrus aged 18, James aged 16, Billy aged 16, Henry aged 11, Joe aged 11, Susan aged 50, Hannah aged 27, Wynnie aged 54, Meary aged 20, Cynthia aged 3, and Fanny aged 15 years." From records filed with the County Register, it is difficult to determine the total price or down payment for both land and slaves, but a later document indicates that in the two transactions Forrest pledged to pay notes totaling $18,371.35 plus interest. The land he thus acquired was possibly a shrewd addition to the Memphis business; working in tandem, it and the downtown slave-trading operations could maximize each other's profits.[10]

In this, he seems to have been following the examples of role models in the New Orleans market, which was not only a larger version of the Memphis slave-trading scene but also similar in its hot and not-always-healthful climate: "[m]ost of the New Orleans traders believed in quick sales, large profits, and leaving the risks to others; and negroes not sold by late spring were commonly disposed of at reduced prices, to avoid the jeopardy of close confinement and illness during the depressing heat of a New Orleans summer."

One prominent New Orleans slave-trading firm "made a virtue and a profit out of a very different practice; they established a farm in a healthy and accessible region about 80 miles north of New Orleans, where the slaves that were not sold by June could cheaply and profitably be kept and trained while becoming acclimated." On this rural farm the "little children, the 'breeding women,' and the ailing of all kinds (also) could be cared for until most salable," affording the farm's proprietor the luxury of advertising Negroes for sale at all times. He also could "reopen his yard in October with a supply of 100 [slaves] that were able-bodied, fully acclimated, and very valuable." Similarly, another New Orleans trader kept "a farm or large slave-yard in the piney woods, nearer and more accessible." Such operations doubtless were studied by Forrest, who has to have visited New Orleans many times in his slave-trading travels. He must have been highly interested in this system whereby slaves not selling rapidly could be used on a plantation to earn other, agricultural profits

while awaiting sale and maintaining their health, or perhaps restoring it,
through the exercise of farm work.[11]

He made another, much different land purchase on November 10, 1856.
For $2,000 down and $1,000 notes due January 1, 1857, and January 1,
1858, he bought from wealthy physician Elbert A. White a lot fronting
fifty feet on Linden Street at the corner of St. Patrick. This purchase seems
to have been a minor real estate speculation, in which he apparently
dabbled as a sideline. The site must have been in a lower-class area of the
city, for less than two years later the Board of Aldermen considered an
ordinance describing an unspecified lot at the same intersection as a
"nuisance" and ordering the city marshal to "abate it."[12]

His slave sales in 1857 were often in four-figure sums: $1,400 for a
woman and two small children, $1,200 for a thirty-year-old man, $1,300
for a female house servant, $1,250 for a sixteen-year-old boy, $1,000 for
a twenty-one-year-old man, and $3,575 for what appear to have been two
parents and their three young daughters. Five years following his move
to the metropolis from little Hernando, he was challenging the city's
largest slave merchants. Within another twelve months, a violent chain of
events would make him preeminent.[13]

7

ANOTHER HOMICIDE. — JAMES MCMILLAN was yesterday severely
wounded by ISAAC BOLTON, at the slave depot of BOLTON & CO., with
pistol shots. BOLTON shot four times at McMillan, wounding him
twice. MCMILLAN used no weapon. MCMILLAN was wounded in the left
thigh, the ball passing around into the groins. The other wound was
in the fleshy part of the hip. MCMILLAN is lying in a dangerous
condition. BOLTON surrendered himself to an officer, and was tried
before ESQ. RICHARDS, who put him under bonds to appear at the next
term of the Criminal Court, with a forfeiture of $12,000. He gave the
required bond and was released. . . . The difficulty arose out of the
sale of a free negro, whom BOLTON alleges MCMILLAN sold him for a
slave. The negro recovered his freedom in a suit at law, and BOLTON
was required to refund the purchase money. MCMILLAN alleges that
he acted as an agent of BOLTON in the purchase of the negro.

P.S. — Since writing the above article, we learn that MCMILLAN has
died from the effects of his wounds.[1]

A SLAVE TRADER from Kentucky, James McMillan died in Forrest's home. McMillan sometimes bought slaves for Forrest on a commission basis in Kentucky and, accompanied by a partner named Hill, had come this time to Memphis with a few whom he quartered for safekeeping in Forrest's slave jail. Advertised in local newspapers as "one of the most complete and commodious establishments of the kind in the Southern country," Forrest's facility housed a business that at the time was excelled in the thriving Memphis marketplace only by that of Bolton, Dickins & Co., which boasted affiliates in New Orleans, Vicksburg, Mobile, and Lexington, Kentucky.[2]

The incident with the free Negro no doubt damaged the Bolton firm, costing senior partner Isaac Bolton much credibility. The infuriated Bolton invited McMillan to his slave yard on the false pretense of wishing to buy a "fancy" houseboy for his wife, and when McMillan, doubtless suspicious, asked Forrest what he should do, Forrest advised him to take a likely slave to the Bolton offices. When McMillan arrived there shortly after 9 A.M., Bolton began cursing and told him to refund the price of the free Negro or be killed. According to testimony in the trial that ensued, Bolton drew a pistol and fired three shots at his unarmed guest, severely wounding him, then denied him water or any other comfort as he lay suffering on the floor. The victim ultimately was taken to Forrest's, where he died about 5 P.M.[3]

This virtual assassination produced public revulsion toward the Bolton firm, whose volume of trade quickly fell behind Forrest's and soon collapsed altogether. Isaac Bolton initially jumped bail, then returned to Memphis and was indicted and jailed in an atmosphere so charged that a change of venue was granted. After seven attorneys were hired by the defense, the matter moved toward trial very slowly. As Forrest waited to testify for the prosecution, another killing shook Memphis. A businessman named Everson was murdered on the street by John Able under circumstances which brought "an immense crowd" to the jail. There fifty men were appointed to stand guard against Able's escape while the rest convened an angry public meeting.[4]

Able, reputed to be a "notorious gambler," claimed to have been drunk when he drew a pistol and shot Everson in front of the Worsham House hotel for "insult[ing] my mother" at the end of a conversation that apparently began over money Able owed Everson. Hundreds of Memphians, already disturbed by other gamblers' "outrages" and McMillan's recent murder, demanded a hanging. At the public meeting to determine the circumstances and quiet the crowd, resolutions were passed unanimously appointing a committee of three to notify another gambler and murderer, Joe Able—John Able's father—"to leave the county of Shelby before 12 o'clock tomorrow, never to return"; ordering all gamblers to leave Memphis within ten days, and authorizing their expulsion by force if necessary; and mandating the closing of all "gaming houses" within the city. The *Daily Appeal* named "Bedford Forrest" as a member of the three-man committee.[5]

Considering Forrest's own gaming proclivities, it is interesting to speculate why he was one of those chosen to go and see Joe Able. No hint remains in available records, but his involvement in the Able affair by no means ended with his service on the get-out-of-town committee. The next day, June 25, was comparatively quiet, a municipal election day on which Memphians chose a new mayor and aldermen. As soon as the polling places closed, however, Able came to the forefront of the public consciousness again. A June 26 mass meeting was held to name a committee of vigilance and mollify the crowd until a trial could be convened. A prominent citizen, Colonel John L. Saffarans, was named chairman and "[o]n a motion, Messrs. F. TITUS, D.B. TURNER, N.B. FORREST, and W.E. MILTON were selected as Vice Presidents."[6]

Forrest's elevation to this vice-presidency is as mysterious as his committee appointment two days earlier, but this time there is at least a hint as to how it may have occurred. His authorized biographers, who apparently exaggerated his considerable part in the incident, say believably that almost as soon as the murder had been committed, Forrest, whose slave yard was in the same neighborhood, had been among those drawn to the Worsham House by rumor of the crime. When he saw the mob's intent to lynch Able, these biographers continue, Forrest "[c]ounsel[ed] with the mayor and some other prominent citizens." The mayor, newly elected, was R. D. Baugh, later a political ally of Forrest's and possibly already a personal acquaintance. Forrest's paternal grandmother, wife of the first Nathan Forrest, was originally Nancy Baugh, and an R. D. Baugh is in the 1840 census records in Marshall County, Mississippi, an area with which Forrest was intimately familiar from his mid-teens through his early thirties. Even if he and Baugh weren't cousins, which seems impossible to determine now, they probably got to know each other years before the Able affair. In a lynch-mob atmosphere, a brand-new mayor no doubt would call on all dependable help he could find, especially from someone as manifestly fearless as the former Hernando constable.[7]

The June 26 mass meeting named its officers, defeated a motion to double the city's police force, and passed a resolution to name one man from each of the city's six wards as a committee of vigilance. Then, however, "a citizen of Arkansas, a non-resident of Memphis," took the floor and said that "if one hundred men would follow him, ABLE would be hung in ten minutes." The Arkansan summarily left, followed noisily by most of the crowd. The throng descended on the jail, forced its doors, extracted Able "in his nightclothes and bare-footed" and hauled him two blocks to the Memphis Navy Yard to carry out the hanging. At the Navy Yard, however, the crowd encountered its intended victim's wife, mother, and sister. A rope encircled Able's neck "when his mother rushed in and plead [sic] for the life of her son, and succeeded." The prisoner was returned to jail, but the crowd tried again that evening to take him and was dissuaded only by "several speeches" — one of which may well have been made by Forrest, although no surviving newspaper account names all the speakers who dispersed the third lynching attempt.[8]

Whatever else he did in the Able incident (and there is no surviving evidence to indicate he single-handedly saved Able, as his authorized biographers later claimed), Forrest doubtless made enough of a name for himself that Memphians began to see him as more than just a slave trader. He probably added to his rising public profile in the Bolton trial, which convened in nearby Covington, Tennessee, in April 1858. Even as reflected in the markedly imperfect newspaper reporting of the time, his testimony was characteristically abrupt, succinct, profane, and without fear of the powerful business competitor whom his testimony was helping consign to ruin.

He testified he was on a corner in front of Planter's Bank, perhaps a half mile from Bolton's slave yard, when he heard of the shooting of McMillan, a "middle-sized, delicate, spare man." Forrest immediately went to Bolton's, but by then McMillan had been taken away. McMillan had been in Memphis "six or seven days," having come down with partner Hill and "eight or 10 Negroes" from Maysville, Kentucky, where he lived. McMillan "has transacted business for me," Forrest added, and had been a guest in the Forrest home "a month in all" over the years; they had met in Lexington, Kentucky, in January 1853, and Forrest had "traveled with him in Kentucky" and "never saw him with a weapon." He also found "no weapon about him" when "I assisted to undress him" after the shooting, at which time McMillan remarked "he knew he should die." About 2 P.M., some four hours after being brought to the Forrest residence, McMillan sent for him and "asked me candidly about his condition. I said he would die, he said he knew it." He "wished me to arrange with his wife about some money." At this time, Forrest said, McMillan told "several times" the story of what had happened to him.

> *He stated he had gone to Bolton's mart to sell him Mr. Ridge-*
> *way's negro boy, when Bolton shot and killed him. When he got*
> *in the house, he found Bolton and Patrick Duffy* [a Bolton employee]
> *sitting there. The latter desired him to be seated, and asked him*
> *if that was the boy. He replied yes. Bolton then said he was a*
> *d—d rascal, and had sold him a free negro. He required him to pay*
> *up the value of the negro. He said pay, you G—d d——d rascal,*
> *or I will kill you. He (McMillan) said he would go to Forrest's*
> *and see his partner, Hill, and try and fix it up; but he had no money,*
> *and nothing to [write a] check upon. Duffy got up and went into*
> *the room in the rear. As he was passing out, Bolton drew a pistol*
> *and fired three times, by which he (McMillan) was wounded. Duffy*
> *then returned, and Bolton drew a bowie-knife and threw it upon*
> *the floor near him, and said to Duffy, there is the d——d son of*
> *a b——'s knife; I had to shoot him, or he would have killed me.*

Forrest testified that before Bolton fired the shots, McMillan had told him that Washington Bolton—a Bolton, Dickins & Co. partner who operated the firm's business in Lexington—"knew all about the free negro," an indentured servant whose unexpired term the Kentucky Bolton had acquired through McMillan. Forrest added that when Duffy got up to go into the back room of the Bolton establishment, he did so at Bolton's direction and that Bolton wanted him to take McMillan with him, but McMillan didn't go. McMillan told Forrest he "had no weapon with him but a four-bladed [pocket]knife." After the shooting, and after McMillan had been denied water or a pillow by Bolton and his employees, McMillan told Forrest, "he said to Bolton, you have killed me. Bolton replied, You d——d s—n of a b——h! you ought to have been killed twenty years ago."[9]

Incredibly, Bolton was acquitted by the Covington jury, but under outrageous circumstances that could only have made Forrest more publicly admired. Evidence emerged that a buyer for Bolton, Dickins & Co. had paid several Kentucky witnesses to testify against McMillan's character. Jury bribery was charged in the newspapers, and estimates of the expenses of the defense ran as high as "nearly $300,000."[10]

Forrest's business connections with a man who would join with others to sell an indentured servant into slavery (if that is in fact what McMillan meant to do) don't reflect well on him, and there is further evidence that he may not have been a complete stranger to such transactions. Louis Hughes, whose wife's mother and seven children he reported to have been sold in Forrest's Memphis slave yard, claimed that the mother and children all were entitled to "have been free under the old Pennsylvania law." Hughes wrote that two of his mother-in-law's brothers, subject to the same law, had won their freedom thanks to abolitionist attorneys, but as soon as this happened, the owner of the mother and her children put them in the hands of slave traders in Lexington for sale "down the river" in "a deliberate attempt to keep them from their rights." They became part of a drove of slaves taken by traders named Woods and Collins to Memphis, where upon arrival they were put in Forrest's yard and sold. The eldest daughter, Hughes adds, was sold "seven times in one day" because "the parties that bought her, finding she was not legally a slave and that they could get no written guarantee that she was, got rid of her as soon as possible." It should be added here that the whole of Hughes's account of his wife's experience with Forrest's yard suggests at least a possibility that Matilda Hughes and her family were only lodged in the Forrest slave jail, rather than sold by the Forrest firm. If Woods and Collins were just renting space in Forrest's busy facility and did their own selling, there is no reason Forrest need have had intimate knowledge of the circumstances.[11]

However questionable his business dealings, his forthright behavior on the side of law and order in both the Able affair and the Bolton outrage was admirable and must have seemed particularly so in the Memphis of that era. In light of it, the events that quickly followed aren't so surprising, even involving a slave trader. On June 22, 1858, the "Local Matters" column in the *Appeal* reported that "the voters of the Third Ward will hold a meeting tonight, at eight o'clock, at Forrest's Yard, on Adams Street, for the purpose of nominating candidates for Aldermen." Five days later, the *Appeal* printed the Third Ward vote results in the aldermanic election: "Coleman 158, Kortrecht 168, Forest [sic], 196, Brooks 47."[12]

8

FORREST JOINED THE city council at a precarious municipal time. Memphis had indebted itself trying to provide passable streets, police protection, and public peace for a population growing as the area's agriculture developed and boomed. The 1858 city canvass increased the number of aldermanic districts from six to eight and for the first time elected sixteen aldermen instead of twelve. A few days after the sixteen new ones were chosen, however, the city register estimated that the municipality's revenues for the year would fall $29,396 short of expenditures.[1]

Forrest didn't run for the Board of Aldermen for the salary it paid; there was none. Just attending the meetings—let alone making whatever preparations they required, individually and in committees—was time-consuming and boring if newspaper accounts of them are even marginally trustworthy. In addition to the regular meetings, which seem to have occurred every couple of weeks and often lasted for several hours, there also were frequent extra sessions because of business overflow. In contrast to many long-winded peers, Forrest was the same speaker who testified in the Bolton trial: forceful, succinct, practical, and markedly unawed by the merchants, attorneys, and other city fathers with whom he served. They, on the other hand, seem to have recognized early that he was a man possessed of certain skills and insights the rest of them lacked. Almost immediately, doubtless because he had been operating one of the most successful slave jails in the region for the past five years, he was appointed to a body overseeing the affairs of "Courthouse and Jail" as well as to four other standing committees: Finance, Vigilance, Improvements, and Markets.[2]

In assuming his duties, Forrest exhibited the demeanor of a man unfamiliar with parliamentary procedure and the gray formality of assemblages employing it. One can imagine chuckles in the city's prime Front Row business district over a paragraph in the July 21 *Appeal* regarding a council debate on how best to control the municipality's burgeoning population of stray dogs. After noting that other aldermen had recommended everything from poison to shotguns to deal with the problem, the *Appeal* reported: "Alderman Forrest suggested that there was a Mexican in town who would lasso the dogs for a dime each." Chuckles or no, the man who knew there was such a Mexican demonstrably knew Memphis and the common people who made it run, and most of his recommendations were not laughable, even if sometimes humorous. At the same meeting, the council was asked to pay for a barrel of "Dean's best whisky" that had been used by the city engineer. Another alderman explained that the whisky had been required "on an extraordinary occasion—fixing the [city's] street railroad." The *Appeal* added: "Alderman Forrest said the liquor was wanted last February when a great deal of cotton had to be moved by a great many Irishmen." The bill was ordered paid.[3]

Forrest's observations were to the point and sometimes acerbic and politically bold. For example, he challenged the stringent Sabbath blue laws by proposing that livery stables be allowed to do business on Sundays. During the same meeting, he proposed the construction of a new bridge and added that the one being used at the time would "fall down in three weeks." Of the city's expensive and ill-fated street-graveling projects, which a modern Memphis historian says engender suspicion that officials of the period 1858–60 were "in league with local gravel contractors," Forrest seems to have been an early opponent. As he neared the end of his first term on the board in June 1859, he attacked the jail, calling its "state so abominable that the prisoners ought not to be kept there another night."[4]

One of the more important early aldermanic matters in which he became involved was a committee to investigate how jail personnel had come to release a thief named David Adams. In an incident typical, in different ways, of council committees and Forrest, the five-man body released a majority report, a minority report, and Alderman Forrest's report. In the last-mentioned, Forrest appeared to defend the administration, saying he believed Adams's release resulted from an "oversight" and that "censure or reprimand"—not the suspension or firing of three policemen recommended by both the majority and minority—would be sufficient. When three-term alderman Thomas J. Finnie accused the whole council of a "coward-like" refusal to do its duty in the Adams matter, he quickly found he had used a word not employed by the prudent in reference to any group that included Forrest. The fire in the eye of the latter smoulders through the bland *Appeal* report: "Alderman Forrest said he did not think Alderman Finnie meant him, in his attack, for he [Finnie] knew he was a fighting man."[5]

After that, Forrest was handled a little differently by the chairman. In a heated discussion of whether the property of "charitable societies" such as the Masons and Odd Fellows should be untaxed along with that of churches, "several members made remarks from their seats, and engaged in conversation; for this, the President fined Alderman Robinson, Alderman Kortrecht, and Alderman Forrest $5 each. On explanation, the fine of Alderman Forrest was remitted." Forrest, a member of the Odd Fellows since 1847, did end up with a five-dollar fine for talking during that meeting, but it came later. Forrest apparently incurred the fine for talking to Mayor Baugh and Kortrecht, who also were fined five dollars each; by that time the chair had even levied a five-dollar fine on itself.[6]

The Finnie affair was not the only reported instance of Forrest's anger.

Early in August, as a member of the Markets Committee, he began working on a proposal to give the city a new Market House. The affair dragged on until the latter part of March, and after a down payment finally had been made on property he recommended, the protest of a prominent widow against locating the market near her home caused the council suddenly to reverse its position and order a new site to be found. Forrest threatened to resign from the committee if the change was made (he "was sick of the subject," the *Appeal* quoted him as saying), but the council persisted. He protested that he was "surprised at the manner in which the Board dilly-dallied upon the subject," but a vote was called for and another location chosen. He immediately resigned from the Market House Committee and said he "would never again, he believed, serve on a special committee." Characteristically, he later cooled, and two months later agreed to be appointed to bodies studying street paving and selling the Memphis and Charleston Railroad a strip of publicly held land.[7]

Forrest's original Market House proposal hints that he had forged a close relationship with the Memphis & Charleston, one of the area's more powerful interests. Four years earlier, he had apparently sold some slaves to the railroad's president, Sam Tate, and he got on closer terms with Tate soon after assuming public office, if not before. His initial, unsuccessful Market House plan was to build the facility near the Memphis & Charleston depot, a measure that would have benefited the railroad, which at the time was still laying track. As his aldermanic tenure wore on, Forrest increasingly assumed the role of spokesman for the Memphis & Charleston, bringing the board several communications from Tate. In October he voted against selling the city's $500,000 stock in the Memphis & Charleston at a loss; the sale was to be to Tate and several other prominent citizens and was proposed because the city was $42,000 in arrears on its payment of interest on the bonds. The measure carried eight to six, however, and the following April, Forrest himself bought $50,000 worth of the bonds from the city. He later said he sold them within a year for a sizable profit—of $10,000 or more.[8]

There were also, of course, the mundane street-paving, lamppost-constructing, gas-main-digging, and similar ward-heeling measures in which any alderman necessarily deals, and in a few of them Forrest's actions were implicitly self-serving. Early in his first term, for instance, he proposed that any auctioneer selling slaves along with other merchandise be required to "take out a [$300] negro trader's license." Six weeks later, Kortrecht offered Forrest's proposal in the form of an ordinance, and

Forrest rose in favor of it, saying "that he knew of several companies who proposed to come here and establish regular negro auction houses, if protected in their business in the manner proposed by the ordinance."⁹

His vocation came up again in a discussion of the need for a decent cemetery for paupers. The *Appeal* reported that "Alderman Forrest said a potter's field ought to be provided; he had lost several negroes lately and had to pay from $25 to $75 to bury them." The insensitivity of this observation, the only one like it that appears in *Appeal* accounts of his aldermanic tenure, is possibly attributable to anger. It occurred during the same meeting of, and a few minutes following, his stormy resignation from the Market Committee.¹⁰

Late in Forrest's first term, the street commissioner made a ward-by-ward report of amounts spent in repair work by his office; the Third was the only one in which no work had been done. Whether that reflected Forrest's and Kortrecht's freshman status as aldermen, or whether there just happened to be no such work that badly needed doing in the Third Ward during that period of straitened finances, is uncertain, but it apparently shouldn't be taken as an indication that he and Kortrecht weren't doing the jobs for which they were elected. The more important things Forrest did included, toward the end of his first term, offering a resolution (on behalf of Mayor Baugh) establishing the city's first paid fire department. In late June of 1858, both he and Kortrecht were renominated for their positions, and on July 1 the *Appeal* reported that they had been reelected with more votes than they had polled a year earlier: Forrest 201, Kortrecht 188. Their closest opponent received 101.¹¹

The new council elected Kortrecht its president, and Forrest was named head of the Finance Committee. Before he could do much in that position, however, he suddenly resigned, citing plans to move out of the ward. A day or two prior to his resignation, the following advertisement by his former partner, Byrd Hill, began running in the *Appeal*:

HILL, WARE & CHRISP.
A NEW FIRM.

A GRAND and complete arrangement—having bought of Mr. Bedford Forrest his new and splendid residence, and the commodious and well arranged Negro Mart building attached thereto, I have also associated as partners, Messrs. Ware and Chrisp, and in this business we flatter ourselves that we can give general satisfaction to all who favor us with their patronage. We will also receive to board, and for sale on commission, any negroes consigned to our care.

HILL, WARE & CHRISP.

Adams street.[12]

Forrest had by then been engaged for a year and a half in a complicated series of real estate transactions, acquiring more and more prime agricultural and residential property not only in Memphis but in Mississippi and, for a brief time, in Arkansas. On January 28, 1858, he paid $1,600 for another 100 acres near the 797.5 purchased two years earlier in suburban Shelby County. Then, less than two weeks later, he sold for $12,075 a total of 805 acres in this area to future Memphis mayor John W. Leftwich. A week after being elected to his first term in city council, he paid $3,125 for a 3.08-acre lot on Pigeon Roost Road and, on August 16, enlarged his Adams Street compound by acquiring eighty-five more feet of frontage between Second and Third for $10,000; part of the latter sum was to be paid via certain notes due in 1858 and 1859. The largest purchase came on October 16, 1858, when he bought 1,900 acres of cotton land in Coahoma County, Mississippi, from H. C. Chambers for $47,500. Two weeks thereafter he paid James C. Tappan about $47,000 for another 1,346 acres in Phillips County, Arkansas—roughly across the Mississippi River from the Coahoma County tract. The Tappan transaction may have included a swap of properties, because early in 1859 he deeded to Tappan the 3.08 acres on Pigeon Roost Road, along with 20 acres he recently had bought 2.5 miles north of Memphis; the two tracts together were valued in the deed at $12,000, a total of $4,875 more than he had paid for them a few months before. On July 7, 1859, two weeks before he resigned his aldermanic seat and the same day he sold his slave yard to Byrd Hill for $32,000, he bought from Hill for $13,000 a lot at the corner of Second and Adams.[13]

These are the facts, but Forrest's aims at the time are unclear; maybe they were so even to him. Five weeks after his resignation, he was back on the city council, welcomed by his colleagues. Perhaps he had planned to move to the remote Coahoma County plantation—on which the quarters were decidedly less grand than the "splendid residence" mentioned in the Hill, Ware & Chrisp advertisement—and Mary Ann had balked. Whatever his intention, it was short-lived; he moved only down the street, from a home at 85 Adams Street to one on the south side of Adams between Third and Fourth.[14]

Where he acquired the resources to make this series of real estate transactions isn't so problematical. In 1858, his slave business had expanded into a busy Mississippi office at Vicksburg, apparently headed by his younger brother Aaron; its title was A. H. Forrest & Co. For eighteen months or more, that firm—often using the aid of other Forrest brothers—imported sizable "gangs" of slaves, significant numbers of them from Missouri and evidently bought there by William H. (Bill) Forrest, who was active in St. Louis. The senior, Memphis-based brother sometimes was brought in to witness certain documents attesting that the slaves being imported into Mississippi included no felonious lawbreakers. Other younger brothers such as Jesse and Jeffrey Forrest seem to have been engaged in these Mississippi operations, too, either selling slaves on their own or acting as agents for sellers in Memphis. Between 1858 and early 1860, more than forty Forrest transactions were entered in the Warren County Chancery Clerk's records in Vicksburg, with the eldest brother named in a handful, usually as a witness to certificates written in Memphis by a commissioner appointed by the governor of Mississippi. As late as August of 1860, the Vicksburg firm was advertising a pressing need for "150 likely young negroes for the Mississippi and Louisiana market. . . ."[15]

By the late 1850s, the primary Forrest's annual net income from slave trading alone—forgetting the yields of his cotton plantations—has been estimated minimally at from $50,000 to $96,000, "a fabulous income" at the time. With slave sales conservatively estimated to number more than 1,000 a year during the late 1850s, even the $96,000 figure is probably low, since a "20 per cent profit on only 600 at $800 each would be a net gain of $96,000." Forrest sales recorded in Memphis in 1859 average not $800 but, rather, more than $1,100 each, and his advertisements appeared in newspapers from the South's eastern coast to its southwestern frontiers.[16]

He withdrew his resignation and was restored to his seat on the Memphis Board of Aldermen on September 8, 1859, just in time to participate in a lively debate on a referendum to decide whether the Memphis & Charleston Railroad should be given a right-of-way through the city to the river. He voted with slim majorities which passed the measure and then turned back an attempt to kill it. Two weeks later, he rose in opposition to a measure proposing to confine policemen's rewards to no more than five dollars and prohibiting them from going outside the city's limits in pursuit of fugitive slaves. One alderman complained that "some of our policemen consumed their entire time, to the neglect of their other duties, in search of runaway negroes." Forrest, who surely had paid policemen for such services, was reported by the *Appeal* as hoping "that the ordinance would not be passed, arguing that it was unconstitutional. He said that such perquisites as the policemen received for arresting slaves were necessary to their support."[17]

A couple of days after this council meeting, he was involved in an abortive illegal duel, conducted across the river in Arkansas to evade authorities. It involved two candidates in a Mississippi election held a few days later, and Forrest served as second for John M. Dockery against Felix Labauve, a prominent politician and newspaper publisher from Hernando. The combat was aborted when Forrest, who had not been present when the challenges and ground rules were issued, noticed at the dueling site that Labauve's rifle was shorter and thus deadlier than had been agreed upon. He offered to let Labauve and his second, S. S. Minniece, have time to locate a proper weapon, but the affair disintegrated amid mutual charges of a "back-out."[18]

A month thereafter, the *Appeal* printed impressive evidence of how far the slave trader had elevated himself in both the society and the sporting circles of his adopted city:

> The semi-annual meeting of the Memphis jockey club, at the Worsham House last evening, was . . . called for the election of officers and for making regulations for the approaching races. Gen. Thomas H. Bradley was chosen president by acclamation for the ensuing year, and Messrs. J. J. Worsham, J. Knox Walker, N. B. Forrest, J. M. Rodgers and James Goslee were elected vice presidents. . . .[19]

9

FALL OF A BUILDING ON ADAMS STREET. — The new brick building, on Adams street, between Second and Third, occupied by Messrs. Forrest, Jones & Co., as a negro mart, fell to the ground about 7 o'clock yesterday. The building was occupied at the time by a number of slaves, no less than six of which number were buried beneath the ruins. A large party of citizens at once commenced a diligent search for the remains of the dead and dying, and in a short time recovered the lifeless bodies of Jeff and Frank, who had been suddenly killed by the catastrophe. Four other negroes, more or less injured, were extricated from the ruins, one or two of whom, it is feared, will die of their wounds. None of the slaves who were killed outright belonged to the proprietors. Jeff was the property of a Mr. Brown, and Frank belonged to a Mr. Thornton. The loss by the accident is about $5,500, including the death of the slaves and the destruction of the building.[1]

THIS STRUCTURE, WHOSE collapse occurred on a "horrible" day in early January 1860 during which rain had fallen "all day and night," must have represented an enlargement of facilities, reflecting the steady growth of business up until about this time. In the Charleston, South Carolina, *Courier*, as well as the Memphis *Avalanche* and other newspapers across the South in the winter of 1859–60, Forrest announced that he was doing business, "BUYING AND SELLING NEGROES, both on commission and on private account," in new quarters with "Mr. S. S. Jones, of DeSoto, Mississippi, and my brother, Wm. H. Forrest, of Memphis. . . . Our buildings are located at 89 Adams Street, next door east of my old Mart; they are spacious, combining convenience, comfort and safety — are superior to any establishment of the kind in the State, and equal to any that I have ever inspected." The advertisement added that the company would "board, and sell on commission, and keep constantly on hand, a good assortment of Virginia, Georgia and Carolina negroes. 500 NEGROES WANTED. I WILL PAY MORE THAN ANY OTHER PERSON, for No. 1 NEGROES, suited to the New Orleans market. . . ."[2]

Forrest's work on the Board of Aldermen continued, and apparently to more avail than in his first term. The Third Ward jumped from last place to third among the eight in its receipt of municipal street expenditures, getting $117.62 of the city's money. The local political climate, though, appears to have been changing, with Memphians becoming more concerned about the city's finances. Forrest was one of but two aldermen reelected in late June of 1860, and accounts of the meetings during this period reflect mounting tension.[3]

On July 10, with his third term barely begun, the Finance Committee chairman became testy in ramrodding several municipal measures through. One provided that a "first-class engineer" be hired to oversee the work of paving streets by affected property holders. First-term alderman J. B. Robinson denounced the measure as "a magnificent absurdity . . . that would cost the city $25,000 a year." The *Appeal* report indicates Forrest replied hotly: "Alderman Forrest said the previous speaker was the worst scared man he ever saw, and his exaggerations had doubled the expenses spoken of."[4]

The *Appeal* itself was growing increasingly critical of the city administration's methods of handling monies. A lengthy August 3 editorial commended the appointment of a special council committee—of which Alderman Robinson was a member—to ascertain the state of the city's finances. As the council's curiosity about the matter grew, one member introduced an ordinance to hire a city controller to straighten things out. Another offered a measure of possibly retroactive proportions: a resolution to appoint a committee "to investigate, with the city attorney, the sale of the city's stock in the Memphis & Charleston railroad" in 1858, and to ascertain "whether it was legal and valid."[5]

The only member of the 1858–59 council still on the Board of Aldermen, as well as the only member of that council to have bought some of the bonds in question, was Forrest, and he naturally became a central figure in the discussion. The *Appeal* reported that "Ald. Forrest explained that he had . . . taken $50,000 of the stock purchased from the city. He held it twelve or eighteen months and then sold it, making $10,000 on the transaction." He said he thought the city's sale of the bonds was "all right, although he was opposed to it at the time; it was better to leave the matter where it was." When it became obvious that some council members weren't going to do that, "Ald. Forrest advised that good counsel should be employed, and that five or ten thousand dollars be appropriated to pay them, for it would cost much to contest the sale. . . ."

An alderman named Hughes "thought the sale was illegal; the matter should be settled; it was much talked of in the streets." Forrest agreed with an Alderman Martin that no examination of the legality of the sale had been made by the council that passed it, but he added that "nine-tenths of the citizens" had favored it at the time; "more than twenty business men came to him and wished him to favor the sale. In reply to a question, Ald. Forrest stated that the stock in question had paid sixty per cent, since the city parted with it, but had paid no cash dividend before that time."[6]

Three days after this probing discussion, he submitted his second aldermanic resignation. According to the *Appeal*, he explained that "things were in such a fix—so much difference and wrangling—. . . that he saw no possibility of escaping going to protest [i.e., a contest of the bond sale], all of which, he believed, was owing to proceedings of members of the board." Therefore, he said, he would quit. "Several" aldermen "appealed to Mr. Forrest not to," but he ignored them, saying he had "found such difficulties in raising money for the city" because of the "late proceedings, that he must withdraw. He had two plantations to attend, and could not spare the time required at the board." Alderman Robinson, the freshman councilman he a month earlier had branded "the worst scared man he ever saw," moved that his resignation be accepted.[7]

Did Forrest, though, really want it to be? His seniority—he was one of just three three-termers in the council—and the way this resignation followed by a year another in which he was restored triumphantly to his original position, suggest that this second one may have been an impulsive and arrogant ploy to stop debate on the railroad bond sale. He apparently had nothing to lose in the continuing investigation; he, after all, had fought the sale when it was made, and there were no published allegations of wrongdoing on his part. So his motive in trying to force the council to drop its attempt to revoke the sale was seemingly the responsible civic one of opposing a process likely to cost the depleted city treasury still more money. Actual resignation, however, may have been a step farther than he intended to go, or so hints a sentence in the *Appeal* report of a council meeting two weeks later. A vote had to be taken to fill his vacated chair, and after Alderman Robinson named four possible successors, "[t]he mayor said he believed Mr. Forrest would consent to re-enter the board if re-elected." In two council ballots that followed, Forrest received just two votes out of twenty-two cast. Two weeks later, after a successor had been named, he seems to have defended himself against any possible besmirching of his honor in the accepted public way, publishing a "card" no longer extant but referred to in the reply of Alderman John Martin, one of the council's seekers of wrongdoing in the bond controversy; Martin replied that he had not intended to place blame on any individual.[8]

Forrest's public office-holding career was over, but his interest in politics wasn't. Five days before his resignation, the hotly secessionist Memphis *Avalanche* had named him first of fifteen men appointed by the Shelby County Democratic Association "to make arrangements for a Grand Mass Meeting" on August 14. Secessionist William L. Yancey of Alabama, an advocate of reopening the African slave trade, was principal speaker, and Forrest and the other fourteen organizers apparently did their jobs well. The *Avalanche* reported that Yancey spoke for four hours to a crowd estimated at 10,000, "the largest meeting that ever gathered in Memphis."[9]

Forrest's participation in the preparations for the Yancey speech may not necessarily indicate that he was an advocate of extreme secessionist views (something he would deny repeatedly years later); it perhaps reflects no more than his stature as an influential local Democrat. Yancey was an important national figure, particularly that summer, and therefore one whose views were informative to any audience interested in America's rapidly worsening sectional divisions. In the spring, Yancey had led forty-nine Deep South delegates out of a national Democratic convention in Charleston and advocated Southern revolt against a Northern majority who refused to support slavery in the party platform. Six weeks later, after Abraham Lincoln had been nominated in May by the Republican convention in Chicago, Democrats tried to convene a second national meeting in Baltimore; this time 110 Southerners walked out and held their own Southern Democratic convention. They nominated retiring vice president John C. Breckinridge of Kentucky, while Northern Democrats chose Stephen A. Douglas of Illinois, and holders of formerly Whig sentiments, most from the upper South, formed an antisecession Constitutional Union Party, naming as their standard-bearer John Bell of Tennessee.

Forrest's views regarding the four candidates cannot be stated with certainty. His authorized biography describes him as "always a strong . . . States Rights Democrat" who nevertheless "had become deeply attached . . . to the Union." Like most prominent Southerners of the period, he surely had friends pushing him in different directions. One had to have been Matthew C. Gallaway, the Memphis *Avalanche* editor whose publication was vociferously backing Breckinridge and secession and whose closeness to Forrest is hinted by the fact that the latter used four Gallaway notes as part of his down payment on part of the Mississippi land he bought from H. C. Chambers. A member of the Democratic state central committee, Gallaway surely acquainted himself with the men in charge of the 1860 rally addressed by William L. Yancey—if, indeed, he had not already cultivated Forrest because of the latter's prominent role on the Board of Aldermen. On the other hand, Forrest's former mentor and probable kinsman, Memphis mayor R. D. Baugh, was a very active vice president of the local Constitutional Union Party, and Mary Ann Forrest's distant relative, Sam Houston, publicly supported the Bell ticket in Texas.[10]

With no further aldermanic duties and two plantations to attend to, Forrest suddenly was without many of his former reasons to remain much in Memphis. Perhaps the building collapse in January caused him to begin thinking along new occupational lines that appeared more and more attractive as the year progressed; or perhaps it merely resolved him to take a direction he had abortively selected when he resigned from the council the first time, in 1859. Possibly Mary Ann prevailed on him to take up a more gentlemanly calling, or his business acumen discerned in the increasingly warlike headlines of Memphis newspapers the impending doom of the business of selling humanity. Whatever the cause, his slave business started winding down. He had apparently stopped selling to Memphis buyers the year before, possibly restricting his business to the more profitable course of supplying the New Orleans market cited in the Forrest, Jones & Co. advertisement. His last slave sales recorded in the Shelby County Register's office were dated in early 1859. The sales of his younger brother Aaron's company in Vicksburg apparently stopped in 1860.[11]

Forrest seems to have been spending much more of his time in the comparative wilds of Coahoma County. The census taker who interviewed him on June 5, 1860, listed his occupation as a "Planter" who owned $171,000 in Memphis real estate and another $90,000 in "personal estate." By October of that year, he held title to at least 3,345 acres in Mississippi, having traded in his recently purchased 1,346-acre Phillips County, Arkansas, plantation—valued at $33,000—on 1,445 more Coahoma County acres valued at $100,000. In this purchase, he paid $10,000 in cash, a $17,000 tenement, and a batch of notes payable over the next three years.[12]

One wonders why a man earning as much as Forrest seems to have been would have to stretch himself so thinly to buy such property. In acquiring the Arkansas land (along with twenty-eight slaves) on November 1, 1858, for a price of approximately $47,000, he was similarly mortgaged, paying only $7,000 in cash accompanied by $20,000 worth of "certain property in the city of Memphis," and notes of $6,430, $6,796, and $7,156 due each November 1 for the next three years. If he was earning as much by slave trading as has been estimated, he must have been spending much on other things. He is reported to have been paying for the college education of his youngest brother, and, if his earlier conduct can be taken as fair indication, he probably was supporting members of his own and his wife's extended families. He perhaps was gambling heavily, too. The sporting members of the Memphis Jockey Club must have been substantial bettors. After the war, in comparatively impoverished circumstances, he is reported to have casually played cards for stakes totaling thousands.[13]

The Forrests' Mississippi plantation probably wouldn't have impressed his fellow officers of the Jockey Club. A few years later a neighbor described it as a "six-room dwelling, not beautiful but well-built and comfortable," sitting "in a grove of magnificent oak trees and facing the public road. . . . [B]ack of [it] were the slave quarters, consisting of two rows of cabins facing each other, forming a sort of avenue. Conveniently located near these were several large cisterns." The slave schedule accompanying the 1860 Census disclosed Forrest had thirty-six slaves living in twelve houses here.[14]

The Coahoma plantation appears to have been very profitable, although nowhere near as much so as slave trading; after the war, Forrest claimed to have harvested there in 1861 more than 1,000 bales of cotton—valued at $30,000 by a later estimate. The pace in Coahoma County was slow compared to that of Memphis, and he sought ways of compensating for that. In early 1861, local authorities indicted him on a charge that sounds trivial and yet significant. It held that he "did play at and bet upon a certain game of cards."[15]

10

. . . LET THE SOUTH ALONE—RESTORE THE FRATERNAL SPIRIT THAT GAVE IT [the Union] BIRTH AND CHANGE THE HEARTS OF THE NORTH-ERN PEOPLE. . . . Do this, and there is some chance for the good old Union of Washington and Jefferson. . . . Alas, the task is more than this motley crowd of compromisers dare to undertake! What but omnipotence itself can reunite the scattered fragments of the golden bowl of brotherly love that has been broken? Who can breathe into the dead body of the sundered Union, the breath of life that abolition traitors have trampled out of it? It is too late. . . .[1]

INDEED. ON THE day in January 1861 on which this appeared in the *Avalanche*, the legislatures of five states—South Carolina, Florida, Alabama, Georgia, and Forrest's own Mississippi—already had voted to quit the Union. Five days after the *Avalanche* editorial, Louisiana's legislators did the same, and those of Texas followed within a week. On February 9, 1861, delegates to a convention in Montgomery, Alabama, finished drafting the constitution of a new nation christening itself the Confederate States of America. They also would name its provisional president and vice president: former U.S. senator Jefferson Davis of Mississippi and former U.S. congressman Alexander Stephens of Georgia.

Thus a Union that had strained its seams over the issue of slavery since the presidency of Andrew Jackson finally had come undone, split asunder by tensions that heightened in Kansas during the mid-1850s, exploded eastward with John Brown's insurrectionary raid on Harper's Ferry, Virginia, and culminated—thanks to the split between the Democratic Party's Northern and Southern wings—in the minority election of Abraham Lincoln to the presidency of the disuniting States. The *Avalanche* regarded Lincoln's inauguration as the ultimate constitutional desecration, "a dark day in the history of the . . . Republic. During the next few hours an Abolition ignoramus" from "the wilds of Illinois . . . will be propped in the chair sanctified by Washington and consecrated by Jefferson. The heart of the patriot bleeds and sickens. . . ."[2]

These words probably were written by Forrest intimate Matthew Gallaway, one of two proprietors of the *Avalanche*. Describing himself as an "infidel, radical, ultra Democrat," Gallaway was both a crusader for the rights of Caucasian Southerners and a talented journalist who knew how to pick prose fights to his paper's advantage with the more moderately Democratic *Appeal*. The *Appeal* accused Gallaway of being fanatical, dishonest, immature, politically treasonous, and disrespectful of his seniors in journalism and politics. Gallaway, whose newspaper's early lack of a political following in moderate Memphis was balanced by its enthusiastic acceptance in more bellicose northern Mississippi, retorted that the *Appeal* represented "the mistletoe Democrats — the excrescence which had become a fungus growth to this party."[3]

Now in the midst of a protracted process of paying off his Mississippi cotton kingdom, Forrest would have preferred to enjoy a period of continued national peace in which to do it. Notes owed on his Mississippi property, payable through early 1863, included ones for $12,400 due January 28, 1862, and $12,471.85 due February 28, 1863. If Forrest possessed the money to pay off these notes, he may have been hoarding his cash for the uncertain months ahead. Mississippi had seceded, but citizens of Tennessee — long the center of his sphere of interest — had voted overwhelmingly, in a referendum held on the very day Davis and Stephens had been elected provisional leaders of the Confederacy, against calling a secession convention. The March 4 edition of the *Avalanche* carried not only the disgusted commentary cited above on the inauguration of Lincoln but also articles on postal rates in the Confederate States of America and "confident" expectations from Little Rock that an Arkansas state convention would pass a secession ordinance.[4]

It was a confusing time. On April 28, about three weeks after Southern troops under General P. G. T. Beauregard captured Fort Sumter in South Carolina, the *Avalanche* reported that — despite the fact that Tennessee had not seceded — General Gideon J. Pillow, a Tennessee-born Mexican War hero of modest proportions, was "now in our midst," given "the important duty of providing for the military defense of Tennessee. We had an interview with Gen. Pillow yesterday, and he assured us that he would not leave this state until everything was placed in a safe and defensible position. . . ." Directly beneath the Pillow report, under a headline reading "CORN! PROVISIONS!", appeared an agricultural item: "Again we would impress upon the people of the South the necessity of planting large crops. The war may be of long duration, and we should be prepared for the worst."[5]

Four days after this issue of the *Avalanche*, Forrest bought a forty-two-acre farm seven miles north of Memphis and installed on it his mother and his stepfather, James H. Luxton. On June 24 he conveyed to the Luxtons title to the property for five dollars. By then, two more critical watersheds had been passed, one national and one individual. On June 8 Tennesseans held another referendum on secession and, in response to Lincoln's call for troops to quell rebellion in South Carolina six weeks earlier, voted two to one to endorse a state legislature resolution to leave the Union. On June 14, Forrest—along with his youngest brother, Jeffrey, and his fifteen-year-old son, William—"repaired to Memphis with the intention of joining the Confederate force then engaged in fortifying the position of Randolph, Tennessee," near Memphis. Once again, he characteristically acted on a spur of the moment. Reaching Memphis, "following the strong bent of his nature for cavalry, he at once attached himself . . . to the 'Tennessee Mounted Rifles,' a company which he found forming . . . under Dr. Josiah S. White, and in less than a week afterward he became a part of the garrison at Randolph, whither his company was ordered."[6]

Nathan Bedford Forrest, his brother, and his son all signed on at the same rank: private.[7]

Part III

SOLDIER

11

FORREST DID NOT remain a private very long. In fact, just one eyewitness glimpse of his service at that rank remains. Fellow private John Milton Hubbard, a West Tennessee schoolteacher who had volunteered with an ambitious crowd of would-be cavalrymen calling themselves the Hardeman Avengers, had ridden in with them from Bolivar, Tennessee, and camped near Randolph in a wasp-infested area quickly dubbed Camp Yellowjacket. Nearby, Hubbard later recalled, were posted two Memphis cavalry companies. He was riding near the area of these companies one day, he wrote, when "I met a soldier speeding a magnificent black horse along a country road as if for exercise and the pleasure of being astride so fine an animal. On closer inspection I saw it was Bedford Forrest, only a private like myself, whom I had known ten years before down in Mississippi."[1]

Exactly how Forrest came to be promoted from private to lieutenant colonel is lost to history. One story has it that a delegation of prominent Memphians went to Nashville "a few days after" his enlistment to see Governor Isham G. Harris and departmental commanding general Leonidas Polk and prevailed on them to give Forrest a larger role, and that his commission followed about July 10. It is documented that Harris, "knowing Forrest well and having a high regard for the man," sent a telegram commanding Forrest to meet him in Memphis, where the latter was discharged as a private and commissioned to recruit a battalion of mounted rangers. There is evidence that the commission and the order to recruit a mounted battalion came separately during public, third-party lobbying on Forrest's behalf; apparently, prominent friends won him the commission first and then began calling for a command suited to him.

On July 23, almost two weeks after his authorized biographers date his promotion to lieutenant colonel, the *Avalanche* of Matthew Gallaway (who in addition to being senior proprietor of the newspaper was the Memphis postmaster and a member of the state executive committee of the Democratic Party) printed an article headlined "MILITARY NECESSITY" suggesting that in addition to several regiments of cavalry already in Confederate service in western Tennessee, "we want a regiment of rangers" who "could make forays upon the enemy's camp or country . . . in advance of the regular army, and deal death and destruction on every side." The article added that men of West Tennessee and North Mississippi could make up such a force "as would become a terror to the foes of the South" under "a leader of known skill and bravery, and such an one might lead them to the very jaws of death." Then it came to the point. It had made this suggestion, it continued, because of "numerous applications made to us to know of such a force" by men who wanted to serve in it — and who "expressed a desire that our fellow citizen Col. N. B. Forrest should be at their head. Those who know Col. Forrest, who are acquainted with his reckless bravery controlled by a fund of sound and logical sense — in short, those who know the man will not be surprised at the wishes of so many to be led by him." The writer went on to add that such a Forrest-led regiment undoubtedly would be received into service by Jefferson Davis. "We hope he [Forrest] may undertake it under any circumstances."[2]

This article — indicating that as soon as Forrest enlisted, some of the recruits at Randolph expressed a preference to be commanded by him rather than by their superiors, and that other prospective volunteers were awaiting his elevation to appropriate rank — was well timed to make an impression on Governor Harris; an item in the same *Avalanche* issue noted that the governor "arrived in the city yesterday, and is stopping with his family." Harris, at that moment campaigning hard for reelection, may have needed no huge push to pull Forrest from the ranks. With Tennessee's northern border virtually undefended at the time, he had to have troops and men to lead them, and any reasonable plan to induce influential people to raise more units was probably welcome. He also "knew" Forrest, as his own words attest — if not as a past patron of Forrest's slave yard, then certainly as a mutual guest at some of the same Memphis Democratic functions Forrest had attended as alderman. Like Forrest, Harris had based his business — a law practice — in Memphis for several years, and he and Forrest may well have been longer-term acquaintances. Three years older than Forrest, the governor not only had been born in the same county as Mary Ann Forrest but in his late teens had spent two years as junior partner in a mercantile business in Ripley, Mississippi, seat of Tippah County.[3]

However close they were personally, the *Avalanche* soon could claim to have exerted successful public pressure. Two days later, under "Local Matters," it declared itself "pleased to learn that Gov. Harris has commissioned our fellow citizen, Col. N.B. Forrest, to raise a battalion of Mounted Rangers. No better man could have been selected for such a duty. Of known courage and indomitable perseverance, he is a man for the times." Colonel Forrest went about raising his troop with diligent speed. A day later, the *Avalanche* printed an advertising notice from him:

A CHANCE FOR ACTIVE SERVICE——MOUNTED RANGERS

Having been authorized by Governor Harris to raise a battalion of mounted rangers for the war, I desire to enlist five hundred able-bodied men, mounted and equipped with such arms as they can procure (shot-guns and pistols preferable), suitable to the service. Those who cannot entirely equip themselves will be furnished arms by the State. . . . Those wishing to enlist are requested to report themselves at the Gayoso House. . . . N. B. Forrest[4]

Within a week after receiving orders, he departed for Kentucky to buy Northern arms and other equipment for his new unit and to recruit men for it as well. He assumed that in that officially neutral but Southern state he could get recruits more easily than in Tennessee, where——since the Confederate capture of Fort Sumter in South Carolina on April 6 and the Confederate victory at Bull Run in Virginia three days before he got his orders——the eagerest volunteers had already rushed to the colors. He therefore left his home state to scour such Kentucky towns as Paris, Lexington, Mount Sterling, and Frankfort, but found "comparatively few" of their residents "prepared to take up arms at that moment." Moving on to Louisville, he first clandestinely bought with his own money some 500 Colt navy pistols and 100 saddles and similar cavalry gear, then hurried westward twenty-five miles to Brandenburg to muster in the Boone Rangers, a ninety-man unit forming to join his regiment. Ordering much of this company divided into detachments of two to six men, he sent them south by different and little-traveled routes to Nolin, a central-Kentucky railway station, where he planned to meet them. He then returned to Louisville, where, under their linen dusters, he and two Kentuckians smuggled the 500 pistols into a livery stable where the saddles and other equipment had been gathered. From there the pistols, disguised as sacks of potatoes, were taken in a market wagon to a Southern sympathizer's farm, and the horse equipment to a tanyard as leather. A few of the Boone Rangers then loaded the goods onto wagons and headed them south toward Nolin. Forrest himself, watched suspiciously by Union officials, rode in the opposite direction of the wagons for some distance before circling and catching up with them after nightfall.[5]

Two days later, at the Nolin station, he received word that two Union "Home Guard" companies were awaiting him fifteen miles south at Munfordville. Encamped beside tracks of the Louisville & Nashville Railroad, which ran through Munfordville, Forrest drew up beneath his Confederate flag — in plain sight of a southbound train — not only the Boone Rangers but also a considerable collection of friends, parents, and other relatives who were accompanying the new soldiers for a few days. Then, knowing that word of his seeming strength would precede him, he continued southward across the Tennessee line without incident. This first of many Forrest military tricks had much in common with those to follow. First and foremost, a precedent for it wasn't apt to be found in any textbook. It also cannily employed third-party witnesses, the train's passengers, to impart what would be taken as an objective estimate of his strength; it skillfully skewed that estimate by making his strength appear larger than it was; and it all occurred a hundred or so miles outside the lines of the new Confederacy.[6]

The man who could conceive such unschooled ruses may have hoped from the beginning to distance himself a little from the aristocratic, well-educated Confederate military hierarchy to which such stratagems would never occur. First hinted in the *Avalanche* article calling for a force to strike the enemy "in advance of the regular army," this conclusion is more strongly suggested by a notice he placed in the *Appeal* and *Avalanche* on August 29, soon after he and his Kentucky company arrived back in Memphis:

FOR ACTIVE SERVICE!

A few more companies are needed to complete a mounted regiment, now being formed here for active service. There is also room for a few more recruits in a company of independent rangers not to be attached to any regiment unless on the option of the members. Applicants for membership in the Rangers to furnish their own arms and horses. To those desiring to engage in the cavalry service an excellent opportunity is offered. Now, freemen! rally to the defense of your liberties, your homes and your firesides!

N. B. Forrest[7]

Forrest had returned from Kentucky to find the ranks of his prospective regiment already swelling. Charles May, a Memphis livery stable owner and former North Mississippi sheriff, had recruited another ninety-man company he called the Forrest Rangers. The Forrest and Boone Rangers went into camp at the fairgrounds, and soon were joined by similar units from Texas, northern and southern Alabama, and Kentucky. The Alabama companies joined Forrest's group because the commander of one of them became impressed with Forrest's ability to slice through military red tape. Its captain, a Methodist-minister-turned-soldier named David C. Kelley, recalled years afterward that he had taken his independent company to Memphis to be outfitted and found himself competing for supplies with a number of other, similar cavalry units. Wary of attaching his force to a higher commander until he found one he deemed worthy, he soon encountered a prospect. He later wrote that in trying "to get my requisitions through the various departments I found that persistent watchfulness enabled me to accomplish what I desired ahead of any officer with whom I had to contend, except when I came in contact with the requisitions of N.B. Forrest." Instrumental in getting three other Alabama units to sign on, Kelley was elected major, Forrest's second-in-command, in a 650-man battalion of eight cavalry companies — four from Alabama, two from Kentucky, one from Texas, and one from Memphis. Half of these troopers were armed with double-barreled shotguns they had brought from home.[8]

By the end of October, Forrest had received his first marching orders — to proceed to a rustic redoubt then being hastily thrown up a few miles south of the Kentucky border. His friend Sam Tate of the Memphis & Charleston Railroad mentioned this assignment in a letter he wrote November 4 to General Albert Sidney Johnston, the new Confederate commander of the western theater. To information concerning the guns and other supplies he could cause to be gathered or manufactured for Johnston, the railroad executive added the following prescient postscript:

"Colonel Forrest's regiment of cavalry, as fine a body of men as ever went to the field, has gone to Fort Donelson. Give Forrest a chance and he will distinguish himself."[9]

12

HOPKINSVILLE [Kentucky], November 14, 1861

W. W. MACKALL, Assistant Adjutant General:

I have been operating with my command of eight companies near Fort Henry and Fort Donelson, by order of General Polk. Finding the country impracticable for cavalry, and with scant subsistence, I moved a part of my command to Canton [Kentucky], north side Cumberland River, leaving two companies at Dover [Tennessee]. I am of no use south of Cumberland; desire my command united, and can do vast service with General Tilghman. Will you so order?

N. B. FORREST,
Commanding Tennessee Cavalry.[1]

FORREST'S FIRST MILITARY dispatch to come down through history sounds characteristically independent, decisive, sparing of words, and undeferential—and unusually literate. The document may have been written by Major Kelley, since Kelley is known to have been the writer of a lengthy and impressive report to General Johnston dictated by Forrest less than two months later. Kelley recalled after the war that although Forrest "was indisposed to the use of the pen himself, he had clear and exact ideas of what he wanted written, and few were more exacting in requiring a precise statement of the ideas furnished."[2]

His correspondence with superiors soon increased in volume. Although his unit's earliest work was of little strategic consequence, it indicated the sort of soldier he could become. He first moved forward into Kentucky, where more than a third of his battalion was sent by General Tilghman to intercept a Union force seeking to seize a large shipment of Confederate hogs; he himself, meanwhile, took the main body of his troopers to Princeton, Kentucky, where they detained a Union transport steamer and captured its sugar, coffee, blankets, and other supplies. Then, riding thirty-two miles in eight hours at night, he returned to Canton, Kentucky, to prevent a Union gunboat, the *Conestoga*, from taking Confederate clothing stored there. Unsuccessful in an attempt to lure the *Conestoga* crew ashore, Forrest's sharpshooters ended up winning a match with the boat's heavier guns; at least, Forrest lost no men, and after several hours of enduring potshots into its portholes, the *Conestoga* closed them and retired.[3]

The command lost its first man in early December, on a reconnaissance in force that Forrest asked permission to undertake during bad December weather; it took him and 450 men all the way to the Ohio River, despite the illness of many of his recruits with measles. The manner in which the first casualty was incurred, and Forrest's response to it, can be read as a forecast of not only the kind of war that would be fought in the West but the charmed life he would lead in it and the lengths to which he would unflinchingly go. Unlike the eastern theater, which until 1864 would be characterized by pretensions at chivalry, the war in the West from its onset was a mean-spirited death duel which, in the upper South, was multiplied in ferocity by its frequent division of brothers, relatives, and neighbors.

As Forrest approached the western Kentucky town of Marion, he learned that a Confederate sympathizer there had been arrested at the instigation of a Unionist neighbor. Forrest decided to respond by seizing the latter, but when he and a small detachment approached the man's house, the regimental surgeon, wearing a uniform more resplendent than his commander's, was shot dead from the house. The man they sought, who probably had assumed that the well-dressed surgeon was the force's commanding officer, then fled out the rear of the place. Unable to apprehend the assailant, Forrest seems to have been ineffectual until one of his detachments encountered ten Unionist Baptist ministers returning from an Illinois church association meeting. Forrest took eight of them hostage and sent the other two back across the Ohio River, ordering them to achieve the release of some Confederate-sympathizing Kentuckians recently abducted by Illinois Unionists. He warned the two he let go that if they didn't return with the kidnapped Kentuckians in twenty-four hours, he "would hang the remainder [of the clergymen] all on one pole." The threat reportedly accomplished its purpose, after which he is said to have released the other ministers.[4]

Interestingly, nothing of the incident with the ministers appears in a report he filed for this period, and the soldier-clergyman Kelley, who talked considerably about Forrest after the war, seems never to have mentioned it; the tactic was so irregular that Forrest and his staff may have deemed it best untold at headquarters. It was also inconsistent with his usual attitude toward the clergy. Except for the times he chased the ministerial student away from Mary Ann Montgomery back in 1845, and this wartime incident sixteen years later, his normal treatment of men of

God is reported to have been markedly respectful, despite his nonacceptance of the faith.

His units spent Christmas in Hopkinsville in the kind of accommodations he would provide for his men ever after: the best available. In this case, they consisted of "good floored tents," with himself quartered in one with Mary Ann and their son, Private Willie. He treated his soldiers in the practical, usually humane way he long had tended livestock and slaves, as personal possessions of great value never to be wasted. As a soldier, he conserved his men and their energies wherever possible, so they would have the optimum left for battle, where he demanded everything they had. "Shoot any man who won't fight," he routinely ordered subordinates. Kelley later wrote of this period that Forrest's men quickly found that his "single will, impervious to argument, appeal, or threat . . . was ever to be the governing impulse in their movements. Everything necessary to supply their wants, to make them comfortable, he was quick to do, save to change his plans, to which everything had to bend."[5]

He fought his initial military battle three days after Christmas. On another reconnaissance on which about 260 of his troops were joined by forty more from Russellville, Kentucky, under Lieutenant Colonel J. W. Starnes, he found word of the enemy near the small town of Rumsey; 500 Union soldiers reportedly had been there earlier that morning. The news evoked "jubilant and defiant shouts" from the Confederate ranks—partly prompted, no doubt, by the fact that "the women from the houses [in Rumsey] waved us forward." In one of the more romantic declarations his military secretaries ever wrote for him, his official report added that his column was met by "a beautiful young" horsewoman "smiling, with untied tresses floating in the breeze . . . just before our advance guard" encountered the Federal rear. The sight of her, he said, "infus[ed] nerve into my arm and kindl[ed] knightly chivalry within my heart."

The Confederate advance sighted the Union rear guard one mile south of the village of Sacramento, and the Union troopers stopped momentarily, until Forrest himself fired at them with a rifle; then they clattered off to join their main body. Later officially reported to number 168, it moved to the top of a hill and formed a battle line. Forrest kept coming, and the Federals "commenced firing from the time we were within 200 yards of them. When we had moved 120 yards farther I ordered my men to fire." Discovering "that my men were not up in sufficient numbers to pursue them with success," he observed that "they showed signs of fight" and "ordered the advance to fall back." This caused the Federals, "supposing we were in retreat," to "move towards us" in "greatly animated" fashion.

They had come more than 100 yards and appeared "to be forming for a charge, when, the remainder of my men coming up, I dismounted a number of men with Sharp's carbines and Maynard rifles to act as sharp-shooters; ordered a flank movement upon the part of Major Kell[e]y and Colonel Starnes upon the right and left, and the detachments from the companies under my command, still mounted, were ordered to charge the enemy's center."

The Confederates "sprang to the charge with a shout," and even though the undergrowth along the sides of the road "impeded the flank-ers" under Kelley and Starnes, "the enemy, broken by the charge and perceiving the movement on their flanks, broke in utter confusion, and, in spite of the efforts of a few officers, commenced a disorderly flight at full speed, in which the officers soon joined." A Union report of the action says that at about this moment "some dastard unknown shouted 'Retreat to Sacramento!' Most of the men fled . . . without stopping at Sac-ramento." Just as it seems not to have occurred to Forrest to simply charge headlong at the enemy without employing simultaneous flank attacks at the critical moment, it also appears not to have occurred to him not to charge headlong once the opponent began to break. He later reported pressing "closely on their rear . . . until we reached the village of Sacramento, when, the best mounted men of my companies coming up, there commenced a promiscuous saber slaughter of their rear, which was continued at almost full speed for two miles beyond the village, leaving their bleeding and wounded strewn along the whole route."[6]

In a discrepancy common to Confederate and Union reports of the same battles, Forrest claimed his own loss at two killed — including a captain, C. E. Meriwether — and three "slightly" wounded. He estimated his enemy's casualties at 100, "about 65" of whom were killed or mortally wounded. The Union, by contrast, listed its killed at eight along with "perhaps 13" captured, with no mention of wounded, while saying the Confederates were known to have lost at least one officer and four men killed. Forrest's report also recalled that during the chase beyond Sac-ramento two of the Union officers "were run through with saber thrusts, and [Federal] Captain Davis thrown from his horse and surrendered as my prisoner, his shoulder being dislocated by the fall." Exactly who sabered the two officers is unspecified in the report, but later accounts indicate it was Forrest. Kelley afterward wrote that after running through a Federal captain named Bacon and disabling Davis by "a heavy blow on the sword-arm," Forrest resumed his pursuit of the other Federals so reck-lessly that he collided with the horses of the two fallen Federals and himself "fell headlong some twenty feet in advance of the heap of horses." Although his official account of the battle offered no hint of these exploits, one filed ten days later by Brigadier General Charles Clark to General Johnston did. Clark called Forrest's report "a modest recital of one of the most brilliant and successful cavalry engagements which the present war has witnessed" and said he had learned "from private and unofficial sources" that Forrest's summary of Union casualties "is not overestimated." He added that Forrest's "skill, courage, and energy" were "entitled to the highest praise," "officers and men" having reported that "throughout the entire engagement he was conspicuous for the most daring courage; always in advance of his command. He was at one time engaged in a hand-to-hand conflict with 4 of the enemy, 3 of whom he killed, dismounting and making a prisoner of the fourth."[7]

His superiors weren't the only ones who noticed that this unheralded and unschooled new cavalry colonel from Memphis took to fighting that day the way most men take to talking about it. Kelley, in notes written soon after Sacramento, recalled that this battle was "the first time I had seen the Colonel in the face of the enemy, and, when he rode up to me in the thick of the action, I could scarcely believe him to be the man I had known for several months." Forrest's face, Kelley said, was so "flushed" that "it bore a striking resemblance to a painted Indian warrior's, and his eyes, usually mild in their expression, were blazing with the intense glare of a panther's springing upon its prey. In fact, he looked as little like the Forrest of our mess-table as the storm of December resembles the quiet of June."[8]

After Sacramento, morale among his men soared, but some of them worried about this "panther" and where it might lead them; Kelley was one of the worriers. He would reflect after the war that in his first battles Forrest "was so disregardful of the ordinary rules of tactics, so reckless in personal exposure, that I felt sure his career would be short." Kelley reasoned that "a skilful opponent . . . would . . . utterly cut" Forrest's command "to pieces. So fierce did his passion become that he was almost equally dangerous to friend or foe, and, as it seemed to some of us, he was too wildly excitable to be capable of judicious command."[9]

Forrest's "passion" for war impressed superiors, however. After a few more uneventful reconnaissances, during a period in which a tenuous Confederate grip on southern Kentucky was slipping, he was given command of all cavalry covering a retreat from Hopkinsville toward Nashville. He then was ordered to take his troopers to Fort Donelson on the Cumberland River just south of the Tennessee border. There, under

General Pillow, some 15,000 Confederates were gathering to fend off Federals whose gunboats already had taken Fort Henry on the Tennessee River ten miles to the west. Forrest was given charge of all cavalry within Confederate lines that formed a three-mile arc from above the fort on the north to below the town of Dover on the south.

Ordered to reconnoiter the Fort Henry road to see how fast the Federals were moving up, he chased a Union cavalry detachment almost back to its own lines. The following day, keeping watch on the same road, he fought a heavy, five-hour skirmish with advancing Union infantry before being ordered back inside Confederate entrenchments. On February 13 the Union troops, under the as-yet-unheralded brigadier general U. S. Grant, attacked Confederate fortifications with artillery from the west and a few gunboats from the river to the east, as well as with rifle fire.

Forrest himself picked off a Federal sniper in a tree with a Maynard rifle hastily borrowed from an enlisted man. Meanwhile, an unusually balmy Tennessee winter got suddenly nasty; rain turned to heavy sleet and snow, and temperatures dived into the teens. February 14 featured more probing, this time along snow-covered roads and among trees covered with ice. The day's highlight was a terrific cannonade by Union gunboats. Forrest had never seen anything like the struggle between the gunboats and Donelson's single heavy gun. Finding a point at which both the boats and the Confederate battery were in full view, he watched almost continuous explosions of Union shells within and around the walls of Donelson with frank fear of their effect. Kelley later recalled riding up to him as the shelling was at its height and having Forrest turn to him and yell: "Parson! For God's sake, pray. Nothing but God Almighty can save that fort!"[10]

Confederate gunners, though severely endangered themselves, managed to cripple and drive off the gunboats, and Donelson's problem turned out to be not the much-feared naval vessels but its own commanders. There were too many of them. Brigadier General Bushrod Johnson had been put in command of the place February 7, succeeded by Brigadier General Pillow on the 9th, Brigadier General Simon Buckner during a brief absence by Pillow on the 12th, and Brigadier General John B. Floyd on the 13th. All four were still there together, and two of them—Buckner and Pillow—had nursed a mutual grudge since the Mexican War.

At a February 13 meeting of most of the fort's principal officers, including Forrest, it was determined that constant reinforcements had swelled Grant's force to at least twice the size of their own, and that the best course was to break out and move seventy miles southeast to Nashville, where General Albert Sidney Johnston meant to concentrate Confederate men and supplies preparatory to still further retreat. With Floyd in overall command, Pillow on the left, and Buckner on the right, it was decided to strike from the Confederate left below Dover and try to open the Nashville road, along which the Union right was anchored. The cavalry was to lead the breakout attempt, which began on the 14th. Forrest briefly left the entrenchments with Pillow's infantry before the gunboat cannonade, but Pillow canceled the attempt in early afternoon, saying it was too late in the day. At another council that evening, the same course was adopted for the following morning.

The next day saw a sweeping, but incomplete, victory by exhausted Confederate soldiers, who had been virtually sleepless for three days. Pillow attacked on the left in the "gray of the morning," with Forrest's troopers in his advance and protecting his left flank. After a two-hour fight that stained the snow with blood, the Federals began to fall back "through undergrowth . . . so thick that I could scarcely press my horses through it," Forrest reported a few days later. The Union troops re-formed briefly beyond an open, marshy field, and Forrest's cavalry prevented them from flanking the advancing Confederate infantry. Evidently realizing that the Confederates "would cut them off," the Federals began to retreat again and "in haste," having been driven "near a mile." Here, Forrest contended after the war, their retreat could have been made a rout. Pillow having gone to the right to confer with Buckner, Bushrod Johnson was the senior commander on that area of the field, and Forrest later said the West Point–educated Johnson refused him permission to charge the disorganized Federals.[11]

Forrest then drifted off rightward with the heart of the battle. Seeing a Federal battery of six guns "which had kept several of our regiments in check for several hours, killing and slaughtering a great many of our men," he charged and captured it, "killing most of the men and horses." Then he struck the flank of the stiffening Federals, who "finally gave way, our infantry and cavalry both charging them at the same time, committing great slaughter." He pushed "still farther to our right" and "found a regiment of our infantry in confusion, which I relieved by charging the enemy to their front. . . . General Pillow, coming up, ordered me to charge the enemy in a ravine." The ensuing onrush "completely routed the enemy, leaving some 200 dead . . . , accomplishing what three different regiments had failed to do. Seeing the enemy's battery on our right about to turn on us, I now ordered a charge on this battery, from which we drove the enemy, capturing two guns."

He then ordered forward some scouts who reported more Federal troops moving up the road from Fort Henry. These Union reinforcements would have been too late had the Confederate commanders been decisive. Pillow, however, said there wasn't enough time, again pleading shortage of daylight, and ordered the victors back within their own lines at 2:30 P.M. Forrest said in his initial report that his own troopers and the infantry "had driven the enemy back without a reverse from the left of our entrenchments to the center, having opened three different roads by which we might have retired if the generals had, as was deemed best in the council the night before, ordered the retreat of the army."[12]

In charging the battery in the ravine, Captain May of the Forrest Rangers was killed, Forrest's youngest brother, Jeffrey, endured a painful fall from a horse under fire, and Forrest's own mount—having already sustained some seven wounds—dropped dead from blood loss. Forrest quickly mounted another and rode a few minutes further to the right, reconnoitering, before an artillery shell passed through the second horse's body just back of the saddle blanket. Forrest then ran back to his men, reaching them as Pillow was beginning to call the Confederates back to their lines. By the end of the day's action a half hour later, his overcoat bore fifteen bullet marks.[13]

The remainder of the afternoon, Forrest and his men were busied by Pillow bringing in Confederate wounded and picking up captured Federal arms, blankets, packs, and so on. After dark, back inside the lines, he told his troops to get what sleep they could. He followed this order himself, but was awakened around midnight for another council of war. At the Dover Inn beside the icy, rain-swollen Cumberland, he was thunderstruck to find Floyd, Pillow, and Buckner discussing surrender. Pillow told him the Federals were reoccupying the ground the Confederates had taken from them during the day, and Forrest, who had been on that ground supervising the collection of wounded and captured matériel until dark, "told him I did not believe it." Pillow said scouts had reported it, and he directed Forrest to send out two soldiers of his own to check the condition of the southeast-running river road on which they had marched out to fight that morning. These scouts soon reported that "from their examination and information obtained from a citizen living on the river road the water was about to the saddle skirts, and the mud about half-leg deep in [a] bottom where it had been overflowed. The bottom was about a quarter of a mile wide and the water then about 100 yards wide."[14]

They also said they had "returned without seeing any of the enemy, only fires, which I believed to be the old camp fires, and so stated to the generals; the wind, being very high, had fanned them into a blaze. . . . The enemy could not have reinvested their former position without traveling a considerable distance and camped upon the dead and dying, as there had been great slaughter on that portion of the field. . . ." By the time Forrest's scouts had returned, however, the three generals—fearing the continual reinforcements reported to be pouring into the Federal camp—were bent on surrender. Buckner's men had been moved during the day from their positions on the right to be ready to protect the escape route Pillow's men had fought to open on the left, and late in the day Buckner had seen his depleted right attacked by a hugely superior Union force, which captured a small portion of his trenches; he estimated that on the following morning he wouldn't be able to hold his position more than half an hour. He added that three-fourths of Donelson's defenders would be lost in any attempt to break out now, and that to order them to do so would be unconscionable. When Forrest eventually got a chance to express an opinion, he disagreed absolutely; offering to cover Buckner's withdrawal with his cavalrymen, he said he hadn't come to Donelson to surrender. Pillow "then said I could cut my way out if I chose to do so, and he and General Floyd agreed to come out with me."[15]

He determined to go out by the flooded road, but Floyd, Pillow, and Buckner decided that only cavalry could safely use this route; as a later Forrest report would concede, "a great many of the men were already frost-bitten, and it was the opinion of the generals that the infantry could not have passed through the water and survived it." Expressing a view diametrically opposed to Buckner's, he told the generals that if his command would follow him, he would cut his way out even if doing so "saved but one man."[16]

One of the more bizarre proceedings in American military annals had taken place by this time. Floyd, who a few months earlier had been U.S. secretary of war under President James Buchanan, would not surrender himself to a Union which since then had indicted him for malfeasance in office and accused him of deliberately sending war matériel south to be seized by secessionists. Pillow, having dramatically promised on first entering Donelson that he wouldn't surrender, also refused to do it. So Floyd gave up his command of the fort to Pillow, who passed it immediately to Buckner, who in turn—having once lent money to General Grant years before—consented to do the surrendering after Floyd and Pillow had time to escape. By the time Forrest's men were ready to depart, Pillow already had left with his chief of staff in an old scow, and Floyd was about to escape with four-fifths of his brigade in a commandeered steamboat.

Forrest reported a few days later that he "moved out by the road we had gone out the morning before. When about a mile out crossed a deep slough from the river, saddleskirt deep, and filed into the road" leading toward Nashville.

I ordered Major Kell[e]y and Adjutant Schuyler to remain at the point where we entered this road with one company, where the enemy's cavalry would attack if they attempted to follow us. They remained until day was dawning. . . . More than two hours had been occupied in passing. Not a gun had been fired at us. Not an enemy had been seen or heard. . . . I am clearly of the opinion that two-thirds of our army could have marched out without loss, and that, had we continued the fight the next day, we should have gained a glorious victory. . . . our troops were in fine spirits, believing we had whipped them. . . .[17]

13

FORREST ESCAPED THE Fort Donelson lines with about 500 men from his own unit, plus "a company of artillery horses . . . and a number of men from different regiments." Minus more than 300 men killed, wounded, or captured in the previous days' fighting, as well as one cavalry unit which failed to accompany him out of Donelson, he "made a slow march with my exhausted horses to Nashville. . . ."[1]

On the way, he had no patience for a hysterical defeatism that suddenly ran rampant through the wide expanse the Confederates were abandoning. At the village of Charlotte the morning after the Donelson breakout, he threatened a state senator with instant punishment for disseminating "false intelligence" that the Federals were in possession of Nashville and had loosed 10,000 cavalry to cut off and capture the retreating Confederates. He himself could hardly have known the senator's story was false, but he reassured the locals somewhat by lingering a few hours in Charlotte to have some of his horses shod. Just south of the village that afternoon, he had his troops discharge and reload their pistols and shotguns to prepare them for whatever Nashville offered—and thus panicked another regiment of Confederate cavalry just ahead of them. This regiment, having heard not only about the Donelson surrender but also the state senator's story, fled at a gallop, discarding along the road cookware, food, tents, and baggage, then finally even wagons wrecked by haste. Forrest's troops, having had to leave some of their own equipment behind at Donelson, claimed as much of this windfall as they could carry.[2]

That night, February 17, they halted eighteen miles out of Nashville at the home of a prosperous Confederate sympathizer. This friend provided for both men and horses and set a lavish dinner for the unit's officers, but the commander was in no mood for prolonged refreshment. Discovering some of his subordinates preparing to occupy the civilian's proffered beds, he ordered them back to their men, and all slept outdoors in the February cold with horses saddled and weapons at hand.[3]

They were on the road again early the next day, scouts having established by then that Nashville was still in Confederate hands. They rode on in, and Forrest reported first to General Johnston, who was just leaving for Murfreesboro farther south. Then he reported to the man Johnston had directed him to: his all-too-recent commander at Fort Donelson, John Floyd. Johnston had left Floyd in charge of removing from Nashville the stockpiled "subsistence stores and whatever else of public property he can," and Floyd appears to have been about as good at protecting property as he was at commanding a fort under siege. He initially ordered Forrest to patrol and guard Nashville's inner environs. This order evidently impressed Forrest little; he didn't comply with it until a day later, pleading fatigue of his men, while he concentrated on getting the rest of his horses shod. Reporting February 20 with his patrol detachments, he found Floyd again in a hurry to abandon a post, this time leaving for Murfreesboro; on the verge of suspension for his conduct at Donelson, Floyd instructed Forrest to stay in Nashville until the next afternoon, then to follow the rest of the Confederates to Murfreesboro.[4]

Intending to outfit his men as completely as possible from the Nashville commissaries and then to load the rest of the supplies for removal, Forrest apparently found he should have responded quicker to Floyd's order to patrol the city. All but one of the commissaries were no longer supervised by the appropriate officers and had been left to the mercies of a throng of civilians. When the looters ignored his warnings, he "had to . . . charge the mob before I could get it dispersed so as to get wagons to the doors of the departments to load up the stores for transportation." The charge was made with drawn sabers, which ejected the looters from the warehouses and allowed the doors to be locked. Almost as soon as he left to attend to other duties, however, the thieves broke in again, and when he returned, a "stout Irishman" rushed up, seized his collar, and shouted that he and the civilians were as entitled to the stockpiled goods as the colonel or anybody else. Forrest responded by striking the man on the head with his pistol and again drove him and the others from the warehouse, this time stationing guards in front of it. When he left yet again on other errands and the mob tried to overpower the guards, he hit on an innovative solution perhaps suggested by his aldermanic familiarity with municipal equipment; he turned a fire hose of ice-cold water on the pillagers, who finally retreated.[5]

Instead of leaving for Murfreesboro as Floyd had directed, Forrest remained in Nashville, gathering and shipping valuable matériel. He later reported collecting "some 700 large boxes of clothing . . . 700 or 800 wagon loads of meat . . ." and "30 odd wagon loads of ammunition." The "greater part of these supplies were actually sent off by rail," and more would have followed had not "high water destroyed the bridges so as to stop the transportation over the Nashville and Chattanooga Railroad." Nashville's mayor, wishing to surrender the city undamaged to Union general Don Carlos Buell, finally asked that Forrest leave his city. Only after entraining the last load of ammunition and dispatching a wagon convoy of other supplies southward did the colonel quit the Tennessee capital the afternoon of February 23.[6]

Arriving in Murfreesboro that same evening, Forrest was immediately ordered by Johnston to fall back further south to Huntsville, Alabama, to rest and replenish his depleted force. Reaching Huntsville February 25, he gave his troops a two-week furlough. All returned from this leave March 10, many accompanied by new recruits; the latter included a company raised by Forrest's younger brother Jesse, who became its captain. At Burnsville, Mississippi, to which they were ordered to report to General John C. Breckinridge, they were greeted by yet another new company, this one raised in rural southwestern Tennessee by a former Forrest lieutenant, C. H. Schuyler, the unit's captain. The additional companies made the battalion a full regiment, whose leader now was elected full colonel.[7]

Forrest had been ordered to Mississippi as part of a massing of all available Confederate troops around Corinth, an important railroad junction. Situated just west of the southernmost turn of the Tennessee River, a principal artery up which Union troops and gunboats were steaming into the Deep South, Corinth was chosen by Johnston as a staging base from which to try to throw back two Federal armies advancing at a leisurely pace under Grant, who had been proceeding more or less due south from Forts Henry and Donelson, and Buell, moving southwestward from Nashville. At the end of March, on the basis of Forrest scouting reports that showed Buell heading for a junction with Grant, Johnston — who had been waiting for another 15,000 men from the trans-Mississippi—decided to attack Grant with the 40,000 he already had rather than allow Grant's 40,000 to be reinforced by Buell's 30,000.[8]

Johnston's attack, delivered just north of the Tennessee border near a log meetinghouse called Shiloh Church, was a surprise. Accustomed to Southerners who had been retreating steadily for two months, the Federals had camped lackadaisically between two creeks, the Owl and the Lick, with their backs to Pittsburg Landing on the Tennessee River. After a rainy march and nightmare delays, the Confederate assault struck at dawn of April 6, twenty-four hours later than planned. Forrest's troops were posted at Lick Creek on the far Confederate right, guarding against prospective Union attack from another landing to the southeast called Hamburg. Early that morning, Johnston had sent Colonel George Maney's First Tennessee Infantry to the same area, giving Maney command of Forrest's troops and another regiment of Tennessee infantry under Colonel D. H. Cummings. Maney's instructions from Johnston were "to watch and resist any demonstration of the enemy against the extreme right flank or the rear of the army from the direction of Hamburg." Johnston's orders, Maney officially reported three weeks later, "left me at liberty, in case I became perfectly satisfied that no enemy was in my direction, to . . . join in the main battle; and about 11 a.m., having from diligent observations been unable to learn the presence of any enemy toward or at Hamburg and the battle continuing to rage, I left Colonels Forrest and Cummings to carry out their instructions existing before my presence with them, and recrossing the creek with the five companies of my regiment, directed their march toward the battle, then seeming about 4 or 5 miles distant." He had gone only about a mile when a courier from Forrest brought word that "it was not certain but that a portion of the enemy was in the direction of Hamburg." Maney halted briefly, then learned that General Beauregard, Johnston's second-in-command, had ordered "all troops . . . brought to the scene of action, and that both Colonels Forrest and Cummings were near at hand on their way forward. I then moved directly with my five companies toward the battle."[9]

Forrest was taking seriously his orders to cover any Hamburg threat, but after Maney left for the roar of the guns he got itchy. He moved his troops to the northwestern side of the Lick and sent forward a request for orders to advance. Apparently he received none for a while, if ever. Gilbert V. Rambaut, a former Memphis hotelkeeper who had become a commissary officer in Forrest's cavalry, later remembered that his commander had "just returned from his outposts," probably making one last check of the Hamburg road. Now "he rode to the front of his regiment, having drawn them in line of battle, and addressed them in these or similar words: 'Boys, do you hear that rattle of musketry and the roar of artillery?' A yell, 'Yes, yes.' 'Do you know what it means? It means that our friends and brothers are falling by hundreds at the hands of the enemy and we are here guarding a d——n creek. We did not enter the service for such work, and the reputation of this regiment does not justify our commanding officer in leaving us here while we are needed elsewhere. Let's go and help them. What do you say?' A yell, 'Yes, yes,' and with this reply he moved his command at a gallop into the fight."[10]

He seems to have headed toward the nearest portion of the Confederate line engaged in the hardest fighting, a part of the field near what afterward became known as the Hornet's Nest. There he came up in the rear of much-bloodied Confederate troops under Major General B. F. Cheatham, who had just charged and been savagely repulsed. Union artillerymen saw the Confederate horsemen arrive and opened fire on them, and Forrest spurred his way to Cheatham. He said that to escape the cannons he had to move his men either forward or backward and proposed a joint charge. Knowing all too well the strength of the Federal position, Cheatham demurred—probably testily, very possibly considering the newly arrived Forrest presumptuous.

"I cannot give you the order, and if you make the charge, it will be under your own orders," Cheatham said.

"Then I will do it," Forrest retorted. "I will charge under my own orders."[11]

Forrest's charge failed to reach its objective, bogging down in soft ground forty yards short, but Cheatham's men followed and the Union position was taken, with Forrest's unit detouring around the marsh and falling on the Federal infantry and artillery as they began to run and scatter. Interestingly, Cheatham makes no mention at all of Forrest in his official report of the battle. Neither does Maney, who seems to have been in the same area of fighting. Shiloh, fought in scattered fields and orchards in heavily wooded country, was not the kind of battle in which cavalry could be used very effectively; rather, it was a maelstrom of smaller fights, and it is possible that nobody who made a report saw much of what Forrest's men did that day. Of this first charge, Rambaut theorizes that Cheatham "took possession of . . . guns" Forrest's men had overrun, "not knowing the injury we had inflicted on the enemy or the consternation we had caused in their ranks. . . ."[12]

After a brief rest, during which he was ordered to "mask the battery to our rear and move it up," Forrest was directed to bring his cavalry to help on the right. There, in furious fighting, a Federal division under Brigadier General Benjamin M. Prentiss saved Grant's army by digging into a sunken road at the center of the Hornet's Nest and holding off the Confederates for six hours. Forrest's men, apparently in the advance of Southern units which finally got between Prentiss and the Union reserves, were in on the capture of the Union general and some 2,200 of his men. It was after 5 P.M. by that time, but Forrest's men continued, following the fight to the battle's Confederate high-water mark: the slopes of a hill overlooking Pittsburg Landing, where Union generals had massed more than fifty guns in an effort to stop the Southern juggernaut.

There Forrest's troopers, along with a brigade of Mississippi infantry under Brigadier General James R. Chalmers, were unable to go further, although both units tried uncoordinated, unsuccessful moves on this last hill as daylight waned. Forrest sent word to Major General Leonidas Polk, from whom his last orders had come, that a concerted assault could dislodge the guns' defenders and throw them into the river; soon, however, the Union batteries and gunboats opened on the advancing Confederate reinforcements, and Polk ordered Forrest's men to the comparative cover of a wooded ravine next to the river just south of Pittsburg Landing. They stayed there, under shelling from the gunboats, until the fall of darkness, after which they were ordered to fall back and camp for the night.[13]

Forrest, though, seemed reluctant to stop fighting. Momentarily distracted by news that his fifteen-year-old only son was missing, he started a fruitless search of the field for him (Willie and two similar-aged companions eventually turned up herding some fifteen Federal prisoners), but later that night he had a few of his men don captured Union overcoats and ride up the bank of the Tennessee River. Proceeding to within sight of Pittsburg Landing, they saw Buell's men arriving in a steady stream and being ferried by steamboat across the river to the battlefield. With this information, Forrest began trying to find the army's commander, no small task in the middle of the night. For one thing, the battle plan, which Johnston had entrusted to Beauregard, had spread two Confederate corps across the three-mile front one behind the other, so that their right, center, and left components soon became separated and thus all but ungovernable after several hours of hard fighting. For another thing, Forrest may not have known who the commander of the army was anymore. For morale purposes, the Confederate generals were keeping secret the fact that full command had passed to Beauregard; Johnston had been killed in midafter-noon, bleeding to death from a wound in the leg.

The first superior officer Forrest could find was Chalmers, a well-educated North Mississippi lawyer whose tent Forrest approached de-manding to see its occupant. It is an indication of Forrest's standing at the time that his midnight visit goes unrecorded in Chalmers's official report, but the attorney recalled it after the war. He didn't invite his visitor into his tent, instead going "out in[to] the darkness" to inquire what he wanted.

"I want to know if you could tell me where I could find the command-ing officer of the army," Forrest said.

Chalmers said he didn't know and asked what news Forrest had, "if any."

"I have been way down along the river-bank, close to the enemy," he remembered Forrest replying. "I could see the lights on the steamboats and hear distinctly the orders given in the disembarkation of the troops. They are receiving reinforcements by the thousands, and if this army does not move and attack them between [now] . . . and daylight, and before other reinforcements arrive, it will be whipped like hell before ten o'clock tomorrow."[14]

Chalmers's memory, recorded long afterward, didn't quite reflect actual events. Forrest didn't see and hear the Union troops personally; at least, he didn't tell his authorized biographers he did, because they say the scouting expedition was headed by a Lieutenant Sheridan. Chalmers also says Forrest "found the commander-in-chief, told him what he had seen and heard, and the unlettered colonel was told to go back to his regiment." Forrest was indeed instructed to go back to his regiment, but not by Beauregard. He was able to find only John C. Breckinridge and William J. Hardee, both corps commanders, and Hardee told him to take his information to Beauregard. Unable to find Beauregard in the "woods and darkness," he returned to his men and sent out another scouting party. At 2 A.M. it came back with news that the arrival of fresh Federal troops was continuing. Forrest went again to find Hardee, who this time told him to "return to his regiment, keep up a vigilant, strong picket line, and report all hostile movements" — and, like Chalmers, didn't find Forrest's noctur-nal visits worthy of official mention.[15]

Considering the reactions of Chalmers and Hardee, Beauregard and his staff might not have believed the "unlettered" Forrest had he found headquarters. Indeed, the captured Union general, Prentiss, did tell them exactly what Forrest wanted to—that Buell was crossing the Tennessee to reinforce Grant—and they paid him no attention. They had received a telegram from a Confederate colonel in North Alabama saying Buell had changed his line of march and was headed in that direction.

For their commanders' refusal to take Forrest and Prentiss more seriously, the Confederates paid bloodily the next day. Buell's fresh Federal troops attacked at dawn and drove the exhausted and outnumbered Southerners back over the ground they had won the day before. After first capturing "some 50" Federal pickets deceived by his men's blue overcoats, in the morning Forrest fell back slowly onto the infantry of Hardee, who ordered him to retire behind it. After that, he busied himself collaring and redirecting stragglers until about 11 A.M., when Breckinridge told him to cover his right flank. There he helped ward off three Union attempts to break the Confederate line, then was ordered by Beauregard to the center, where he dismounted his regiment and helped repel the last Union charge. By midafternoon, the Confederates had begun an orderly retreat back toward Corinth, Breckinridge's corps and Forrest's cavalry covering the rear. The Federals made no pursuit that day, and that evening Forrest took several squads of troopers back to Lick Creek to see that no pursuit came from there.

The morning of April 8, Union general William T. Sherman gave belated chase. About four miles from the battlefield on the road to Corinth, just beyond a 200-yard expanse of timber felled in a civilian logging project, Sherman saw an "extensive" Confederate camp in which cavalrymen were visible. He wrote to Grant that evening that he had been advancing on this camp when—despite the fact that the "ground was admirably suited to a defense of infantry against cavalry, it being miry and covered with fallen timber"—Confederate cavalry "came down boldly to the charge, breaking through the line of skirmishers," and an infantry regiment behind the skirmishers "without cause, threw away their muskets, and fled." An Illinois cavalry unit behind the fleeing infantry also "began to discharge their carbines and fell into disorder," and Sherman had to send "orders to the rear" for a following brigade "to form line of battle."[16]

All this consternation was caused by a sudden assault by a motley collection of 350 Confederate troopers. They consisted of Forrest and about 150 of his own men and some 200 others from independent commands of Mississippians, Kentuckians, and Texas Rangers. That their attack was savage Sherman eloquently testifies, and out of several conflicting Confederate reports of it rises one of the most striking examples of

Forrest's prowess at hand-to-hand combat. No report of his part in the battle of Shiloh was filed, but his authorized biography says he was at the head of this charge against Sherman and, overcome by zeal, so far outdistanced the rest of the attackers that he found himself surrounded by Union troops. As he turned to shoot his way out with one of his pistols, he took a rifle ball in the left side just above the hipbone, and it lodged on the left side of his back near the spine. "His right leg, benumbed by the blow, was . . . left hanging useless in the stirrup." Federal soldiers were yelling "Kill him! Shoot him! Stick him! Knock him off his horse!"—but he managed to turn, clear a path for himself with a pistol, and gallop out of danger without being otherwise hit by a hail of bullets fired at his back. In 1902, a Memphis biographer, who claimed to have been aided by Forrest's son, added the information that after being shot and turning to flee, the colonel "reached down, caught up a rather small Federal soldier, swung him around and held him to the rear of his saddle as a shield until he was well out of danger, and then gladly dropped his prisoner, who doubtless saved his life."[17]

That a man with a spinal wound so serious that his right leg was numb would be able to snatch a man—albeit a "rather small" one—off the ground and onto a horse's back, even aided by the adrenalin of battle, is miraculous, but it is the only plausible explanation of how a man nearly six feet two could ride out of the midst of a regiment of hostile soldiers and be struck by only one bullet. It is also possible that his wound was more potentially dangerous than immediately grave. The only official Confederate record, a report by a Texas Ranger major, says "Colonel Forrest was, I learn, slightly wounded." Since Forrest is reported to have left the field immediately for the nearest hospital, the Texan may not have known the extent of his wounds and may have assumed they were minor if Forrest could seek the hospital under his own power. Given the major's task of reporting the activities of his own unit, he also can reasonably be expected not to have reported any such extrinsic exploit as Forrest's single-handed escape from a surrounding Union regiment.[18]

His commissioned biographers say field surgeons were unable to find the lodged bullet and advised him to go to the rear, which he did. Breckinridge then ordered him to Corinth, where he went primarily on horseback, which proved less painful than riding in a jolting wagon. His horse, also wounded in the battle, died a few hours after carrying him to Corinth, and the next day he left for Memphis on a sixty-day furlough. Recuperating for just three weeks, he returned painfully to his regiment because of reports of commissary problems. The next month, while "reconnoitering Federal lines" around Corinth, jumping a horse over a log caused him such pain that his regimental surgeon—Mary Ann Forrest's first cousin J. B. Cowan—removed the bullet without anesthetics, and he again absented himself from command for another two weeks.[19]

The charge at "the fallen timbers" stopped all Union pursuit of the Confederates and added to Forrest's growing stature. It also showed that, in contrast to most other Southern cavalrymen, he was a soldier first and a cavalryman second. Unlike Confederate guerrilla John Hunt Morgan, who not only was present at Shiloh but even participated in the rearguard strike against Sherman, Forrest was no guerrilla, at least not during a fight. During the battle proper, Morgan's sole contribution was a single charge; the rest of the time he and his men sat safely in the rear. Morgan biographer James A. Ramage cites Forrest's decision to charge under his own orders on the first day, and to keep charging wherever possible afterward, as early proof that Forrest, unlike Morgan, was much more than a dashing guerrilla. Forrest, Ramage writes, "could lead guerrilla raids behind enemy lines and harass the enemy with great success. But when there was a fight, he was never content to hold his ground, and he could not flee to avoid getting whipped. . . . Forrest's inclination to battle tenaciously was not in the guerrilla tradition."[20]

Shiloh was a fitting field for his tenacity. Resting his aching back in Memphis a few days later, he could reflect that he had survived the greatest battle of American history up to that time. It had produced more American casualties—13,047 Federals killed, wounded, and captured plus 10,694 Confederates killed, wounded, or missing—than the Revolution, the War of 1812, and the Mexican War combined.

14

200 RECRUITS WANTED!

I will receive 200 able-bodied men if they will present themselves at my headquarters by the first of June with good horse and gun. I wish none but those who desire to be actively engaged. My headquarters for the present is at Corinth, Miss. Come on, boys, if you want a heap of fun and to kill some Yankees.

N. B. Forrest
Colonel, Commanding
Forrest's Regiment[1]

FROM THE TONE of his earlier recruiting advertisements, there is a discernible change in this one published during the period he was home recuperating from his spinal wound. It abandons some of the high-flown formality found in his earlier efforts, which probably were written by journalistic friends such as Matthew Gallaway. Instead, it adopts more of the no-nonsense vernacular more typical of the advertiser himself. The last sentence, had it been written by most recruiters in the war's early days, might be taken as coarse naïveté concerning the horrors of war; but it was written by a man who had been thrown from a horse after personally killing and capturing Federal officers at Sacramento, had ridden out of Fort Donelson's fighting with fifteen bullet marks in his overcoat, and had survived unparalyzed a shot near the spine at Shiloh. In short, the advertiser was a man who already had seen personally more military combat than most soldiers ever do. He was either a man who wanted to deceive his prospective recruits into thinking "kill[ing] some Yankees" was going to be "a heap of fun" or a man who actually felt it was.

The marked move away from a stiff military manner may also have indicated a change in, or perhaps a deepening commitment to, his own attitude. Never having been one to defer much to the authority of others in civilian life, he possibly decided there was little reason to do so in the Army, either; doubtless, he had begun to deduce from the examples of Floyd, Pillow, and Buckner at Donelson, as well as of Cheatham, Chalmers, Hardee, and Breckinridge at Shiloh, that, although not nearly so well schooled, he was at least as intelligent, resourceful, and victory-directed as any superior he so far had encountered. Such reflection could only have made him more impatient with many of the seemingly petty rules of war and warriors, unwritten laws of cavalierish gallantry which seemed oblivious to the awesome imperativeness of winning. To him, everything always had depended on final triumph, not on the gentlemanly gamesmanship so many affected in seeking it. Like all the frontier fights he had made, this was not a game. It was a struggle for no less than survival — this time, not only individually but collectively and nationally. After Shiloh, he seemed to begin to wage war more nearly the way he had lived the rest of his life: not only single-mindedly, but confident in his own counsel and following his own rules. His apparent revelry in the work can be seen in his personal reply, mere weeks after the Shiloh wound, to a letter from a Memphis acquaintance requesting payment of his annual dues to the Independent Order of Odd Fellows. After asking to know the exact amount he owed, he went on to write:

*. . . I had a small brush with the Enamy on yesterday I Suceded
in gaining thir rear and got in to thir entrenchments . . . and
Burned a portion of thir camp. . . . they wair not looking for me I
taken them by Suprise they run like Suns of Biches. . . . this army
is at this time in front of our Entrenchments I look for a fite soon
and a big one. . . . Cant you come up and take a hand this fite wil
do to hand down to your childrens children. . . .[2]*

Beauregard, the commander he tried so hard to find that crucial night
at Shiloh, quickly became an admirer of this "unlettered colonel" who had
scouted the Tennessee riverbank and was such a fighter he wanted the
army to renew its attack in the dark. A few weeks later, complying with
a request from an influential cavalry officer operating near Chattanooga,
the Louisianian persuaded a reluctant Forrest to be transferred to southeastern Tennessee, away from the troops he had raised. The purpose was
to galvanize disparate cavalry units there into a force capable of helping
fend off Federals, again under Buell, who were proceeding slowly across
northern Alabama toward Chattanooga's vitally important rail junction.
Beauregard's authorized biography recalls that Forrest "hesitated at first,
modestly alleging his inability to assume such a responsibility; but yielded,
finally, when again urged . . . and after receiving the promise that his old
regiment should be sent to him as soon as it could be spared from the
Army of the Mississippi."[3]

He no doubt was influenced somewhat also by the promise of a promotion; a request for one was forwarded to the War Department to make him
the senior cavalry officer in the Chattanooga department. With a brigadier
general's star in his immediate future, he left Mississippi for Chattanooga
June 11 with an escort of some two dozen officers and men from his old
regiment. He arrived in Chattanooga a week later and was given command
of a cavalry brigade made up of the Eighth Texas and some Georgia and
Kentucky units who doubtless had heard little of him and apparently
weren't impressed with his nonmilitary reputation. One of his authorized
biographers, ex-Beauregard chief of staff Thomas Jordan, recalled talking
with "an officer of rank who had left Chattanooga just as Forrest was
leaving" on his first operation from there and being told that Forrest's
planned expedition was "rash, inconsiderate, and likely to lead to disaster."[4]

The expedition he had in mind was indeed a bold one, especially for a
command with which he was unfamiliar. Ordered to try to disrupt Buell's
drive against Chattanooga, he had determined to return to Murfrees-

boro — just southeast of Nashville, more than a hundred miles from Chattanooga, and well in Buell's rear — and fight a Union force close to the size of his own. He probably had been mulling this operation for weeks. Late in June he is known to have had conversations with John Hunt Morgan regarding their mutual wish that the Confederate War Department swap Forrest's Kentucky troopers to Morgan for some other cavalrymen from Tennessee. Murfreesboro was much on the mind of Morgan, who then was courting his second-wife-to-be, the daughter of a former U.S. congressman there. Less than a week after Morgan's July 4 departure on his first raid into his native state, he cut telegraph wires near the Kentucky town of Horse Cave, assumed a name, and sent, ostensibly from a U.S. provost marshal at Nashville, a bogus and cavalier message to the Federal provost at Louisville. It presumed to inform the latter that Forrest, with a brigade, "attacked Murfreesborough, routing our forces, and is now moving on Nashville. Morgan is reported to be between Scottsville [Kentucky] and Gallatin [Tennessee], and will act in concert with Forrest, it is believed. Inform general commanding."[5]

One wonders how Forrest, had he known, might have taken the sending of this telegram, which put his impending operation at risk in furtherance of Morgan's own. On the day it was sent, Forrest was one day out of Chattanooga heading for Murfreesboro with plans to do exactly what Morgan's message was reporting he already had done. Forrest's official report later would recall leaving Chattanooga July 9 with the Texas Rangers and the Second Georgia Cavalry and making "a forced march of nearly 50 miles, reaching Altamont [Tennessee] on the night of the 10th instant." They rested at Altamont for a night before moving on to McMinnville, "where I was joined on the night of the 11th by a portion of the First Georgia Cavalry, two companies of Colonel Spiller's [Tennessee] Battalion . . . and two companies of Kentuckians," bringing his total strength to 1,400 men. He reported that "both horses and men were much jaded and worn by their long travel," but "[a]fter feeding and refreshing for a single day and being joined by some few volunteers I left on the 12th at 1 o'clock for Murfreesborough," more than 50 miles farther on. From that point, "there was no halt except for a short time to feed the men and horses."[6]

The feeding stop was made well after dark at Woodbury, where he found female residents exceedingly glad to see him. They reported that most of the town's men had been arrested suddenly by Federals the night before and taken to Murfreesboro on charges of aiding the Confederacy. Forrest informed them they could expect the return of their menfolk by the end of the following day, and the women gratefully supplied his troopers with food and fodder. Here, probably, he made a short speech telling the troops that dawn would mark his birthday and he wanted to observe it with a victory at Murfreesboro.[7]

The march covering the final eighteen miles was resumed at 1 A.M. Reaching Murfreesboro's outskirts at 4:30 A.M., his vanguard captured all of the fifteen Federal pickets without a shot. Forrest scouts by now had ascertained that they were about to encounter the Ninth Michigan and Third Minnesota infantry regiments and part of the Seventh Pennsylvania Cavalry, as well as an artillery battery, and when a company of the Texas Rangers approached the pickets, they pretended to be part of the Seventh Pennsylvania arriving to join the rest of the command. Allowed to pass, they quickly surrounded the pickets and took them prisoner with drawn pistols.[8]

Forrest had been informed that there were two camps, "one in Murfreesborough of one infantry regiment and the cavalry, the other [infantry regiment] with the artillery about a mile distant, and a small force with the officers in the courthouse and private houses around the public square. I decided immediately to attack the camp in town and the buildings, while the camp with the artillery should be held in check until the first was stormed and surrendered." He ordered Colonel Wharton and the Texas Rangers to assault the downtown camp, and Wharton "moved forward in gallant style" despite the fact that, because some of his Rangers were detached to storm the individual buildings, he had just two companies. Nevertheless, he and these "charged over the tent ropes right into the camp."[9]

Day was just dawning as they slammed into a waking detachment of approximately eighty men of the Seventh Pennsylvania, bivouacked in a field beside the Murfreesboro–Woodbury road. They captured most of them there and pursued the others into the nearby camp of the Ninth Michigan infantry. "[T]he enemy, mounted and some 1,200 strong, with terrific yells, dashed upon us from three directions, armed with double-barreled shot-guns and Colt's navy revolvers," the Ninth Michigan's lieutenant colonel, John G. Parkhurst, later reported. His unit, commanded by Colonel W. W. Duffield, had been reduced to five companies a week earlier when four companies had been detached and sent to Tullahoma, and yet another was quartered on the courthouse lawn. Duffield was wounded in the initial Confederate rush, shot both in the groin and the left thigh, but remained with his command until it repelled the attack. Then, "fainting from pain and loss of blood," he was carried from the field. His men, now under Parkhurst, eventually charged the Confederates, driving them out of their camp and beyond it, where the Michigan troops found and improved "quite a formidable position" behind "a cedar-post fence."[10]

Meanwhile, other elements of the attacking force long since had swept past them into the public square, site of both the courthouse and the jail. Several of the prisoners in the latter had been scheduled to hang later that morning. One, a Baptist minister from five miles north of Murfreesboro, recalled many years later that a Federal soldier had been killed near his home, and he and four secession-sympathizing neighbors had been arrested by order of Tennessee's new military governor, Andrew Johnson; in retribution for the soldier's murder, the minister recalled, they had been sentenced to die. Another of those set for execution that morning was Confederate captain William Richardson, who had been wounded and captured at Shiloh and then paroled by the Federals in Indiana. He was trying to get from Nashville southward with a guide who, when both were captured near Murfreesboro, turned out to be a Confederate spy carrying incriminating papers. Richardson later recalled that he and the spy, James Paul, finally had fallen asleep in their cell on the eve of their supposed doom when he was awakened by Paul "about daylight. [Paul] . . . caught me by the arm and was shaking me, saying 'Listen, listen!' I started up, hearing a strange noise like the roar of an approaching storm." They leaped onto a box "to look . . . out through the small grating of our prison window. The roar grew louder and came nearer, and in a very few seconds we were sure we could discern the clatter of horses' feet upon the hard turnpike." Then, "on the morning air there came to our ears with heartfelt welcome the . . . rebel yell. . . . Almost before we could speak, the advance-guard of the charging troopers came into sight and rushed by us on the street, some halting in front of the jail."[11]

Fighting ensued, and Richardson recalled that when the Federal company guarding the prison yard saw it was being surrounded, several of its soldiers took shots at the prisoners before fleeing; the inmates had to dive into a forward alcove of the cellblock to escape. Then a final Federal guard lit a bundle of papers with a match and shoved it under some loose planks in the floor of the front hall. By the time the Confederate troops reached the still-locked door, flames were high, and only by means of a "heavy iron bar" applied by the troopers to a lower corner of the heavy jail-door were the prisoners rescued, dragged out under the door while lying flat on the floor. Then, Richardson wrote, Forrest himself "dashed up and inquired of the officer in charge if he had rescued the prisoners. He said that they were safe, but added that the jail had been set on fire in order to burn them up, and the guard had taken refuge in the courthouse. Forrest said, 'Never mind, we'll get them.' " Richardson added that he would "never forget the appearance of General Forrest on that occasion; his eyes were flashing as if on fire, his face was deeply flushed, and he seemed in a condition of great excitement."[12]

The fire in the jail wasn't the only one. Duffield and other Federal officers later reported that the Michigan infantry company held out on the upper floor of the courthouse until "the enemy had possession of the lower story of the building and had started a fire, with the evident intention of burning them out." Forrest's own report indicates the same, saying that following "two or three hours' hard struggle the courthouse was fired," after which it was "surrendered to Colonel Morrison" and the Second Georgia. The private houses were taken, and Brigadier General Thomas Crittenden and his staff captured. Part of the Second Georgia stormed the jail, "releasing many prisoners confined for political offenses; [it] also took the telegraph office, capturing the operator."[13]

All this transpired by about 8 A.M. His mood no doubt unimproved by news that the prisoners in the jail had been nearly burned alive (the Michigan soldiers in the courthouse, after all, had the alternative of surrendering), Forrest turned to the rest of his task with grim zeal. A Union report filed six days later would say the three different Federal forces had been posted "beyond supporting distance in sudden emergency" because of "[j]ealousy of officers," and that "bad picketing, lack of skill, vigilance, and personal courage on part of officers" also came into play; Forrest set about capitalizing on these deficiencies. While the Texas Rangers were keeping Parkhurst's smaller Michigan unit pinned down, he went to join the First Georgia and his Tennessee and Kentucky troopers in the attack on the Minnesotans, worrying that from their position so far from the town they might escape. When his troops first found them, they had marched about half a mile toward the sounds of the fighting in Murfreesboro and had taken a defensive position in a field. They and the Confederates had been sparring since just after dawn. Forrest took personal command and "charged the rear of the enemy into their camps and burned their camps and stores, demoralizing their force and weakening their strength. . . . After the courthouse and private buildings were surrendered and the fight had lasted five or six hours, I prepared my whole force to storm both camps and summoned them to surrender."[14]

What Forrest really did, according to his authorized biographers, was change his plans when the Minnesotans drew up on a hill that would have been costly to storm. Instead, he left a strong force in their front and hurried back across town to dispose of Parkhurst's Ninth Michigan— while some of his officers, fearing the arrival of Federal reinforcements from Nashville, "urged Colonel Forrest to rest content with what had been accomplished and quit the field without further and, as they were satisfied, fruitless yet costly efforts to carry the Federal position." Ignoring this counsel, he dismounted one of his units and sent it forward against the front of the Michigan regiment, then dismounted another and positioned it for a charge on the Federal right flank while a subordinate wrote a message to be taken to Parkhurst.[15]

By now wounded in the lower leg, Parkhurst later reported having repeatedly sent couriers to the commander of the Minnesota regiment, Colonel H. C. Lester, requesting reinforcements, but said he never received a reply. The Parkhurst report says his troops "maintained our position, despite the frequent attacks and desperate efforts of the enemy to destroy us, until 11:30 o'clock, when a flag of truce was sent to us, with a demand for surrender, of which the following is a true copy . . . :

Murfreesborough, July 13, 1862.

COLONEL: I must demand an unconditional surrender of your force as prisoners of war or I will have every man put to the sword. You are aware of the overpowering force I have at my command, and this demand is made to prevent the effusion of blood.

I am, colonel, very respectfully, your obedient servant,

N. B. FORREST,
Brigadier General of Cavalry, C.S. Army.[16]

Parkhurst sent Forrest's note on to Duffield, but Duffield returned it "with a message that he should leave the matter entirely to my discretion." In the meantime, Parkhurst "had ascertained that General Forrest had concentrated his entire force, save one squadron . . . in the immediate vicinity of my camp, hemming us in on all sides, and . . . preparing to make a charge upon us with his entire command . . . evidently intending, with this overwhelming force, to execute the threat contained in his demand for a surrender."[17]

At noon Parkhurst, after fighting for nearly eight hours and having just 134 men left, surrendered, and Forrest immediately returned to the west of town to deal with the Third Minnesota. Sending Lester substantially the same surrender-or-die ultimatum he had given Parkhurst, he consented to Lester's request to come into town under a flag of truce and confer with

Duffield, who by now was a Confederate prisoner. Brigadier General Crittenden later reported that on this trip Lester "saw the enemy, who had not dared to come within range of his artillery, and was so impressed with what he saw that he returned determined to surrender." What Lester observed was an "ostentatious . . . display . . . [of Forrest's] several commands along the path Colonel Lester was led in going to and returning from the interview with Duffield, so as to make an appearance of greater numbers than were really present." It worked. Lester surrendered, and not only he, but a Federal board of inquiry charged with finding the cause of the Murfreesboro debacle, later officially estimated Forrest's force to number 2,600, almost twice its actual size.[18]

Forrest preliminarily estimated his loss in the battle at "about 25 killed and 40 to 60 wounded," which was apparently lower than it ultimately turned out to be; no later report was ever filed. Federal reports indicate the Union loss at approximately 20 killed and 170 wounded and missing at the time they surrendered. Forrest sent superiors in Chattanooga word that he not only had captured 1,200 men but "burnt $200,000 worth of stores; captured sufficient stores with those burned to amount to $500,000, and brigade of 60 wagons, 300 mules, 150 or 200 horses, and field battery of four pieces; destroyed the railroad and depot at Murfreesborough. Had to retreat to McMinnville, owing to large number of prisoners to be guarded."[19]

Several of the Federal prisoners helped drive the wagon train of captured supplies and artillery vehicles to McMinnville in exchange for a Forrest promise to parole all but the commissioned officers there; given two days' rations, they headed northward for home and relatives with a parole exempting them from further service for a while. The officers were taken initially from McMinnville to Knoxville under a small guard. Parkhurst reported that on the march from McMinnville to Knoxville "I was ordered to dismount and surrender my horse, which General Forrest instantly appropriated." Forrest mentioned no such incident. Interestingly, his report and even the account of the battle by his biographers failed also to mention the nature of the surrender ultimatums he made to Parkhurst and Lester. His report also didn't include another of his personal combat victims. This one supposedly was a "negro camp-follower" who fired four shots at him, including one that "cut his hatband" as he led the charge into the camp in the rear of the Third Minnesota. "[J]ust as the negro was about to fire the fifth time, Forrest killed him with his pistol at the distance of thirty paces."[20]

During or after the fighting, he may have killed more than one black.

Later he would be charged in a Union general's hearsay account with "deliberately" drawing his pistol at Murfreesboro and fatally shooting in the head a captured free mulatto who declared himself to be a servant to a Federal officer. Also, a Confederate cavalryman eventually would claim to remember that when he brought Forrest a similar capture during the battle [a "fine big Buck Negro dressed in federal uniform"], Forrest "gave me a Cussing" for not killing the black, but finally ordered the human prize taken to the officer in charge of prisoners. And a civilian diarist wrote soon after the battle that slaves were avoiding contact with Federals since they "heard" that Forrest had hanged blacks captured bearing weapons at Murfreesboro and nearby Gallatin. Blacks had not been officially placed under arms by the Lincoln government at that time, but some of the liberated slaves, wishing to destroy their chains once and for all, may have been volunteering for unofficial Union duty.[21]

There apparently was another significant incident that he failed to report. Captain Richardson, the erstwhile Murfreesboro jail inmate, recalled later that "after the fighting had ceased and the Federal prisoners were all brought together, General Forrest came to me and said: 'They tell me these men treated you inhumanly while in jail. Point them out to me.' "

> *I told him there was but one man I wished to call his attention to, and that was the one who had set fire to the jail in order to burn us up. Forrest asked me to go along the line with him and point that man out. I did so. A few hours later, when the list of private soldiers was being called, the name of this man was heard and no one answered; Forrest said, "Pass on, it's all right."*[22]

15

FORREST'S TROOPERS WERE joined in late 1862 by a young artillery chief ordered there by Braxton Bragg, the new western departmental commander. The arrival of this unimpressive lieutenant — small and spare John W. Morton Jr., nineteen-year-old son of a refined Nashville physician — evoked acid defiance from Forrest. "I have a fine battery . . . under Captain Freeman," he brusquely responded to Morton's introduction of himself, "and I don't propose to be interfered with by Bragg." Morton, abruptly dismissed, left the interview crestfallen; he had served with distinction at Fort Donelson, been surrendered there, and after being exchanged, had pulled strings to get himself assigned to this cavalry leader who had refused to participate in the Donelson capitulation. After Morton walked away in mortification, Forrest turned to an aide and began to curse. "I'd like to know why in the hell Bragg sent that tallow-faced boy here to take charge of my artillery," he said. "I'll not stand it. Captain Freeman shan't be interfered with."[1]

He was so incensed that, on December 3, 1862, he fired off a contentious letter to his superior, Brigadier General Joseph Wheeler, saying that he had "no objections to receiving Lieutenant Morton in my command, provided he is willing to come under command of Captain Freeman; but I am unwilling to exchange Captain Freeman (who has made a reputation at Shiloh and before Nashville, and proven a gallant and efficient officer) for any other officer"; instead, he asserted, he would as soon "return the battery." He also pointedly said he hoped the order assigning Morton to him "has been made without your knowledge and consent, and that you will not permit any changes, but allow my command to go on as organized. You are well aware of the trouble and dissatisfaction caused by these [types of] changes, and I hope none will be made. . . ."[2]

The Murfreesboro victory not only sent shock waves through Federal commanders across the upper South and beyond, it seemed to affirm in Forrest's own mind his fitness for not only waging but planning battles. His superiors encouraged this assumption, approving his commission to brigadier general just eight days after the raid. The capture of the Murfreesboro garrison virtually halted the Chattanooga drive of Buell, some of whose troops were recalled to the Nashville area while others were detached to guard the most vulnerable points along his railroad lines of supply. This sudden change in Union attitude much aided Bragg. Having succeeded Beauregard soon after Forrest was sent east from Tupelo, this dour disciplinarian recognized that Chattanooga was the door to the Deep South's eastern half and that Buell was knocking on it. With no Federal interference, he quickly moved most of his army there from Tupelo by rail and, to recover Confederate territory lost since the fall of Donelson, began planning an ambitious northward thrust that would be aided no little by the moves of Forrest.

For two months after Murfreesboro made his name demonic in the minds of Federals, Forrest had enlarged on this reputation, playing small-scale but bloody hide-and-seek with Union commanders in central and eastern Tennessee. On July 18, he took 700 troopers within sight of downtown Nashville, capturing pickets and burning railroad bridges. Two weeks later, he struck at Manchester, killing three Federals, capturing fifteen, and spreading fear along the railroad toward Chattanooga; then he dropped out of sight. Union major general William Nelson complained, with more truth than he may have known, that chasing Forrest and the also-active Morgan with infantry in the hot Tennessee summer was "hopeless," especially as they were "mounted on racehorses." In early August, four Federal units totaling several thousand men tried unsuccessfully to corner Forrest as he was reported now and again at such east-central Tennessee towns as Sparta, McMinnville, Smithville, Woodbury, and Murfreesboro. Meanwhile, mistakenly thinking he detected the beginnings of a Federal retreat from Nashville, he urged Bragg to attack there. Soon he received his first reproving note from Bragg. Assuming him incapable of operating in the face of the large Federal forces in that vicinity, Bragg on August 22 ordered him to "return and act according to instructions you have previously received." Which were: to move southeast into Sequatchie Valley where, Bragg said, "the enemy is reported advancing." Forrest did as instructed, eluding three converging Union columns near Altamont, but by September 3 Bragg was moving toward Kentucky in concert with an advance into Maryland by Robert E. Lee's Army of Northern Virginia.[3]

Forrest joined Bragg under orders to operate on the far left flank in the territory he had just been ordered out of. Charged with harassing Buell's Federals while Bragg slipped northward past them, Forrest headed from Sparta west to Lebanon, then south to Murfreesboro. He pushed northward himself then, annoying Union forces at Tyree Springs, Tennessee, and Franklin, Kentucky, while Buell began to try to overtake Bragg. On September 14 Bragg placed Forrest over all cavalry supporting Leonidas Polk, commanding the army's right wing. In that capacity, Forrest helped surround a 4,000-man Union garrison which surrendered at Munfordville September 17.

Things then turned sour for Forrest as well as Bragg's Kentucky thrust. Polk ordered Forrest to bring his troops back to Munfordville from Elizabethtown as quickly as possible because Bragg anticipated a Federal attack there. The next day, Polk notified Forrest his own troops were moving to Bardstown and ordered him not only to protect his—Polk's—flanks "thoroughly" but also to "break up the railroad connection between Elizabethtown and Louisville." Forrest protested the order to strike the railroad, informing Polk it was "impossible for me to carry out your orders on account of the condition that my horses are in" and adding that he himself was "disabled," all his available men were on picket duty, he was "threatened with the enemy" and, in the absence of the majority of his troops that had been ordered back to Munfordville, would confine himself to trying to "defend the wagon train." Polk on September 24 ordered him forward again, and Forrest grumbled that he had "not a full company in the command, having furnished several guards and pickets, but I will send from the different companies a sufficiency to report, as you ordered."[4]

The next day, for the second time in three months, he was ordered to give up troops he had seasoned. This time, Bragg ordered him to turn over his men to Wheeler, the twenty-six-year-old (and West Point–trained) new commander of the cavalry of the left wing. Forrest's assignment was to return to central Tennessee to raise recruits—two cavalry regiments and four of infantry—and then to "operate against the enemy wherever found, but especially at Nashville, Clarksville, &c., cutting off supplies, capturing trains, and harassing them in all ways practicable." These orders may have resulted partially from Forrest's temporary disability, a dislocated right shoulder and "great" bruising by a debilitated horse which fell and rolled over on him. They also possibly reflected Bragg's worries about his own advanced position. Bragg had hoped Generals Sterling Price and Earl Van Dorn, left behind in Mississippi with separate commands when Bragg moved to Chattanooga, would "clear away our rear and open a base" for him. "Otherwise we may be seriously embarrassed," he wrote Richmond the same day he issued his order to Forrest. In the Richmond dispatch, Bragg also complained that few Kentuckians had come forward to swell his thin ranks. He soon became so preoccupied with his rear—or something—that, pleading lack of subsistence around Munfordville (there was a drought in central Kentucky that summer), he stepped aside to Bardstown and let Buell pass him to reach the protection and reinforcements of Louisville. Bragg thus tossed away his chance for a great Confederate victory in Kentucky and, instead, settled for a costly draw October 8 at Perryville, where he lost 3,400 killed, wounded, and missing out of 15,000 Confederates engaged. Bragg withdrew from Kentucky after Perryville—a few days after Van Dorn and Price were repulsed at Corinth, Mississippi, and a couple of weeks after Lee staggered back to Virginia from similarly indecisive slaughter at Antietam.[5]

Riding 165 miles in five days from Bardstown, Forrest and his small escort arrived back at Murfreesboro in central Tennessee. At LaVergne, they found 1,700 untrained and underequipped Tennessee militia and 1,000 cavalrymen, all newly recruited, while at Murfreesboro there were posted a regular infantry regiment, the Thirty-second Alabama, and a battery of two six-pounders and two twelve-pounders commanded by

Captain S. L. Freeman. Soon after Forrest ordered the Thirty-second Alabama to reinforce the troops at LaVergne, that regiment and the rest were attacked and driven from the field by Federals from Nashville October 7. Having arrived only a few days before, Forrest began a continual pleading for additional troops from his departmental superior, Major General Samuel Jones at Knoxville. Jones apparently sent all the troops and arms he could find, which were few. Jones's dispatches indicate the new brigadier general was very nervous at Murfreesboro, continually expecting a Federal attack and—especially after the Union assault at LaVergne—threatening to retreat if unreinforced. Jones gave him provisional permission to "fall back to Tullahoma [Tennessee], and farther if necessary" but added: "If the enemy's force is as small as represented the cavalry ought to be able so to harass the enemy as to prevent their advancing to Murfreesboro."[6]

When Bragg retired from Kentucky in late October, Forrest again was relieved, this time of his short-lived central Tennessee infantry-and-cavalry command, and was assigned as commander of cavalry cooperating with Breckinridge. When leaving Kentucky, he had been allowed to keep the four Alabama companies that had signed on with his first regiment in 1861, and to these were added the Fourth Tennessee under Colonel James W. Starnes, who had participated with him in the battle of Sacramento; Colonel George G. Dibrell's Eighth Tennessee, which included Forrest's youngest brother, Jeffrey, a major (along with Lieutenants Jesse and William Z. Beck, who were probably cousins); Colonel J. B. Biffle's Ninth Tennessee; and some thirteen other companies. In all, they totaled some 3,500 men ill armed and ill supplied, and, with Forrest—in a pronounced reversal of recent stance—again urging an attack on Nashville, Breckinridge sent them on an extensive, infantry-supported demonstration against Nashville in early November. When Bragg arrived back in central Tennessee, headquartering at Tullahoma, Forrest was ordered to report to young General Wheeler. Wheeler had been given command of all of Bragg's cavalry: three "regular" brigades plus those of Forrest and Morgan, whom Bragg considered only irregulars.[7]

The tone of Forrest's early dispatches to Wheeler hints that he wasn't happy at being placed under him. He sounds, in fact, as if he—not Wheeler—were the commander:

Murfreesborough, Nov. 15, 1862 . . .

GENERAL:
You will order the following companies to report to Colonel Carroll,

*inspector-general, at Spencer's Springs, 3 miles west of Murfrees-
boro. . . . I would suggest that you order your brigade to Stewart's
Creek. . . .*

Tullahoma, Nov. 20, 1862

*General Wheeler:
Can you spare my brigade? If so, order them up to Murfreesborough
with the battery and all their transportation on Sunday. Answer . . .*[8]

It was shortly after Bragg's Kentucky withdrawal that Lieutenant Morton arrived and was curtly dismissed from Forrest's presence. The next
day, Forrest relented slightly. He said he would allow Morton to join his
command, although not as chief of artillery, on the expectation that some
artillery pieces for him and his squad of artillerymen to fire soon would
be captured—but he would do so only if Wheeler would so order. To
get the order Forrest demanded, Morton rode from Columbia, Tennessee,
where Forrest then was camped, fifty-two miles to LaVergne, where
Wheeler was. He then returned immediately to Columbia, making the
whole journey in twenty-three hours without changing horses. Perhaps
grudgingly impressed, Forrest let the "tallow-faced boy" and his squad
accompany the first expedition of his new troopers.[9]

Forrest received orders from Bragg on December 10 to begin a march
into West Tennessee. It was an important assignment designed to relieve
Federal pressure on Confederate forces in Mississippi, and Forrest asked
Bragg for "better supplies." Despite the fact that Bragg himself had
reported a surplus, he refused the request and ordered Forrest into motion;
he apparently wasn't willing to outfit units he considered only partisan
guerrillas. Forrest was forced to leave Columbia for West Tennessee
without firing caps for the shotguns and pistols borne by his approximately 2,000 troopers. Lacking even tents for shelter, he and his men
crossed the wide and icy Tennessee River at Clifton December 13–15 in
a hard rain in skiffs and "a large wooden flatboat." They were met on the
opposite shore by an unidentified "citizen" who, under previous orders
from Forrest, somehow had procured from far behind Union lines 50,000
firing caps for the shotguns and pistols. Now more prepared for work, the
troopers approached the town of Lexington and, encountering Federal
pickets December 18, attacked and routed an artillery unit and some 1,000
Federal cavalry and infantry there; in the process, they also captured
Colonel R. G. Ingersoll of the Eleventh Illinois Cavalry, about 150 other
U.S. soldiers, and two cannon thereafter assigned to Morton. The attack

was made in the casualty-cutting manner becoming usual with Forrest, strong forces being sent against the enemy flanks after a demonstration had been launched at the center. Ingersoll later reported that Confederates were "pouring in [from] all directions." He also estimated to superiors that Forrest's 2,000 troopers were "at least 5,000 strong."[10]

Ingersoll's overestimation of Forrest's strength was no coincidence. Forrest had brought kettledrums across the Tennessee, which were kept beating to give the impression that large numbers of infantry were present. Many more fires than his troops required were lit and tended at night, and some of his cavalry were dismounted and paraded as infantry in front of his captives. Such measures—along with Forrest's frequent division of his forces in the presence of the enemy, giving the impression he had many more men than he did—not only put fear in the minds of his pursuers but encouraged exaggerated caution, thus providing more time to out-maneuver them.

From Lexington, he moved quickly westward to Jackson, where he drove in Federal pickets on all roads leading into the city and then destroyed railroad tracks coming in from the north and others leading out southward toward Grant's Mississippi bases; Dibrell's Eighth Tennessee Cavalry, doing the destruction north of Jackson, also captured 101 Federals at Webb's Station, burning their stockade with everything in it that couldn't be hauled away. The next day, Forrest advanced on Jackson itself, but found it garrisoned by Federal troops several times his own number and withdrew, heading northwest to Humboldt and Trenton. Starnes's Fourth Tennessee Cavalry was sent to capture Humboldt and did, taking more than 100 prisoners and again thoroughly wrecking a stretch of railroad. Forrest meanwhile personally led an attack on Trenton, sending Biffle's Ninth Tennessee around to the rear of the town before he struck it. On the third volley from artillery under Captain Freeman, the Federals surrendered—400 prisoners of war, 300 blacks, and a large number of arms and supplies that had to be destroyed because there was no means of transporting them.[11]

That night, detachment after detachment of dismounted cavalry were marched repeatedly in front of these prisoners to give the impression that Confederate reinforcements were continually arriving. The prisoners then were paroled, marched to Columbus, Kentucky, and turned over to Union commanders, to whom they spread their misconceptions of Forrest's strength. Within days, Forrest's numbers were being officially estimated by his adversaries at as high as 20,000. The personal image he presented to his foes was as singular as his collective one. When the Union officer in charge at Trenton, Colonel Jacob Fry, surrendered a sword he said had been in his family more than a hundred years, Forrest gave it back with the comment that he hoped its next use would be in a better cause. Instead, he took a sword from among the stored supplies captured at Trenton: an imported one of Damascus steel which he promptly made a symbol of his light regard for the conventions of war. He sharpened not only the usual cutting edge but the regulation dull one as well, and thereafter in battle used both.[12]

He hit Union City December 21, having captured on the way two U.S. companies at Rutherford Station along with twenty-two hospitalized Federals and a colonel of the 119th Illinois at Kenton Station. At Union City, he made more significant captures, this time "without firing a gun" and perhaps by using another tactic considered irregular in the practice of war. His opposing officer, Captain S. B. Logan of the Fifty-fourth Illinois, charged in a subsequent report that Forrest sent forward a flag of truce ostensibly to convey into Union lines Federal prisoners of war already captured and paroled (and on their way to Columbus, Kentucky); then he used that flag of truce as a means to demand an unconditional capitulation by the Union City garrison. Logan protested but, surrounded, surrendered his force of about 100 men. Forrest's report makes no mention of any flag-of-truce incident, while his authorized biography says the large number of paroled prisoners, resembling a hostile force when it came in sight of the Union garrison from about a half mile away, encouraged the Federals to "yield . . . with little parley."[13]

After a short pause to rest his men, Forrest celebrated Christmas Day by disrupting the railroad from Union City southeastward to McKenzie. Large numbers of Federal troops began gathering around him at Trenton, Humboldt, Huntingdon, and Lexington, and he left McKenzie moving southward away from the railroad December 28, hoping to evade action until he could strike the Federals and the railroad another blow south of Jackson at Bethel Station. He had so much trouble getting his artillery and wagons across a rickety and collapsing bridge over the Obion River, however, that he had to use sacks of captured flour and coffee to give traction to the muddy wheels of his wagons and caissons; only by detailing twenty men per wagon, fifty per piece of artillery, and working all night in drizzling sleet, did he get the procession out of the Obion's banks and back in motion. It crawled along thoroughfares of mud until late December 30, when scouts under Captain William Forrest discovered a large enemy force some six miles away moving in their direction from Huntingdon. The scout commander's eldest brother decided that, rather than try to outrun the Federals with his spoils-laden wagons, he would accept an attack, despite the fact that Biffle's regiment had been detached toward Trenton and Starnes's toward Huntingdon.

Forrest was moving southeastward from the village of McLemoresville when he struck a Union force of about the same size coming south along the Huntingdon Road; their routes intersected twelve miles north of Lexington at Parker's Crossroads. Having already sent four Alabama companies cross-country to Clarksburg to warn him of any Federal force approaching from that direction, he closed about 10 A.M. with the Fiftieth Indiana, the 122nd Illinois, the Thirty-ninth Iowa, two companies of the Eighteenth Illinois, and three guns from the Seventh Wisconsin Battery.

"[F]inding that we were able to whip the enemy, [I] dismounted a portion of my cavalry to support my artillery and attack in front while I could flank them on each side and get Col. Russell's [Fourth Alabama Cavalry] in their rear," he later officially reported. The fighting lasted five hours. Confederate cannon under Freeman and Morton fired with such effect that, when the Federals took up a seemingly strong position in the corner of a rail fence, the rails were splintered into flying wooden shrapnel. Both Biffle's and Starnes's regiments returned as the fighting progressed, and the Confederates prevailed, driving the Union troops from the west side of the Huntingdon road to the east. "I was whipping them badly with my artillery . . . had them entirely surrounded and was driving them before me . . . taking it leisurely and trying as much as possible to save my men," Forrest reported. He was "whipping them badly" enough, in fact, that officers of other Federal units arriving about that time remembered that the firing had ceased for a half hour and surrender was being discussed under flags of truce.

Suddenly, Forrest informed his superiors, "to my surprise and astonishment a fire was opened on us in our rear" from the direction in which he had sent the four Alabama companies as a safeguard. Another brigade of Federals roughly the size of the force he had just vanquished, commanded by Brigadier General J. C. Sullivan, had marched from Huntingdon and, in a peach orchard west of the Huntingdon road, had gotten among the Confederates tending the horses of Forrest's dismounted cavalry-turned-infantry. The perilous predicament gave rise to the colorful but apocryphal story that Forrest, to a subordinate asking anxiously how they could solve this sudden two-front problem, responded: "Charge them both ways." The reality was less memorable. Dibrell recalled in his own report that Forrest ordered him "to retreat, which we did in much confusion. . . . [O]ur horse-holders were demoralized, and many men were captured trying to get to their horses. We retreated through . . . [a] large cotton field between a fire from the re-enforcements and the brigade we had just driven back." Starnes and Russell helped stave off disaster by charging the Federal brigade, keeping it from aiding its reinforcements and enabling Forrest to get his artillery and most of his men from between the two Federal forces and hurry them onto the road to Lexington. In addition to more than 300 of his men captured and perhaps 100 killed and wounded, Forrest lost three artillery pieces he had taken—plus six wagonloads of ammunition captured during the campaign "which, by a mistake of orders, were driven right into the enemy's line." Even in this debacle, however, he captured as many men as the Federals and almost certainly inflicted more casualties than he suffered.[14]

On the subsequent and laxly pursued ride to the Tennessee River, which he recrossed New Year's Day on the same boats he had used two weeks earlier, he had ample time to ruminate on the "mistake of orders" to the ammunition wagons—as well as another mistake that had permitted him to be surprised from the rear. The assignment of the four Alabama companies sent to Clarksburg had been vague, calling only for a reconnaissance; they had fallen back in the face of the superior Union force, had gotten lost, and by the time they heard the battle raging and reached the crossroads they found Forrest in retreat. He also had time to reflect on the beginner's lesson in artillery operation he had gotten from an enlisted man as guns were being unlimbered to protect the recrossing of the Tennessee at Clifton. Federals were reported in pursuit, and one battery and a detachment of cavalry had been left in a fortified position, ordered to put up a last-ditch fight if necessary. When Forrest saw the guns being pulled into position and then the horses and caissons rapidly moved backward out of the way, he mistook the movement for a precipitous retreat on the part of the drivers of the vehicles. Striking the lead driver across the shoulders with the flat of his saber, he shouted: "Turn those horses around and get back to where you belong, or by God I'll kill you." The artilleryman responded that he was only doing his job.[15]

Returning to central Tennessee, Forrest found that in his absence Bragg had fought another costly draw December 31–January 2 and retreated from the field, this time at Stone's River outside Murfreesboro. Bragg then moved his headquarters back to Tullahoma and placed Forrest's command at Columbia, where it remained most of the rest of the first month of 1863. Without Forrest's consultation (he may have been on a leave of absence), about 800 of his men then were put under Wheeler on a mission toward Fort Donelson to interrupt the southward flow of Union shipping up the

Tennessee River. The foray was begun in bitter cold, and Forrest had to overtake his men on the road; when he did, he found them woefully undersupplied with ammunition and food. Then the Federals learned of the Confederate presence and suspended boat traffic of their own accord, prompting Wheeler to decide that "nothing could be lost" by an attack on the town of Dover on February 3. Forrest argued against the idea, noting that even if the fort were taken it couldn't be held against Federal gunboats 100 miles behind enemy lines. Should the Confederates succeed in capturing the garrison of 500 or 600 Federal troops, he said, they probably would have to lose 200 or 300 of their own men and expose the rest to unnecessary privation. These remarks reportedly "passed without heed," which troubled Forrest. Saying he would mention it to no one else, he informed two staff officers of his conversation with Wheeler because, if he were killed in the fight and it ended badly, he was "not willing to be held responsible for any disaster that may result."[16]

After a spurned demand for surrender only slightly subtler than Forrest's ultimatum at Murfreesboro (and signed by all three generals — Wheeler, Forrest, and John A. Wharton — perhaps to impress Union colonel A. C. Harding with their strength), Wheeler's battle plan called for sending Forrest against the fort's east side while troops under Wharton struck its west and southwest sides. Wheeler accompanied Forrest's troops to their attack site, then departed to oversee Wharton's, the larger force. Wheeler's report says that just as he left Forrest, Forrest thought Union troops were leaving the fort trying to get to the river and — "being anxious to rush in quickly" and enter the works simultaneously with the pursued Federals — charged, meeting Federal fire so strong that "he was repulsed and forced to retire." Leading this costly charge, Forrest had a horse shot from under him. When it and he went down, his men thought him dead and began retreating, and he had to get up and go quickly after them. Having moved before the 2:30 P.M. starting time of the planned concerted assaults, Forrest dismounted his men and waited this time, but his second forward rush was doomed by another Union movement toward the river and another mistaken assumption as to its meaning. After his men had "occupied the houses on the east side of the town, and had a plunging fire of musketry on the enemy," Wheeler later reported, ". . . the enemy commenced running out toward the river, and our men in the houses seeing this, and thinking it to be a movement on their held horses, abandoned their favorable position and rushed back to protect them. But for this accident, the garrison would have surrendered in a very few minutes. General Forrest then withdrew and discontinued the action."[17]

To Wharton went the few laurels won at Dover — notably, the capture of a Union artillery piece. Both Wharton's and Forrest's men ran out of ammunition, and the three generals decided there was nothing to do but leave before more Union troops arrived. That night in a farmhouse three miles from the battlefield, Wheeler wrote his report while Forrest, severely bruised after his second horse of the day was killed, lay prone on the floor, his upper torso resting on the back of an overturned chair. He protested Wheeler's dictation of the portion of the report concerning his troops' part of the action, and Wheeler responded that his account "does ample justice to yourself and your men." Possibly as angry at his own errors as at Wheeler, Forrest hotly noted his early opposition to the attack and remarked that Wheeler could "say or do" nothing to "bring back my brave men lying dead or wounded and freezing around that fort tonight." He then grew frankly insubordinate, saying that he meant "no disrespect to you; you know my feelings of personal friendship for you; you can have my sword if you demand it; but there is one thing I do want you to put in that report to General Bragg — tell him that I will be in my coffin before I will fight again under your command."[18]

Thanks largely to Wheeler, who apparently liked and admired him, Forrest spoke truly; Wheeler arranged for him always to work under some other commander from then on. The next was Earl Van Dorn, the loser of the battle of Corinth. Van Dorn was transferred to Bragg's army and on February 25 was given command of a cavalry corps consisting of Forrest's brigade and two divisions which had served with Van Dorn in Mississippi. The only other cavalry corps with Bragg's army was commanded by Wheeler.

Van Dorn's new corps debuted in battle March 5 at Thompson's Station, where it encountered Federal colonel John Coburn and four Union infantry regiments supported by a battery of artillery and a cavalry unit. Nearly 3,000 strong, Coburn's force was on its way to join Brigadier General Philip Sheridan at Spring Hill, Tennessee, when it met 6,000 of Van Dorn's Confederates: three dismounted brigades of Brigadier General William H. (Red) Jackson drawn up across the Franklin-Columbia road and Forrest's troopers stationed well to Jackson's right. Coming on cautiously, Coburn soon became "convinced that we were in the neighborhood of an overpowering force," but his cavalry "went off" and left him before he could order them to retreat. His artillery also retired unceremoniously after one of Forrest's guns opened on it. Jackson's units made three charges against Coburn and were hurled back, but from the far right Forrest's men, also dismounted, got into Coburn's rear. Out of ammunition after nearly five hours of fighting, Coburn gave up as a Forrest charge came within twenty feet of the Federal line. The Confederates took 1,200 prisoners.[19]

The battle cost Forrest one of his favorite mounts, and the way this one—named Roderick—died bespeaks the fidelity of his horses. In camp Roderick often followed Forrest like a dog, and at Thompson Station the animal was struck three times while bearing his master on a charge simultaneous with one of Jackson's that rolled up the Union flank. Forrest dismounted and gave the reins to his son, Willie, continuing the charge on the son's mount and telling Willie to take Roderick to the rear. Willie did, but when Roderick was relieved of his saddle and bridle in the horse-holding area, he heard the roar of the battle and galloped back into it, jumping three fences before perishing of a new, fourth wound just as he reached Forrest.[20]

A couple of other, smaller fights quickly followed Thompson's Station. At Brentwood on March 25, Forrest captured two Federal garrisons of 500 and 300 men and many stands of new arms—which he let his men exchange their inferior weapons for. After leaving the field, however, his rear guard was attacked and routed by 700 Union cavalry under Brigadier General G. C. Smith, who drove them several miles before Starnes, involved in other operations close by, attacked Smith's right flank. Forrest, carrying a flag and "cursing a blue streak," gathered up a few hundred of his men and mounted another flank charge of his own. It then became Smith's turn to be chased for miles.[21]

As part of a Van Dorn reconnaissance in force at Franklin April 10, Forrest's troops were attacked in the flank again by Federals under Major General David Stanley as they moved in extended fashion up the Lewisburg road. Freeman's six artillery pieces were with this part of the column and were suddenly captured by the U.S. Fourth Cavalry. Confederate horsemen counterattacked almost immediately, recovering most of the guns and prisoners, but not before a few of the latter were made to run on foot in front of the retiring Union cavalry at pistol point. Freeman, who had injured a knee and was unable to keep up, was shot in the face by a retreating Federal.[22]

Word of Stanley's attack reached Forrest at the front of the column via a courier. "General Stanley has cut in behind you, has captured the rearguard battery and many prisoners, and has now got into [Brigadier General Frank] Armstrong's rear!" a messenger informed him. "You say he's in Armstrong's rear?" Forrest shouted in earshot of some of his troops. "That's where I've been trying to get him all day, damn him! I'll be in *his* rear in about five minutes. Face your line of battle about, Armstrong; push forward your skirmish line; crowd 'em both ways. I'll go to the rear brigade, and you'll hear from me there directly." Forrest is reported to have said later that at that moment he thought his command was done for, but a general on the scene at the time said every enlisted man present believed Stanley had fallen into a Forrest trap. A subsequent Forrest charge broke the Federal attack.[23]

Freeman's funeral on April 11 at Forrest's headquarters in Spring Hill moved the general to rare tears. An attorney before the war, the artillery-man had been much respected by Forrest for his courage, and the way his death occurred suggests a continuing escalation of guerrilla-style war in the West. It also appears to have been almost a random instance. As Stanley's cavalry moved back to Murfreesboro after the Franklin action, one of its unit commanders later officially reported that his men burned "on our way ten dwellings . . . belonging to persons who had sons in the Confederate Army, as per order of General Stanley."[24]

16

FORREST'S FIRST GENERAL'S star had followed the Murfreesboro victory, but for a while afterward his brilliance had dimmed.

During the Bragg invasion of Kentucky he performed in lackluster fashion—perhaps, granted, because he was in great, albeit temporary, physical pain from the horse fall and also was chiefly being used as a supplier of pickets. The resounding defeat of his troops at LaVergne (despite his own absence from the field) made him appear unimpressive in his brief tenure as central Tennessee cavalry-and-infantry commander. The West Tennessee raid was masterly, but it ended with his troops getting surprised and barely avoiding disaster at Parker's Crossroads. At Dover, he made two critical mistakes and then personally revolted against his superior. He worked well enough under Van Dorn at Thompson's Station, but his efforts at Brentwood and Franklin again had to weather enemy surprise attacks. Thus the Bragg view that he was no more than an adept independent raider wasn't without foundation at this stage, when Forrest still was learning how to be an army officer. Bragg's opinion was strengthened, no doubt, by two occurrences which soon followed: another incident with a superior, followed by one of Forrest's greatest independent exploits.

Relations with Van Dorn had deteriorated as a result of the battle at

Thompson's Station and the Brentwood raid. In late April, the two faced each other in the memorable moment in which Van Dorn grabbed his sword from the wall and challenged Forrest. A small man, Van Dorn accused the comparatively huge Forrest of breaking military regulations by letting his men have access to the captured guns at Brentwood and of prompting someone on his staff (possibly former Memphis *Avalanche* proprietor Matt Gallaway, who, now that Memphis was in Federal hands, was acting as Forrest's assistant adjutant general) to write an article for the Chattanooga *Rebel* giving Forrest credit for the Thompson's Station victory. Whether Forrest actually did is not known, but his relations with the *Rebel* may have been close; it was being operated at the time by future Louisville *Courier-Journal* editor Henry Watterson, who previously had served a brief stint on Forrest's staff. There also, however, existed other reasons why Van Dorn and Forrest could have clashed. Mississippi-born Van Dorn was a West Pointer, a representative of the planter class Forrest had so recently entered, and as emphatic a seeker of glory as Forrest himself. Their rivalry, however, was short-lived. A day or so after their confrontation, Forrest was ordered to northern Alabama to counter aggressive Federal moves there, and by the time he returned, Van Dorn had been shot dead in his Tennessee headquarters by a man who claimed the general was courting his wife.[1]

By spring 1863, Federal commanders in the west seemed to have profited from their education the previous year at the hands of Forrest and Morgan. In the same manner in which the two Confederate raiders had run wild and drawn attention away from Bragg's change of base from Tupelo to Chattanooga, the Federals now began a similar ploy to allow Grant's men to gain siege position around Vicksburg, by now the last Confederate bastion on the Mississippi River. In April the Federals themselves sent out two raiders: Colonels Benjamin Grierson, who headed from Memphis deep into Mississippi, and Abel Streight, whose orders sent him from Nashville across northern Alabama to cut Confederate railroads supplying Chattanooga.

Forrest knew nothing of the Federal designs when, on April 23, he received orders to reinforce hard-pressed Confederates under Colonel P. D. Roddey at Tuscumbia, Alabama. Three days later, during all-day skirmishing against an attempted Federal crossing of an Alabama stream called Town Creek, he was told by a Roddey scout that some 2,000 other Federals had passed southward toward the Confederate rear. That force, actually about 1,500 men, was commanded by Streight. The Union colonel had been ordered to mount his infantry on horses and mules at Nashville, proceed by steamers down the Cumberland to a place opposite Fort Henry, march cross-country to the fort, then take other steamers down the Tennessee into northeastern Mississippi. There he was to join some 7,500 Federals under Brigadier General Grenville M. Dodge in northwest Alabama and "march . . . long enough with [him] to create a general impression that you are a part of his expedition." Thereafter, he was to move around the southern flank of Dodge's Confederate resistance and proceed "with all reasonable dispatch" into northwest Georgia, where he was to cut Chattanooga's rail lifeline to the Deep South. Major General W. S. Rosecrans's chief of staff, Brigadier General James A. Garfield, understatingly termed the assignment "highly important and somewhat perilous."[2]

Mounted so badly that some of his horses and mules fell ill or died before he started, and with fifty men still afoot when they left Dodge's command, Streight and his uncomfortable infantrymen struck out in "very hard" rain for Moulton, Alabama, on April 26. Delayed by muddy roads and his transportational deficiencies, he required a day and a half to march the forty miles to Moulton; by the time he got there, though, he had been able to obtain enough additional horses and mules along his route to mount all his men. Before daylight April 30, he had his column moving southwestwardly out of a pass called Day's Gap toward Blountsville, Alabama. Its head "had not proceeded more than 2 miles . . . before [about 6 A.M.] I was informed that the rear guard had been attacked," he later reported. The moment he was given this information, he added, "I heard the boom of artillery in the rear of the column." Knowing "that the gap through which we were passing was easily flanked by gaps through the mountains," he "soon learned that the enemy had moved through the gaps on my right and left, and were endeavoring to form a junction in my advance; consequently, I moved ahead rapidly until we passed the intersecting roads on either flank with the one we occupied. The country was open, sand ridges, very thinly wooded, and afforded fine defensive positions. . . . [W]e dismounted and formed a line of battle on a ridge circling to the rear."

The place was Sand Mountain. Directing his men to lie down atop it, Streight instructed his rear guard to stay in position until the Confederates pressed, then to retreat quickly and try to draw the pursuers into the face of the concealed main Federal lines. It worked. When the rear guard came flying back and passed the front line, the main Union force "rose and delivered a volley at short range." It then "continued to pour a rapid fire into their ranks, which soon caused them to give way in confusion." The

Confederates quickly dismounted and re-formed, though, opening up with a battery of artillery and trying to break the Federal lines with an assault. Noting they had pushed their artillery "to within 300 yards," Streight prepared to charge "as soon as they wavered." He sent the Seventy-third and Fifty-first Indiana, on his left, in an assault "to draw the attention of the battery," then pushed the Third Ohio and the Eightieth Illinois out to capture the Confederate artillery. Briefly but stubbornly, the Confederates resisted, then "fled in confusion, leaving two pieces of artillery, two caissons, and about 40 prisoners . . . a large number of wounded, and about 30 dead on the field. . . . It was now about 11 o'clock. . . . I had learned that the enemy were in heavy force, fully three times our number . . . under General Forrest in person."[3]

They were indeed under Forrest, but they were nowhere near as many as Streight thought. They numbered only about 1,000 men when Forrest attacked at Day's Gap, with another couple of hundred or so catching up gradually as their exhausted mounts allowed; they had covered fifty miles from Courtland, Alabama, in not much more than twenty-four hours. Forrest had left Dibrell's regiment behind near Tuscumbia to harry Dodge into returning to Corinth and had sent Roddey's men hurrying after Streight. He himself stopped at Courtland a few frantic hours to shoe mounts, issue rations, and otherwise prepare for a long ride.

The attack atop Sand Mountain cost Forrest two stinging reverses. The initial charge into the Federal trap was led by scouts under Captain Bill Forrest, who was captured after being unhorsed by a bullet that smashed one of his thigh bones. The Federal countercharge shortly afterward took the two guns, which, because Captain Morton had been left with Dibrell to keep Dodge occupied, were commanded by Lieutenant A. W. Gould, a Morton friend and former schoolmate. Forrest hotly, and possibly unjustly, blamed Gould for leaving these pieces. In the wake of the Federal charge, the irate commander was so determined to get his guns back, as well as so desperate for troops with which to do it, that he ordered all his men to tie their horses to saplings and join in the attack.

Streight prevailed in five hours of fighting on Sand Mountain and moved out again, only to be caught by the Confederates six miles down the road at Crooked Creek. Here, Streight reported, they "pressed our rear so hard that I was compelled to prepare for battle." He stopped at a strong position on another ridge, Hog Mountain, and there fought another pitched battle, using the captured artillery pieces to repel Confederate charges on both his right and his left. Under a bright moon, Forrest kept charging, having ordered his men to "shoot at everything blue and keep up the skeer." During the evening he had three horses shot beneath him, and the superior Federal force again prevailed. When Streight resumed his march in the moonlight, however, he left behind the captured cannons, spiked and disabled. Beyond these ruined prizes, the Confederates encountered another ambush, this one laid by the Seventy-third Indiana under Streight's personal supervision. It caused "a complete stampede" of the Confederates, Streight later reported. Confederate versions of the incident have it that the "stampede" was only by three volunteers sent forward to sniff out an anticipated trap; Confederate artillery then was brought noiselessly forward, and its shells prompted the Federals to move on again.[4]

By 2 A.M., with Forrest again harrying the Union rear, Streight laid another ambush. A sharp skirmish followed, after which the Confederates vanished. Confident that the enemy couldn't escape him now, Forrest had ordered his men to dismount, unsaddle, feed their horses, and take two hours' rest. Streight's men meanwhile plodded on, reaching Blountsville about 10 A.M. May 1, there finally to take two hours' rest themselves. However, moving again by noon, they "had not got fairly in motion before our pickets were driven in," Streight's report says, "and a sharp skirmish ensued between Forrest's advance and our rear guard . . . in . . . Blountsville." The Confederates "followed closely for several miles, continually skirmishing with the rear guard, but were badly handled by small parties of our men stopping in the thick bushes by the side of the road and firing at them at short range, and when we reached the East Branch of the Black Warrior River, the ford was very deep and the enemy pressed so closely that I was compelled to offer him battle before we could cross."[5]

With skirmishers out and artillery covering the crossing, the last of the Federals reached the other side about 5 P.M. They then continued their march toward Gadsden, Alabama, dogged by "small parties who were continually harassing the rear of the column"; by then, Forrest had started sending his men after them in shifts. Seeing his troopers falling asleep on horseback, he determined to rest some while others rode and fought. Halting his main force, he also pared it down to 600, culling all "ineffective men" and animals. He then made a short speech to the remainder, telling them he was confident the end of this marathon was at hand. Refreshed by a few hours' rest, his full force "fiercely attacked" the Federal rear guard at a bridge over deep and supposedly impassable Black Creek near Gadsden.[6]

The Federals crossed and burned the bridge behind them just as Forrest, at the head of the Confederates, galloped up chasing a Union soldier who had arrived too late to brave the flames on the bridge. The man surrendered personally to Forrest, who then turned anxiously to a trio of civilian bystanders: a farm woman and her teenaged daughters. The bridge fire had been kindled from rails from their fence, and as they looked on unhappily, Forrest introduced himself—"I am General Forrest; I and my men will protect you from harm"—and asked where "the Yankees" were. The woman, a widow named Sansom, replied that Federals were lined up on the other side of the burning bridge and "if you go down there they will kill the last one of you." More of Forrest's men were arriving and entering the Sansoms' field to shoot at the Union troops, and, as the Federals fired back, the females ran toward the house. Just as the widow's sixteen-year-old daughter reached the gate, Forrest rode up and asked where he could cross the Black. More than thirty years later, Emma Sansom remembered replying that "there was an unsafe bridge two miles farther down the stream" but that she also "knew of a trail about two hundred yards above the bridge on our farm, where our cows used to cross in low water, and I believed he could get his men over there. . . ." She told him that "if he would have my saddle put on a horse I would show him the way."

He said, "There is no time to saddle a horse; get up here behind me." As he said this he rode close to the bank on the side of the road, and I jumped up behind him. Just as we started off, mother came up about out of breath and gasped out: "Emma, what do you mean?" General Forrest said: "She is going to show me a ford where I can get my men over in time to catch those Yankees. . . . Don't be uneasy; I will bring her back safe." We rode out into a field through which ran a branch or small ravine and along which there was a thick undergrowth that protected us for a while from being seen by the Yankees at the bridge or on the other side of the creek. This branch emptied into the creek just above the ford. When we got close to the creek, I said: "General Forrest, I think we had better get off the horse, as we are now where we may be seen." We both got down and crept through the bushes, and when we were right at the ford I happened to be in front. He stepped quickly between me and the Yankees, saying: "I am glad to have you for a pilot, but I am not going to make breastworks of you." The cannon and the other guns were firing fast by this time, as I pointed out to him where to go into the water and out on the other bank, and then we *went back towards the house. He asked me my name, and asked me to give him a lock of my hair. The cannon-balls were screaming over us so loud that we were told to leave and hide in some place out of danger, which we did. Soon all the firing stopped, and I started back home. On the way I met General Forrest again, and he told me that he had written a note for me and left it on the bureau. He asked me again for a lock of my hair, and as we went into the house he said: "One of my bravest men has been killed, and he is laid out in the house. I want you to see that he is buried in some graveyard near here." He then told me goodbye and got on his horse, and he and his men rode away. . . .*[7]

Having crossed Black Creek, Streight was nearly to Gadsden and hardly more than fifty miles from his objective at Rome, Georgia, but Emma Sansom and her homemade ford had dimmed his prospects. Now, hearing that large numbers of Confederates were moving along north of him, he felt forced "to march all night, although the command was in no condition to do so." He halted at Gadsden only long enough to destroy "a quantity of arms and commissary stores." His unit now was on the verge of disintegration from weariness. He later reported that large numbers of his mounts and troops "were entirely worn out and unable to keep up with the column; consequently they fell behind the rear guard and were captured." He realized that "our only hope was in crossing the [Oostanaula] river at Rome and destroying the bridge, which would delay Forrest a day or two and give us time to collect horses and mules, and allow the command a little time to sleep, without which it was impossible to proceed."

Forrest harried him the rest of May 2, keeping up "a continuous skirmish with the rear of the column," until 4 P.M., when Streight halted at a plantation fifteen miles beyond Gadsden. There he was forced to stop and fight just to be able to feed and rest his men and animals. The Confederates "severely engaged" the Federal rear guard, then drove it in and "at once attacked our main line and tried hard to carry the center." Unsuccessful in this, they "then made a determined effort to turn our right," again unsuccessfully. Afterward, they fell back and, Streight thought, began to mass "as if preparing for a more determined attack." Discovering most of his remaining ammunition had been ruined by deep creek-fording, Streight decided to move on again. Sending 200 of his best-mounted men ahead to Rome to take the crucial bridge and hold it, he laid another ambush in a thicket. This time, it didn't succeed. The Confederates, "who by some means had learned of our whereabouts, commenced a flank movement."

Streight's nightmare worsened as the evening wore on. At Centre, Alabama, he found that some Confederates had gotten ahead of him and were trying to stage an ambush themselves. He had hardly circumvented this trap when he reached the Chattooga River and found his enemy had gotten rid of the ferry. Turning north toward a bridge seven miles away at Gaylesville, his command—"so worn out and exhausted that many were asleep"—became disoriented and wandered most of the night in a maze of wagon trails crossing a logging ground. The cut timber was being burned for charcoal at a nearby iron furnace that manufactured pig iron for the making of Confederate cannon and engines, and a Streight detail wrecked the important furnace. Because of the delays in the logging area, however, "it was not until near daylight that the last of the Union command crossed the river" and burned the bridge.

At 9 A.M. May 3 on the Lawrence plantation, less than twenty miles from Rome, it became necessary for Streight to halt again to feed men and animals. By now, even that was virtually useless, because it was "almost impossible" to keep his exhausted men "awake long enough to feed." Almost immediately, he was told that "a heavy force of the enemy was moving on our left, on a route parallel with the one we were marching on, and was then nearer Rome than we were." Then his pickets were driven in, and he had to order his troops back into line of battle. "[E]very effort," he said, "was made to rally the men to action," but it was useless; "nature was exhausted, and a large portion of my best troops actually went to sleep while lying in line of battle under a severe skirmish fire. After some maneuvering, Forrest sent in a flag of truce, demanding the surrender of my forces."[8]

Streight's subordinate officers urged giving up their futile dash. The colonel himself was not so eager to surrender, even though he had just learned that the 200 men he had sent out had been unable to take the bridge at Rome. An experienced and intelligent soldier, he first refused Forrest's surrender demand unless he could be shown that he was outnumbered. He also insisted that no Confederates be moved any closer to his position while the surrender discussion was in effect. Just as he was making this demand, the two Confederate artillery pieces that had managed to keep up throughout the chase moved into sight, and Forrest acceded to Streight's wishes by sending an aide, Captain Henry Pointer, to move them back.

Unnoticed by Streight, however, Forrest also nodded significantly to Pointer, and over the next few minutes the same two guns began reappearing here and there in Streight's line of vision.

"Name of God!" Streight finally exclaimed. "How many guns have you got? There's fifteen I've counted already!"

Nonchalantly glancing in the direction toward which the Union commander was looking, Forrest replied: "I reckon that's all that has kept up."[9]

As the discussion continued, Forrest periodically interjected orders to Pointer for the handling of phantom units. Doubtless cued by Pointer, the commanders of the few Confederates actually present began marching their men into and out of sight the way the artillerymen were doing with the guns. Streight returned for more talk with his own officers, but about noon he gave in. To fewer than 600 Confederates, who had been riding and/or fighting almost every consecutive day and half the nights since leaving south-central Tennessee April 24, he surrendered 1,466 Federals, plus the 200 soon to be caught returning from their vain mission to the Rome bridge.[10]

The ignominy of this decision quickly became considerable, trumpeted in gleeful headlines throughout the South. One grumbling Federal reminiscence, unable to argue with the fact that it happened, quarreled instead with the Emma Sansom story, contending that the Black Creek ford was shown Forrest by a man, a young Confederate soldier named Sansom who had been captured by Federals that morning and violated his parole by helping Forrest; the anecdote about "beautiful" Emma Sansom was concocted by the Confederates for publicity purposes, this story claimed.[11]

Emma Sansom did have a brother in the Confederate Army, and he indeed had been captured that morning. Decades afterward, though, she retained convincing evidence that it truly had been she, and not her brother, who made the all-important disclosure of the Black Creek ford. The note left on her bureau, written in lead pencil on a stained sheet of account paper, commended her in a high-flown but uncertain scrawl:

Hed Quaters In Sadle
May 2, 1863

My highest Regardes to Miss Ema Sanson [sic] for hir gallant conduct while my forse was skirmishing with the Federals a cross Black Creek near Gadesden Allabama

N. B. Forrest
Brig Genl
Comding N. Ala—[12]

AROUND 6 P.M. on Sunday, May 3, just hours after Streight's surrender, Forrest marched his first contingent of prisoners into Rome and a hero's welcome. Overjoyed to be out of danger from the Federal raiders, the city's women strewed his army's path with flowers and presented a wreath of them to the conqueror himself, who was besieged with proffered handshakes and requests for locks of hair.[1]

Although reported to have gone so far as to kiss a baby, the exhausted celebrity apparently tried to concern himself less with accepting thanks than with finishing the job at hand. He requested food for his men and prisoners, prompting a community-wide "wholesale cooking" which fed Union as well as Confederate troops; a high Federal officer among the captured recalled later that Forrest "furnished us with sufficient rations for our subsistence," and also with comfortable quarters. While also enjoying such overdue comforts themselves, Forrest's men were busied with military tasks. The main body of Streight's men, brought in Monday, had to be guarded and provided for. Some 300 of Forrest's 550 horses had gotten sick or died from the efforts of the long chase, and he replaced them with Streight's best mounts, meanwhile shoeing all that needed it. Tuesday morning, he turned the prisoners over to a detachment sent from Atlanta to escort them to Richmond. He also dispatched the remainder of Streight's horses and mules to Bragg at Chattanooga, asking that they be distributed among the northern Alabama residents from whom so many had been taken by Streight; some 450 of these eventually were returned, many others having died from the hard use they had seen.[2]

The general himself was presented a handsome mount named Highlander by a local citizen — for which, the local newspaper surmised, "he would not on any account have taken the best negro fellow in the State." Funds raised by other Rome residents to buy him a horse were dedicated instead to the care of his sick and wounded troops. He also was interviewed by visiting journalist and old friend George W. Adair, editor and proprietor of the Atlanta daily *Southern Confederacy*. "Intimately associated" with Forrest during the slave-trading days, the editor was a prominent Atlanta businessman who possibly bought and sold slaves for Forrest in Atlanta before the war. In the article written from the 1863 interview, Adair indicated the Forrests had other Georgia connections, noting the Sand Mountain battle wound of "Capt. Wm. H. Forrest, a brother of the general, whom many of our citizens in Atlanta will remember."[3]

The article reports Adair spent twelve hours on a train from Atlanta to Rome, arriving at 7 A.M. May 5. He was walking up a Rome street toward Forrest's hotel headquarters when he passed a camp of guarded prisoners, then the hotel in which the Federal officers were held, and, "a few steps further" in a livery stable, a crowd gathered closely around the "manly form of my old friend Forrest, who had come out this early to look after the welfare of a . . . horse." Adair found him "very plainly dressed" in "an old slouch hat and plain, well-worn gray coat and pants. . . . He is looking something thinner and much grayer than when I saw him last. His heavy, wavy black hair is now worn short, which gives his stern and strongly marked features . . . the appearance of 'Old Hickory' [i.e., Andrew Jackson]. But when he smiles, and you see his beautiful . . . teeth, you almost forget that he is . . . a stern warrior, with the feeling that you are in the presence of a most agreeable gentleman."

Forrest invited Adair to his room, "where he furnished me, in his own . . . modest way, with all the particulars" of the Streight chase. These details seem to have been pretty much the same ones he later officially reported. He emphasized to Adair that Streight had access to all the fresh mounts his men could take from the local inhabitants, leaving none in their wake for their outnumbered pursuers, yet Forrest's Confederates had averaged forty-one miles a day on horses that were fed only ten captured ears of corn apiece between their departure from Town Creek and Streight's surrender five days later. The Emma Sansom story varied only in that the "beautiful young girl," misidentified as "Anna," told Forrest to ride over to a log so she could get up behind him and show him the ford; that her mother disapproved, saying "people may talk about you"; and that the girl replied she was "not afraid to trust myself anywhere with as brave a man as Gen. Forrest. Southern men always protect the innocent and helpless." Forrest told Adair he had less than 500 men present on the field "on worn-out horses" when he demanded the surrender of 1,467 under Streight, which Adair called "the boldest game of bluff on record. . . . For cool audacity, it excels all history or imagination." Interestingly, if Forrest told Adair the unorthodox tactics he employed to prompt Streight's accession to this demand, they do not appear in Adair's account; Forrest obviously planned to use them again.[4]

A great feast for the conqueror and his men was planned for May 6, but early that morning he and his troops suddenly pulled out for Jasper, Alabama; another Federal force was said to have left Tuscumbia heading in that direction. By the time his Confederates reached Gadsden, however, the report had proven false, so Forrest started them back toward their post in Tennessee. At Decatur, Alabama, orders reached him to leave his command on the march, take a train to Shelbyville, Tennessee, and report in person to Bragg. At Huntsville, met by a large crowd and presented another fine horse, he boarded a train and reached Shelbyville May 13.

Bragg, displaying "unwonted warmth and cordiality," informed him he would recommend his promotion to major general. Forrest demurred, suggesting instead that Bragg name someone who had "more capacity for the functions which properly belonged to the rank . . . ," and apparently advancing the name of General Pillow of Fort Donelson notoriety. Pillow told Tennessee's Governor Harris by letter May 9 that he had seen Forrest two weeks earlier at Columbia, Tennessee, and that both Forrest and General W. H. Jackson not only had urged him to seek a cavalry command but had asked to serve under him. At that time, Van Dorn was still alive, and Forrest and Jackson may have been trying to use Pillow's political connections to get free of Van Dorn. By the time Forrest reported in person to Bragg, however, Van Dorn was dead, so there was no need to continue to push Pillow or anyone else unless either Forrest still felt obligated by his earlier overtures or was truly sincere about not wishing the position himself. Apparently he was. By now, he seems to have wanted freedom from Bragg, rather than a place even closer to this commander with whom it was difficult both to get along and to win.[5]

Forrest ended up without Van Dorn's rank but with his command. Bragg ordered him to assume Van Dorn's duties at Spring Hill, putting under him W. H. Jackson and Frank C. Armstrong. Jackson, however, was soon dispatched to Mississippi in response to the pleas of several prominent Mississippians. They visited President Davis May 8 to ask him to assign Forrest to duty there, but Davis referred the matter to Bragg, who sent Jackson instead, saying Forrest's troops were "not in condition."[6]

Ranging across central Tennessee in May and June, Forrest reorganized his forces, but on June 13 he was wounded again, this time by a subordinate. Lieutenant A. W. Gould—who had commanded the guns lost at Day's Gap and, apparently unjustly, incurred Forrest's wrath by his handling of others at Franklin—asked to see his commander to protest an order transferring him to another command. The two met at a Masonic hall in Columbia that was being used by the unit's quartermaster department. An account said to have come secondhand from Forrest himself holds that when Gould asked for an explanation of the order, Forrest said his mind was made up, that he wouldn't discuss it. Gould protested that the order could be construed as reflecting on his courage, and "no man can accuse me of being a coward and both of us live." Forrest is quoted as saying Gould then tried to draw a pistol from the pocket of a long linen duster he was wearing, but the weapon hung in the cloth and discharged before it cleared the pocket, causing the ball to strike Forrest in the left side. Forrest happened to be holding a penknife with which he said he had been picking his teeth when Gould arrived. He had it in his left hand when Gould drew the pistol, and he grabbed Gould's pistol hand with his right and forced it upward to deflect further shots. Then, holding the penknife in his left hand and pulling one of its blades open with his teeth, he stabbed Gould in the right side between the ribs. Gould broke free, exited the door, and lurched off up the street.

"Stop that man!" yelled Major C. S. Severson, Forrest's quartermaster. "Stop that man! He's shot General Forrest!"

Severson's shout was heard by two civilian surgeons, James H. Wilkes of Columbia and Luke Ridley of Murfreesboro. They had charge of a nearby hospital and happened to be coming up the street when they heard the shout and saw a man crossing the street with blood spurting onto his linen coat. Ridley recognized him: "My God, it's Willis Gould." The two physicians hurried to their wounded acquaintance and helped him into the first open door they found, which happened to be to a tailor shop. Wilkes remained, putting Gould on a low table where he could dress the wound, while Ridley ran for surgical equipment.

By coincidence, four Columbia youths saw the struggle in the hall outside the quartermaster's office. Apparently fascinated by the gore, they—at the head of a growing crowd—followed Gould into the tailor shop. One, who eventually became secretary of the Maury County (Tennessee) Historical Society, later recalled that when Gould's shirt "was rolled up under the armpit the stab between the ribs was plainly visible"; as Gould "breathed the blood would spurt out, often spattering us boys, but we could hardly dodge because there was such a crowd behind us." An artery had been cut, "and Dr. Wilkes was bending over him trying to staunch it with his fingers while waiting for Dr. Ridley to bring the proper surgical appliances."

Outside, the Confederate provost marshal, Colonel J. Lee Bullock, spotted a wounded Forrest coming down the street looking for his assailant. Bullock hailed him. "I think you need not pursue Gould, for I believe that he is fatally wounded," Bullock told him. "He is bleeding profusely and losing strength with every step."

"Get out of my way," Forrest retorted. "I am mortally wounded and will kill the man who shot me."[7]

He reached the opinion he was dying by walking to the office of another physician, Dr. L. P. Yandell, immediately after Gould fled. There he was hurriedly examined and given the prognosis that his wound, because of its apparent location near his intestines, was dangerous and in the warm June weather probably fatal. Pushing past Bullock now, he grabbed two pistols from another Confederate officer, crossed the street, and was heading down an alley when he learned Gould was in the tailor shop. Returning from the alley, he burst inside the shop's front door with a pistol in each hand, shouting "Look out! Look out!" The crowd tried to scatter. Gould rolled off the table, his blood again spurting onto the young boys. Dr. Wilkes jumped away from his patient and into a corner, and Gould dived out the back door. Forrest fired, but the bullet struck a brick wall in the alley outside and ricocheted into the leg of a Confederate soldier who happened to be out there. Gould had no strength to go far, though. He fell in a patch of high weeds in the backyard of the shop as Forrest, "in a torrent of rage," ran back outside the shop's front door and down the alley, apparently intending to cut off Gould's escape. When he arrived in the backyard and saw his quarry lying in the weeds, he "touched him with his foot as if to turn him over," then turned and reentered the shop.[8]

The crowd again backed away from him. Noticing Dr. Wilkes, he asked the physician to accompany him and treat his wound, but Wilkes replied that "his first duty was to the wounded man he [already] was attending. [W]ith an oath," Forrest "ordered him to go with him." Outside, they met Ridley, just arriving with medical instruments, and Forrest, "with an[other] oath, ordered the two doctors to get in[to] a carriage at the curb. Forrest himself got in unaided." Picking up a third physician, Dr. Sam Frierson, across the street, Forrest was driven to the nearby home of a Confederate officer while the four young boys who had seen the whole incident tagged along, holding on to the carriage from behind. When they arrived at the house, both the men and boys apparently went inside, for the eyewitness recalls that the physicians tried "to assist the General in getting to his room upstairs, but he did not accept their aid . . . his rage was terrible."

Upstairs, he undressed, and Wilkes probed the wound. He discovered Gould's pistol ball had missed all vital organs and also had gone around the pelvic bone, embedding itself "in the large muscles of the hip." The physicians informed the patient that "it was a mere flesh wound and that the ball could be cut out." Forrest's manner swiftly changed. Telling them to forget about cutting it out ("It's nothing but a damn little pistol ball; let it alone!"), he instructed Ridley to go at once to Gould and, if he were still alive, to take him to the best room in the Nelson House hotel, give him every comfort, and tell the proprietor that he, Forrest, would pay for everything. He added: "And by God, Ridley, when I give such an order I mean it!" After Ridley left—and found Gould already taken to the Nelson House by a member of Forrest's staff—the two other doctors dressed the general's wound.[9]

A popular story has it that Forrest was overcome with remorse at having inflicted Gould's injury, which proved fatal. The lieutenant lingered another couple of days, and this story maintains that an anonymous member of Forrest's staff later saw the two adversaries reconciled at Gould's deathbed. Gould is said to have asked to see Forrest, who was brought to his bedside, where Gould took his hand, requested forgiveness, and said he was "thankful that I am the one who is to die and you are spared to the country." Forrest "wept like a child," the anonymous informant is quoted. According to a relative of Gould who claimed to have attended the lieutenant during his last hours, no such reconciliation ever occurred, and Forrest is reported to have callously remarked immediately after the shooting that had Gould shown as much courage on the battlefield as at the Masonic hall, their violent encounter never would have happened. Later, however, in behavior consistent with his pattern in such instances, he appears to have been shamed by Gould's death, and if he did not actually go to Gould's bedside, he may well have expressed to someone an intention to. In later years he is reported to have said, in reference to it, that "he never wanted to kill anybody except an enemy, and then only when fighting for his country."[10]

Twelve days after taking Gould's bullet, Forrest was back in the saddle, marching hurriedly eastward from Columbia toward Shelbyville to join Polk's corps on June 25. Bragg's whole army was falling back again in the face of a sudden advance from Murfreesboro by William Rosecrans. By the time Forrest reached Shelbyville, Bragg's slimly guarded and hardpressed supply wagons had just crossed a bridge over Duck River, covered by an outmanned cavalry detachment under Joseph Wheeler. Forrest had been ordered by Wheeler to intersect Wheeler's line of retreat between Murfreesboro and Shelbyville, but Wheeler, who had fought in front of and then within Shelbyville on June 27, had been pushed so hard by Federals that Forrest was unable to catch up. Assuming Forrest had crossed the Duck elsewhere, Wheeler was about to torch the bridge when a Forrest aide arrived and reported that his commander was on the outskirts of Shelbyville coming hard, counting on crossing the Duck on that bridge. Wheeler threw his small detachment of 500 men and two cannons back across the bridge and tried to hold it until he was overrun and forced to cut his way out of encircling Union troops. Ultimately, he had to jump his mounted men off a fifteen-foot bluff into the Duck, where fifty or more drowned. Forrest apparently told his authorized biographers that he held his column in a gallop for eight miles trying to catch Wheeler at Shelbyville, but, with Wheeler already reported driven across the river by the time he arrived, he turned west and crossed at another bridge four miles out of town. He carelessly sent no messenger to try to inform Wheeler of his changed plans, although he must have known a fight was in progress; earlier in the day, he reported hearing other Wheeler fighting that was almost certainly farther away.

The alternate crossing allowed Forrest to place his troopers between the Confederate wagon train and its Union pursuers, and by late afternoon the wagons and their escort had reached Tullahoma. There followed two days and nights of skirmishing in a downpour of rain, during which Starnes was killed. Then Bragg ordered them to fall back again toward Chattanooga, with the cavalry protecting the army's flanks and rear. In this capacity, they engaged in small delaying skirmishes with the enemy, fighting and running. In one of these, Forrest and some of his men came flying through his wife's hometown of Cowan, Tennessee, where one of the local women screamed at him as he passed her house:

"You great big cowardly rascal, why don't you fight like a man, instead of running like a cur? I wish old Forrest was here. He'd make you fight."[11]

After Bragg reached Chattanooga, Forrest was ordered seventy miles north to Kingston, Tennessee, where on August 9 he wrote two letters to Confederate adjutant general Samuel Cooper in Richmond. He sent one through Bragg at Chattanooga and the other through President Davis, explaining to Davis that he had asked that Bragg forward the letter "through the proper channel" but "understood that it was likely it would not be forwarded by the general commanding. . . . While I believe the general commanding is unwilling for me to leave his department, still I hope to be permitted to go where (as I believe) I can serve my country best. . . ." That, he added, was along the banks of the Mississippi River, where "I have resided . . . for over twenty years" and had "for many years [been] engaged in buying and selling negroes." He noted that he knew "the country perfectly from Memphis to Vicksburg on both sides of the river," was "well acquainted with all the prominent planters in that region as well as above Memphis," and had "officers in my command and on my staff who have rafted timber out of the [Mississippi] bottom. . . ." Proposing to be accompanied only by some 460 men from the command he then held, he asked to be placed in command "of the forces on the Mississippi River from Vicksburg to Cairo, or in other words, all the forces I may collect together and organize between those points, say in North Mississippi, West Tennessee, and those that may join me from Arkansas, Missouri, and Southern Kentucky." What he proposed, he said, was to "seriously if not [entirely] obstruct the navigation of the Mississippi River, and in sixty days procure a large force now inside the enemy's lines, which without this or a similar move cannot be obtained. . . . I am confident that we could so move and harass and destroy boats on the river that only flat[boat]s heavily protected by gun-boats would be able to make the passage." Saying his proposal was motivated "by the repeated solicitations of numerous friends and acquaintances resident in West Tennessee and North Mississippi," he added that if supplied "with guns and ammunition," he believed he could raise between 5,000 and 10,000 men. He said he was making his proposal "entirely for the good of the service. I believe that I can accomplish all that I propose to do. I have never asked for position. Have taken position and performed the duties as assigned me. . . ." He stretched the truth slightly by adding he had "never yet suffered my command to be surprised, cut up, or defeated."[12]

It turned out that Bragg did, after all, forward this letter—accompanied by a note protesting that loss of Forrest "would deprive this army of one of its greatest elements of strength." Bragg's close friend Davis soon concurred in this opinion, but added a notation that "[w]henever a change of circumstances will permit, the measure may be adopted." Exactly what motivated Forrest here—especially in going over his commander's head—can only be conjectured, aside from an obvious Confederate need to react to the recent fall of Vicksburg. What his Mississippi River plan and his unorthodox pursuit of it most strongly suggest is that he wanted to operate his own way in his own theater and concentrate on what ultimately must win or lose the Confederacy's whole desperate enterprise: his lifelong specialty, fighting. He also, surely, felt shame at his treatment of Wheeler at Dover and Shelbyville and perhaps wished to separate himself both from Wheeler and the army in which his behavior toward Wheeler was best known.[13]

The Federals had maneuvered Bragg out of forage-rich central Tennessee, pushing him back into the mountains around Chattanooga, and now they kept pressing. Forrest was ordered first to drop back from Kingston onto the Knoxville railroad at Loudon, then to move farther southward to Charleston, Tennessee, forty miles northeast of Chattanooga. At Charleston, Bragg made him commander of all cavalry north of Chattanooga—about the time he got into another controversy with headquarters. Having been joined by some 240 survivors of John Hunt Morgan's unauthorized and disastrous raid into Indiana and Ohio in July, Forrest ignored a Bragg order to dismount the Kentuckians and thus deprive them of their identity as Morgan cavalrymen. The colonel of the newly organized unit later wrote that Forrest "ran the risk of trial by court martial by refusing to carry out this policy of Bragg's."[14]

At the moment, Bragg had little time for courts-martial. Federals led by Alexander McCook and George Thomas—under the overall command of Rosecrans—were pouring through gaps in the Alabama mountains southwest of him while he watched another force under Thomas Crittenden threaten Chattanooga from the north. Bragg thought the scattered Union units coming over Sand Mountain into Will's Valley in northern Alabama were aiming for Gadsden or Rome, he wrote Major General D. H. Hill on September 4. Hill, a prewar educator and testy brother-in-law of Stonewall Jackson, had been sent west from Virginia after criticizing Robert E. Lee; his personality notwithstanding, he was a fierce fighter with a grasp of military reality that, in September of 1863, seems to have far exceeded Bragg's. Bragg's expressed opinion as to what the Federals were up to blithely contradicted a September 3 Hill dispatch discerning that "the movement is for Chattanooga, in order to secure the railroad." Hill predicted the Union troops would "work their way up Will's Valley until they get in a position to drive us from Chattanooga. . . . They will then be in condition to hold the country, bring in their supplies, operate among the disloyal portions of East Tennessee and Western North Carolina." The overall Federal design, he thought, was to gain control of East Tennessee, and although he said his own knowledge of the area was "too imperfect" to propose specific action, "I have felt so uneasy about the delay that I cannot refrain from expressing my anxiety. If we wait until the meshes be thrown around, we may find it hard to break through. . . ."[15]

Four days later, Bragg finally acted—and did what Rosecrans wanted him to. Trying to protect his railroad supply line and to assume a position to strike the Federal forces one at a time, he evacuated Chattanooga in favor of LaFayette, Georgia. On September 10, he ordered Hill and Major General T. C. Hindman to attack Thomas, the centermost Federal force, at Pigeon Mountain. Hill was unable to comply because the gaps through which he had to move had been obstructed with timber felled by Confederate cavalry, requiring "several hours" to cross. Bragg then ordered Hindman to attack on the same day, with others joining in at the sound of his guns, but most of the day passed before Hindman's guns were heard, too late. By that time, Rosecrans's forces had fallen back into the shelter of the mountain passes and begun feverishly concentrating around a central point called McLemore's Cove.

While Bragg was worrying over Thomas, Brigadier General John Pegram—commanding cavalry under Forrest—began shooting at Crittenden's infantry around the Georgia-Tennessee border. Forrest moved up to support Pegram and sent urgent messages to both Polk, who had the closest large body of infantry, and Bragg. Then he prepared to slip behind Crittenden and seize the bridge by which Crittenden had left Chattanooga, but no attack order or infantry support came. At midnight he vainly set out to find Bragg, who had gone to LaFayette that evening and taken all the infantry in the area. Bragg didn't turn north to attempt an attack on Crittenden until dawn of September 13, and then Polk loitered until Bragg had to order him in person to attack. Again, the order came too late.[16]

Meanwhile, Forrest and his cavalry tried to impede Crittenden's advance. They fell back slowly in the face of superior numbers until they reached Tunnel Hill, where Forrest suffered a wound obscurely reported to have been "near the spine" as his dismounted troopers stopped Crittenden's advance; faintness and loss of blood caused him to take the "urgent" advice of his unit's chief surgeon, J. B. Cowan, and take a drink of whiskey, but he relinquished neither the field nor command of his troops.[17]

Bragg finally ordered all his forces—which, including reinforcements just arriving from Virginia under Major General James Longstreet, numbered 66,000—to cross Chickamauga Creek to their west the morning of September 18 and engage the Federals, who only slightly outnumbered the Confederates. Once again, delays prevented total action, but Forrest's men opened one of the war's bloodiest battles by passing to the front of Bushrod Johnson's massing infantry and, about 11 A.M., beginning a brisk skirmish with the Federals. The next morning, with Wheeler commanding the cavalry on Bragg's left wing and Forrest that on the right, the battle opened early as the Confederate right moved up to try to turn the Union left and get between it and its newly established base at Chattanooga. That turned out to be difficult to do, because during the night the consolidated Federal line had moved north toward Chattanooga just as the Confederates had been moving south; the Union left actually was turning the Confederate right. Forrest was ordered "to move with my company down the road toward Reed's Bridge, and develop the enemy, which was promptly done, and their advance was soon engaged at the steam saw-mill near that point."[18]

Finding himself opposed by heavy columns of Federal infantry "too strong for General Pegram's [division]," he sent to Polk's headquarters for Armstrong's division. When Polk could spare only Dibrell's brigade, Forrest dismounted both Dibrell's and Pegram's men to try to hold off counterattacking Union infantry. Pegram later reported that they soon faced "overwhelming numbers," which prompted Forrest to send "several messengers" seeking infantry support. Finally, he went off in search of the desperately needed infantrymen in person, ordering Pegram "to hold the position until their arrival"—an order that eventually entailed "loss . . . [of] about one-fourth of the command." Meanwhile, Forrest found the Twenty-fifth Georgia of Colonel Claudius C. Wilson. Wilson later reported that Forrest first "informed me that the enemy in considerable force were engaging his cavalry to the right and front of my position" and "directed me to select a position and form a line of battle on the left of the road." His men hadn't been in line very long when another Forrest order "informed me that the enemy were pressing him sorely in front and directed me to move up on his left." Wilson complied, meeting and driving back Union skirmishers before striking a battle line that "opened upon us a terrific fire." The Georgians, however, continued forward, pouring "into the enemy's ranks a well-directed fire" that soon caused the Federals "to break and flee from the field in confusion, leaving dead and wounded covering the field over which we marched."[19]

Wilson's men, along with Forrest's dismounted cavalry, gradually drove the Federals 700 yards, capturing some Union artillery. A counterattack then pushed them backwards and turned their left, until Brigadier General Matthew Ector's infantry brigade, which also had been summoned by Forrest, arrived. At Forrest's direction, it went in on the right and again drove the Federals until Ector's men were "overpowered by vastly superior numbers," Forrest later reported. "We were compelled to fall back to our first position. A cavalry charge was made to protect the infantry as they retired, which they did in good order, but with loss. We captured many prisoners, but were unable for want of horses to bring off the guns captured from the enemy." Twice in an hour Ector sent an aide to Forrest voicing concern about his flanks, first the right and then the left. The second time, the man carrying Ector's messages later reported, he found Forrest with his artillery, "right in the thickest part of the fight, the battery blazing away and every man fighting like mad. . . . He turned around on me and shouted, loud enough to be heard above the terrible din . . . : 'Tell General Ector that, by God, I am here and will take care of his left flank as well as his right.' "[20]

Forrest's report notes that he "(being the senior officer present) . . . assumed temporary command of the infantry" until the arrival of Major General W. H. T. Walker, commander of the Reserve Corps. Walker was not pleased. He reported that when he reached the battle area "I found that Wilson's and Ector's brigades (Ector having . . . been taken by Forrest without any authority from me) were heavily pressed and from the greatly superior numbers of the enemy were compelled to fall back." Walker himself then sent for reinforcements, and Cheatham's division came up about noon to help. Cheatham battled back and forth with the Federals for the next three hours, but eventually was forced rearward. The first day of savage but inconclusive fighting ended for Forrest as he rushed artillery and the dismounted troopers of Dibrell forward to support the "hard pressed and retiring" infantry brigade of George Maney. Maney's report says Forrest "had been forced in on my right," and Maney thought the Forrest artillery, posted "in rear of the right of my line," "was firing . . . too much in range with two companies of my right regiment." Maney requested Forrest adjust his guns more to the right, "which he did and continued firing. . . . Forrest's battery was some protection to my right flank."[21]

The next day, Bragg won his greatest victory, then failed to consummate it. He had reorganized his army in the middle of the battle, dividing it into two parts under Polk and the just-arrived Longstreet. He neglected, however, to get word of the reorganization to all his unit commanders until after the "day dawn" time specified for renewal of the Confederate attack. Nothing happened until after 9:30 A.M., and Forrest's troops, still on the extreme right, didn't engage again until nearly noon. When they did begin fighting, it was to try to stop the overpowering advance of the Union reserve corps under Major General Gordon Granger. For nearly two hours, most of Forrest's men again fought dismounted, for which they received a compliment from the unimpressionable Hill. Seeing them in action, Hill happened to ask a Forrest aide, Major Charles W. Anderson, what infantry he was watching. "That is Forrest's cavalry," Anderson replied. Hill asked to meet Forrest and, taken to him, raised his hat and congratulated him on the "magnificent behavior" of his troops; he added that in Virginia he had made himself "unpopular with the cavalry" for saying he had yet to see "a dead man with spurs on." Forrest thanked him briefly and wheeled his horse back toward the fight. His men, however "magnificent," could only slow the march of Granger to the relief of the embattled George Thomas farther to the left.[22]

The struggle was decided when Rosecrans, responding in midafternoon to Thomas's calls for aid in battling the Confederate right, withdrew a division from his own right to send to Thomas and neglected to replace it. The Confederates saw their opportunity, and Longstreet plunged through the gap in the line, turned right, and began chasing Federals from the field. Except for a salient held by Thomas on the left-center of the Union line, the Federals fled toward Chattanooga. Well before nightfall even Thomas's men, who had been reinforced by Granger's, also pulled back in that direction, although in more orderly fashion. Thus ended the Battle of Chickamauga, one of the war's bloodiest. It had cost the South's thin western ranks a staggering 18,454 casualties, while the Union suffered 16,170.

At 4 A.M. September 21, Forrest had his men in the saddle on the heels of the retreating Federals. Nearing Rossville, Georgia, he and some 400 troopers sighted and charged a Federal cavalry rear guard, which retreated after firing a volley. A ball struck Forrest's horse in the neck, cutting an artery, but its rider was so intent on his work that he placed an index finger in the wound and kept riding until the Union cavalrymen had been chased from the field. When he removed his finger and dismounted, the horse crumpled and died.[23]

He later reported capturing "many prisoners and arms" as he moved up. His advance was so rapid that he caught some Federal observation troops in a tree, ordered them down, and commandeered their field glasses and lookout. When he came down from their perch, he dictated to Major Anderson a dispatch to a superior:

ON THE ROAD, September 21, 1863

Lieut. Gen. L. Polk:
General: We are in a mile of Rossville. Have been on the point of Missionary Ridge. Can see Chattanooga and everything around. The enemy's trains are leaving, going around the point of Lookout Mountain.

The prisoners captured report two pontoons thrown across for the purpose of retreating. I think they are evacuating as hard as they

*can go. They are cutting down timber to obstruct our passing. I
think we ought to press forward as rapidly as possible.*

> *Respectfully, &c,*
> *N.B. Forrest,*
> *Brigadier-General*

Please forward to General Bragg[24]

Well after the war, Longstreet blamed this dispatch for Bragg's daw-
dling pursuit of the Federals; on the basis of it, Longstreet said, Bragg
decided against a Longstreet recommendation that the victorious Confederates march around Chattanooga and get between Rosecrans and his
supply bases. Bragg decided instead to march through Chattanooga, since
he assumed it would be abandoned to him the following night. Forrest's
conclusion that Rosecrans was abandoning Chattanooga was indeed erroneous, and he corrected it soon afterward. Still before noon, in another
dispatch to Polk, he reported that the Federals seemed to be "fortifying,
as I can distinctly hear the sound of axes in great numbers. The appearance
is still as in the last dispatch, that he [Rosecrans] is hurrying on toward
Chattanooga." Bragg's response to the first of these two dispatches illustrates how widely he and Forrest diverged in their military attitudes. The
main point of this dispatch was Forrest's opinion that the "skeer" was on,
that the Federals could be run as far as Bragg cared to pursue them—but
they had to be pursued; this part of the message seems to have been
correct.[25]

Forrest sent his men, dismounted again, against the Federal blockade
of the gap at Rossville, "but found the force too large to dislodge.
. . . On the arrival of my artillery, opened on and fought them for several
hours, but could not move them." Bragg didn't seem to care whether they
were moved; the rest of his army didn't get into motion until after 2 P.M.
Forrest sought out the commanding general's headquarters that night,
apparently to see what the problem was, and returned nonplussed. "What
does he fight his battles for?" he was overheard to ask no one in particular.
The next morning, with the rest of the Confederate army apparently idle
again, Forrest moved ahead and pursued the Federals nearly into Chattanooga. When infantry under General McLaws of Longstreet's corps
came in sight in early afternoon, Forrest proposed a joint attack, but
McLaws demurred, saying he felt unauthorized to take such a step.[26]

With Bragg's inactivity continuing, Forrest received welcome orders
on September 24 to withdraw ten miles from Chattanooga to feed and rest
his men and horses. The following day he was sent northeast of the city

again, this time to repel a reported move by Major General Ambrose Burnside to come to Rosecrans's aid. Forrest chased a Union detachment northward to Loudon, which angered Bragg. The Confederate commander is reported to have complained to a fellow officer that he had "not a single general officer of cavalry fit for command—look at Forrest; [he] has allowed himself to be drawn off toward Knoxville in a general rampage, capturing villages and towns, that are of no use whatever to me. . . . The man is ignorant, and does not know anything of cooperation. He is nothing more than a good raider." From Bragg, Forrest shortly received orders to move back to Cleveland and relinquish most of his troops to Wheeler for a raid to Rosecrans's rear. Forrest protested in a letter that never has been found, then went to see Bragg, where he is reported to have been told he would get his command back when Wheeler completed his raid. Having little else to do, he took a ten-day leave—for the first time in eighteen months—to see Mary Ann Forrest in La Grange, Georgia. While at La Grange, he received orders from Bragg placing him where he had sworn he would never serve again: under Wheeler. Predictably, he decided to resign his commission.[27]

Accompanied by J. B. Cowan, he went to Bragg's Missionary Ridge headquarters above Chattanooga. Cowan knew nothing of what had transpired, but he deduced that something was wrong from Forrest's unusual quietude on the ride. As they approached Bragg's tent, Cowan later recalled, Forrest uncharacteristically ignored the sentry's salute, and when they went inside and found Bragg alone, he also refused his commander's proffered hand. Instead, he stuck the index finger of his left hand into Bragg's face and addressed him with frank insubordination.

I am not here to pass civilities or compliments with you, but on other business [Cowan later remembered him saying]. *You commenced your cowardly and contemptible persecution of me soon after the battle of Shiloh, and you have kept it up ever since. You did it because I reported to Richmond facts, while you reported damned lies. You robbed me of my command in Kentucky and gave it to one of your favorites—men that I armed and equipped from the enemies of our country. In a spirit of revenge and spite, because I would not fawn upon you as others did, you drove me into West Tennessee in the winter of 1862 with a second brigade I had organized, with improper arms and without sufficient ammunition, although I had made repeated applications for the same. You did it to ruin me and my career. When in spite of all this I returned with my command well equipped by captures, you began again your work of spite and persecution and have kept it up; and now this second brigade, organized and equipped without thanks to you or the government, a brigade which has won a reputation for successful fighting second to none in the army, taking advantage of your position as the commanding general in order to humiliate me, you have taken these brave men from me. I have stood your meanness as long as I intend to. You have played the part of a damned scoundrel, and are a coward, and if you were any part of a man I would slap your jaws and force you to resent it. You may as well not issue any more orders to me, for I will not obey them, and I will hold you personally responsible for any further indignities you endeavor to inflict upon me. You have threatened to arrest me for not obeying your orders promptly. I dare you to do it, and I say to you that if you ever again try to interfere with me or cross my path it will be at the peril of your life.*

Cowan reported that Bragg sank into a camp chair in a corner of his tent and silently endured the continual poking of Forrest's left index finger into his face. When the tirade was finished, Forrest abruptly turned on his heel and strode out of the tent toward his horse, followed by Cowan.

"Well," Cowan remarked as they rode away, "you are in for it now."

"He'll never say a word about it," Forrest snapped. "He'll be the last man to mention it; and, mark my word, he'll take no action in the matter. I will ask to be relieved and transferred to a different field, and he will not oppose it."[28]

18

HEADQUARTERS ARMY OF TENNESSEE
Missionary Ridge, October 13, 1863.

Brigadier-General Lee,
Aide, &c., to President:

SIR: Some weeks since[,] I forwarded an application from Brig. Gen. N.B. Forrest for a transfer to the Mississippi for special service. At that time I withheld my approval, because I deemed the services of that distinguished soldier necessary with this army. As

*that request can now be granted without injury to the public interests
in this quarter, I respectfully ask, in reply to your inquiry, that the
transfer be made.*

   I am, sir, very respectfully, your obedient servant,

                                          BRAXTON BRAGG,
                                          General Commanding.[1]

JAMES CHALMERS, WHO knew both Bragg and Forrest well, would
write after the war that "promotion of Wheeler over Forrest, which
[Bragg], in an honest desire to promote the good of the service, recommended was unfortunate." Wheeler "did not desire it and suffered in
public estimation when it was thrust on him," Chalmers wrote, whereas
Forrest, "though a great strategist, trusted largely for tactics and many
military details to officers under him; and if Wheeler had remained second
to Forrest, as he was perfectly willing to do, a more splendid combination
for cavalry operations could scarcely have been made."[2]

Having chosen the wrong combination, Bragg had to live with it. In
the wake of his bloody and unproductive victory at Chickamauga, he had
larger problems than Forrest to ponder. He had relieved two of his
ranking generals, Polk and Hindman, for tardiness in attacking during the
battle, and, threatening now to dismiss Hill on similar charges, the Confederacy's supreme western commander found himself counterattacked by
many of his senior subordinates. Polk and Longstreet, followed by most
of the others, beseeched the Davis administration to relieve him, creating
a dilemma so thorny that the President himself arrived at Bragg's headquarters for a five-day visit on October 9. In his abrasive and ineffectual
way, Davis interviewed each of the subordinate generals, asked them if
they thought the army needed a change in command, and then, after each
replied in the affirmative, stood by his friend Bragg.

Davis also attended, somewhat more intelligently, to the comparatively
minor matter of Forrest. Nearly three weeks earlier, on September 24,
Governor Isham G. Harris had telegraphed Davis recommending Forrest
be promoted, prompting the president to remind Bragg of Forrest's earlier
request for transfer. After refusing to fire Bragg, Davis left for a tour of
Alabama and Mississippi, having issued to Bragg's mishandled and dis-
gruntled troops an address exhorting them toward "harmony, due subor-
dination and cheerful support of lawful authority." Two weeks later, on
his return journey, he invited Forrest to meet him at Montgomery and
travel with him to Atlanta, and when they reached the Georgia capital, he

wrote Bragg approving Forrest's transfer. He also mentioned Forrest's wish that a few of his present troops be allowed to go with him to serve as a core for new units he planned to raise.[3]

Given the relations between the two generals, it is hardly surprising that not all Forrest's wishes were granted. He had asked for a battalion from the Second Kentucky; instead, he was assigned the regiment of his youngest brother, Colonel Jeffrey Forrest, who had been reported killed the week before in northern Alabama. Colonel Forrest's troops were Alabamians, and General Forrest later reported he had decided to permit these men to remain with Bragg since "it is my impression that they will be unwilling to go" to defend Tennessee and Mississippi soil with their commander dead. Thus with a detachment of 310 men—his own sixty-five-man escort, McDonald's battalion of the regiment Forrest himself first commanded, four artillery pieces, and John Morton's sixty-seven artillerymen (which force, Forrest complained in a letter to Richmond, "is wholly inadequate")—he departed the western theater's mainstream for a comparative backwater.[4]

Headquartering at Okolona, Mississippi, where he quickly learned that Jeffrey was not dead (but, instead, had been wounded, captured, and exchanged), he also found himself now reporting to a more appreciative commander than Bragg. Major General Stephen D. Lee was a thirty-year-old South Carolinian distantly related to the more famous Virginia Lees. As a West Pointer accustomed to artillery command, he evinced great respect for his new subordinate's reputation for fighting. Before ever meeting Forrest, Lee had written Bragg requesting Forrest be assigned to Mississippi, and when he learned the transfer was being made, he sent a markedly deferential letter informing Forrest that "whether you are under my command or not, we shall not disagree, and you shall have all the assistance and support I can render you." Lee said he would be "proud" to "either command . . . or co-operat[e] with so gallant an officer as yourself and one who has such an established reputation in the cavalry service to which I have been recently assigned." He enclosed an order to his own staff officers to fill Forrest's requisitions "as far as practicable and afford you every facility in your new assignment."[5]

The new arrival got to work with his usual speed. On November 25, the day Bragg's army was being chased by Grant out of Chattanooga, Forrest wrote the western theater's other major commander, General Joseph E. Johnston, that he was about to leave Okolona for Jackson, Tennessee, on a recruiting venture well behind Federal lines. Ten days later, he wrote from Jackson to apprise Johnston of his progress: 5,000 recruits already gathered, 50 to 100 a day coming in from Kentucky alone, and "from 4,000 to 6,000 head of good beef cattle for the use of the army" if Generals Lee and Roddey would cooperate with him to bring the animals out of Union territory. He added that "two articles are indispensably necessary — they are arms and money. . . . I have had to advance to my quartermaster and commissary $20,000 of my private funds to subsist the command thus far." He asked Johnston for $250,000 to feed, arm, and pay his troops, and, a couple of days later, dispatched Major M. C. Gallaway all the way to Richmond "to make requisitions and receipt for what is obtainable." He said he was "greatly in need of arms and money, and have sent Major G. to Richmond on purpose to represent more fully than can be done on paper the details necessary to a proper appreciation of the necessity of holding this [western Tennessee] country and the available supplies in it; also to send rapidly forward all the arms, &c., that can be spared me." While waiting for the guns and funds, he sent southward a contingent of recruits who were without arms, moving them away from alerted Union commanders in the area.[6]

His initial hope of holding West Tennessee seems to have dimmed as the Confederacy delayed in sending him the necessary supplies and money, and he began scaling down his earlier forecasts. In another letter to Johnston, he noted that the Federals "are preparing to move against me" and that he expected them to do so by Christmas or so. He said he would have "at least 1,000 head of beef cattle," as well as at least 100,000 pounds of bacon, to move southward by December 25; he asked that the Mississippi-based brigades of Generals Ferguson and Chalmers be sent northward to help him defend and transport these commissary treasures. He added that if he could be reinforced by Ferguson and Chalmers for thirty days, "I shall organize 7,000 troops, besides getting out a great number of absentees and deserters from the army." If Ferguson and Chalmers could not be sent, he said, he requested that "General Lee harass the enemy along the line of the Memphis & Charleston Railroad" to divert Union attention from his southward march, which would be hampered by the cattle, wagons loaded with bacon, and shortage of arms.[7]

Guerrilla-style war was continuing. Forrest's recruiting in enemy-occupied territory turned up such evidence of military maltreatment of Confederate sympathizers that he wrote a letter of protest to Union major general Stephen A. Hurlbut in Memphis on December 13. Hurlbut answered three days later, expressing "regret that the discipline of both armies has not been equal to the task of wholly suppressing these outrages." He added, in wry reference to Forrest's own behind-the-lines kind of operations, that "[a]s you are well aware as a cavalry officer, detached bodies of men on distant service frequently commit these wrongs." Hurlbut said he had received a report "that two women, residing in McNairy County, have been shot by the command of one Wilson because their husbands were in the Union service. If I obtain any accurate information of the parties, I shall forward their names to you for that speedy justice which you promise."[8]

Hurlbut surely was less concerned with Forrest's justice than with his moves. The Union general wrote his superior, Grant, that "Forrest must fight or run," adding "I think we shall cure [him] of his ambition to command West Tennessee." Forrest actually had no options. Facing nearly 15,000 Union troops converging from the north at Columbus, Kentucky, the west at Memphis, the east at Nashville, the southeast at Corinth, Mississippi, and the southwest at LaGrange, Tennessee, and with only 3,500 mostly new troops of his own—with arms for barely 1,000 of them—he could hardly fight. Receiving no response to a December 18 request for Stephen Lee to help him hold West Tennessee, on Christmas Eve (the date atop a letter Lee finally wrote saying he was on his way, and two days before notification was written that the requested troop payment monies had been ordered) Forrest pulled his unwieldy and supplies-laden little force southward out of Jackson.[9]

That day, he received official notice that he had been promoted to major general; he probably didn't learn why, however. Davis had been sending Johnston directives that Mississippi cotton be burned by the cavalry rather than be illegally traded to Northerners; meanwhile, Johnston had been demanding from Davis more cavalry to carry out the directives. Johnston had written Davis that "[w]e require another major-general of cavalry. The frontier is much too long for Major-General Lee's supervision." In reply to another Johnston letter around the same time, Davis indicated Johnston had asked to borrow from the Virginia front Major General Wade Hampton, a prominent South Carolina cavalryman owning vast Mississippi properties. Davis responded on December 3 that Hampton couldn't be "spared," but that Forrest was being promoted to major general "and will I hope supply your wants in North Mississippi and West Tennessee so as to enable you to draw Major-General Lee to the southern portion of your department."[10]

The new major general escaped West Tennessee in a style becoming typical of him: by dividing his slender ranks in the presence of overwhelming Federal force and sending each detachment off with directions to act as if it were the whole Forrest army. For instance, while his men were crossing the rain-swollen Hatchie River at Estenaula, Tennessee, his sixty-man escort rode ahead and, under a cold moon, attacked and drove back some 600 Federals; they did it by deploying in a very wide and loose formation, shouting commands over their shoulders to a nonexistent brigade, and then crashing loudly onto the Union position through a field of dried-up cornstalks. Forrest himself was soon back at the Hatchie, however, overseeing the crossing. When a ferryboat foundered and threw a wagon and mule team into the current, the general himself got chest-deep into the water in an attempt to save the mules. On a bank above this scene, a large conscript—perhaps not realizing his commander was within ear-shot—boasted he could never be made to enter the water on such work. A member of the escort later remembered that Forrest climbed out of the river and up the bank, grabbed the big-mouthed soldier-to-be, and pitched him into the freezing current.[11]

At New Castle, a few miles farther southeast, he met two Union detachments sent north from the Memphis & Charleston Railroad to cut him off. Deploying his force's unarmed contingent as if it were battle-ready, he routed the Federals. Then, instead of continuing his southeast-ward flight toward the Tennessee-Mississippi line, he turned west toward Memphis to baffle his pursuers. He sent fifty armed men and 650 unarmed ones almost into the outskirts of the bluff city, ordering them to cross Wolf River near there and move ostentatiously into Mississippi, thus diverting considerable Federal attention from his bacon and beef and its all-but-unarmed guard. The latter column, meanwhile, he took toward a Union garrison guarding LaFayette Station on the Memphis & Charles-ton, having heard it commanded a usable bridge over the Wolf. There Forrest troopers under Colonel Tyree Bell fired a volley with the 200 rifles they had, and the Federals—apparently (and wrongly) assuming the rest of the Confederates had guns, too—retreated, only to be pursued. Other Federals, though, now were coming hard from Collierville five miles west, Moscow eight miles east, and other farther locations; a Union telegrapher at LaFayette had managed to summon them by sending a message about Forrest's intent to cross the Wolf. When the first Federal troops arrived in a driving rain, the embattled Confederates attacked westward with most of their armed men, leaving a few others to prevent pursuit from the east until dark. With most of his men, wagons, and livestock being pushed hard toward Holly Springs, Mississippi, Forrest drove almost into Collier-ville, where the Federals he was pursuing finally dug in December 27 for a fight the next morning. Day dawned, however, on an empty field in front of the Federals' position; their pursuer had retreated in the darkness to follow the rest of his column into Holly Springs.[12]

Establishing a headquarters New Year's Day at Como, he began organizing his recruits and conscripts. Many of these men previously had been carried on the rolls of other Confederate units, but, asserting that these had been units "upon paper" only, he got permission from Richmond to "annul" the previous orders of those who hadn't joined their regiments within two months after enlistment; he also requested and received command of these troops himself. His authority was growing. Although he remained under the overall supervision of Lee, he was given dominion over "Forrest's Cavalry Department"—North Mississippi and West Tennessee—in a January 13 meeting at Meridian with Lee and Leonidas Polk. A few days later, he referred to it that way in a general order describing his area of authority, adding that all cavalry commanders north of its southern boundary "will at once report to these headquarters the strength and condition of their commands."[13]

About this time, Johnston in Georgia had sent to Polk in Mississippi a colonel charged with restoring to the Tennessee regiments in Johnston's army certain " 'absentees without leave' and deserters . . . supposed to be in the cavalry organizations of North Mississippi and West Tennessee. This number is 2,869, and in addition the absentees from two regiments not yet reported." Polk replied a few days later that he had sent Johnston's letter along to Forrest but had advised Johnston's colonel "that I did not think this is a proper time to attempt to recover those men. . . . They have been so short a time with General Forrest, that any attempt to detach them now would result in a general stampede. They would almost all desert and return to West Tennessee." For his part, apparently after receiving Johnston's letter from Polk, Forrest sent a brief, steely, and not very subordinate message to the latter from Tupelo on February 5: "Have telegraphed General Lee to come up. Desire greatly that you meet him here. If matters are not arranged to my satisfaction I shall quit the service."[14]

He reorganized the department's troops—hailing from such varied states as Tennessee, Mississippi, Kentucky, Arkansas, Missouri, and Texas—into four slim brigades commanded by Brigadier General R. V. Richardson, Colonel Tyree Bell, Colonel Robert McCulloch, and his own youngest brother, Colonel Jeffrey Forrest. Named second in overall command was Chalmers, the Mississippi lawyer to whose tent Forrest had gone looking for Beauregard that Shiloh midnight nearly two years before; Chalmers, whose upper-crust northern-Mississippi beginnings contrasted so sharply with Forrest's, had had his own command in their mutual home section until Forrest arrived there.[15]

To instill discipline in his raw recruits and conscripts, he adopted another forceful tactic similar to his standing battle order that any man who refused to fight be shot on the spot. Having apprehended nineteen new West Tennessee recruits who had set out together illegally to return home, he sentenced them to die by a firing squad February 12, 1864, on the outskirts of Oxford, Mississippi. The condemned were standing in front of coffins, freshly dug graves, and leveled rifles when their general's pardon — long sought by citizens of the surrounding area — arrived at the last moment via a staff officer. "There were no more desertions," an officer wrote later.[16]

By now, things were heating up in the area. General William T. Sherman had returned temporarily from northern Georgia, determined to lead an ambitious Union raid of destruction from Vicksburg due east into the heart of Mississippi. To help accomplish this, he arranged for a diversionary gunboat expedition up the Yazoo River and ordered a 7,500-man cavalry column to join him near Meridian; beforehand, the cavalry-men were to advance southeast from Memphis, laying waste to both potential military foodstuffs and the tracks of the Mobile & Ohio Railroad. This mounted thrust was commanded by thirty-three-year-old Brigadier General William Sooy Smith, an intelligent and even brilliant ex-civilian engineer. Having made his name as a leader of infantry at Shiloh, Perryville, and Vicksburg, Smith was placed by Sherman in charge of all cavalry within the Federal Department of the Tennessee — "which," Sherman wrote Smith on January 27, "I believe to be superior and better in all respects than the combined cavalry which the enemy has in all the State of Mississippi." Sherman's own raid from Vicksburg to Meridian, meanwhile, was to be of the pattern of his later march across Georgia and the Carolinas. His orders made it plain that Smith's mission from Memphis was similar to his own: to "destroy [Confederate] communication from Okolona to Meridian and thence eastward to Selma." Of the "abundance of forage collected along the railroad, and the . . . standing corn in the fields," Smith was to take "liberally . . . as well as horses, mules, cattle, &c. As a rule respect dwellings and families . . . but mills, barns, sheds, stables, and such like things use for the benefit and convenience of your command."[17]

Sherman's timetable called for Smith to rendezvous with him at Meridian in mid-February, but there were delays. Smith lost time waiting for one of his units, numbering some 2,000 men, to make its way south from

Kentucky in the flood season; as a result, he did not leave Collierville, Tennessee, until February 11. Then he moved slowly as his mission of destruction and theft encumbered his column with not only some 3,000 horses and mules but also many hundreds of liberated slaves. Warned about Forrest by Sherman, Smith seemed to take the warning much to heart. An eerie hint of dread pervades a Smith subordinate's description of crossing the Mississippi border into "rough, hopeless, God-forsaken" Tippah County, the homeland of Forrest's youth: "Its hills were steep, its mud was deep, its houses and farms were poor, its streams, torrents of bottomless muddy water, fast swelling from the thaw."[18]

In this area still inhabited by his father's and mother's kin, Forrest naturally heard of Federal movements quickly. On February 4 he alerted Chalmers to a Union force advancing from Friar's Point, near his own 3,000-acre Mississippi plantation. Five days later, he was reading the Federal mind, writing Chalmers in Panola from his Oxford headquarters that "I am of opinion the real move is in direction of Okolona and Meridian." With his scattered troops long since ordered to be ready to move at once, he sent Polk word that "General Smith, with 10,000 mounted infantry and cavalry and 31 pieces artillery, passed Holly Springs on the evening of the 12th, going toward Beck's Spring and New Albany." Noting the dispositions of his own troops, he reported that Jeffrey Forrest had been sent to West Point, Mississippi, to seek the enemy there, while Lieutenant Colonel A. H. Forrest "is on the Yazoo River with one regiment fighting gunboats and transports." His own part of his force, he wrote, was following his youngest brother to West Point, which he expected to reach early on February 19.[19]

With his other brigades on the lookout from Grenada all the way to Columbus, he sidled swiftly southeastward waiting for Smith's direction to become obvious. It did so on February 19, when the Federals began wrecking the Mobile & Ohio Railroad near Okolona. By then, Smith later reported, they had brushed aside at Houston a "rabble" of state troops under Brigadier General Samuel J. Gholson and commenced burning between 1,000,000 and 2,000,000 bushels of corn along the railroad; "there was a line of fire from place to place." Actually, there was more burning than Smith really wanted. On the 19th, he issued orders that any of his men "caught in setting fire to property of any kind without orders shall be arrested" and offered a $500 reward for the first man so caught. His retinue of liberated blacks, infected with military pyromania that went beyond even Sherman's liberal destruction orders, had begun torching plantation buildings from their mansions all the way to their slave cabins;

Smith himself called it "incendiarism of the most shocking kind." His already deliberate pace slowed the farther he moved from Memphis. "Any reverse to my command, situated as it was, would have been fatal," he explained afterward.[20]

Ordered by Polk to combine with Stephen Lee's forces in central Mississippi and prevent Smith from joining Sherman, Forrest rightly assumed that once Smith had begun destroying the railroad tracks, he would attempt to follow them on to Meridian. Accordingly, while planning a junction with Lee's troops, he began gathering his forces and laying a trap. When Smith reached West Point early February 20, he encountered Jeffrey Forrest's brigade, which had made a forced march of forty-five miles to get there first. Jeffrey retreated, attempting to draw Smith into a three-sided box formed by the Tombigbee River on the east and, on the south and west, the muddy valleys of Oktibbeha and Sakatonchee creeks.

Meanwhile, Jeffrey's brother drew up most of the rest of his 2,500 or so Confederates behind the Sakatonchee, intentionally leaving undisturbed a bridge and a raised road across the river bottom. He hoped he might be able to use them to attack when the Federals followed his brother into the box. The problem was, they didn't. Smith later reported that after encountering a Confederate brigade a mile north of West Point, he "drove" them in a "short, sharp fight" but decided "to move back and draw the enemy after me, that I might select my own positions and fight with the advantages in our favor." He explained that "[e]xaggerated reports of Forrest's strength reached me constantly, and it was reported that Lee was about to re-enforce him with a portion or the whole of his command"; in fact, "all the State troops that could be assembled from every quarter were drawn together at my front to hold the Oktibbeha against me, while a heavy force was seen moving to my rear. . . . Under the circumstances, I determined not to move my encumbered command into the trap set for me by the rebels."[21]

As Sherman, ninety miles farther south at Meridian, tired of waiting and turned back toward Vicksburg, Smith launched a two-hour diversionary rearguard attack against Jeffrey Forrest's troops at the Sakatonchee bridge on February 21. This attack, to buy time for the bulk of his "encumbered" column to begin its retreat northward, was in progress as General Forrest and an orderly arrived "out of a cloud of dust" and rode up onto the highway leading across the bridge. Chalmers, sitting a horse there in the rear, had never seen Forrest under fire before, and later recalled that his commander "seemed very much more excited than I thought was necessary under the circumstances." When he asked, in "rather a harsh, quick tone . . . what the condition of affairs was at the front . . . I replied that Colonel Forrest had reported nothing to me beyond the fact that there was some skirmishing." The questioner wasn't impressed.

"Is that all you know?" Forrest said in brusque impatience. "Then I'll go there and find out for myself."

Forrest galloped toward the fighting, and Chalmers followed through "pretty thick" Federal fire across the thirty-foot bridge. On the other side, they met a frightened Confederate "who, dismounted and hatless, had thrown away his gun and everything else that could impede his rapid flight to the rear." Chalmers recalled that Forrest jumped down off his horse, grabbed the frightened trooper, threw him to the ground, and then dragged him to the side of the road, where he began whipping him with a piece of brush. Then, turning him toward the gunfire, he said: "Now, God damn you, you go back there and fight. You might as well get killed there as here, for if you ever run away again you'll not get off so easy."[22]

The Federals struck Jeffrey Forrest's men at eight o'clock, the Forrest battle report subsequently said, and "after a fight of two hours were repulsed with considerable loss. . . . As the enemy withdrew, I followed . . . and . . . soon ascertained, after a few well-directed shots from our artillery, that the enemy had begun a rapid and systematic retreat, and [I] dashed on after them."[23]

"It was not my intention to attack them or bring on a general engagement, but to develop their strength, position and movements," Forrest explained in another report. However, when he "found the enemy had begun a systematic retreat, . . . being unwilling they should leave the country without a fight, [I] ordered the advance of my column." Discerning that the "skeer" was on, he quickly turned the action into a shorter version of the Streight chase. Ordering his much smaller force to dog the Federals' flanks and heels, he goaded them into turning to fight about four miles above West Point, in a patch of timber accessible by another highway and bridge. There he employed his usual tactic, dismounting his troops and sending part of them around to attack from the rear while the rest struck the front. This twofold assault dislodged the Federals, and the Confederates swept after them. They "made several stands, but . . . we continued to charge and drive them on, killing and wounding fifteen or twenty of them and capturing a number of prisoners." After nightfall, they "kept so close" to the Federals that "my men mistook each other for the enemy and fired a volley at each other, without, however, doing any damage." Forrest's authorized biography says there actually was damage, that one man was killed while a bullet passed through the clothing of the general himself; perhaps the casualty was forgotten by the time his report was filed almost a month later—or perhaps he was reluctant to report the mortal extent of the confusion. Anyway, "[f]earing a recurrence of such mistakes," he and his men made camp, planning to resume the chase at daylight the next morning.[24]

Smith's Federals meanwhile marched until 2 A.M., then were given a four-hour rest three miles south of Okolona. The Confederates were moving again by daylight, and Forrest and his escort company found and charged the Federal rear guard four miles south of Okolona, driving it through the town only to find an imposing Federal battle line drawn up on the other side. Outnumbered ridiculously, he left his escort in a skirmish line and joined Bell's brigade on the Union flank. "Where is the enemy's whole position?" he hurriedly asked Colonel C. R. Barteau, who was temporarily commanding the brigade because Bell was ill.

"You see it, General, and they are preparing to charge."

"Then we will charge them," Forrest said, ordering Bell's men to mount their horses and ride toward the Union position.[25]

When this maneuver was momentarily unsuccessful—"they received us with a volley and charged with yells," he later wrote—he took Barteau's own regiment, the Second Tennessee Cavalry (Confederate), moved it around to the flank, and with his familiar "Come on, boys!" led it on a second charge. In the wake of the first Confederate onrush, the Second Tennessee Cavalry (Union) and the Fourth U.S. Cavalry had charged "gallantly back on the enemy into town," their commander reported. There they were struck by Forrest's second charge. In the words of their commander, "being about to be outflanked, [they] were forced to retire in haste upon the column." In fact, they ran pell-mell into a position newly occupied by the Third Tennessee Cavalry (Union), "and all three of the . . . regiments became entirely disorganized by being mixed up."[26]

A wild rush toward the Union rear ensued. Smith tried to get part of his column moving northward again while the fight was in progress. Lieutenant I. W. Curtis of a First Illinois artillery company reported that after "we arrived at Okolona and formed ready for a fight, . . . [we] were soon ordered to march on. We had not proceeded very far when we were unexpectedly surprised by the presence of fleeing cavalry on both sides of us. They were in perfect confusion; some hallooing, 'Go ahead, or we will be killed'; while some few showed a willingness to fight." Union colonel L. F. McCrillis, Smith's Third Cavalry Brigade commander, moved up and "formed the Fourth Tennessee on our left and the Fifth Kentucky on our right" when the Confederates, by moving on their flanks, "forced them to retire to prevent being cut off from the main column." McCrillis reported afterward that the Thirty-second Indiana, farther to his right, was "pressed back by the Second and Third Tennessee and Fourth Regulars and stragglers, who broke his line, and he had to fall back after giving the enemy a momentary check."[27]

Lieutenant Curtis reported receiving "an order, purporting to come from headquarters, for me to try and save the artillery by marching through the field to our right." The field was gashed by a series of ditches, one of which was six feet deep, and only one gun could be pulled over safely before the horses were exhausted; another was broken in the crossing and had to be spiked and abandoned, along with four others, after its ammunition had been destroyed. Curtis went on to note the loss of thirty horses during the expedition, some "in the stampede, but most . . . worn out on the march. . . . I lost my 5 packsaddles. The men and negroes, they say, were ordered to leave them in the stampede, and I couldn't find them any more."[28]

Colonel George Waring, commanding the Union First Cavalry Brigade, reported that five miles north of Okolona "a message was received from the rear . . . that the Fourth U.S. Cavalry had found the enemy too strong and had been forced to retire with much loss, and that the Seventh Indiana Cavalry and the whole of the Third Brigade had been unable to resist the onward march of the enemy, and were retreating upon the main column." Waring said he "immediately formed my brigade in line, and remained in this position until the Third Brigade passed through, portions of it in such confusion as to endanger the morale of my whole command." He then was ordered to fall back another mile to a "stronger position . . . on a farm called Ivey's Hill," where he watched "other brigades retiring," he said, "and the immense train of pack-mules and mounted contrabands [liberated slaves], which had been corraled in a field near the road, swarmed up with such force as to carry past the line of the Second New Jersey and the Second Illinois Cavalry, which were then marching to this position." Other regiments from other Union brigades made a stand with him there, and the pursuing Confederates "soon attacked us with heavy musketry fire, which was replied to with good effect by the battery of the Fourth Missouri Cavalry."[29]

In this last pitched battle of the Smith expedition, troops under Jeffrey Forrest, the general's youngest and favorite brother, along with other troops under McCulloch, had taken over the vanguard of pursuit from Bell's men, who on foot had chased the Federals nine miles since morning. Fifty yards in front of the Federal position, Jeffrey Forrest was struck by a ball in the throat. The general rushed to him, raised his head off the ground, and spoke his name several times, "melt[ing] with grief," artillerist John W. Morton later recalled. This moment "was of short duration, however. Placing the dead man's hat over his face, he called to Major Strange . . . to take charge of the body, and looking around called in a ringing, passionate voice to the bugle to sound the charge once more."[30]

Once again the front-and-flank attack was pressed, as Forrest sent his brother's brigade around to the left while he himself took other troops and struck the front with such fury that Strange wondered if grief for his brother had made him decide to die also. The Federal line quickly retreated under pressure of the dual thrusts. Forrest followed up quickly, driving them with only his sixty-man escort, until he reached a place where a broken piece of artillery had slowed the Union retreat. There about 500 Federals had formed another battle line to deal again with the pursuit, and Forrest and his escort tore into it in a savage and hugely outnumbered assault. J. B. Cowan later remembered reaching where Jeffrey Forrest had fallen and hearing Strange urge him, "Doctor, hurry after the general; I am afraid he will be killed!" Cowan spurred his mount, and "in about a mile, as I rounded a short turn in the road, I came upon a scene which made my blood run cold. There in the road was General Forrest with his escort, and a few of the advance-guard of the Forrest brigade, in a hand-to-hand fight . . . with Federals enough . . . to have pulled them from their horses."[31]

At that moment, the vanguard of McCulloch's brigade came into sight, but the disparity of numbers was still so great that McCulloch's men hesitated. When they did, McCulloch himself started waving a bloodily bandaged, wounded hand above his head. Urging his horse toward the fighting, he shouted: "My God, men, will you see them kill your general? I will go to his rescue if not a man follows me!" His troops did follow, and the Federals turned and retreated hastily again. By the time they did, Forrest is reported to have personally killed or incapacitated three of them in the fight in the road.[32]

One last time, the Federals formed for battle around sunset a little farther on, about ten miles southeast of Pontotoc, attempting to fend off their pursuers while the wagons, mounts, and liberated slaves made their escape. As Forrest arrived with only his advance elements, he found the Federals "formed in three lines across a large field on the left of the road, but which a turn in the road made . . . directly in our front." The Union lines "were at intervals of several hundred paces, and the rear and second lines longer than the first." As Forrest's point elements advanced, the

Federals opened with artillery. The Confederate "ammunition was nearly exhausted, and I knew that if we faltered they would in turn become the attacking party, and that disaster might follow."[33]

Dr. Cowan again was riding beside the general, and he urged Forrest to "get out of the road." Forrest refused almost contemptuously: "Doctor, if you are alarmed, you may get out of the way; I am as safe here as there." A moment later, the general's horse was killed, struck by five balls almost simultaneously while its saddle was shattered by another three. As its miraculously unhurt rider was being provided another mount, he and Cowan noticed a terrified farm woman and her children trying to shield themselves from shells and bullets behind a small log cabin's chimney. Forrest noted a hole in the ground where clay had been dug to build the chimney, and he sent Cowan over to lead them to that better refuge. "In there," he told Cowan, "they will be perfectly safe." He had not ridden the new horse more than 150 yards before it, too, was killed — just as his twelve-year-old, iron-gray gelding King Philip was brought to him from the rear; King Philip, an otherwise sluggish animal distinguished by a habit of rushing furiously at blue-clad troops with his ears back and his teeth bared, himself took a shot in the neck that afternoon, but lived.[34]

In the face of the lines of mounted Federals waiting to receive him now, Forrest reported having only 300 men of his Second and Seventh Tennessee, most of whom had been fighting dismounted and had not had time to get to their horses again. As this small force advanced, the Federals suddenly "charged down at a gallop" to defend Smith's fleeing column. It was, Forrest said in his report, "the grandest cavalry charge I have ever witnessed." Getting his men into a gully crossing the field, he delivered a volley that sent the first Union line "reeling rearward, and strewed the ground in front with a number of dead and wounded horses and men." Successive waves met the same fate, but each wave was larger in size and pushed closer. The last reached the gully, and many Confederates tossed aside empty rifles and began using their pistols in another hand-to-hand melee. At one point, Major Thomas S. Tate of Forrest's staff flung his empty carbine at the head of a Federal officer aiming a pistol at him and then was saved when Forrest himself rode up "and with a sweep of his saber, nearly severed the Federal officer's head from his shoulders. The man toppled to the ground, and as he did so, Tate, taking the revolver from his hand, swung himself into the vacated saddle. . . ."[35]

After the final Federal charge had been repulsed, Forrest happened upon a hastily made Union-hospital area in which a yelling, wounded Federal had been left behind by his surgeon halfway through the amputation of a leg; the physician had left so quickly that the amputation saw had been left in the bone. Forrest quickly "saturated a cloth with chloroform and applied it to the nostrils of the sufferer," then ordered Dr. Cowan to complete the surgery.[36]

Forrest later explained his small loss (of 144 killed, wounded, and missing, compared with Smith's reported 388) in the battles around West Point and Okolona by saying that "we kept so close to them that the enemy overshot our men." His abandonment of pursuit he explained by the "broken down and exhausted condition of men and horses, and being almost out of ammunition." The chase hadn't been abandoned altogether, though. Major General Sam Gholson's "comparatively fresh" Mississippi troops, having arrived the night of February 22, were given the duty of pursuit "and when last heard from [were] still driving the enemy, capturing horses and prisoners."[37]

Smith arrived back in Memphis on February 26. He had returned from West Point in half the time he had taken to get there.

19

HEADQUARTERS,
Demopolis, Ala., March 3, 1864

. . . The lieutenant-general commanding takes pleasure in congratulating the officers and men of the commands of Major-General Lee and Major-General Forrest upon the brilliant and successful campaign just closed. It marks an era in this war full of honor to our arms and calculated to teach a useful lesson to our enemies. They came by thousands with glistening bayonets and confident of their strength. . . . They have been forced to return, beaten and distracted and pursued by our cavalry. . . .

THOS. M. JACK,
[General Polk's] *Assistant Adjutant-General*[1]

THE UNION COMMANDERS were as chagrined by the "campaign just closed" as Leonidas Polk was happy about it. After the war, Sherman would recall that Smith had permitted Forrest "to head him off and defeat him with an inferior force," while Grant would write that the Smith-Forrest encounter was "decidedly in Forrest's favor." Contemporaneously, Union general Hurlbut at Memphis said the Smith stampede "demoralized the cavalry very seriously." However, a Confederate general noted that Forrest's victory wasn't as total as it might have been. Stephen Lee, who helped contest Sherman's march to Meridian and then tried vainly to get his troops up from central Mississippi in time to join Forrest's and destroy Smith, later recapitulated in his official report that his command "was much disappointed with the result of this action, having anticipated a fight with their own arm of the service and with equal numbers." He said Forrest's dispatches had "led [him] to believe . . . that the force of the enemy was superior to our combined commands, and that the difficulty was in avoiding a general engagement till my arrival." He had not received Forrest's report, he added, and thus "am not able to explain his move on the 19th to fight the enemy, and again retiring before him without concentrating and giving battle with his entire force. I feel confident, however, that this gallant officer acted with judgment and to the best interests of the service."[2]

By Forrest's "move on the 19th to fight the enemy" and retirement "before him without concentrating and giving battle with his entire force," Lee must have referred to Jeffrey Forrest's skirmishing retreat from West Point to the Sakatonchee early on the 20th; the reason Jeffrey's older brother didn't concentrate "and giv[e] battle with his entire force" was simply that he was unable to—in fact, was still trying to mass his scattered units at the Sakatonchee when Smith started retreating. The importance of Lee's remarks, however, lies in their perception that although the pursuit of Smith was spectacular, it certainly wasn't the crushing victory the pursuit and capture of Streight had been. The Smith chase did relieve Federal pressure on interior Mississippi, but it didn't destroy the force applying the pressure. That force was left able to apply it again.

In significant Confederate quarters, the Smith stampede apparently even escaped notice. Forrest's slippage from general view when he left Bragg's army is indicated by Richmond notations appended to a letter he wrote to President Davis over the heads of his superiors on February 5, regarding his new Cavalry Department of West Tennessee and North Mississippi. More than two weeks after his pursuit of Smith, an assistant adjutant general in the Richmond inspector general's office noted that Forrest's letter to Davis had been sent on to Bragg and that the "Cavalry Department of West Tennessee and North Mississippi is not known within this office." A week later, another notation from another assistant adjutant general, this time Bragg's, added: "An inspection of this command has been ordered."[3]

With Smith back in Memphis, Forrest located his troops in the eastern Mississippi towns of Columbus and Starkville and prepared for another advance into West Tennessee. In late February, he and Lee were called to Polk's headquarters at Demopolis, Alabama, where Forrest received further reason to go north. Polk informed him he was assigning to his command three small Kentucky regiments in need of horses. To command them, Polk also gave him Kentucky brigadier general Abraham Buford, a West Pointer and Mexican War hero who knew Bluegrass horseflesh and with whom Forrest probably was personally acquainted; between 1854 and 1862, Buford had raised racehorses at his plantation in Versailles, Kentucky. Not surprisingly, Forrest's plans now began to extend north of Tennessee.[4]

On this raid, he was ordered to take only a necessary portion of his command, leaving his artillery and wagon train "to be refitted" and the rest of his troops in position to protect northern Mississippi. Having just reorganized his men into two divisions, he was on the verge of heading northward when an ugly incident rocked his officer corps. On March 9 Forrest ordered the new First Division commander, Chalmers, to direct his two brigade commanders to prepare their troops to move — because that day he summarily relieved Chalmers himself from duty and told him to report to Polk for orders.[5]

A small and cultured man ten years his commander's junior, James Chalmers was a United States senator's son who had been born in south-central Virginia and educated at South Carolina College before practicing law in Holly Springs, his hometown since childhood. There he quickly became a community leader, a district attorney and fire-eating delegate to the secession convention in 1860. Promoted to brigadier general in early 1862, he seems to have stalled there, despite a reputation for competence and gallantry. After the war he would say that he was more attached to Bragg, his first brigade commander, "than any General under whom I served," so when Forrest stormily left Bragg and was given the North Mississippi command then held by Chalmers, the latter no doubt was doubly displeased.[6]

A flurry of communications concerning Forrest's relief of him proceeded quickly. "Write me the reasons for relieving the officers named in your dispatch of today," Polk wrote Forrest March 10, referring to Chalmers and Brigadier General R. V. Richardson, who had been brought up on charges by a subordinate. Polk soon got notes from both Forrest and Chalmers. Forrest said he had dismissed Chalmers from his duties because he was "satisfied that I have not and shall not receive the cooperation of Brigadier-General Chalmers, and that matters of the smallest moment will continue, as they have heretofore done, to be a source of annoyance to myself and detrimental to the service. . . ." Chalmers's communication dealt in specifics: "General Forrest took my only tent from me and gave it to his brother. I wrote him a letter which he considered disrespectful, and he has relieved me from my command and ordered me to report to you. . . ."[7]

The Chalmers affair apparently became as embarrassing for Forrest in the Confederate military hierarchy as it was unworthy of him. Polk wrote Richmond for a decision in the case, adding his own opinion that Forrest "has exceeded his authority. . . . Please answer." Confederate adjutant and inspector general Samuel Cooper replied briefly and emphatically: "General Forrest has no power to relieve an officer and order him to report in person to the department commander. The officer should remain with the command and be tried if amenable to charges." Polk's office then ordered Chalmers to "resume command of his division and report to Major General N. B. Forrest. . . ." Forrest at that point seems to have dropped the charge.[8]

Chalmers rejoined his unit and gradually moved it northward to Jackson, Tennessee, a 150-mile trek through land "laid waste . . . by the enemy and by roving bands of deserters and tories." Particularly was this so between Tupelo, Mississippi, and Purdy, Tennessee, the hometown of Colonel Fielding Hurst of the Sixth Tennessee Cavalry (U.S.). Familially rooted in the Unionist eastern section of the state, Hurst was a vengeful partisan in his mid-fifties who is reputed once to have torched a church and then watched it burn while praying and singing. Forrest reported to Polk on March 21 that Hurst "and his regiment of renegade Tennesseans" repeatedly had been reported as perpetrators of "wanton destruction of property," and that a month earlier Hurst, by threatening to burn Jackson, had extorted $5,139.25 from its residents; the sum, Forrest charged, was to be used to pay damages brought against Hurst by a female Jackson resident and adjudged payable by Memphis Federal authorities. Forrest wrote those same authorities on March 22, complaining that "within the past two months seven cases of deliberate murder have been committed in this department, most of them known and all believed to have been perpetrated by the command of Colonel Hurst." To be more specific, he enclosed findings by a Confederate investigative officer that included two McNairy County–connected murders of Forrest troopers recruiting behind enemy lines, a couple of similar killings in other western Tennessee counties, and the following graphic evidence of just how brutal the guerrilla war in West Tennessee had become:

> *Lieut. Willis Dodds . . . collecting his command, was arrested at the home of his father in Henderson County, Tenn., on or about the 9th of March, 1864 . . . and put to death by torture. Private Silas Hodges, a scout . . . states that he saw the body of Lieutenant Dodds very soon after his murder, and that it was most horribly mutilated, the face having been skinned, the nose cut off, the under jaw disjointed, the privates cut off, and the body otherwise barbarously lacerated and most wantonly injured, and that his death was brought about by the most inhuman process of torture.*[9]

One of Forrest's reasons for returning to Tennessee was to round up more of its residents who had deserted Confederate ranks or managed to avoid service in them altogether. Confederate recruiters now had to be especially forceful; with the odds of victory looking longer and longer, some West Tennessee Confederates were changing sides, becoming so-called "homemade Yankees," while others were just staying home to help their families cope with a famine now spreading over this area so often visited by armies of both sides. Accompanied now by fugitive governor Harris, Forrest announced on March 22 "to whom it may concern" that because of alleged "outrages" and Federal refusal of Confederate demands for redress, he was declaring "Fielding Hurst, and the officers and men of his command, outlaws, and not entitled to be treated as prisoners of war falling into the hands of the forces of the Confederate States." To Federal commanders, he also complained he had learned "that many citizens of this portion of the State are now held in confinement by the U.S. authorities" despite having no charge lodged against them; one such detainee, he said, was "the Rev. G.W.D. Harris of Dyer County, Tennessee, now in confinement at Fort Pillow."[10]

There now was yet another complication of the Tennessee military situation, this one explosively sociological. Union commanders, followed by throngs of overjoyed slaves on every incursion they made into the Deep South, had been authorized to put this human ex-property to use by giving it arms with which to seal its freedom. Most Southerners regarded this as insanity, incitement of the Armageddon of slave insurrection they had been taught to fear all their lives. On May 1, 1863, the Confederate Congress enacted an official policy of returning captured slaves to their owners — and of putting to death white officers and noncoms of the new black units.

Less than three months before Forrest began his move northward, however, hard-fighting Major General Patrick Cleburne—born in Ireland and having become a Southerner only well into adulthood—had proposed giving slaves arms and freedom in return for service in Confederate uniforms. Cleburne predicted that so doing would rob the North of not only its numerical superiority but also the political advantage in which it was masquerading as humane, while actually using the slavery issue as "merely the pretense to establish sectional superiority and a more centralized form of government, and to deprive us of our rights and liberties." Jefferson Davis quickly scotched any public discussion of Cleburne's proposal, "[d]eeming it . . . injurious to the public service that such a subject should be mooted, or even known to be entertained by persons possessed of the confidence and respect of the people." Brigadier General James Patton Anderson, once a boarder in Forrest's home at Hernando, confidentially wrote Polk about this "monstrous proposition . . . so revolting to Southern sentiment, Southern pride, and Southern honor. . . . If this thing is openly proposed to the Army the total disintegration of that Army will follow in a fortnight."[11]

Prospects of large-scale collision between the armed ex-slaves and soldiers of the slaveholder government grew more imminent. Into the teeth of these prospects—and no doubt conscious of agitation over an approaching U.S. election to determine whether the embattled Lincoln would be replaced by a Democrat inclined to reconcile with the South— Forrest and his separated units moved north toward Kentucky in the spring of 1864. Fielding Hurst and other bitter enemies had been ordered to dog their heels, "cut[ting] off and captur[ing] . . . foraging parties, stragglers, etc." On March 24, the day this order was issued to Hurst, the northwestern Tennessee hamlet of Union City and 475 Federals fell to 320 Forrest troopers under Colonel W. L. Duckworth.[12]

A physician and Methodist minister, Duckworth expertly played the role of his commander, sending in over Forrest's name a typical surrender-or-else ultimatum to Union colonel Isaac Hawkins; this followed hours of Forrest-like maneuvering in which horse holders cheered the arrival of apparent reinforcements, who then galloped into Federal view for a long look at the highly adequate Union fortifications. When Hawkins—who had surrendered to Forrest once before, in December 1862—demanded to meet his old adversary face-to-face, Duckworth quickly returned another forged Forrest note saying he wasn't accustomed to meeting lesser officers in such circumstances—but that he would send Duckworth, "who is your equal in rank." After a five-minute deliberation, Hawkins returned a note of surrender.[13]

By then the real Forrest, with most of the rest of the 2,000 men of Buford's Division, was on his way northward to Paducah, Kentucky. On the evening of March 25, his force pushed Paducah's defenders into an earthwork at the town's western edge, near the Ohio River. There followed an attack that seems to have lasted several hours as Forrest's men took possession of the town and availed themselves of "a large amount of clothing, several hundred horses, [and] a large lot of medical stores for the command, burning a steamer, the dock, and all cotton on the landing." These prizes weren't without cost. Colonel A. P. Thompson, a lawyer to whom Paducah was home, assaulted the fort with the Third and Seventh Kentucky and was bloodily repulsed, Thompson himself sustaining a mortal wound from a shell possibly fired by one of two Federal gunboats participating. Before Thompson's death, Forrest presented Federal colonel Stephen Hicks one of his characteristic demands for surrender, informing Hicks that he was accompanied by "a force amply sufficient to carry your works and reduce the place, and in order to avoid the unnecessary effusion of blood, I demand the surrender of the fort and troops, with all public property. If you surrender, you shall be treated as prisoners of war, but if I have to storm your works, you may expect no quarter."[14]

Hicks spurned the demand. He recalled a few days later that during a truce for the presentation and answer of Forrest's message, Confederate troops "were engaged in taking position and planting a battery." Union newspapers soon charged not only that Forrest had used a flag of truce to gain advantage but even that some of his men had placed five female nurses from a local hospital in front of themselves to discourage Federal fire while taking positions during the truce. According to Hicks's and another Union report, the battle raged in varying proportions, with Confederates making three charges and then continuing to keep the fort under fire from nearby town buildings until 11:30 P.M. Forrest, by contrast, reported only that the Confederates "held the town for ten hours" and "[c]ould have held the place longer," but "found the smallpox was raging and evacuated the place."[15]

That the attack wasn't made by Forrest's whole force, as later Confederate accounts maintained, is supported by a proclamation Buford issued three days later at Mayfield, Kentucky, congratulating his troops on "the valor your skirmishers displayed in their attack upon the fort at Paducah. . . . With a force less than that of the enemy within the stockade, you in an exposed situation, with your skirmishers, silenced his guns, caused one of the gunboats to withdraw from the action . . . captured and destroyed immense stores, quartermaster's commissary, and ordnance, and inflicted upon him a loss of 27 killed and 70 to 80 wounded besides capturing 64 prisoners, your own loss being 10 killed and 40 wounded." The order also mentioned that these Kentucky Confederates had made a significant contribution toward rescuing their native state "from the iron heels of abolition, despotism, and the rule of the negro."[16]

Here, apparently for the first significant time, Forrest's men fought black troops: 274 men of the First Kentucky Heavy Artillery (Colored), comprising more than a third of the 665 Union soldiers within the fort. The blacks apparently made their presence felt. "[P]ermit me to remark that I have been one of those men who never had much confidence in colored troops fighting," Hicks, a Mexican War veteran, informed superiors toward the end of his account, "but those doubts are now all removed, for they fought as bravely as any troops in the fort." It doubtless was galling to the Confederates to be repulsed by such a force after demanding surrender.[17]

Up to now, Confederates in the West seem to have regarded black soldiery, which the Federals had begun to institute nearly two years before, as something between cold-blooded incitement toward wholesale murder and a diabolical joke. Although the Richmond government branded black soldiers escaped slaves who should be returned to their former masters, where they faced an unpleasant fate at best, there also were other avenues open to their captors. James M. Williams, one of Forrest's fellow Memphians, headed a party of seven scouts which surprised and captured some black Federals in camp near Memphis in May 1863. Spiriting them away behind Confederate lines to Meridian, Mississippi, they there were approached by "[a] Negro trader, from Montgomery, Ala.," who "proposed to buy the twenty-four negroes. . . . [T]he neat little sum of $36,000 in cool cash [good Confederate bills] was counted out to the boys . . . ," recalls a postbellum account. It adds that Williams reputedly "lived in royal style the balance of the war. . . . His mess was the best in the camp, the menu the best that could be had. He still has a lot of that nigger money on hand, which he keeps as a souvenir of the happy days of long ago."[18]

By this time, Sherman—amassing supplies at Nashville for his impending campaign to split the Southeast, driving through Georgia to the sea—was getting nervous, and with reason: Forrest had discerned what he was up to. Indulging in what seems to have been a developing penchant for circumventing the chain of command, Forrest wrote Joseph Johnston in Georgia that he believed "everything available is being concentrated against General [Robert E.] Lee [in Virginia] and yourself. Am also of the opinion that if all the cavalry of this and your own department could be moved against Nashville that the enemy's communications could be utterly broken up."[19]

Meanwhile, Forrest continued with his original plan. At Mayfield, Buford furloughed his Kentucky commands to return to their homes, get clothing and horses, recruit fellow Kentuckians, then return to West Tennessee for the raid's next phase. On April 3 his troops entered Trenton, Tennessee, where Bell's brigade of Tennesseans was similarly re-equipping itself. By this time the Thirteenth Tennessee Cavalry of Chalmers's division, moving northward out of Mississippi at Forrest's direction, had "whipped" the hated Hurst near Bolivar and killed and wounded "a great many" of Hurst's Sixth Tennessee Cavalry (U.S.), according to a Federal account; according to Chalmers's, the Thirteenth Tennessee "drove Hurst hatless into Memphis, leaving in our hands all his wagons, ambulances, papers, and his mistresses, both black and white."[20]

By now, the Confederates were beginning to read in Union newspapers — no doubt with chagrin — excited accounts of their "defeat" at Paducah. The Louisville *Journal* reported that the "rebels" had been "in large force," "gloriously drunk, and but little better than a mob" which, with "wild cheers and blasphemous oaths . . . thronged the streets and commenced an indiscriminate pillage of the houses." When Forrest finally "succeeded in rallying [t]his force and, forming the regiments in battle line," the *Journal* said, "several desperate charges were made upon the fort. The Federals met them with a withering fire, and in each onset the rebel columns were broken and driven back in confusion."[21]

From Cairo, Illinois, a Chicago *Tribune* account reported that an initial Confederate charge had preceded the presentation of Forrest's demand for surrender. After its rejection, the *Tribune* went on, the Confederates "now formed anew, made an attack, and were again repulsed: made a third effort and were repulsed the third time. They now broke up established lines, and occupied buildings in swarms . . . but were steadily held back from advance." A *Tribune* correspondent at Paducah reported that Colonel Thompson had fallen in the second charge, felled by a "musket-ball" in the forehead, "and whilst falling, a cannon-ball struck him on the body, mangling and exposing his person in a dreadful manner." The account in the emancipationist *Tribune* continued: "The rebels were repulsed at each assault, and about 9 o'clock P.M. skedaddled, after killing as many negroes as they could, which seems to have been their primary object in coming to Paducah." Some of the Northern press, Forrest's authorized biographers would complain three years later, even made the unsupported assertion that the musket ball that struck Thompson in the forehead was fired by a black soldier.[22]

That the Confederates read such accounts and were stung by them is indicated by the fact that in early April Buford reported to Forrest having seen "in a Northern newspaper" a report that horses the Confederates captured at Paducah had belonged to the Southern-sympathizing townspeople, whereas about 140 U.S. military animals had been safely secreted in an old foundry in the city's outskirts. Buford asked permission to take his Kentucky brigade back to Paducah to get these others, and Forrest so ordered—partly, no doubt, because he wanted just such a force to divert Federal attention from another operation he was planning. Four days before Buford and his Kentuckians galloped away on their second Paducah raid in less than three weeks, Forrest wrote Polk on April 4 that he was holding all of Kentucky and Tennessee lying between the Mississippi and Tennessee rivers, that he would appreciate having Morton's Artillery sent him from Mississippi to facilitate "destruction or capture of boats," and that he planned to attack at least one fort on the Mississippi: "There is a Federal force of 500 or 600 at Fort Pillow, which I shall attend to in a day or two, as they have horses and supplies which we need."[23]

At Jackson, Forrest apparently had been visited by a "delegation" of West Tennesseans who "earnestly besought him to leave [in West Tennessee] a brigade for their protection against" the "nest of outlaws" at Fort Pillow. Many of the members of the Thirteenth West Tennessee Cavalry (U.S.), headquartered there under the command of Major William F. Bradford, reputedly had deserted Confederate ranks—"and the rest were men of the country who entertained a malignant hatred toward Confederate soldiers, their families and friends." Bradford, a West Tennessee attorney born in Forrest's native Bedford County, was particularly unpopular. He had, "[u]nder the pretense of scouring the country for arms and 'rebel soldiers,' . . . traversed the surrounding country with detachments, robbing the people of their horses, mules, beef cattle, beds, plate, wearing apparel, money, and every possible movable article of value, besides venting upon the wives and daughters of Southern soldiers the most opprobrious and obscene epithets, with more than one extreme outrage upon the persons of these victims of their hate and lust. . . . [M]any of his [Forrest's] officers, uniting with the citizens of the country in the petition, begged to be permitted to remain, to shield their families from further molestation."[24]

If he planned to continue using West Tennessee as a source of Confederate recruits, conscripts, and supplies, Forrest had to neutralize the influence of Fort Pillow. His scouts knew virtually everything about the place; if they were aware that "500 or 600" troops were there (580 exactly), they must also have known that about half of these (292) were black, sent north from Memphis. The black soldiers seem to have been dispatched as an offhand safeguard in response to Forrest's moves; Federal general Hurlbut, commanding in Memphis, informed their commander, Major Lionel F. Booth, that "I think Forrest's check at Paducah will not dispose him to try the river again, but that he will fall back to Jackson and thence cross the Tennessee; as soon as this is ascertained I shall withdraw your garrison." Hurlbut also told Booth, a Regular Army officer, that he was to take command of the fort from Bradford, "whom you will find a good officer, though not of much experience."[25]

To deal with Booth and Bradford, Forrest chose Chalmers. At Forrest's order, Chalmers had moved north from Panola, Mississippi, at the end of March to conduct southward 600 prisoners already harvested by the West Tennessee–Kentucky campaign. Chalmers's forces remained in West Tennessee, Neely's brigade divided between Brownsville and Somerville, while McCulloch's was posted at Jackson. When, on April 10, Forrest ordered the attack on Fort Pillow, Chalmers directed Neely to move southward from Whiteville, Tennessee, spreading reports that he was leading Forrest's whole command in an attack on Memphis. Afterward, if unpursued by Federals, he was to conduct a conscription that can hardly have been less rigorous than Federal ones, deploying "your command in every direction with orders to arrest and bring to you at Brownsville all men between the ages of eighteen and forty-five years, and all officers and soldiers absent from their commands without proper authority"; he also was to "send out proper officers to impress horses to mount your dismounted men. . . ." Chalmers sent similar instructions to Colonel John McGuirk's regiment of state cavalry at Holly Springs, ordering him to advance on Memphis from that direction and convey the impression that "Major-General Lee was advancing from the south. . . ."[26]

Chalmers himself took command of a patchwork division composed of McCulloch's brigade from his own command and Bell's from Buford's, then dispatched this force from Jackson and Brownsville toward Fort Pillow. At Brownsville at 2 P.M. on April 11, Chalmers was overtaken by

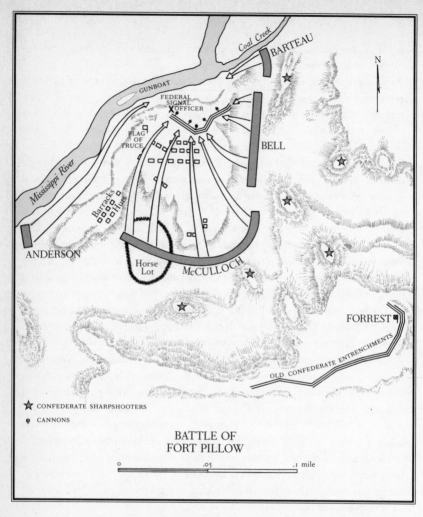

**BATTLE OF
FORT PILLOW**

CONFEDERATE SHARPSHOOTERS

CANNONS

0   .05   .1 mile

'THERE ARE NOT MANY—WE MUST TAKE THEM'—Atop a bluff more than 300 precipitous feet high, protected by gorges across its front, Fort Pillow and its 580 black and white Federals are surprise-attacked by 1,500 Forrest troopers. McCulloch works his way northward past the horse lot while Bell presses from the east, and detachments under Barteau and Anderson go to waterside to fend off Federal gunboats. Following the Union garrison's refusal to surrender, these detachments enfilade Federals fleeing down the bluff in the aftermath of the Confederate charge. The gunboat *New Era*, whose captain had agreed to aid the Federals with canister, steams away at the decisive moment.

Forrest and ordered to move by forced march to reach Fort Pillow as early as possible the next day. Chalmers complied impressively, riding thirty-eight miles in a soaking rain. His lead elements under McCulloch reached their destination before dawn and captured most of the fort's pickets. Succeeding units went on to invest the fort, and, at daylight, the Confederates attacked.

Fort Pillow, located beside a hamlet and a stretch of the Mississippi River channel narrow enough to be commanded by musket shot, was constructed in 1862 by Gideon Pillow, but it turned out to be too large for full use by most forces later stationed there, Confederate or Union. It possessed three lines of fortifications: long parapets 600 and 300 yards in front of, and ringing three sides of, a small core facility. This central stronghold, containing not only Federal troops but also several dozen Union-sympathizing civilians of both races and sexes, was situated on a bluff that fell sharply away to the river. It wasn't impregnable, though. Federal troops on the morning of April 12 abandoned the second of the two lines of outer parapets and fell back first onto a commanding ridge, then to a shorter line of just-dug trenches protecting three rows of barrack huts occupied by Union cavalrymen. McCulloch's men and other arriving Confederates gradually gained possession of points within the exterior fortifications that stood higher than the walls of the central fort, excellent sites for sharpshooters. Before long, 300 or so yards in front of the barrack huts, McCulloch's troops had advanced under cover of a ravine and were threatening the pens of Federal horses Forrest had come after. First Sergeant Henry F. Weaver of Company C, Sixth U.S. Heavy Artillery (Colored), commanding a battery at the south end of the fort just after dawn, reported that he "was firing at the advancing enemy as they came in sight." Meanwhile Company B, Thirteenth Tennessee Cavalry, had left its camp "on a hill in front of our main fort and came rushing back in disorder, leaving their horses and all their camp equipage behind. The rebels soon commenced running off the horses. . . ."[27]

McCulloch's men advanced from the south, under orders to get as close to both the river and the core fortress as possible, while Bell's brigade employed Forrest's favorite tactic of simultaneously swinging around to come in from the side and rear: that is, the east and northeast toward where swollen Coal (or Cold, as it is now usually spelled) Creek flowed into the Mississippi some fifty yards north of the fort. The northern end of the facility was "understood [by the Confederates] to be very weak and vulnerable," but "it was found impracticable to reach the river along Coal

Creek, and a new plan of attack had to be arranged." This was the situation about midmorning, when Forrest, having ridden seventy-two miles in twenty-seven hours, reached the field—and when, coincidentally, Federal major Booth, walking near one of the fort's battery ports encouraging his garrison, was struck in the chest and killed by a Confederate bullet. Knowing nothing of Booth's death, Forrest ordered more Confederate sharpshooting from any cover that could be found. Then he began a personal reconnaissance so intensive that a horse was killed beneath him, the first of two that day; this one died so frantically that it reared and fell onto its rider, badly bruising him. Federal fire became so heavy that Captain Charles W. Anderson, acting adjutant general, suggested that Forrest dismount and make the rest of his reconnaissance afoot. He replied no, that he was "just as apt to be hit one way as another, and . . . could see better" on horseback.[28]

His close inspection of the field, which required more than an hour, was productive. He discovered on the north side, within seventy-five yards of the fort's walls, another ravine like that protecting McCulloch's men to the south; the northern one ran almost parallel to the walls. While awaiting the belated arrival on the field of his ammunition wagons, which had been unable to keep up with his forced march overnight, he sent one of Bell's units, Colonel C. R. Barteau's Second Tennessee, on a difficult trek around Coal Creek's bluffs into this northern ravine. Sergeant R. R. Hancock later recalled being near Forrest momentarily, and that the general was intent on doing more than just the horse capturing and plundering he had done at Paducah; as he passed Hancock's position, he was overheard to say: "There are not many—we must take them."[29]

When he got Barteau's men into the ravine and more sharpshooters into commanding positions, Forrest began moving the rest of Bell's men toward the same protected position, covering the advance with the sharpshooters' fire. While Bell was advancing, so was McCulloch on the other end of the Confederate semicircle. Before retreating Federals could set fire to more than one line of the barrack huts, McCulloch was into these and the newly dug rifle pits, chasing out their occupants and setting up a galling small-arms fire. The deep ravines the Confederates had infiltrated on the south, east, and north kept the Federal artillery from getting at them. By midafternoon, all these positions had been reached, and Forrest suddenly sent forward a flag of truce with a message somewhat different from most others he had used in previous situations. Whereas at Paducah he may not have known he faced black troops at the time he offered to

treat them the same as white Federals, he made the same offer this time
with that knowledge:

> *HEADQUARTERS, FORREST'S CAVALRY,*
> *Before Fort Pillow, April 12, 1864.*

Major Booth, Commanding United States Forces, Fort Pillow:
*   Major,— The conduct of the officers and men garrisoning Fort
Pillow has been such as to entitle them to being treated as prisoners
of war. I demand the unconditional surrender of this garrison, pro-
mising you that you shall be treated as prisoners of war. My men
have received a fresh supply of ammunition, and from their present
position can easily assault and capture the fort. Should my demand
be refused, I cannot be responsible for the fate of your command.
Respectfully,

> *N.B. Forrest,*
> *Major-General Commanding.*[30]

Captain W. A. Goodman, Chalmers's adjutant general and bearer of the
note, said later he clearly remembered the offer to treat the entire garrison
as prisoners of war "because, when the note was handed to me, there was
some discussion about it among the officers present, and it was asked
whether it was intended to include the negro soldiers as well as the white;
to which both General Forrest and General Chalmers replied, that it was
so intended."[31]

As the flag of truce went forward, Forrest noticed Federal steamers
ascending the river. One of them, the *Olive Branch*, was crowded with
blue-uniformed troops and artillery apparently heading for Fort Pillow.
To keep reinforcements from landing, he sent Anderson with three companies of McCulloch's men down through the little riverside town and into
old Confederate trenches at the base of the bluff, where they waited
beneath the southern end of the surrounded fort. At the same time, he
moved forward some of Barteau's men on the north side of the fort for
the same purpose. Later, many Federal eyewitness accounts would swear
Forrest illegally used the truce to improve his men's position, but if he
did—and the new positions the Anderson and Barteau detachments took
did prove critical later—he was only protecting himself by responding to
what appeared to be another incipient violation. The Federal steamer,
however, got no signal from the fort and passed on by, eventually to dock
at Cairo, Illinois.[32]

Above Anderson on the bluff, the fort's reply to Forrest's demand eventually came. With Major Booth's name forged at the bottom, it requested an hour for Booth to consult with his officers and those of a gunboat, the *New Era*, standing offshore. Forrest, several hundred yards south of the truce party on the bluff, assumed the Union commander was stalling for time to receive reinforcements from the several boats then in sight on the river. He quickly replied in writing that he demanded only the capitulation of the fort, not the gunboat, and that he would allow twenty minutes for a decision. A Federal officer in the truce party suggested that Forrest might not be on the field, that his name again was being used as it had been by Duckworth to induce the Federal surrender at Union City. When word of this reached Forrest, along with speculation that proof to the contrary might influence the Federal decision, he rode forward and was introduced to Federal Captain John T. Young of the Twenty-fourth Missouri Cavalry and another man who knew him by sight.

> *At the same time . . . the parapets of the fort were thronging with negro soldiers, intently watching the course of events, and some of whom were heard also to say, it was useless to deny that General Forrest was before them, for they "knew him too well for that." And so close meanwhile were the Confederate lines, that the white men of both sides were bantering each other from their respective positions, while some of the negroes indulged in provoking, impudent jeers.*[33]

A Confederate sergeant in the Twentieth Tennessee said the Federals "threaten[ed] . . . that if we charged their breast works to show no quarter," while a Confederate news correspondent reported them to say "with an air of insulting defiance that he [Forrest] could not take the place, and that they asked for no quarter." About then, the *Olive Branch* reached a point in the river directly opposite the fort, which Captain Goodman pointed out to Forrest. "She won't land," Forrest replied, knowing his instructions to Anderson. After two or three shots across her bow by Anderson's men, which the Union officer commanding the *Olive Branch* construed as coming from "some stragglers or guerrillas," she moved on upriver. The *Olive Branch* commander later reported having been instructed by an officer from the *New Era* that "he did not want any boat to stop; [he] ordered us to go on to Cairo." The reason the *New Era* asked for no assistance may have been that its captain felt he had the situation in hand; he later reported he had an arrangement with Bradford. They had "agreed on a signal that if they had to leave the fort they would drop down under the bank, and I was to give the rebels canister."[34]

On the bluff, Bradford's answer, again signed "Booth," was returned penciled on a plain scrap of dirty paper: "Your demand does not produce the desired effect." Forrest read it quizzically. "This will not do," he protested. "Send it back, and say to Major Booth that I must have an answer in plain English. Yes or No." As this message was sent in, the "menacing" manner of black soldiers along the fort's parapets prompted Confederate subordinates to prevail on Forrest to move to the rear again. A few minutes later, Goodman brought him an unequivocal answer: "General: I will not surrender. Very respectfully, your obedient servant, L.F. Booth, Commanding U.S. Forces, Fort Pillow."[35]

Forrest now surely felt left with no choice. "We must take them," Sergeant Hancock had heard him say; the reasons why were obvious. Not only did he need to neutralize Fort Pillow to retain his influence in West Tennessee; his previously feared give-up-or-die ultimatum had been flouted at Paducah and his attackers driven off — if it happened again, all such subsequent demands were likely to be snubbed. Almost as soon as he received word that he had been spurned again this time, he ordered a general charge, meanwhile directing Anderson beneath the bluff to "hold the position against anything that might come by land or water" and sending brigade commanders Bell and McCulloch the message that he would "watch with interest the conduct of the troops; that Missourians, Mississippians and Tennesseans surrounded the works, and I desired to see who would first scale the fort."[36]

Less than a half hour later, he again would come within Hancock's hearing, this time to say: "When from my position on that hill I saw my men pouring over these breastworks, it seemed that my heart would burst within me." Although he later contended that any course besides capitulation was useless, the Federals had stymied them for six hours and remained behind walls four feet thick and eight feet high and a ditch six feet deep and twelve feet wide. Now, however, his sharpshooters had them pinned down, and, at the first notes of the bugle, his troops howled the rebel yell, charged into the ditch, boosted each other up over the wall, and leaped among their aghast foes. Lieutenant Mack Leaming of the Thirteenth Tennessee (U.S.) said the Confederates seemed to "ris[e] . . . from out the very earth on the center and north side, within twenty yards of our works." They received the first Union volley, "wavered, rallied again and finally succeeded in breaking our lines. . . ." First Sergeant Wilbur Gaylord of the Sixth U.S. Heavy Artillery (Colored) would recall afterward that he "was wounded with a musket-ball through the right ankle" as the Confederates were coming over the wall. He estimated that some

200 "passed over the works . . . by me while I lay there." One Confederate noticed that Gaylord was alive "and shot at me again and missed me. I told him I was wounded and that I would surrender, when a Texas Ranger stepped up and took me prisoner." At that moment he "saw them shoot down 3 black men who were begging for their lives, and who had surrendered."[37]

When the Confederates came over the wall, Private John Kennedy, a member of the Second U.S. Colored Light Artillery, "heard Major Bradford give the command, 'Boys, save your lives.' " Kennedy said Lieutenant Bischoff of the Sixth Heavy Artillery protested to Bradford, " 'Do not let the men leave their pieces; let us fight yet'; but the major, turning around and seeing the rebels coming in from all sides, said, 'It is of no use anymore'; whereupon the men left their pieces and tried to escape in different directions and manners." Corporal William Dickey of the Thirteenth Tennessee said the Confederates "had no sooner obtained the top of our walls when the negroes ran, and the whites, obtaining no quarter, ran after them. The rebels followed closely, shooting down all who came in the way, white and black."[38]

Daniel Stamps of the Thirteenth Tennessee's Company E, long since sent under the bluff as a sharpshooter to oppose the Confederate drive down Coal Creek, later remembered that "when the negroes had given way on the left, I saw them run out of the fort down the bluff close to my vicinity."

> Then I saw the white soldiers coming down after them, saying the rebels were showing no quarter. I then threw down my gun and ran down with them, closely pursued by the enemy shooting down every man black and white. They said they had orders from Forrest to "kill the last God damn one of them." While I was standing at the bottom of the hill I heard a rebel officer shout out an order of some kind to the men who had taken us, and saw a rebel soldier standing by me. I asked him what the officer had said. He repeated it to me again. It was, "kill the last damn one of them." The soldier replied to his officer that we had surrendered; that we were prisoners. . . . The officer replied, seeming crazy with rage that he had not been obeyed, "I tell you to kill the last God damned one of them." He then turned and galloped off. . . . I saw 2 [white?] men shot down while I was under the bluff. They had their hands up; had surrendered, and were begging for mercy. I also . . . saw at least 25

negroes shot down, within 10 or 20 paces from the place where I stood. They had also surrendered, and were begging for mercy.[39]

"The slaughter was awful," Sergeant Achilles V. Clark of the Confederate Twentieth Tennessee wrote his sisters a week later.

The poor deluded negroes would run up to our men fall upon their knees and with uplifted hands scream for mercy but they were ordered to their feet and then shot down. The white men fared but little better. Their fort turned out to be a great slaughter pen. Blood, human blood stood about in pools and brains could have been gathered up in any quantity. I with several others tried to stop the butchery and at one time had partially succeeded but Gen. Forrest ordered them shot down like dogs, and the carnage continued.[40]

It was worst under the bluff. Those who fled there, and managed to pass alive between the flanking fire of the Anderson and Barteau detachments, received no help from the gunboat. The *New Era* reportedly fired at least 260 rounds at the Confederates during earlier stages of the battle, but then, its log says, the fort's flag came down "and an indiscriminate massacre was commenced on our Troops, the enemy firing volley after volley into them while [they were] unable to resist, at the same time turning their fire on us[;] the enemy being in overwhelming force we proceeded up the river."[41]

Along the banks the pursued dived into the Mississippi trying to reach refuge in nearby barges, one to the north that had carried some women and children to safety above Coal Creek in the early morning and a beached coal carrier on the southern end of the riverbank. Three weeks after the battle, a Confederate newspaper correspondent recalled that "several hundred" were shot on the barge and in Coal Creek. He said the river was so full of Federals that "they resembled a drove of hogs swimming across the stream." None, he added, escaped, their heads presenting "beautiful" targets. "The Mississippi River was crimsoned with the red blood of the flying foe. Our soldiers grew sick and weary in the work of slaughter, and were glad when the work was done."[42]

A significant number of Confederates were horrified. Several Federals who survived recalled instances of being protected by their individual captors. Lieutenant Mack Leaming, for instance, reported being spared because he was a Mason and happened to be taken by a fellow member of the order. Nevertheless, out of the 580-man garrison, 66 percent of the blacks and 35 percent of the whites were killed. Most of these casualties seem to have occurred during the melee immediately after the Confederates entered the walls, but not all. One of the dead whites was Major Bradford, the Federal commander, who was killed a day or so later while in Confederate custody—trying to escape, Forrest reported he was told when he learned of it more than a week after the fact; assassinated, said a Union sympathizer claiming to be an eyewitness.[43]

It had been just twenty minutes from the sounding of the charge until a Confederate pulled down the fort's Union flag and Forrest ordered a cease-fire; Confederate partisans later would make much of that, saying the butchery was so great because the fort hadn't been surrendered, but Federals running for their lives had little time to concern themselves with a flag. Soon after the cease-fire was ordered, Hancock recalled being inside the fort and hearing Forrest make a short speech that appeared brashly jubilant. After describing how his heart had "swelled" as they scaled the walls, he added:

> Men, if you will do as I say I will always lead you to victory. I have taken every place that the Federals occupied in West Tennessee and North Mississippi except Memphis, and if they don't mind I'll have that place too in less than six weeks.[44]

Even after the Union colors were struck, the horror continued. Surviving Federals claimed the killing went on sporadically into the next day as Confederates burned the place and supervised the burying of dead. Some men were buried alive, Federals charged, and a Confederate participant later seemed to substantiate this at least partially in a jocular newspaper column; he said Southerners at Fort Pillow had to bury some Federals alive to accomplish a "resurrection" of those playing dead.[45]

Before nightfall of the day of the battle, Forrest, exhausted "by hard riding and bruises received" in his fall from the dying horse, started back toward Brownsville, leaving Chalmers in charge of mopping up. Early the next morning, U.S. Navy acting master William Ferguson shelled Confederate pickets out of his way and landed the steamer *Silver Cloud* below the bluff, taking aboard some twenty Union soldiers who had managed to hide along the bank. About 8 A.M., under a flag of truce, the Confederates proposed that the Federals come ashore to remove wounded and assist in burials. Ferguson agreed and soon saw a scene he would long remember, finding "about 70 wounded men in the fort and around it, and buried, I should think, 150 bodies."

*All the buildings around the fort and the tents and huts in the
fort had been burned by the rebels and among the embers the charred
remains of numbers of our soldiers . . . could be seen. . . . Bodies
with gaping wounds, some bayoneted through the eyes, some with
skulls beaten through, others with hideous wounds as if their bowels
had been ripped open with bowie-knives, plainly told that but little
quarter was shown to our troops. Strewn from the fort to the river
bank, in the ravines and hollows, behind logs and under the brush
where they had crept for protection from the assassins who pursued
them, we found bodies bayoneted, beaten, and shot to death, showing
how cold-blooded and persistent was the slaughter. . . .*[46]

During the truce, Chalmers invited Captain John G. Woodruff of the
113th Illinois Infantry and other Federal officers to visit the fort. Woodruff said the Federal party "saw the dead bodies of 15 negroes, most of
them having been shot through the head."

*Some of them were burned as if by powder around the holes in
their heads, which led me to conclude that they were shot at very
close range. One of the gun-boat officers who accompanied us asked
General Chalmers if most of the negroes were not killed after they
[the enemy] had taken possession. Chalmers replied that he thought
they had been, and that the men of General Forrest's command had
such a hatred for the armed negro that they could not be restrained
from killing the negroes after they had captured them. He said they
were not killed by General Forrest's or his orders, . . . that both
Forrest and he stopped the massacre as soon as they were able to do
so. He said it was nothing better than we could expect as long as we
persisted in arming the negro.*[47]

Forrest himself adopted a similar tone in his own reports of the battle.
Filed three days later, one said he "hoped" the battle's outcome would
"demonstrate to the Northern people that negro soldiers cannot cope with
Southerners." It added a line he would paraphrase later, in another proud-
sounding speech to troops, referring to the large number of Federals killed
after they jumped into the Mississippi: "The river was dyed with the blood
of the slaughtered for 200 yards." That the battle's aftermath constituted
a massacre, which Confederates later disputed, was granted and even
proclaimed by Southern observers until an outcry erupted in the Northern
press. Forrest trooper W. R. Dyer laconically penciled in his pocket diary

for April 12: "We arrived at Ft. Pillow and attacked the same early in the day. The Fort was defended by about 450 blacks and 250 whites. We captured about 40 Blacks & 100 Whites and killed the remainder. We demollished the Place." The Memphis *Appeal,* then being published in Atlanta, ran front-page headlines April 18 that exulted in the "CAPTURE OF FORT PILLOW. General Slaughter of the Garrison"; it went on to report such details as: "One hundred prisoners were taken and the balance slain. The fort ran with blood."[48]

How much of the fault lay with Forrest himself? Whether he actually intended this time to carry out the no-quarter threat he had made so many times before, and whether he actually ordered his soldiers to do it, will likely never be learned for certain. Although there is the contemporary Confederate evidence from Sergeant Clark indicating he "ordered them shot down like dogs," there is also other contemporary evidence indicating just the opposite. Confederate Samuel H. Caldwell, who wrote his wife that the Fort Pillow battle "was decidedly the most horrible sight that I have ever witnessed," went on to add that "[t]hey refused to surrender—which incensed our men & if General Forrest had not run between our men and the Yanks with his pistol and sabre drawn not a man would have been spared." Federal Captain Young of the 24th Missouri Cavalry, captured during the battle, later was quoted by a Union naval officer as telling fellow Federals during the battle's aftermath that Forrest actually "shot one of his own command for refusing quarters [sic] to our men"; Young's veracity, though, may be open to question, as will be seen later.[49]

Nevertheless, one black soldier at Fort Pillow, Private Ellis Falls, soon would attest that Forrest ordered the Confederates to "stop fighting," and another Fort Pillow Federal, a Private Major Williams, would remember hearing a Confederate officer shout that the blacks should be killed and hearing another Confederate officer contradict him, saying Forrest had said the blacks should be captured and "returned to their masters." Forrest, though, plainly was in no very magnanimous mood—as, with the combat still raging, he could hardly be expected to be. One captured Federal, Charles Fitch, urgently requested Forrest's personal protection at the top of the bluff because of violence he had seen perpetrated against surrendering Federals down below. He identified himself as Fort Pillow's surgeon, to which he recalled Forrest retorting, "You are a surgeon of a damn nigger regiment." When Fitch said he wasn't, Forrest said, "You are a damn Tennessee Yankee then." When Fitch pronounced himself an Iowan, Forrest then said: "What in hell are you down here for? I have a great mind to have you killed for being down here." Luckily for Fitch,

Forrest resisted the impulse, instead commending the physician to a Confederate soldier with orders that he be kept safe.[50]

Can the same Forrest have "ordered them shot down like dogs" and have "run between our men and the Yanks with his pistol and sabre drawn," perhaps even shooting one of his own men? Possibly. His temper may have undergone one of its characteristic waxings and wanings. Angered by the taunts of the black soldiers and especially by the Union refusal to surrender, necessitating the paying of more precious Confederate lives for this victory he had to have, he may have ragingly ordered a massacre and even intended to carry it out—until he rode inside the fort and viewed the horrifying result. Then, begged for his protection, he was probably both vain enough to be flattered and sensitive enough to respond.

Even if Clark's assertion stemmed from a false assumption and Forrest ordered no massacre, he probably didn't have to; there was enough rancor between his men and the armed former slaves, as well as the Tennessee Unionists, that about all he had to do to produce a massacre was issue no order against one. This seems particularly true in view of the terms of his habitual demand that the enemy surrender or die.

Why did Chalmers invite Federal officers to tour the fort afterward if he and Forrest had not decided they wanted the Federals to see for themselves how "negro soldiers cannot cope with Southerners"? The question is driven further home by a sham surrender demand presented at Columbus, Kentucky, the day following the Fort Pillow battle. Buford, it will be remembered, had ridden back to Kentucky to get the Paducah garrison's horses after a council of war with Forrest and Chalmers at Jackson. That, in the wake of their earlier repulse, the three generals initially decided to promulgate a policy of selective extermination against black troops (in an effort to intimidate others and drive a wedge between them and their white Union counterparts) is suggested by the fact that on April 13, as Buford sent a small force to demonstrate vigorously at Columbus, covering the Paducah move, one of his staff officers carried to the Columbus garrison a flag of truce and a surrender demand offering to return "the negroes now in arms . . . to their masters. Should I, however, be compelled to take the place, no quarter will be shown to the negro troops whatever; the white troops will be treated as prisoners of war."[51]

That same day, Forrest was arriving at Jackson to find his brother Aaron, lieutenant colonel of a Mississippi cavalry regiment, dead of pneumonia contracted three weeks earlier during the first Paducah operation. If Aaron was the brother for whom Chalmers complained his tent had been commandeered by Forrest a few weeks before, at least the object of this high-handed act seems to have needed the tent. Maybe that realization had something to do with a sudden reversal in Chalmers's attitude toward his commander, at least publicly. On April 20 he issued a proclamation congratulating his troops on their "success in the brilliant campaign recently conducted in West Tennessee under the guidance of Major-General Forrest, whose star never shone brighter, and whose restless activity, untiring energy, and courage baffled the calculations and paralyzed the arms of our enemies."[52]

Forrest seems to have accepted this roundabout but effusive apparent apology. In an official report he filed from Jackson on April 26, he acknowledged the "prompt and energetic action of Brigadier-General Chalmers, commanding the forces around Fort Pillow. His faithful execution of all movements necessary to the successful accomplishment of the object of the expedition entitles him to special mention."[53]

20

A MAY 23 joint resolution of the Confederate Congress "cordially tendered" that body's gratitude to Forrest and his troops "for their late brilliant and successful campaign in Mississippi, West Tennessee and Kentucky—a campaign which has conferred upon its authors fame as enduring as the records of the struggle which they have so brilliantly illustrated."[1]

The Fort Pillow campaign's renown was certainly "enduring," but "fame" hardly described it. Union newspapers and periodicals already were making it notorious, a savage war's preeminent atrocity. Just six days after it, in a speech in Baltimore, Abraham Lincoln promised "retribution" if the "painful rumor" of a "massacre" at Fort Pillow proved true. Forrest quickly attained in the Northern public mind a status as repugnant as it was prominent. The Chicago *Tribune* published the following article attributed to the New York *Tribune*:

THE BUTCHER FORREST AND HIS FAMILY.
All of them Slave Drivers and Woman Whippers.

Knoxville, E[ast].T[enn]., April 18, 1864.
The news of the capture of Fort Pillow by Forrest, and the cowardly butchery which followed of blacks and whites alike, has produced a profound sensation here. The universal sentiment is "Let

no quarter be shown to these dastardly butchers of Forrest's command while the war lasts."

These Forrests, the oldest of whom, Gen. Bedford Forrest, has by this and other atrocities obtained such a record of infamy, were all negro traders. There were four brothers — Bedford, who kept a negro pen for five years before the war on Adams Street, in rear of the Episcopal Church, Memphis; John, a cripple and a gambler, who was jailor and clerk for Bedford; Bill Forrest, an extensive negro trader at Vicksburg; and Aaron Forrest, general agent and soul driver to scour the country for his older brothers. They accumulated large sums of money in their nefarious trade, and Bedford won by that and other influences a natural promotion to a Brigadier in the women-whipping, baby-stealing Rebel Confederacy. He is about 50 years of age, tall, gaunt and sallow-visaged, with a long nose, deep-set, black, snaky eyes, full black beard without a mustache, and hair worn long. He usually wore, while in the "nigger" trade in Memphis, a stovepipe hat set on the back of his head at an angle of forty-five degrees. He was accounted mean, vindictive, cruel and unscrupulous. He had two wives — one white, the other colored (Catharine), by each of which he had two children. His "patriarchal" wife, Catharine, and his white wife had frequent quarrels or domestic jars.

The slave pen of old Bedford Forrest, on Adams street, was a perfect horror to all negroes far and near. His mode of punishing refractory slaves was to compel four of his fellow slaves to stand and hold the victim stretched out in the air, and then Bedford and his brother John would stand, one on each side, with long, heavy bull whips, and cut up their victims until the blood trickled to the ground. Women were often stripped naked, and with a bucket of salt water standing by, in which to dip the instrument of torture, a heavy leather thong, their backs were cut up until the blisters covered the whole surface, the blood of their wounds mingling with the briny mixture to add torment to the infliction. One slave man was whipped to death by Bedford, who used a trace-chain doubled for the purpose of punishment. The slave was secretly buried, and the circumstance was known only to the slaves of the prison, who only dared to refer to the circumstance in whispers.

Such are the appropriate antecedents in the character of the monster who murdered in cold blood the gallant defenders of Fort Pillow.[2]

The article clothes itself in enough truth to merit interest; the rest can only be pondered. Such, however, was the fame Fort Pillow earned

Forrest among Unionists, one considerably more enduring than that of the military victory so lauded in Richmond. The ugly headlines swiftly spawned a U.S. congressional investigation of the Fort Pillow Massacre, as it was dubbed. Originating with Secretary of War Edwin Stanton, the order passed through General Sherman to Brigadier General Mason Brayman at Cairo, Illinois, where many of the Fort Pillow survivors were taken. Dozens of witnesses were interviewed, and, with a U.S. presidential election looming in the fall, the issue quickly became political on both sides. Union Republicans seeking fodder for assailing Democrats soft toward the Confederacy, and Confederate politicians hoping to avoid the growing Fort Pillow opprobrium, hurled wilder and wilder charges at each other the further the date of the battle receded. Southerners began to contend that the fort's garrison refused to surrender and had to be killed because its men were all drunk, while the Federal congressional investigation turned up allegations that Forrest's men shot down women and children (no such corpses were ever found) and burned prisoners alive.

On May 3 Lincoln informed his cabinet that the fact of a massacre "is now quite certain" and asked for their recommendations as to an appropriate response; the one ultimately adopted recommended that no "extreme" action be taken until the result of Grant's Wilderness offensive in Virginia became evident. Some observers have assumed that the fact that no Union reprisal was ever ordered by Lincoln or taken by Sherman is proof that neither was convinced a massacre really had taken place; the reality, however, probably was that Sherman was one of the least sensitive toward blacks of all the supreme Federal commanders, and Lincoln was facing a tough November election in which many voters seemed to feel much as Sherman did.[3]

In no small part because of his primary prewar vocation, no doubt, Forrest became the national scapegoat for policies that, if not exactly ordained by Richmond, certainly seem to have been encouraged by it. The Confederate congressional policy of putting to death white officers commanding black units apparently sanctioned the assassination (if that was what it was) of Bradford, who technically had become a commander of blacks by virtue of the death of Booth. Actually, killing all captured blacks wearing U.S. uniforms was the declared policy of the Confederacy's trans-Mississippi commander, Lieutenant General Kirby Smith, one against which Richmond remonstrated only weakly. Other Confederate commanders had taken no black prisoners for some time, occasionally hanging the few who did turn up.[4]

Now Forrest began to worry about a prospective massacre of his own troops, and with reason. At Memphis less than a week after the battle, newspapers reported black U.S. troops had fallen on their knees vowing to "Remember Fort Pillow," to fight Forrest's men to the death, and to give them no quarter. He possibly also knew that such vows were not being taken cavalierly. As early as the battles of Port Hudson and Milliken's Bend, Louisiana, in 1863, black units had felt the scourge of racial atrocity on the battlefield—and had begun replying in kind. Especially after Fort Pillow and Poison Springs, Arkansas, they were widely reported to be taking no Confederate prisoners. If he had deliberately encouraged the Fort Pillow excesses in the expectation of frightening Federal black units, his tactic now seemed counterproductive. Time, though, would tell more about that.[5]

Meanwhile, his old enemy Braxton Bragg continued to snipe at him from the rear. Ever since he had quit Bragg's army at Chattanooga and President Davis had given him the West Tennessee–North Mississippi command, Forrest had been going outside military channels with letters to Davis and Johnston, recounting his moves and offering pointed opinions as to how Federal drives in the West might be met. Sometimes he went so far as to suggest orders to be given to his immediate commander, Stephen Lee, and once—soon after the Fort Pillow battle, apparently—he ordered a "beautiful" captured Union battle flag to be sent to Davis's wife. These extra-channel efforts were probably attempts to counteract the powerful influence of Bragg, who—after voluntarily leaving his command following the defeat at Chattanooga—had been given supervision of Confederate operations on all fronts. They also may have been prompted by communications from his current commander, Leonidas Polk, who reprimanded him sharply at least twice within a month. Polk had informed him tartly on March 14 that two North Alabama regiments were "not . . . under your orders," commanding him to "revoke your orders to them, and allow them to do the duty on which they were sent." A month later, Polk wrote of his disappointment "in not being frequently advised of your movements. . . . I have not heard from you in two weeks." Forrest wrote Davis on April 15 questioning new Polk orders pulling him out of Tennessee to counter an anticipated Federal thrust into Alabama; he disputed the likelihood of this threat and suggested that instead he and Lee be sent into Middle Tennessee and Kentucky to "break up" Federal strategy in the area, a move that would have interrupted Sherman's Georgia operations at a critical time.[6]

This Forrest letter was referred to Bragg, who appended to it an acid note accusing Forrest of exaggerating his conscription efforts and illegally persuading Tennesseans and Mississippians enrolled in units far from home to quit their proper commands and join his ranks nearer their families and firesides. The stated "strength of this command [some 5,000 men, Forrest had reported] is very surprising after the verbal reports sent here of the number of men raised in the first visit to West Tennessee," Bragg wrote. He went on to say that two of Forrest's "four brigades were transferred under Brigadier-General Chalmers from General Lee's command, one (Richardson's) was raised by him and Colonel Bell before Forrest went to the department, and one large regiment and one battalion of five companies were sent by me from the Army of Tennessee, and General Polk has assigned three small regiments of Kentucky infantry. But little is left for the men raised by General Forrest." Bragg then got even testier, writing that the person who had taken Forrest's letter to Davis, a member of a Louisiana battery, "is employed by the general without authority, and is one of the cases of men enticed from their commands and employed in violation of orders. He [the messenger] should be arrested and sent to his proper command, and General Forrest made accountable for his unauthorized absence."[7]

Meanwhile, on orders from Polk, Forrest arrived back in Mississippi, where he began refitting his units. On May 17 Morton's battery unanimously passed a resolution to "take the lead" in reenlisting; a copy of the resolution was then sent to the Memphis *Appeal* and other newspapers. During this period, Forrest's ranks were swelled by the addition of Mississippi state militiamen under Gholson, who were transferred to the Confederate army and assigned to Chalmers's division.[8]

Sherman, assembling forces at Nashville for his great push through Georgia, was so preoccupied with the threat of Forrest against his supply lines that he changed both his Memphis commander and his head of cavalry there in late April. He urged their replacements to "hold Forrest and as much of the enemy as you can . . . until we strike Johnston [in Georgia]." In a dispatch to the new Memphis commander, Major General C. C. Washburn, a Sherman subordinate wrote: "It is of the utmost importance . . . to keep his [Forrest's] forces occupied, and prevent him from forming plans and combinations to cross the Tennessee River and break up the railroad communications in our rear." The new Memphis cavalry commander, Brigadier General Samuel D. Sturgis, finally marched out of the city with 3,400 men and, as ordered, made a seemingly half-hearted lunge at Forrest as the latter's troops moved past him into Mississippi. Sturgis followed them as far south as Ripley, where he ceased pursuit because of lack of forage rather than Confederate resistance.[9]

By then, a chorus of pleas had gone to Richmond to loose Forrest and his troopers onto the Nashville-Chattanooga-Georgia rail line supplying Sherman's campaign against Joseph Johnston; the suggestions had come not only from Johnston but from Bragg. Richmond, however, appeared more interested in inspecting Forrest's controversial command than in sending it anywhere. Its commander hardly had arrived back in Mississippi in May and reorganized his new conscripts and recruits before two Richmond inspectors, Brigadier General George B. Hodge and Colonel George William Brent, arrived. They found his horses "in tolerable condition," his "arms and equipments very deficient . . . need[ing] quite 3,000 guns and accouterments," and his reorganization "irregular and without authority." Brent's report added, however, that, except for the brigade Chalmers had led before being elevated to division command, Forrest had inherited a "chaotic, disorganized" force just a few months before, and that he necessarily had had to reorganize "all these scattered, disorganized, and fragmentary bodies" "claiming to be followers of different leaders." Thus, the report went on, Forrest had "assum[ed] and exercis[ed] the power of appointing both field and staff for many of these commands." The origin and subsequent history of some of these, Brent found, were "impossible to trace. . . . It is equally so to reinstate them in their original condition. To do so would produce endless confusion and controversy." Therefore, the inspector concluded, "the good of the service would be best promoted by accepting the existing organization."[10]

Brent himself, however, doesn't seem to have accepted Forrest's reorganization entirely. Finding that about 650 men in the Forrest units were listed as infantry deserters from Johnston's Army of Tennessee, he ordered them returned to Johnston. Forrest protested in vain to Lee, who had just been named departmental commander (because Polk and most available infantry had been sent to Johnston against Sherman). On May 22, about 650 men from ten of his regiments were arrested and conveyed under guard to Johnston—and that evening alone, as he had predicted in his letter of protest to Lee, 126 of 1,629 men in three newly organized regiments deserted.[11]

Soon afterward, Richmond took more of his men. Chalmers's division, as well as Gholson's brigade, were detached to Alabama to counter a threat of Federal raids from Georgia. Although belatedly approved, the much-sought Forrest foray against Sherman's rear never eventuated. Just as it was about to get into motion, Lee called it off May 17 because of a threatened enemy incursion from Memphis into Mississippi. Sherman was making sure Forrest was kept off his line of supply. From Georgia on May

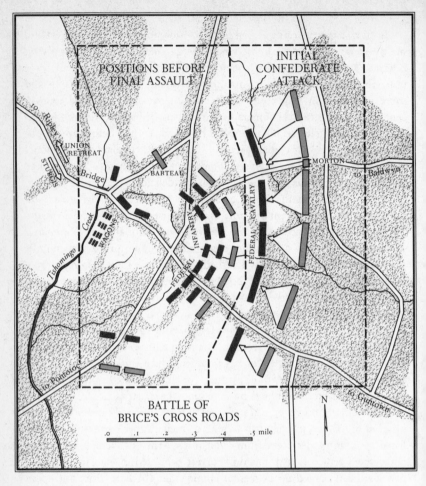

POSITIONS BEFORE
FINAL ASSAULT

INITIAL
CONFEDERATE
ATTACK

to Ripley

UNION
RETREAT

STUBB

Bridge

BARTEAU

Tishomingo Creek

WAGONS

FEDERAL INFANTRY

FEDERAL CAVALRY

MORTON

to Baldwyn

to Pontotoc

BATTLE OF
BRICE'S CROSS ROADS

to Guntown

N

.0   .1   .2   .3   .4   .5 mile

'IT IS GOING TO BE HOT AS HELL'—A mile out the road toward Baldwyn
from Brice's Cross Roads, Forrest troops collide with Federal
cavalrymen. Some 4,800 Confederates, arriving piecemeal, drive
3,200 Union cavalry west along and between the Baldwyn and
Guntown roads, finally striking 3,600 Federal infantry who have
run uphill through blistering heat from beyond Tishomingo
Creek bridge to the junction. When the Federal line at the crossroads breaks in the face of Morton's cannons, elements of Barteau's Second Tennessee—whom Forrest had ordered Bell to send
down a farm road into the Union rear early in the day—help panic
the retreating Federals. Black infantry wagon-guards desperately
keep the rout of the 8,300 Federals from becoming annihilation.

23 he wired instructions calling for "a threatening movement from Memphis on Columbus, Miss., to prevent Forrest and Lee from swinging over against my communications." Forrest, in northern Alabama with 2,200 men, was just beginning a Middle Tennessee expedition when fruits of Sherman's wire began manifesting themselves. Countermanding Forrest's orders, Lee sent him back to northern Mississippi with a new assignment: meet 8,300 Federals advancing slowly through his old hometown of Salem.[12]

Hastening back from Alabama to Tupelo, Forrest initially was perplexed by Federal movements. Sturgis on June 5 sent a 400-man detachment ahead to Rienzi, Mississippi, to disrupt Confederate rails while the main Union force slogged slowly from Salem to Ripley. The Union commander's deliberate pace was prompted not only by bad weather but by the onset of forebodings like those that had beset ill-fated Sooy Smith a few months earlier. Delayed and worried by eight days of almost incessant rain and flooding streams, miry roads that wore out his wagon teams, and a lack of forage to refresh these animals, Sturgis understandably began to wonder "whether or not I should proceed any farther. The rain still fell in torrents. The artillery and wagons were literally mired down, and the starved and exhausted animals could with difficulty drag them along." He thought of the "utter hopelessness of saving our train or artillery in case of defeat," a probability discussed and endorsed at a council of his ranking subordinates at Ripley on June 8. They couldn't very well just turn around again, however. ". . . It was urged . . . (and with some propriety, too) that inasmuch as I had abandoned a similar expedition only a few weeks before . . . it would be ruinous on all sides to return without first meeting the enemy."[13]

Not knowing whether Sturgis was headed east to join Sherman in Georgia or south to devastate the grain-rich Mississippi prairie, Forrest kept his available units fanned out. Joined by Lee on June 6, he moved 500 men north to Baldwyn, 1,500 to Booneville, and 2,800 to Rienzi. The Union aim disclosed itself on June 9 when, after two days of skirmishing with a Confederate regiment under Colonel Edmund Rucker, Sturgis's main force encamped twelve miles from Ripley at a farm called Stubbs's; obviously, it was heading southeast toward Tupelo through the railroad hamlet of Guntown. That night, hours before this intelligence arrived, Lee departed southward to gather other, scattered units and combine them with those of Chalmers in the open terrain around Okolona. He directed Forrest to get between the Federals and Tupelo by marching southwestward from Booneville toward Pontotoc through Brice's Cross Roads, a route that bisected the Federals' southeasterly Ripley-Guntown path six miles west of Guntown.

Lee's plan was "to fall back with the whole force toward Okolona, so as to effect a junction with Chalmers, and such other forces as he hoped to be able to glean from Mobile, before grappling with the enemy," thus drawing Sturgis as far as possible away from his Memphis supply base before launching an attack. He left Forrest with discretionary authority, however, and Forrest seems to have already gotten another idea — one that illustrates his ability to spot an enemy's weakness and maybe also his own disinclination, given reasonable alternative, to go into combat under someone else's command. After the war, perhaps sensitive to an appearance of disobeying orders, he seems to have told his authorized biographers that the Federals "were about to intercept his line of march" and that he saw "no way of avoiding this contingency." More likely, he didn't care to. Colonel D. C. Kelley later said Forrest indicated on June 8, the day before Lee's departure, that he planned to fight June 10 at Baldwyn or Brice's Cross Roads.[14]

Such an intent had its justifications. Fighting at Brice's Cross Roads would keep the Federals from reaching the precious crops around Okolona, and it was almost certain to surprise Sturgis, who obviously expected no pitched battle before reaching the railroad and open terrain. There was a more personal reason, too. By now, Forrest had learned that Sturgis's force included some 1,200 black troops who had sworn to avenge Fort Pillow. Forrest trooper William Witherspoon later remembered that from Memphis to Ripley Union officers had told citizens along their route that "they were carrying the negroes along to guard Forrest and his men back to Memphis, and that they [Forrest and his men] would fare as did the negroes at Fort Pillow."[15]

If Forrest indeed intended fighting at Brice's Cross Roads, he let advance units of Sturgis's troops, who were much closer to the junction than most of his own, beat him to the battle site. He had Colonel H. B. Lyon's brigade of 800 Kentuckians moving out of Booneville, eighteen miles away, by 4 A.M. on June 10, yet by the time he reached Old Carrollville four miles northeast of Brice's, scouts reported that Federal cavalry were also four miles from the crossroads on the other road. Forrest then sent forward "a few men from the Seventh Tennessee Cavalry," who reported meeting advance Federal units a couple of miles farther on, between the Confederates and the crossroads. Ordering Lyon's brigade forward to "develop the enemy," he sent a dispatch back to Buford between Booneville and Old Carrollville "to move up fast and fetch all he's got"—or, as his official report later put it, "to move up with the artillery and Bell's brigade as rapidly as the condition of the horses and roads would permit." He also ordered Buford to send a regiment of Bell's brigade from Old Carrollville cross-country to the Federals' route on the Ripley–Guntown road, hoping to strike them in the flank or rear.[16]

In contrast to so many of its immediate predecessors, the day had dawned sunny. Having instructed Lyon to probe the Federals without giving pitched battle, Forrest began hurrying up brigades of 700 and 500 men respectively under Rucker and Colonel W. A. Johnson. Many of his men had farther to go to reach the battlefield than did the middle and rear elements of the five-mile-long Federal column, but, unlike the Federals, Forrest's men were all mounted, and he had been able to send his wagon trains southward out of harm's way, well back of the railroad. Galloping forward beside Rucker, he disclosed how he planned to oppose almost 8,000 Federals with only some 2,000 Confederates then in close proximity to the field. Rucker later quoted him:

> *I know they greatly outnumber the troops I have at hand, but the road along which they will march is narrow and muddy; they will make slow progress. The country is densely wooded and the undergrowth so heavy that when we strike them they will not know how few men we have. Their cavalry will move out ahead of their infantry and should reach the crossroads three hours in advance. We can whip their cavalry in that time. As soon as the fight opens they will send back to have the infantry hurried up. It is going to be hot as hell, and coming on a run for five or six miles, their infantry will be so tired out we will ride right over them.*[17]

Lyon's probe of the field struck skirmishers of the Third and Ninth Illinois Cavalry in a huge, dense thicket of small blackjack oak trees almost a half mile north of the crossroads. With Rucker and Johnson hurrying forward, Forrest ordered Lyon to forget his earlier instructions and attack before the Federals did, doubtless to conceal his numerical weakness. Lyon began driving the Illinoisans, pushing them backward 300 yards along the road to the rear edge of a field a quarter mile from the crossroads. Men of the Seventh Tennessee Cavalry, hearing gunfire as they approached, "rode in a gallop to the field on the left of Lyon's men and, dismounting in a skirt of woods, were immediately formed and marched into [the] open field, where they, with the Eighteenth Mississippi Regiment, went under fire and immediately prepared to charge the enemy."

The Federals "occupied a wood on the far side of the field, with a thicket fence greatly strengthened with rails and logs and garnished with an abatis of such bushy trees as could be cut across the fence." It had gotten to be midday and was "very hot and sultry" by the time the Confederates charged. As they surged forward, "the fence and abatis were ablaze with the fire of the enemy's breech-loaders, and the men began to fall thickly on the field. . . . the regiment was staggered." They dropped to the ground and sought cover "in small gullies, when Lieut.-Col. [W. F.] Taylor, who was mounted, dashed down the line, ordering them up." Rising again, "with loud cheers [they] rushed up the slope to the defenses of the enemy, leaving the ground strewed with fallen comrades in their rear." When they reached the brush and fallen trees protecting the Federal line, they "hesitated, as there seemed no way of getting over the obstructions, and the enemy's fire was more deadly than ever at not more than 40 feet range." Then "someone cried out, 'Pull out a tree, boys,' and with the vehement energy of battle some of the men . . . seized one of the brushy-topped blackjacks in the abatis and pulled it bodily into the field." The Confederates, "shouting, poured pell-mell" through the hole in the Federal defense "and found themselves at once mixed up with the hitherto unseen enemy. . . . a deadly struggle at arms length began. . . . Guns, once fired, were used as clubs, and pistols brought into play. . . . Never did men fight more gallantly for their position. . . ."[18]

The Union troops were the Seventh Indiana Cavalry and, just behind them, the Second New Jersey Cavalry. Both were fighting dismounted because "the character of the ground would not admit of cavalry movements," their commander, Colonel George E. Waring, later reported. Waring had reached the crossroads at 9:45 A.M. and, hearing that Forrest and Lee had passed there a couple of days earlier bound for Baldwyn, had sent a scouting squadron of the Fourth Missouri northward along the Baldwyn-Pontotoc road. These men collided with the first detachment from the Seventh Tennessee that Forrest dispatched southward from Old Carrollville. Meanwhile, Waring sent urgent dispatches back to the Federal infantry—which, to reach the field, had to cross the rain-flooded Tishomingo Creek valley on a narrow causeway and bridge, then proceed up slowly rising, heavily thicketed ground to reach a low plateau and the crossroads. Waring's line, which also included the Fourth Missouri on the west side of the Baldwyn-Pontotoc road, successfully breasted Lyon's opening demonstration, but found the attack launched by the Seventh Tennessee and the Eighteenth Mississippi more powerful. Equipped with repeating carbines, the Federals discovered that in hand-to-hand fighting their sabers were no match for the pistols carried by Forrest's men.

Waring's initial position was carried at about 2:20 P.M., he later reported, by a Confederate attack he described as "exceedingly fierce" and "apparently numbering 4,000 men."[19]

With only 75 of its original 350 men still able-bodied, the Seventh Tennessee hung on at the brushy fence at the south side of one of the battleground's few open fields. In fact, the Seventh moved back onto the north side of the obstruction in anticipation of a Federal counterattack. By now, both Federals and Confederates were feeding units to the fire as fast as they could bring them up, and Forrest was moving from the defensive-offensive to the purely offensive. A little after 1 P.M. Bell's 2,800-man brigade, reaching the field just behind Morton's artillery, came in on the left of the Seventh Tennessee and was thrown across the Guntown-Ripley road. Before long, however, the advanced remnant of the Seventh could see Bell's force being pushed backward in the face of steadily advancing U.S. flags. Colonel Taylor told his Seventh troopers that, rather than retreat, they would stay where they were behind their fence come what may. Then suddenly Forrest, on a dappled gray horse, crashed through the dense thicket and into their position. With his shirtsleeves rolled up and his military coat thrown across the front of his saddle, he quickly ordered them to turn leftward and charge "the damned Yankees in the rear," Witherspoon later wrote.[20]

"I notice some writers on Forrest say he seldom cursed; well, the fellow that writes that way was not where the Seventh Tennessee was that day," Witherspoon continues. Taylor pointed out to Forrest that he had just seventy-five men, but Forrest again ordered them into line for a charge. When they hesitated before this chilling prospect, "he would curse, then praise, then threaten to shoot us himself, if we were so afraid the Yankees would hit us." As he profanely exhorted these troops, he sat "on his horse in the open field; the Yanks espied him, and then what a deluge of grapeshot, canister, bomb shells, ricochet shots plowed up the ground to the front, to the rear, to the sides, above and under old Dapple Gray, but Forrest and old Dapple Gray did not seem to care. . . . I expected every moment to see Forrest and horse torn into fragments. . . . [He] finally said, 'I will lead you.' [He] ordered us to give the yell and follow."

However, instead of leading them, Forrest suddenly turned as they started their charge perpendicularly across the open field toward another fence at the left rear of the charging Federals. He galloped back to Bell's retreating troops "and urged them to rally; told them he had the damned Yankees whipped, was charging them in the rear and [with] one more rally . . . he would have them." Believing him, Bell's men gave him the rally he demanded, stunning "the apparently victorious Yanks." Hearing the rebel yell and firing in their rear and not knowing that its source was the handful of men of the Seventh Tennessee, the Federals "halted," and "Bell's men . . . with a yell charged. . . . [H]ere came the Yanks back in a long, sweeping trot," and the men of the Seventh—who had had to charge fence-protected Federals so short a while before—now "had our fun shooting through the cracks of a fence."[21]

After holding their position some three hours, Waring's Union cavalrymen had fallen back, relinquishing their positions to several Illinois infantry regiments. The latter, finally arrived on the battlefield after a brutal forced march of four miles, were in no condition for combat. The commander of the 113th Illinois later reported that by then "one-third of my men were so completely exhausted as to be scarce able to stand; several were sunstruck." They came under hot fire as soon as they reached the battle line. Within a half hour their ammunition was running low and, "being overpowered by superior numbers, [they] . . . were reluctantly compelled to fall back." Forming another line, they held until their ammunition was expended, then retreated, "I am sorry to say . . . in great confusion."[22]

By now, with all his 4,800 troopers on the field, Forrest glimpsed victory. All that was needed, he thought, was one more charge all along a thin line of Confederates that outdistanced the thick Federal column at both ends. Buford, having traveled twenty-five miles since mounting his horse that morning, was given command of the right, Bell of the left. Large in Forrest's plan loomed Morton's eight small cannons, long since dubbed the Bull Pups. In the anxious moments just before Buford and Bell arrived, Forrest had approached Morton's guns, dismounted, and walked up to the cannons. "Bullets were striking the guns and occasionally killing a cannoneer," Morton later remembered, and he called to Forrest: "General, you'd better get lower down the hill; they'll hit you there." He then apologized for having presumed to advise his commander, "expect[ing], nevertheless, to be invited to attend to his own damned business; but to his surprise the chieftain replied mildly, 'Well, John, I will rest a little,' and, retiring to the root of a tree, he made himself comfortable for a short time."[23]

Forrest and the fearless young captain he once had scorned had become like father and son; recently the general had lent Morton $750 to buy a horse—and also had refused him nocturnal passes from camp, fearing they might lead to precipitous matrimony. Today, in sultry heat that was felling both enlisted men and regimental commanders, Morton thought

Forrest looked fatigued and suggested the rest, and Forrest accepted the notion. A little later, he told Morton his plan for the blow that would seize victory: The whole Confederate line would charge, Buford's right moving as soon as it heard the fire of Bell on the left—while Morton's guns, double-shotted with grape and canister, were thrown forward to fire at as near point-blank range as possible. He instructed Morton to "charge right down the road . . . get as close as you can" and "[g]ive 'em hell." Morton later wrote that he believed this was the first time "in the history of warfare" that an artillery commander was ordered to charge without the support of accompanying cavalry or infantry. When he noted this daunting fact at the time, Forrest laughed lightly and said he would "like to see the Yanks capture you." Soon Forrest was explaining the plan to other, battle-exhausted troops on Buford's right side of the line. One recalled hearing him say more than once: "Get up, men. I have ordered Bell to charge on the left. When you hear his guns, and the bugle sounds, every man must charge, and we will give them hell."[24]

This charge, a two-hour push southward down both the Guntown-Ripley and Baldwyn-Pontotoc roads and the space between them, didn't proceed with precision—Forrest himself had to go find Buford and personally order the positioning and engagement of artillery—but it finally reached the crossroads and broke the back of a third Union stand. Crowded "40 deep" in the face of Morton's roaring cannons, most of the Federal lines disintegrated and streamed toward the rear, which now was under attack from the Second Tennessee Cavalry unit Forrest had ordered onto Sturgis's flanks early in the morning. Because of the activity of this force on their rear, the Federals fleeing in disorder back down the Guntown-Ripley road toward the little bridge at Tishomingo Creek found no cavalry to shield them from their pursuers. Meanwhile, the whooping Confederates finally encountered a prey they had sought all day. Witherspoon later remembered:

> [S]hortly after the terrible havoc by Morton's Bull Pups, a cry rang out not far off, "Here are the damned negroes!" We had been fighting from 9 a.m. to 4 p.m. constant; although we fought like fiends, we . . . were feeling pretty well fagged out, but when the cry rang out, "Here are the damned negroes," new life, energy and action coursed through our bodies and we bounded forward. . . .[25]

The Fifty-fifth and Fifty-ninth U.S. Colored Infantry, commanded by Colonel Edward Bouton, had spent the expedition guarding Sturgis's 250 wagons. Forbidden to drink from most of the farm wells and cisterns used along the way by their white comrades, they perpetrated "outrages" (insulting and boorish behavior, stock shooting, and food stealing) at some of the civilian residences to which their superiors allowed them access. Witherspoon glibly says that in the "maddening rush of the infuriated Rebs," the blacks "threw down their guns, without firing a shot, and bounded off with the fleetness of a deer," but this appears to be grossly oversimplified exaggeration. Although another Confederate fighting man's reminiscence of the battle similarly mentions that "in many instances" the blacks "ceased their war cry of 'Remember Fort Pillow' and, throwing away their [Remember Fort Pillow] badges, took to the woods," this appears to have occurred later. Forrest's own authorized biography notes that the fighting in the "part of the field" where the blacks were in line was such that just one of the Confederate regiments, the Seventh Kentucky, "lost 30 officers and men killed and wounded." Actually, the black troops—who, Forrest would complain officially, "evidently expected to be slaughtered when captured"—may deserve credit for keeping the Union rout from becoming annihilation.[26]

Leaving the wagon train where it was being gathered in a field just across the Tishomingo bridge, the black infantrymen were sent forward by Bouton without orders when he saw the Union cavalry, artillery, and infantry streaming backward. He "gathered two companies from the head of the column . . . and threw them forward into what seemed to be a gap in the First Brigade," a position they held "with great firmness until they were much reduced by loss and virtually crushed back by overwhelming numbers." Bouton then sent up "seven companies of the Fifty-fifth Regiment . . . which I put into position a little to the rear and the right of the first two companies, so as to cover as well as possible the retreat of the brigade on the left of the road." In veteran fashion, the black companies "gave way to allow the troops in front to pass through to the rear, [after which] they immediately closed up and opened a steady and well-directed fire on the enemy, which for a time seemed to hold in check his right and center. . . . [They held this] position against fearful odds, until . . . ordered to fall back to a new position, which [they] did in good order."

In another retreat that quickly followed, one of Bouton's guns was lost because several of its horses had been killed. Two of his companies positioned obliquely to the left of the Ripley-Guntown road poured an enfilading fire into the front of massed Confederates advancing along the thoroughfare, "for a time checking the column," but his "line . . . then bec[a]me closely engaged; my right was forced back and flanked, which soon caused us to fall back gradually and in good order some 200 yards, the men facing about and firing as they retired." They "fought . . . in this manner for about 800 yards, forming and holding our position at every ditch, ridge, or skirt of timber of which we could take advantage, until just at sundown we were formed on high ground, with timber in our rear and an open field in front, through which the enemy were advancing. The right and center of our line . . . here rallied and charged, driving the enemy back with bayonets and clubbed muskets nearly 400 yards, leaving great numbers of his dead on the ground."

As Bouton's right charged, however, a white Federal infantry unit on his left—the Ninth Minnesota—apparently retreated, and as darkness fell, Bouton's left was "cut off, flanked, and broken, my right flanked by great numbers and in danger of being entirely surrounded, [but] my remaining forces retreated in good order." Bouton himself, no doubt conscious of being one of those white officers of black troops whom Confederate law held punishable by death, was on the "extreme right with a few skirmishers trying to keep the enemy on our flank from closing in our rear as my column moved out, [when] I was left entirely cut off and surrounded by several hundred of the enemy." His troops, "gathering around me, fought with terrible desperation. Some of them, having broken up their guns in hand-to-hand conflict, unyielding, died at my feet, without a thing in their hands for defense." Bouton himself finally "escaped . . . about 9 p.m., and by making a large circuit through the woods joined the retreating column on the Ripley road about 11 p.m."[27]

Colonel William L. McMillen, Sturgis's infantry commander on this ill-fated expedition, reported that Bouton's "colored regiment fought with . . . gallantry . . . bravery and endurance," and that their effort "checked the pursuit and ended the fighting for that evening." It certainly didn't end the pursuit, though. On the Ripley-Guntown road, the yipping Confederates swarmed past Bouton's remnants and headed for the little Tishomingo Creek bridge, where so many Federal horses, artillery, wagons, and soldiers were trying to cross at once that many Federals plunged into the creek, many to be felled on the other side by the fire of relentlessly pursuing Confederate artillery. Confederate cavalrymen meanwhile overtook the wagons on the bridge and cleared it by pushing them off into the water.[28]

The battle now degenerated into another pell-mell Forrest chase. Taking the comparatively fresh one-quarter of his men who had held the horses of the others during the battle, he sent them against the fleeing Federals while ordering the balance of his exhausted force rested until 1 A.M. While most of these napped, he and Buford led the pursuit detachment, letting their hungry troopers stop to rifle food-loaded Federal wagons "but not to unsaddle." Soon, before they had finished gorging themselves, they were ordered to remount and resume the chase. To try to keep their commissary riches from falling into Confederate hands, some Federals had been setting fire to disabled wagons on the road; the blazes lighted the narrow thoroughfare and incensed a booty-hungry Forrest. He wrathfully drove his men forward to put out the fires and save the treasures with an imperious question: "Don't you see the damned Yanks are burning my wagons?"[29]

About 11 P.M. Bouton's black troops caught up with Sturgis at a marshy crossing of a small fork of the Hatchie River, several miles from Brice's Cross Roads. There the last of the Union supply wagons, along with ambulances and artillery, had become hopelessly enmired. Surely knowing that he and his officers were dead men and his soldiers at best reenslaved if they fell into Confederate hands, Bouton begged Sturgis "for God's sake let us not give it up so." He implored Sturgis to give his men the ammunition "that the white troops were throwing away in the mud, and I would hold the enemy in check until we could get those ambulances, wagons and artillery over that bottom and save them." Sturgis, however, was whipped. "For God's sake, if Mr. Forrest will let me alone I will let him alone," he fretted to Bouton. "You have done all you could and more than was expected of you, and now all you can do is to save yourselves."[30]

For the Confederates the rest of the night, especially after 1 A.M., was a matter of staying on the Federal rear and flanks and gathering up exhausted Union prisoners. Both Witherspoon and John Milton Hubbard, who wrote men-in-ranks accounts of Confederate service at Brice's Cross Roads, recalled that Forrest led the pursuit himself and that the succeeding groups of surrendering Federals were told to go to the rear while Forrest's small but bellicose vanguard swept on to capture more. In staying on their very heels, Forrest was following one of his homely but spectacularly effective combat aphorisms, one that he stated again to Morton while riding in the pursuit at 3 A.M.: "Get 'em skeered, and then keep the skeer on 'em."[31]

By then, a couple of hundred Federals, wounded and otherwise, had been captured at the Hatchie Bottom. Forrest was pressing his advance down roads so narrow they could accommodate just four riders abreast, which benefited the few pursuing more than the many pursued. At one point, Witherspoon recalls, a lieutenant informed the general that the whole remainder of the Union army was immediately in front of him while the entire Confederate force immediately to hand numbered ten. "That is enough," Forrest responded. "Ten good men can whip 1,000 in the fix we have them." They continued to press so close they sometimes were mistaken for Federals. Witherspoon says one Union trooper riding along "fell in with me and remarked: 'Old Forrest gave us hell today.' . . . [W]ith the click of my navy six [pistol] and it pointing dangerously near him, I said, 'You are now with Forrest's men. Hand over your arms and roll off that horse.' "[32]

The Confederates ended up chasing the Federals at least fifty miles, with many of the latter saving themselves by dissolving into squads and scattering through the woods to elude organized pursuit. Forrest ordered Buford to follow them as far as La Grange, Tennessee, then to turn southward again and pick up what prisoners and matériel he could while returning to the battlefield; he gathered another "several hundred" of the former, Forrest's official report says. The final toll shows a Federal reported loss in killed, wounded, and missing of 2,165 — including 512 black troops — as compared to a total of 492 for Forrest's forces. Spoils reported taken by the Confederates included "250 wagons and ambulances, 18 pieces of artillery, 5,000 stand of small-arms, 500,000 rounds of ammunition, and all [the enemy's] baggage and supplies." Not all of the latter would find their way to Confederate commissaries, however. "I regret to say," Forrest's report added, "that during our pursuit the abandoned wagons, &c., of the enemy were pillaged and plundered by citizens and stragglers of the command. . . . [B]ut for fire and robbery, the entire outfit could have been saved."[33]

A month short of his forty-third birthday, after three years of war, even Forrest could not fight and pursue forever. On the afternoon following the day of the battle, near his boyhood hometown of Salem, he was still in pursuit but was noticed by his escort to be riding asleep. A dispute arose as to who should have the unpleasant and possibly dangerous duty of waking him, but the matter settled itself when his horse, possibly also asleep with exhaustion, walked out of the roadway and into a tree, knocking its rider to the ground, where he lay unconscious for a time. He finally went to bed that night near Salem in the home of Orrin Beck, brother of his mother.[34]

Three days later, back at Brice's Cross Roads, he initiated a vitriolic correspondence with the Federal commander at Memphis, Washburn. His concern was over the attitude toward him which Federal officers seemed to have instilled in their troops, particularly black ones. Apparently smarting under the scourge of controversy that had been lashing him since Fort Pillow, he wrote Washburn that "recent events" finally had "render[ed]

. . . necessary, in fact demand[ed]" protest. He had heard the reports "that all the negro troops stationed in Memphis took an oath on their knees, in the presence of Major-General Hurlbut and other officers of your army, to avenge Fort Pillow, and that they would show my troops no quarter." He also had it "from indisputable authority that the troops under Brigadier-General Sturgis, on their recent march from Memphis, publicly and in various places proclaimed that no quarter would be shown my men." Then as Sturgis's "troops were moved into action on . . . [June 10] the officers commanding exhorted their men to remember Fort Pillow, and a large majority of the prisoners we have captured from that command have voluntarily stated that they expected us to murder them." For that reason, he continued, the battle at Brice's Cross Roads "was far more bloody than it would otherwise have been[;] both sides acted as though neither felt safe in surrendering, even when further resistance was useless. The prisoners captured by us say they felt condemned by the announcement, &c., of their own commanders, and expected no quarter."

Going on to say he had conducted all his wartime operations "on civilized principles," he inquired of Washburn whether the latter intended to treat captured Forrest troopers "as other Confederate prisoners"—or, by inference, to show them no mercy. Five days later Washburn responded, affirming that the black troops had taken a no-quarter oath concerning Forrest's men and that they had made other such public proclamations, adding that "the affair of Fort Pillow fully justified" their expectation of murder at Forrest's hands. Washburn said he had "received with satisfaction the intimation in your letter that the recent slaughter of colored troops" at Brice's Cross Roads "resulted rather from the desperation with which they fought than a predetermined intention to give them no quarter." He added that Forrest "must have learned by this time that the attempt to intimidate the colored troops by indiscriminate slaughter has signally failed, and that instead of a feeling of terror you have aroused a spirit of courage and desperation that will not down at your bidding." Washburn then asked of Forrest "the course you and the Confederate Government intend to pursue in regard to colored troops. . . ." Forrest replied that Washburn's denunciation of him "as a murderer and as guilty of the wholesale slaughter of the garrison at Fort Pillow" was "unfounded and unwarranted by the facts." He went on to note that the question of how captured black troops would be treated was a matter which the United States and the Confederate States, rather than "their subordinate officers," must "decide and adjust." In a second letter to Washburn, he added: "I slaughter no man except in open warfare, and . . . my prisoners, both white and black, are turned over to my Government to be dealt with as it may direct."[35]

He went on to forward copies of his correspondence to Federal officers during the Fort Pillow battle, as well as other papers connected with it. One, signed by Captain John T. Young of the Twenty-fourth Missouri, professed to have seen "no ill-treatment of the wounded on the evening of the battle [of Fort Pillow] or the next morning," adding that "[a]mong the wounded were some colored troops." Three months later, Washburn would receive another, lengthier communication from Young himself. It would repudiate the earlier statement, saying it had been "extorted from me while under duress" as a Confederate prisoner "about April 27 [1864]." At a Confederate prison in Macon, Georgia, Young said, he suddenly had been isolated from his fellow Union officers and taken to Cahaba, Alabama, "having fresh in my mind Fort Pillow, and the summary manner the Confederate officers have of disposing of men on some occasions." At Cahaba, he found himself repeatedly pressed to sign "certain papers handed me, made out by General Forrest, for my signature." Young told Washburn a judge finally "prevailed on" him "to sign the papers you have in your possession, pledging himself that if I wished it they should only be seen by General Forrest himself; that they were not intended to be used by him as testimony, but merely for his own satisfaction.

"I hope, general, that these papers . . . extorted from me . . . will not be used by my Government to my disparagement. . . ."[36]

21

THIS WAS THE summer of the Confederacy's last chance. It was the summer preceding the 1864 presidential election that would decide whether a pacifist Democrat could wrest leadership of the war-weary North from Abraham Lincoln. Lincoln badly needed a victory of sufficient scope to show that a final one was in prospect, and the mood on both sides, especially in the Confederacy's increasingly sundered western theater, reflected the desperation of the moment.

By now, Forrest was being more and more widely regarded as the West's most aggressive cavalryman. With Sherman driving Johnston down into the heart of Georgia, several prominent Southerners—from Georgia governor Joseph E. Brown and Georgia congressman-turned-general Howell Cobb to Johnston himself and even his cavalry commander, Joseph Wheeler—urged Davis and Bragg in Richmond to briefly relieve the Tennessean from his task of protecting Mississippi's grain fields to, instead, wreak his havoc on Sherman's tenuously guarded 300-mile supply line through North Georgia and East and Middle Tennessee. When Brown formally requested Forrest be given command of Johnston's cavalry for a strike on Sherman's flanks and rear, Davis refused. At least some of his reasons are reflected in an exasperated letter he wrote about this time to Johnston, contending that if Forrest's troops left the area, Union units from Memphis "might lay waste the stored and growing supplies of the Tombigbee Valley, and the main body, liberated from the protection of Memphis and free from flank attack, could (and probably would) move rapidly on to re-enforce Sherman or cover his line of communication. . . ."[1]

Davis's attitude may have stemmed less from a mental fixation on Mississippi, his home state, than from his personal assessment of the military capacity of Forrest. After the war, he would confess that Forrest's exploits—even at Brice's Cross Roads—were "not understood at Richmond." Noting that Forrest's commanders regarded him as only "a bold and enterprising partisan raider and rider," he added that the Brice's Cross Roads stampede went unstudied, assumed to be merely "another successful raid." Under the daily influence of Bragg, the Confederate president doubtless was swayed by his fellow West Pointer's jaundiced views of Forrest's lack of training, his volatile vanity and penchant for self-promotion, and his difficulty in working under supervision. Such views led Davis to deny Johnston, whom he disliked, the one Confederate in the western theater whose quick and lethal style of work might have obstructed Sherman. Forrest's faults notwithstanding, his worth was recognized much more fully by the only other military giant operating in the western theater at that time: Sherman himself. His name filled the dispatches of the Union general, who increasingly saw in Forrest's savage cunning the only real threat to his own bold plan to split the southeastern Confederacy. In a letter to Secretary of War Edwin Stanton after Brice's Cross Roads, Sherman termed Forrest "the very devil," adding that his—Sherman's—plans were to "order . . . a force . . . [to] go out and follow Forrest to the death, if it cost[s] 10,000 lives and breaks the [Federal] treasury. There never will be peace in Tennessee till Forrest is dead."[2]

To President Lincoln a few days later, Sherman sent word that he was ordering two Union generals "from Memphis to pursue and kill Forrest"—candidly adding that he had promised the junior of the two that if the effort proved successful he would use "my influence to promote him to a major-general." He began employing many thousands of troops to keep Forrest out of Georgia and Tennessee by occupying him in Mississippi. To a subordinate he wrote on July 2: "I see Forrest is at Tupelo, that the enemy has detected that a heavy force, under A. J. Smith, is moving out of Memphis, as they suppose, to reinforce us. This will hold Forrest there." To another subordinate on July 6: "General A. J. Smith is out from Memphis with force enough to give Forrest full occupation." To Grant, stymied at the moment by Robert E. Lee in Virginia, he wrote on July 12 that he had "now fulfilled the first part of the grand plan. Our lines are up to the Chattahoochee [in Georgia] . . . and we have kept Forrest employed in Mississippi." He went on to say that Sturgis's defeat "was unfortunate; still, he kept Forrest away from us; and now A. J. Smith is out with a force amply sufficient to whip him."[3]

The object of these ploys was not enjoying life as the hero of Brice's Cross Roads. His constitution ravaged by the exertions and privations of three years of war, Forrest seems to have approached his forty-third birthday suffering both in body and in mind. Less than three weeks after his great victory, he learned of the promotion of his superior, Stephen Lee, to lieutenant general, and he sent Lee a curt note on June 28: "Allow me to congratulate you on your promotion. I am suffering with boils. If the enemy should move out I desire you to take command of the forces. Our force is insufficient to meet this command. Can't you procure some assistance?"[4]

The crisp tone of this message—of superior to subordinate, instead of the opposite—suggests understandable resentment of Lee's promotion. It also suggests that the "boils," or at least Forrest's abrupt command-deferring response to them, may have had something to do with that; if it was Lee who was to enjoy promotion, then Lee could have the risk of commanding. That way the world could compare Lee's results with those his underappreciated subordinate already had produced at Brice's Cross Roads. Lee had been upset momentarily at Forrest for the stampede of William Sooy Smith at Okolona, and Forrest probably knew it. He also could hardly help seeing (and, given his personality, resenting) that Lee, the department commander, was being credited in Richmond for victories Forrest himself was winning. These suppositions seem bolstered by reminiscences Lee published nearly four decades later. He said Forrest "should have had supreme command [in the battle that followed]" because he "had just won his splendid victory at Brice's Cross Roads . . . and his troops had confidence in him." He said Forrest, however, "insisted on General Lee . . . , the department commander, assuming the responsibility and being present." Lee claimed he "insist[ed]" that Forrest "command . . . the field, but he said no; that the responsibility was too great, and that his superior in rank should assume and exercise the command. . . ."[5]

Lee had many more problems than Forrest's boils. His department was under pressure from not only the threatened advance from Memphis but the weakness of the Confederate garrison at Mobile, an important port visited by blockade runners plying the Gulf Coast. Lee's communications with Bragg and Major General Dabney H. Maury, the Mobile commander, indicate he felt obligated to use as quickly as possible some "7,500 cavalry, 1,500 dismounted men, 20 pieces artillery" hastily concentrated under Forrest, so as to be able to disperse them quickly to other threatened points. Having seen two previous Memphis expeditions whipped so soundly, he and others under him may have assumed that defeating A. J. Smith would be as easy as beating Sooy Smith and Samuel Sturgis had been; according to William Witherspoon, Forrest's men certainly thought so.[6]

While Lee gathered all the Confederate troops he could, getting Richmond to expedite activation of 2,000 reserves in Mississippi, Forrest was busy handling administrative problems, posting the men he then had, and fending off an attempt by Gideon Pillow, now reduced to conscript duty, to reclaim four regiments of Colonel Tyree Bell's troops whom he accused Forrest of appropriating for his own. On July 3 Forrest also issued orders pasturing all "unserviceable" horses and forming their erstwhile riders into an infantry unit that would remain such until the horses were rehabilitated. He went on to propose "rigid" inspections of all troops within the department with the aim of arming noncombat soldiers and combining them with this temporary infantry force; he estimated that another 2,000 men might thereby be mustered to help meet the new threat then already launched from Memphis.[7]

In late June, Smith and some 14,000 men began moving eastward and southward into Mississippi to try to lure Forrest north to the vicinity of Corinth, defeat or at least hold him there, send a cavalry force around him to tear up Confederate rails supplying Mobile, and "punish" Confederate citizenry — for their aid of Forrest — by burning their property. Smith appeared to take all aspects of the assignment seriously. After shoving aside a small Confederate force three miles north of Ripley, his soldiers burned many of Ripley's principal buildings on July 8 and moved on, torching a swath reportedly ten miles wide. They came slowly, though, in a column so compact and well guarded that Confederates hanging on its flanks and rear were ineffectual. This Federal force crossed the Tallahatchie River at New Albany on July 9 and a day later pushed McCulloch's brigade of Missouri cavalry out of Pontotoc. Then they stopped as Lee, who had arrived on the scene on July 8, and Forrest were massing their troops to fight further south at Okolona.[8]

Unwilling to attack a Confederate position on a hill behind two creeks south of Pontotoc, Smith turned eastward from Pontotoc on July 13 and suddenly raced for Tupelo. A few miles short of there, he was struck hard in the flank at a hamlet called Barrow's Shop by Chalmers, who later reported that he and his men "took [the enemy] by surprise, and got possession of his train at first, and killed the mules, so that he was forced to abandon and burn 7 wagons, 1 caisson, and 2 ambulances." However, the Federal infantry—black troops under the same Colonel Bouton whose men had guarded the Federal wagons at Brice's Cross Roads—"rallied, and by superior numbers forced us to retire." Pushing on toward Tupelo, Smith stopped his train and drew a battle line around it two miles west at Harrisburg, an abandoned town rendered obsolescent by construction of the railroad through Tupelo. The Federal position, two miles long, was concentrated on both sides of the Pontotoc-Tupelo road but extended southeastward to also cover another road to Tupelo from the town of Verona. The whole two miles bristled with artillery.[9]

On the evening of July 13, while Confederate camp talk held that Forrest favored flanking the Federals via the slimly guarded Verona road, Forrest himself appeared at headquarters around dusk and, according to artillerist Morton, spread his coat on the ground and lay down on it in his shirtsleeves. He appeared both "absorbed in thought" and "greatly exhausted from the heavy work and intense heat," and his staff kept its distance. Suddenly he sprang up, put on his coat, mounted his horse, and called to a staff member, Lieutenant Samuel Donelson, to accompany him. They "made a wide detour through the woods" and, about an hour later, came within the Federal lines from the rear. There they "soon found themselves among the Union wagons and teams. The . . . darkness concealed the Confederate uniforms and, keeping well away from the campfires, the two . . . officers rode through nearly every portion of the enemy's camp." As they started to return to their own lines, however, they were challenged by two Federal pickets. "Riding directly up to these men, General Forrest, affecting intense anger, said, 'How dare you halt your commanding officer?'—and, without further remark, put spurs to his horse, an example quickly followed by Lieutenant Donelson." As they dashed into the darkness, Forrest and Donelson both crouched low over their horses and spurred them into a "full gallop" before the pickets wildly

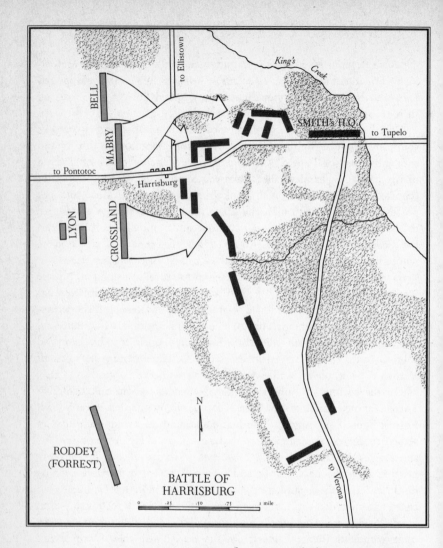

BATTLE OF HARRISBURG

RODDEY (FORREST)

BELL

MABRY

LYON

CROSSLAND

SMITH's H.Q.

to Ellistown

to Tupelo

to Pontotoc

Harrisburg

to Verona

King's Creek

N

0   .25   .50   .75   1 mile

'WE'LL WHIP 'EM IN FIVE MINUTES'—After Forrest declines command, S. D. Lee orders a frontal assault by some 7,500 Confederates against 14,000 heavily entrenched Federals at Harrisburg. When Crossland meets withering fire in the Confederate center, Forrest on the right abandons the Lee battle plan and holds Roddey's men out of the fray, leaving the Union left to enfilade Lee's center. Mabry's advance veers left of its target, and Bell is ordered to fill the gap between Mabry and Crossland. The massive Union countercharge Forrest expects never materializes—but the Union retreat he also has predicted comes the next day.

fired. Back in camp, Forrest told the story "with great gusto, declaring . . . that a bullet might have done him good, as it might have opened one of his boils, which would have been a relief."[10]

The next morning Forrest suggested that the Federals were too well entrenched, especially to be attacked by little more than half their number, and asked Lee to wait until Smith moved, which had to be soon. When that happened, he said, he hoped to be permitted to employ the chase technique he had perfected against Streight, Sooy Smith, and Sturgis. His assistant adjutant, Major Anderson, later said he heard him tell Lee that all he wanted was "to be turned loose with my command," promising that if Smith tried "to cross the country to Sherman, turn south to devastate the prairies, or return to Memphis, I will be on all sides of him, attacking day and night. He shall not cook a meal or have a night's sleep, and I will wear his army to a frazzle before he gets out of the country." Lee, though, was in a time squeeze. At Mobile, Maury had only 2,000 troops under threat of attack by 20,000 Federals reported to be marching from New Orleans, and Lee had written to Richmond three days earlier that he expected to be able to send Maury at least 2,000 of the men at Harrisburg as soon as he could fight Smith. So he decided—in a move Forrest himself, judging from all his others, almost certainly would never have made—to assault the Federal position frontally if the enemy couldn't be coaxed into making an immediate attack.[11]

Forrest's acquiescence in this decision, as later asserted by both Lee and Chalmers, remains a matter of dispute. His own report is silent on the matter, and Lee himself never made one—to a friend after the war, he explained that if he had it would in his view have prompted an investigation that "could have paralyzed [Forrest] and his command." In a reminiscence written thirty-seven years after the battle at Harrisburg in an effort to safeguard his reputation, he claimed that Forrest and he had been in "perfect accord" on the plan of battle, and that Forrest had "urged immediate attack" after two scouts rode up and reported the Federals preparing to retreat toward Ripley via a northwesterly road out of Harrisburg through Ellistown; curiously, though, Lee also said that Forrest "considered the Confederate troops inadequate to defeat Smith." Chalmers's story was that as he rode to the front the next morning with Lee, Forrest, and Buford, Buford advanced the unsought opinion that they were "going to be badly whipped" by the dug-in Federals—and that "Forrest replied sharply: 'You don't know what you are talking about; we'll whip 'em in five minutes.' "[12]

Perhaps Buford, having heard the camp talk that Forrest favored a flank attack along the Tupelo-Verona road, was trying to give him an opening to present that plan; and perhaps Forrest, who is reported to have spent "the night and morning . . . in consultation" with Lee, was tired of presenting it. There are other possibilities. Having seen Smith veer off from Pontotoc toward Tupelo, and having seen him form a battle line near the junction of the Pontotoc-Tupelo road with a Harrisburg-Ellistown thoroughfare leading back to Ripley, Forrest may have interpreted these movements as preparations for another retreat like that of Sooy Smith; if so, he may have assumed that any sort of Confederate attack would initiate another Union rout that could be hounded for the next several days. On the other hand, in his physically weakened condition, he still may have been brooding over Lee's promotion and sullenly intent on forcing Lee to make all the decisions here, even — perhaps especially — when he thought they were wrong. Or perhaps he was just putting up a good front in the interest of morale.[13]

Whatever his motives, this blisteringly hot day would turn out to be Forrest's most questionable on any battlefield, including that at Dover when he botched the ill-advised attack by Wheeler. The plan at Harrisburg, almost certainly Lee's, was to concertedly strike the strong Federal position with three elements: Mabry's brigade on the left, the Kentucky brigade of Buford's division in the center, and Roddey's small division on the right. Behind these forward units would be positioned Chalmers's division and 2,100 temporary infantry under Lyon. Lee was to supervise the left and center, while Forrest, who had been given his choice of command responsibility, chose the right and Roddey's troops, with their task of turning the Federal left. Forrest's report later said the Federals "had selected a strong position on a ridge fronting an open field, gradually sloping toward our approach. During the night [they] had constructed fortifications," and their "naturally strong" position became "almost impregnable." Lee ordered the Confederates forward, "and directed me to swing the right around on the enemy's left." He said he "immediately repaired to General Roddey's right with all possible speed, which was nearly a mile distant, and after giving him the necessary orders in person I dashed across the field in a gallop for the purpose of selecting a position in which to place his troops, but on reaching the front I found the Kentucky brigade [to his left] had been rashly precipitated forward, and were retiring under the murderous fire concentrated upon them."[14]

Buford — who, when ordered to attack that morning, "modestly expressed the opinion that the attack should not be a direct one, but the majority of forces should be thrown on the Verona and Tupelo road, and a vigorous assault made on . . . [the Federal] left flank"—reported that "in front of the enemy's position, the country was open, there being no timber in front for a distance of 100 or 200 yards at different points of his line." He said that when the Kentucky Brigade crossed this open space, reached the edge of the timber and discovered the Union position, they "rais[ed] . . . a shout [and] charged." The Federals did not shoot "until our men were in close range," but then "poured upon them a galling fire." The Confederates kept coming, though, in the face of Union artillery "fired with great rapidity, charged with canister." Noticing that the Confederates "on our extreme right (Roddey's) did not advance, the enemy turned the fire of his batteries . . . in Roddey's front, on the advancing Kentuckians, and they, under a galling fire of musketry and artillery both in front and obliquely from the enemy in Roddey's front, were compelled to fall back."[15]

Morton, commanding all Confederate artillery on the field that day, apparently wanted to use a Forrest-like tactic and was refused. He later said he had proposed to gather all his guns in the left center and not only occupy Federal artillery in that sector but blast a hole in the line through which the Kentucky Brigade might have charged; he added that Lee vetoed this proposition and instead dispersed the Confederate artillery throughout all his units. The most controversial decision of the day, though, with the exception of that of deciding to attack at all, was Forrest's. Colonel Ed Crossland, commanding the Kentucky Brigade, later reported that the "failure of Roddey's division to advance, and thus draw the fire of the enemy on my right flank, was fatal to my men. . . . The ranks were decimated; they were literally mowed down." Instead of rushing Roddey's men forward, Forrest rode to the front of the Kentuckians "and seized their colors, and after a short appeal ordered them to form a new line," he would later report. He would contend that the withering volleys "poured" into Crossland's men "showed that the enemy were in overwhelming numbers in an impregnable position, and wishing to save my troops from the unprofitable slaughter I knew would follow any attempt to charge his works, I did not push forward General Roddey's command when it arrived, knowing it would receive the same concentrated fire which repulsed the Kentucky brigade."[16]

Anticipating the sort of move he himself certainly would have made had he been in Smith's position, he worried that the repulse of Crossland left the whole Confederate rear open to a countercharge by the Union center. Roddey later recalled that Forrest "ordered an immediate retreat to the place where the horses were left, saying at the same time, that Buford was badly cut up, and his only reliance for the protection of his stores, lay in keeping my troops in position to keep the enemy from capturing them." He added, Roddey recalled, "that he had no other troops he could spare or rely upon for such purposes."[17]

For the next two hours, several of the thin Confederate units were fed piecemeal into the battle. Despite his earlier refusal to command, Forrest began issuing orders to troops in the center and the rear as well as in his designated area of responsibility on the right. Chalmers reported that as soon as the battle began he "was ordered to advance, and while moving received three different orders." One from Forrest directed him to move "to the right to support General Roddey"; meanwhile Lee instructed him to "move to the left and support Colonel Mabry"; while from Buford came an order "stating I should move, by direction of General Lee, to relieve him on the center." The directive he decided to follow, he went on, was that of Forrest, "my immediate superior," but before he "had reached the desired position another order from General Lee in person divided my command, leaving McCulloch's brigade in reserve and moving Rucker's brigade to the left to charge at the double-quick. . . ."[18]

Lee's postwar reminiscence of the battle says Forrest already had driven in the skirmishers on the Federal left at the time he saw Crossland's Kentuckians bloodily engaged; it adds that "before Crossland was repulsed Mabry and Bell [on the Confederate left] pushed up to the enemy, fighting desperately, holding their position two and a half hours." Noting that Forrest "was not directly in charge of Crossland's Brigade," Lee said that as soon as Forrest saw Crossland "repulsed" he took it upon himself to "change . . . the entire plan of battle perfected by General Lee and himself, withdrew Roddey, and with Crossland formed a new line of battle, leaving the left wing of the enemy unengaged, and allowing them to concentrate their fire on the troops immediately under Lee." In his third-person account, Lee went on to recall that he could not "drive in the center of the enemy's line" and therefore "ordered up Chalmers to put him in on the extreme right of the enemy." When Chalmers did not arrive, Lee went looking for him and "found he had been moved to extreme right by order of Forrest, who did not report to Lee his change in agreement, nor his order to Chalmers to reenforce Roddey, who was doing no fighting." When he found Chalmers and learned of Forrest's order, Lee said, he still supposed Forrest would carry out the original battle plan and therefore "divided Chalmers's command, sending Rucker's brigade to extreme left to attack enemy, sending Neely to Forrest, as he wanted reenforcements, and holding McCulloch in reserve." With the Union left remaining "unengaged and concentrating their fire on his troops," Lee finally went to the right and sought out Forrest, "who . . . told him what he had done. It was then too late to remedy matters, and under cover of McCulloch's brigade, he (Lee) withdrew Bell, Mabry, and Rucker. . . ."[19]

The assault, for all its murderous meandering, impressed their Federal opponent with its dedication if not its skill. Smith's report would recall that the Confederates "started from the edge of the timber in three lines," and initially "their lines could be distinguished separately, but as they advanced they lost all semblance of lines and the attack[ers] resembled a mob of huge magnitude." It looked to Smith like "a foot race to see who should reach us first. They were allowed to approach, yelling and howling like Comanches, to within canister range. . . . Their charge was gallantly made, but without order, organization, or skill." Like ocean waves against a shore, they "would come forward and fall back, rally and [come] forward again, with the like result. Their determination may be seen from the fact that their dead were found within thirty yards of our batteries."[20]

They lost 1,310 killed, wounded, or missing out of 3,500 troops actually engaged (compared to 674 total Union casualties), and they finally pulled back in the face of a hesitant and ultimately abortive Federal advance. Then they drew up into what Lee described, in a dispatch to Richmond, as a "strong position" to await the expected Federal counterattack. They waited the rest of the day in vain. That night, Forrest is reported to have tried to absent himself from a meeting of Confederate unit commanders on grounds of illness but was summoned by Lee. When asked by Lee if he had any "ideas" on what had transpired, he is reported to have replied hotly: "Yes, sir, I've always got ideas, and I'll tell you one thing, General Lee. If I knew as much about West Point tactics as you, the Yankees would whip hell out of me every day."[21]

The following morning, with no Federal attack having come, Buford and Chalmers were sent out at 11 A.M. to probe the right and left. When Chalmers's men came in sight of the Ellistown-Harrisburg road, they saw Smith's victorious Federals in retreat, leaving a lot of torched Tupelo houses in their wake; Smith's report subsequently and lamely explained that "much" of the bread he had brought with him was found to have been "spoiled when drawn from the commissary depot" and that his artillery ammunition was down to "only about 100 rounds per gun." Lee ordered the Confederate pursuit to be commanded by Forrest, who didn't refuse this time. He quickly directed Mabry, Chalmers, and Buford to follow "and make a vigorous assault upon . . . [Smith's] rear as soon as it could be overtaken."[22]

Four miles north at Old Town Creek, the Federals made a stiff stand reminiscent of the one at Harrisburg. Forrest reported they occupied "a strong position on the crest of a hill," which Bell's and Crossland's men attacked, only to be repulsed. In the process of rallying his retreating men and trying to advance his column's left, Forrest was struck in his right big toe by a rifle ball. This third and most painful gunshot wound of the war prompted him to order Chalmers to take command and withdraw the troops. Attempting to comply, Chalmers ordered Buford to form his troops for retreat, but Buford was under such Federal pressure that he finally replied he could form only three companies of his men. Chalmers eventually found "Lieutenant-General Lee . . . striving to rally Buford's division and determined not to withdraw."[23]

Forrest was taken to the rear — where, during treatment of his foot, he was told that, probably because of his unusual absence from the battlefield, a dismaying rumor had spread among the troops that he had been killed. As soon as his bleeding was stanched and the wound bandaged, he remounted his horse and, without pausing to put on his coat, rode "in his shirt-sleeves" among the troops, telling them his injury was minor. "The effect produced upon the men by the appearance of General Forrest [was] indescribable," a private in the ranks later remembered. "They seemed wild with joy. . . ."[24]

By now Lee must have been wondering what had happened during the past two days to this vaunted leader of men. Surely, he suspected that part of the problem was Forrest's resentment over the fact that, despite the disparity in the number of victories the two had won, he, Lee, was the newly promoted departmental commander while Forrest himself remained a subordinate all but persona non grata in Richmond. Lee's and Forrest's relations during and after the war are frequently characterized as based in friendship and mutual admiration, as are Forrest's relations with Wheeler, but Lee's postwar observations about Forrest's behavior at Harrisburg are at best clipped and restrained. Of the reasons Forrest left Roddey, rode to Crossland's shattered Kentuckians outside his area of command, and then withdrew both Roddey and Crossland, Lee wrote in 1902 that Forrest "was evidently disconcerted at the repulse of Crossland, and assumed prerogatives of commander-in-chief, when he only had person-ally the supervision of the right wing." He then "changed the order of battle and moved reserves without informing the commanding general. The facts are stated as pleasantly and as complimentarily to Forrest as circumstances will permit." Lee added that Forrest's "staff and followers" were "devotedly attached and loyal to him," and "criticized General Lee" the evening after the battle. Lee wrote that he himself confronted Forrest, who "disavowed the criticism, and said it was his fight, and said he would make an example of those who had done the talking. Again at Okolona General Lee called [Forrest's] attention to the conduct of his staff; [Forrest] became angry and said he would hold them responsible for their words, as they certainly misrepresented him and his actions during the battle."[25]

If Lee's recollections nearly four decades later are true, it would appear that Forrest's remark about West Point tactics at the July 14 command meeting never happened. True or not, when Forrest was among his own subordinates and out of Lee's company he seems to have disavowed any responsibility for the Harrisburg defeat. Trooper John Milton Hubbard recalled that the day after the battle he was sitting a horse beside a Harrisburg road when Forrest, "riding in an open buggy," passed him, "[j]ust from the battlefield . . . suffering with a wound . . . [and] somewhat excited." Hubbard said he "remember[ed] well the sentiment he uttered. It was that expressed by the words: 'Boys, this is not my fight, and I take no responsibility for it,' or words tantamount to these."[26]

A reason for such behavior on Forrest's part could have been cannily practical; he had never been beaten in a battle in which he commanded the field, and he surely knew such a record made it easier for him to recruit troops. Chalmers indicated after the war, however, that Forrest's main consideration in repudiating any responsibility for Harrisburg stemmed from a vain unwillingness to admit mistakes. Of Forrest and the Harrisburg battle, Chalmers wrote: "Forrest was a great general; but he never rose to that greatness and dignity of soul which enabled Robert E. Lee at Gettysburg to assume the responsibility of a failure."[27]

Forrest's mistakes at Harrisburg can be overstated, though. Having already demanded that Stephen Lee command the field, he thus prevented himself from making the sort of flank-and-rear attack for which he was becoming famous; that, perhaps, was his worst error. When he saw Crossland's brigade all but destroyed because of its premature advance, he instinctively ordered a defensive move against the counterstroke Smith should have made; had Smith made this move, Forrest's reaction would have saved Lee's army from annihilation. The fact that Forrest refused to order Roddey's brigade forward to the same punishment Crossland's received may be grounds not so much for censure of Forrest as of Lee, who was so inflexible as to leave Crossland under murderous fire for more than two hours. What it does illustrate, though, is that Forrest was too much of an individual tactician and too accustomed to making instantaneous decisions under fire to be able to operate very effectively under anybody else's hands-on command, especially that of someone as unimaginative as Lee was that day.

Forrest and Lee were soon parted. Within days after Harrisburg, the latter was sent east to become a corps commander in the Atlanta-based army of General John B. Hood, while Forrest remained assigned to northern Mississippi to fend off comparatively minor Federal raids designed specifically to keep him where he was. Sherman, preparing for a series of battles around Atlanta, complained over the fact that Smith had retreated home from Harrisburg and insisted he "pursue and keep after Forrest all the time." "[I]f Forrest goes toward Tennessee," he added, "General Smith must follow him." Washburn reported to Sherman from Memphis on August 2 that Forrest was alleged to have died of lockjaw as a result of the wound at Harrisburg. "Is Forrest surely dead?" Sherman inquired on August 7. "General Forrest is not dead, but was in Pontotoc four days ago," Washburn replied on August 11.[28]

By then, A. J. Smith was in Mississippi again. No sooner had he returned from the Harrisburg expedition than Washburn ordered him out in compliance with Sherman's insistence that he "again move against Forrest." By early August, he was advancing with more than 20,000 men, an even larger force than he had commanded at Harrisburg. To meet him this time, however, were only about 5,000 Confederates. Now, though, they were to be commanded by Forrest—who, although not dead, was showing war's ravages. Rattling around in a buggy with his right foot elevated, he was, in the description of one eyewitness, "sick-looking, thin as a rail, cheekbones that stuck out like they were trying to come through the skin, skin so yellow it looked greenish, eyes blazing."[29]

Major General Dabney H. Maury had succeeded to temporary command of the department. A highly cultured and West Point–educated Virginian who was a friend of Lee's, Maury doubtless had reflected on the causes and results of Harrisburg. He wrote Forrest a cordial and solicitous letter saying he was "intrust[ing] to you the operations against the enemy threatening an invasion of North Mississippi." He added that he "would not, if I could, interfere with your plan for conducting those operations, but must confine myself to the duty of sending you the means, so far as I can, of accomplishing the successful results it has been your good fortune so constantly to achieve." The Confederates in their area, he said, "must do the best we can with the little we have, and it is with no small satisfaction I reflect that of all the commanders of the Confederacy you are accustomed to accomplish the very greatest results with small means when left to your own untrammeled judgment."[30]

Forrest probably resented being made subordinate to Maury, but he wrote back sympathizing with his new commander regarding "the responsibility of your position and the difficulties . . . [of] command[ing] . . . a large department with forces inadequate for its defense." He also made a sobering report. Following the costly fighting at Brice's Cross Roads and Harrisburg, he said, Colonel T. H. Bell was the sole experienced brigade commander he had left, "and in Bell's brigade the greater number of field officers are wounded or killed." He said he no longer had a force adequate "to risk a general engagement," but would "resort to all other means in my reach to harass, annoy, and force the enemy back. . . . I can take the saddle with one foot in the stirrup." He hinted that he, too, may have done some reflecting on Harrisburg: "You may rest assured, general, of my hearty co-operation in all things and at all times."[31]

Smith's column had marched eastward from Memphis to Grand Junction, Tennessee, where it was transported south to Holly Springs by rail. August was proving strangely rainy for Mississippi as Forrest scattered his units from Okolona and Pontotoc in the east to Abbeville in the west to learn which way Smith would move this time. He had been completely familiar with this area since late boyhood, and he was making use of civilian relatives; he wrote Chalmers at Oxford saying he was dispatching the regiments of Duckworth and Kelley to try to cut the railroad behind Smith, adding: "Send the Beck boys to report to Duckworth and Kelley as guides."[32]

When, on August 8, Smith crossed the Tallahatchie River heading for Oxford, it was obviously time to rush the Pontotoc and Okolona troops westward. Chalmers wired from Abbeville recommending they be sent south of Oxford to Water Valley or even Coffeeville, but Forrest ordered him to hang on as long as possible near Abbeville and not to "fall back to Oxford if you can possibly help it." Facing a force so overwhelming it would have been suicide to fight it conventionally, Forrest surely was engaged overtime in his habitual solitary planning sessions. He wrote Chalmers cryptically about a situation farther westward: "What facilities for crossing the river at Panola? How many boats are there?" Late on the night of August 10, Forrest brought his eastern units to Oxford, which the Federals had momentarily occupied and then abandoned when they learned he was arriving. He and Smith then spent a rain-soaked week of watching each other around the small college town while the Federals amassed supplies. The Confederate attempt to cut the railroad behind Smith with the aid of the "Beck boys" materialized on August 13 and was unsuccessful, primarily because the countryside was infested with Federal cavalry and, even in this region of Forrest's youth, "citizens refused to give information of any kind for fear of the Yankees."[33]

A desperate move was called for, and near dusk five days later Forrest made one. Leaving Chalmers the unenviable task of keeping the Federals occupied and ignorant at Oxford, he gathered four cannons and less than 2,000 of his best-mounted men and led them west toward Panola. There on the morning of August 19, after culling two cannons and some 100 men "for lack of serviceable horses," he crossed the Tallahatchie and turned north for Memphis, more than sixty miles in Smith's rear. It was to be no easy journey. Just beyond Senatobia the next morning, they encountered rain-swollen Hickahala Creek, where they made another culling of 500 more unsuitably mounted men and sent them back to Oxford under the command of artillery commander Morton. Morton later cited this move as another instance of Forrest's military brilliance: "Should a rumor of his departure have reached General Smith, the return of this body would indicate . . . abandonment of his plan."[34]

They then crossed the Hickahala's sixty-foot width with Forrest ingenuity, using a single flatboat, cedar telegraph poles, planks gathered from the floors of nearby cotton-ginning houses, and a lot of large wild grapevines with which to lash these materials together. In little more than an hour, his troops fashioned a bridge that supported not only themselves and their horses in columns of two, but also two cannons carried across by hand. The same method was used to bridge the Coldwater River seven miles farther on, trooper John Milton Hubbard later wrote. He added that, when a wagon full of ears of corn "was thought to be too heavy for the bridge . . . General Forrest ordered the corn thrown out of the wagon and corn carried over by hand. He was the first man to carry an armful across."[35]

The aim of the expedition was "by a sudden *coup de main* [to] threaten if not capture the city of Memphis, with the effect . . . of forcing General Smith to return to the relief of that place." He hoped to heighten Federal consternation by freeing military detainees in Irving Prison and capturing three important Union generals then residing in Memphis: Brigadier General R. P. Buckland, who commanded the Memphis garrison itself; Major General Stephen A. Hurlbut, former commander of the West Tennessee district; and the current West Tennessee district commander, Washburn.[36]

In a thick fog that muffled gunfire, the Confederates charged into

Forrest's home city about 4 A.M. via the road from Hernando, another of his hometowns. They had ridden the last four miles in total silence behind Captain Bill Forrest, who was back in the saddle despite the bullet-smashed thigh that had caused his capture at Sand Mountain. One of his eldest brother's most trusted scouts—and reputed among Forrest troopers to be the only man alive whom that brother feared—Bill Forrest with ten men preceded the rest of the troops by sixty yards. Ordered to observe silence, the Confederates captured two picket posts, but several gunshots at the second shattered the quiet; unable now to be restrained, they raised the rebel yell and clattered into the heart of this city that had been under Federal occupation a full two years.[37]

The degree of surprise at their appearance in such a place is reflected in the report of General Buckland, who recalled being awakened by shouts and "loud raps" from a sentinel at his front door. "General, they are after you!" the sentinel said.

Buckland leaped out of bed and shouted out a window, "Who are after me?"

"The rebels," he was answered.[38]

Meanwhile, Bill Forrest rode straight for—and into the lobby of—the Gayoso House hotel, where General Hurlbut had a room; fortunately for Hurlbut, he happened to be staying that night in the quarters of a colonel friend and thus missed capture. Lieutenant Colonel Jesse Forrest simultaneously made for the Union Street headquarters of Washburn, who fled in his nightclothes to Fort Pickering, a half mile away—"without having given any command as to what should be done by our troops," a subordinate later officially complained. His unceremonious exit from his quarters is said to have prompted Hurlbut to make one of the wittier remarks of the war: "They removed me from command because I couldn't keep Forrest out of West Tennessee, and now Washburn can't keep him out of his own bedroom!"[39]

Buckland seems to have been the only one of the three Union generals who did anything of note. Dressing quickly, he ran to a nearby barracks and began forming a line of troops, then ordered the firing of an alarm gun. By then, he was told the Confederates had been to his door, where his sentinel shot at them, killing one of their horses and driving them off. Because nothing had been heard from Washburn, Buckland assumed his superior had been captured and so made arrangements to attack a band of Confederates storming Washburn's headquarters. Learning that Forrest—the major general, not one of his subordinate brothers—was personally commanding the Confederates, Buckland then organized several

Federal elements and was concentrating them when Washburn finally was reported "safe in the fort." Washburn soon appeared and "assumed general direction of affairs" shortly before the Confederates began heading back toward the Hernando Road.[40]

By then it was approaching 9 A.M. They had been denied most of the prizes they had hoped to claim, from the generals to the inmates of Irving Prison, but on many of their memories seems to have been etched forever the brief glimpse of not only the bluff city but also, apparently, much more female flesh than was normally to be seen in public in that era. "[T]he women—young and old—forgetting the costume of the hour, throwing open their window-blinds and doors, welcomed their dear countrymen by voice and smiles, and every possible manifestation of the delight inspired by such an advent."[41]

As the Federal opposition firmed up, the foray ended fitfully; the Confederates, in fact, had to retreat from the city in groups as small as twos and threes. Washburn reported killing twenty-two Confederates, severely wounding at least fifteen more, and capturing twenty-five. In addition to some eighty horses, Forrest's troopers had killed fifteen Federals and wounded sixty-five more, according to Washburn's count. They also had captured 600 prisoners, including some 200 adjudged to be either civilians or too sick or disabled to travel; these 200 eventually were turned loose on the road to Hernando—after Forrest, under a flag of truce, first proposed that all his prisoners be exchanged for others Washburn held. When Washburn claimed to have no such authority, Forrest said that since they had been captured in nightclothes and Washburn wouldn't exchange them, humanity dictated that the Union general send out suitable attire for them to wear marching southward. After receiving the demanded clothes, Forrest used a similar argument to persuade Washburn to send these prisoners two wagonloads of food—which he then made them share with his hungry troopers. During negotiations for these unusual gifts, he sent Washburn the Federal general's own uniform, which had been captured by Jesse Forrest's men. Washburn graciously responded by conveying to Forrest enough "gray cloth with buttons and lace to make Forrest and his staff full uniforms."[42]

On August 23, after spending a full day in Hernando, the Confederates left for Panola. Back in Oxford, Smith had received (via wires intentionally left open by Forrest) three Washburn telegrams concerning the Memphis exploit and Washburn's urgent instructions as to how Smith could intercept Forrest's exhausted troops on their way back to rejoin Chalmers. "The whole affair was an utter failure on his [Forrest's] part,"

Washburn blustered in his official report. He was deluding no one but himself. Smith's slow southward progress suddenly halted — just after Chalmers asked and was denied, by department commander Maury, permission to evacuate the Oxford environs and fall back to Water Valley. That same day, according to a Confederate captain of the Oxford garrison, Smith "retired . . . after burning 34 stores and business houses, courthouse, Masonic Hall, 2 fine large hotels, besides carpenter, blacksmith, and other shops; also 5 fine dwelling houses. . . ."[43]

Forrest once more had managed to meet his primary obligation of protecting the grain-laden Mississippi prairie. Sherman, however, had again accomplished a goal of his own. Forrest had been kept out of Georgia and Tennessee.

22

"A TRAIN FROM the north, bringing Forrest in advance of his troops, reached Meridian [Mississippi], and was stopped; and the General, whom I had never seen, came to report," Confederate lieutenant general Richard Taylor, son of President Zachary Taylor and brother-in-law of Jefferson Davis, would later remember of a day soon after the Memphis raid. Forrest, he wrote, "was a tall, stalwart man with grayish hair, mild countenance . . . slow and homely of speech," and Taylor quickly told him "that all of our energies must be directed to the relief of Hood's army, then west of Atlanta. The only way to accomplish this was to worry Sherman's communications north of the Tennessee River, and he [Forrest] must move his cavalry in that direction at the earliest moment." Taylor was surprised to find the reputedly intrepid cavalryman exhibiting "no stomach for the work," noting the "many difficulties" of the task and "ask[ing] . . . numerous questions: how he was to get over the Tennessee; how he was to get back if pressed by the enemy; how he was to be supplied; what should be his line of retreat in certain contingencies; what he was to do with prisoners if any were taken, etc." Then, however, "having isolated the chances of success from causes of failure with the care of a chemist experimenting in his laboratory," his "whole manner . . . changed." He announced his needs "in a dozen sharp sentences . . . said he would leave a staff officer to bring up his supplies, asked for an engine to take him back north twenty miles to meet his troops, informed me that he would march with the dawn, and hoped to give an account of himself in Tennessee."[1]

Although he himself had suggested a return to his native state several times — the latest being a telegram to President Davis on September 5, the very day he met Taylor — his troops, exhausted from the long Memphis ride or the hard work of holding the Federals around Oxford, had just begun to get a little rest. There was also the fact that he, better than anyone else, knew his brilliant dash on Memphis was really the result of ominous deficiency: Brice's Cross Roads and Harrisburg had cost him men whose like and number even his iron-fisted conscription never would be able to muster again. He may have learned, too, that Atlanta had fallen to Sherman September 2 — that, in other words, the Confederate high command had waited far too late to loose him onto the Tennessee railroads. Plus he doubtless was in no mood to be taken for granted by another departmental commander.

Having eluded Smith's attempt to turn and capture the Memphis raiders returning to Oxford, Forrest had been summoned south to Mobile by the urgent appeals of Maury. Apparently both Forrest and his wife attended a dinner there given in his honor by Mrs. Maury, who had "invit[ed] some lady friends who were desirous of meeting this great hero," Maury later remembered. Forrest displayed "natural deference" to females characterized by great courtesy, Maury proceeded, "and in their presence was very bright and entertaining. He had for women that . . . respect that marks the truly brave man. . . . [H]e was their defender and protector from every sort of wrong. His wife was a gentle lady, to whom he was careful in his deference."[2]

As Forrest was preparing for his Tennessee trek, Hood in Georgia was demanding that the cavalryman finally be ordered onto the Tennessee railroads as quickly as possible — while Wheeler was failing at the same assignment. From his own army below Atlanta, Hood had sent Wheeler toward Tennessee and the Federal rear, and Wheeler's subsequent assault on the Federal rails was so superficial that it hardly interrupted Sherman's supply traffic. In the process, Wheeler depleted down to a mere sixty men Forrest's old brigade; Forrest claimed in a letter to Taylor that it had numbered 2,300 when he turned it over to Wheeler the previous November.[3]

Now from West Point, Mississippi, to Cherokee Station, Alabama, Forrest led three brigades totaling just 3,500 men, leaving Chalmers in Mississippi with another brigade plus additional troops. At Tuscumbia, Alabama, Forrest met Wheeler on September 20 and reported to Taylor that Wheeler's men were "demoralized" and "I can expect but little assistance, but will nevertheless go ahead." Reinforced by another 900 men from Roddey, he left Cherokee Station the next morning, and two days later appeared before an imposing Athens, Alabama, blockhouse guarding the Central Alabama Railroad.[4]

Out to accomplish more than Wheeler had, Forrest and his men first drew the attention of the blockhouse by "tearing up the railroad about five miles south of Athens." The Federals sent 150 men down to drive them off and claimed to have done it, but not for long; battle erupted when the Confederates torched a quartermaster's building and tried to get control of Athens. The Federal troops, more than 600 in number, moved that evening into the railroad blockhouse, "[a]n earthwork 180 by 450 feet, surrounded by an abatis of brush and a palisade 4 feet high, and a ditch 12 feet wide . . . 18 feet from the bottom of the ditch to the top of the parapets." This facility was, in the words of a Union inspector of such defenses, "one of the best works of the kind I ever saw." Garrisoned almost totally with black troops of about one-third the number of their attackers, it resembled Fort Pillow more than a little, a resemblance not lost on men of either side. Lieutenant Colonel William F. Prosser of the Second Tennessee Cavalry (U.S.) arrived with 500 men about 9 P.M. Prosser refused, however, to charge Confederates in the town's public square and drive them away from the railroad depot when ordered to by the Athens commander, Colonel Wallace Campbell of the 110th U.S. Colored Infantry; Prosser said "he could not sacrifice his horses." After moving all his own troops inside the blockhouse and burning all Federal property outside it, Campbell ordered Prosser to remain "at or near" the blockhouse; Prosser again refused to obey, "saying he did not think with his force the fort could be held." Campbell finally had to content himself with using Prosser as the bearer of a message to Brigadier General Robert S. Granger at nearby Decatur, to which Prosser soon retired.[5]

Morton's twelve-pounder guns opened on the blockhouse about 7 A.M., September 24, and kept up a fire for two hours. Bell's and Buford's brigades advanced while Kelley's sat at the southeast end of town, covering the railroad and preparing to fend off more reinforcements reportedly hurrying from Decatur. After two hours and the firing of some sixty shells, which killed one Federal and wounded two, Forrest sent forward a flag of truce. "Knowing it would cost heavily to storm and capture the enemy's works, and wishing to prevent the effusion of blood I knew would follow a successful assault, I determined to see if anything could be accomplished by negotiations," he later reported. "Accordingly, I sent Major Strange, of my staff, with a flag of truce, demanding the surrender of the fort and garrison."[6]

Strange—and fellow staff member M. C. Gallaway, who accompanied

Strange into Federal lines—underscored the parallel with Fort Pillow. According to Campbell, they said they knew "from conversation held with General Forrest . . . he was determined to take the fort, and if he was compelled to storm it no lives would be spared." Campbell, who already had been told by two Confederate prisoners that Forrest's troopers numbered at least 10,000, then received a request from Forrest for a "personal interview." Campbell granted it and "immediately met General Forrest . . . [who] told me he was determined to take the place; that his force was sufficiently large, and have it he would, and if he was compelled to storm the works it would result in the massacre of the entire garrison. He told me what his force was, and said myself and one officer could have the privilege of reviewing [it]."

Campbell returned to his own officers and agreed that if Forrest was found to have "8,000 to 10,000 troops, it would be worse than murder to attempt to hold the works." Taking along an artillery officer, he then "rode round his [Forrest's] entire line, thereby satisfying myself and the captain accompanying me that there were at least 10,000 men and nine pieces of artillery." The two Federal officers received this impression of overpowering strength from typical Forrest maneuvering. Morton recalled that Forrest himself took them on the tour and perpetrated much of the deception in person, pointing out dismounted cavalry as infantry, horse-holders as cavalry, and two batteries of artillery; unknown to the Federal officers, each of these elements then was viewed several more times on different parts of the field, "until the whole place seemed to be swarming with enthusiastic troops and bristling with guns."[7]

For three hours, Campbell stretched out the negotiations, hoping for arrival of the reinforcements from Granger at Decatur, but finally Forrest refused to give him more time. With Kelley's brigade holding off and capturing some 700 Federal troops from Decatur in a three-hour running fight (in which Lieutenant Colonel Jesse Forrest was so severely wounded in the thigh that he was out of action the rest of 1864), Campbell surrendered the force inside the blockhouse. Two other nearby block-houses, both south of Athens along the track toward Decatur, were added to the captures. One of these capitulated as soon as asked, the other after Morton's artillery skillfully fired three shots into gaps between its shrunken oak timbers, killing and wounding several Federals inside.[8]

At the latter, Morton later remembered, a German-born officer initially declined surrender, telling Forrest's emissary to return to his own lines immediately or the Federals would "shoot your damned head from your shoulders off!" Forrest, incensed by this reply, "made the atmosphere blue for a while," at one point asking a subordinate if the Federal officer wanted "to be blown up[.] Well, I'll blow him up, then. Give him hell, Morton — as hot as you've got it, too." After Morton's second shot killed and wounded several Federals, a white cloth was stuck out a porthole of the blockhouse 300 yards away, and Morton ordered a cease-fire. "Go on, John, go on," Forrest protested. "That was bully. Keep it up!" When Morton pointed at the cloth floating from the porthole, Forrest responded gloweringly that he could not see it. "Keep on firing," he added. "It'll take a sheet to attract my eye at this distance." A larger white flag soon was produced by the defenders, and Forrest let them surrender.[9]

In all, at Athens Forrest captured "1,300 officers and men, 38 wagons, 2 ambulances, 300 horses, two trains of cars loaded with quartermaster's and commissary stores, with a large quantity of small arms and 2 pieces of artillery." Campbell's capitulation was roundly abhorred by both superiors and subordinates. Brigadier General John Starkweather up the tracks at Pulaski, Tennessee, reported it was done "much to my disgust and to that of his [Campbell's] whole command," while a document condemning it was signed by thirty-one officers under Campbell; they said that just two officers among them had advised surrender and that neither of the two had men inside the blockhouse.[10]

While the Federals assessed blame, Forrest sent his prisoners and spoils south toward Florence and continued northward along the railroad toward Pulaski, taking and burning blockhouses as he went. The first two were surrendered quickly after he sent in with his capitulation demands the German-born Union officer who had first refused, then begged, to surrender south of Athens; "his description [of Morton's artillery attack on his fortress] produce[d] the effect for which he had been carried along."[11]

Early on September 25 some ten miles north of Athens, Forrest's force invested the 100-yard-long, seventy-two-foot-high trestle at Sulphur Branch. It was the largest trestle on that part of the Central Alabama Railroad and, as such, was guarded by two imposing blockhouses with forty-inch walls and garrisons totaling 200 Indiana cavalry, 400 Tennessee Union cavalry and 400 black infantry; these blockhouses, however, were overlooked by hills taller than they were. Posting Morton's eight guns on the surrounding ground, Forrest sent a request for surrender, and when it was abruptly refused, Morton's guns opened a furious cannonade. They fired a total of 800 rounds, killing the Federal commander and, after two hours, silencing the guns to such an extent that they "made no show of resistance." Again Forrest demanded surrender: this time he got it. "The enemy suffered severely in this assault," he later reported. ". . . Almost every house [within the Federal fortifications] was perforated with shell, and the dead lay thick." He went on to number his captures at "700 stand of small-arms, 2 pieces artillery, 3 ambulances, 16 wagons, 300 cavalry horses and equipments, medical, quartermaster's and commissary stores." In his wake as he left, the blockhouses and the huge trestle all were "consumed by fire."[12]

These activities prompted considerable Federal correspondence. Major General Lovell H. Rousseau in Tullahoma, Tennessee, wrote Sherman in Georgia that Forrest appeared to have 8,000 men and twenty-four pieces of artillery and that "he is here [in Tennessee] to stay unless routed by a superior cavalry force." Rousseau then added a shrewd observation that should have caused him to reassess his report of Forrest's numerical strength: "[His] movements are much more cautious than formerly. He has attacked no place held by white men, but every post held by colored troops has been taken. . . ." Rousseau noted that Forrest's "destruction of [the] railroad was most thorough," adding: "This is more than a raid. I regard it as a formidable invasion, the object of which is to destroy our lines, and he will surely do it unless met by a large cavalry force and killed, captured, or routed."[13]

Forrest pushed on toward Pulaski on September 26. At Brown's Plantation a few miles south, he encountered a "Government corral" of "commissary stores and medical supplies" principally populated by "about 2,000 black civilians." From this Union commissary, Forrest was able to issue to his men "several days' rations," including "as much sugar and coffee as they needed." He noted that "[t]he negroes were all ragged and dirty, and many seemed in absolute want," adjectives that connote pity but probably were intended only to indict the Federals who had liberated the blacks into such squalor. He quickly rendered their condition even worse, as he himself reported: "I ordered them to remove their clothing and bed clothes from the miserable hovels in which they lived and then burnt up this den of wretchedness. Near 200 houses were consumed."[14]

The next day he continued in the face of growing Union resistance, pushing Federal troops into Pulaski itself during what he termed "seven hours of constant fighting." Satisfying himself that "the enemy was strongly posted with a large force," he "therefore determined to make no further assault"; instead, he withdrew his troops, built huge campfires that night, then slipped away to the east toward a long-sought target, Sherman's Nashville-to-Chattanooga rail line. From Fayetteville, he sent detachments to cut that line above and below Tullahoma, but at the Mulberry community the next day he learned that the Federals held

Tullahoma and "all other vulnerable points in that direction" with "strong force." With Federal reinforcements "from Atlanta, Chattanooga, and other points . . . being hurried forward . . . not less than 15,000 troops sent forward to intercept my movements," and with his artillery ammunition seriously depleted, he was forced to quickly abandon Sherman's rail line and "operat[e] . . . where there was a prospect of accomplishing some good."

The raid then degenerated into a series of smaller-scale actions. About 1,500 men under Buford were ordered back to Huntsville, Alabama, to threaten the city and to "destroy the Memphis & Charleston Railroad from Huntsville to Decatur." Forrest himself took the rest of his force, with no artillery, and headed first for Columbia, twelve miles north of which he captured 120 more Federals and burned four more blockhouses and three more railroad bridges. He went on to threaten Columbia itself on October 2, but withdrew after ascertaining that the town was held by a large Federal garrison that he couldn't dislodge without artillery. For offensive purposes, the raid was all but over.

Forrest rode hard to Lawrenceburg on October 3, and for the next two days continued toward Florence, Alabama. There he hoped to cross the Tennessee River before being caught by several converging Union forces that had what Sherman described as the Federals' best "chance at him." At Florence, he found a rain-swollen Tennessee River and also Buford, who had made his move toward Huntsville and Decatur and then spent the previous thirty-six hours getting his artillery wagons and most of his troops across the rising river on three small ferryboats. Buford had requested the surrender of 1,200 Federals and been rebuffed; he then had sent in another demand to which Forrest's name had been forged, threatening an "attack . . . tomorrow morning from every rock, house, tree, and shrub in the vicinity." When even this threat didn't work, he and his troopers abandoned the charade a little after midday and headed westward toward Athens.[15]

By the time Forrest reached Buford and the Tennessee, Federals under Brigadier General J. D. Morgan were pushing him. More than 1,000 Confederates were still on the northern banks on October 5, and Forrest was forced to order "all troops on the north side of the river, with the exception of one regiment, to mount their horses and swim them across a slough about 70 yards wide to a large island, which would afford them ample protection and from which they could ferry over at leisure." The excepted regiment, commanded by a Colonel Windes of Roddey's division, was left to hold off pursuit until the swimmers had made it to the island. Windes remained behind three days, annoying a reported force of 15,000 Federals and "retir[ing] to the hills when pushed," until the rest of Forrest's force had been gotten across the river. Then, after the Federals left in disappointment, Windes ferried his regiment across "unmolested."

Forrest dispatched Kelley's brigade and a section of artillery to East-port, Alabama, on October 9 to prevent an expected Federal attempt to cross at another point, and the next day Kelley ambushed a small flotilla of two gunboats and three transports; the artillery blew up a transport and "partially disabled" a gunboat. For the first time, though, a Forrest raid had had to avoid combat repeatedly at almost every turn. He had made impressive captures and torn up a long stretch of Federal railroad, but none of the latter was on the crucial line supplying Sherman in Georgia. As one of his opponents noted, he was markedly less fierce than before, and the reasons are understandable. The Confederacy now was so strapped that he had to send back details of his own men with captured troops and matériel, and his thin ranks were made up of ever greater numbers of conscripts and therefore were less reliable than those of Brice's Cross Roads and Fort Pillow. Discipline, never one of his units' strongest features, became even more lax as he made allowances for officers and noncoms who could hold his men together.[16]

Morton later recalled that on the march from Fayetteville toward Tullahoma, the rural thoroughfares were very muddy, and Forrest came upon a group of artillerymen blocking a road as they struggled to move a captured caisson. Intent on getting to the Nashville-Chattanooga rails before the Federals could protect his target, he impatiently asked who was commanding the men. A Captain Andrew McGregor said he was.

"Then why in the hell don't you do something?" Forrest shouted.

Jumping up, McGregor shouted back, "I'll not be cursed out by anybody, even a superior officer." Furiously, he grabbed a torch and rammed it into the caisson.

Forrest "seemed stupefied for a moment by the insanity of thrusting a lighted torch into a caisson full of powder," John Morton later remem-bered. He "clapped spurs to his horse and rode away as fast as he could, shouting a warning to the others. Reaching his staff, he asked: 'What infernal lunatic is that just out of the asylum down there? He came near blowing himself and me up with a whole caisson full of powder.'" Members of his staff happened to know that the caisson contained no powder and burst into laughter, which Forrest joined as soon as he understood it. He never, however, cursed McGregor again.[17]

He remained quick, however, to discipline any officer whose example seemed likely to increase disaffection among the troops. As they were being ferried from the island to the other side of the Tennessee during the escape at Florence, all were ordered to assist on the ferries' oars and poles. Forrest, engaged in these exertions himself, turned to a lieutenant who wasn't and asked him why. According to an eyewitness, the "lieutenant responded that he was an officer, and did not think he was called upon to do that kind of work as long as there were private soldiers sufficient." Whereupon Forrest slapped the young officer so hard across the face that he was sent "sprawling over the gunwale and into the river." After he was retrieved and pulled back into the boat, Forrest told him: "Now, damn you, get hold of the oars and go to work! If I knock you out of the boat again, I'll let you drown."[18]

Long accustomed to personally performing such menial command duties as checking picket posts and rounding up stragglers, Forrest was worn out. Just a day or so after getting the last of his men across the Tennessee at Florence, he wrote General Taylor from Cherokee expressing his bone-weariness:

> GENERAL: *I have been constantly in the field since 1861, and have spent half the entire time in the saddle. I have never asked for a furlough for over 10 days in which to rest and re[gain health] . . . , and except when wounded and unable to leave my bed have had no respite from duty. My strength is failing and it is absolutely necessary that I should have some rest. I left a large estate in Mississippi and have never given my private affairs a day's attention at any one time since the war began. . . .*

He would go ahead, however, with an expedition into West Tennessee, he said, after which he hoped that "as soon thereafter as you can do so you will relieve me from duty for twenty or thirty days to rest and re[habilitate] . . . which in my present state of health is absolutely necessary. . . ."[19]

The next day, a Taylor aide wrote him that Taylor believed movements by Hood, moving past Sherman's right flank and into his rear, would keep the Union commander busy "and that Western Tennessee will be left unprotected or [un]occupied by the enemy. He therefore desires me to urge you, if possible, to get out of that section all the supplies you can . . . ; these supplies to be . . . paid for by the Confederate States." Forrest replied on October 12 that he was "satisfied the amount of supplies in that region has been greatly exaggerated. I can subsist my command there, and will be able to gather up some wheat and hogs, but not in amounts large as has been supposed." The sentiments of West Tennesseans had taken a further turn toward the Union in the half year since the Fort Pillow raid, undoubtedly because of the economic and political reality of the Confederacy's decline. Forrest reported that Confederate "currency cannot be used in that region, and the people instead of collecting their surplus supply of hogs will scatter them in the woods to prevent their falling into our hands." However, if Taylor could "furnish salt, or anything the people could use at home, I am satisfied they would interest themselves in hunting up and furnishing the Government with every article of supply that they could possibly spare."[20]

He went on to inform Taylor that more than Confederate supplies was on his mind; he was intent on getting at Sherman's well-stocked larders at the end of that railroad he had been unable to damage in central Tennessee. He told Taylor that the Federals derived "much" of their "supplies from the Northwestern railroad, which are shipped up the Tennessee River and thence to Johnsonville and Nashville. It is my present design to take possession of Fort Heiman, on the west bank of the Tennessee River below Johnsonville, and thus prevent all communication with Johnsonville by transports." He said he believed new artillery he had requisitioned "are of sufficient caliber to prevent the operations of their gunboats" and added that the Tennessee River supply route must "be interrupted if not entirely destroyed, as I learned during my recent operations in Middle Tennessee that it was by this route that the enemy received most of his supplies at Atlanta." This letter also cryptically indicated his command's war crimes against blacks — whether assassination or unauthorized sale back into slavery — were continuing, and that he was concerned. In reporting the results of his Middle Tennessee incursion, he wrote: "I have captured on the road upward of 1,000 negroes. I understand only about 800 have reached you. This matter should be investigated, and I shall endeavor to learn where the blame should rest and punish the delinquent."[21]

Hardly pausing after his letter demanding rest, he moved toward West Tennessee, meanwhile endeavoring to get back former subordinates and units reassigned elsewhere. Complaining that he had had to leave behind 500 men (apparently those of Windes) during the Middle Tennessee raid, he did manage to reclaim Chalmers, who recently had been in Mississippi. At Forrest's request, Taylor ordered Chalmers northward with all the men he could take; Forrest reported on October 21 that Chalmers's force had brought his unit total to "about 3,000." In mid-October, Forrest entered West Tennessee and soon reopened his Jackson headquarters. He entertained notions of crossing the Tennessee—"[i]f I succeed in capturing one other boat in Tennessee River, which I think I can do"—and "push[ing] forward to Nashville." This idea seems to have quickly passed, however, perhaps because of temporary illness among his troops and the fact that Federal general Hatch was in position to gain his rear if he crossed the river and made for the Tennessee capital.[22]

Joined at Jackson by Chalmers, Forrest sent him northeastward to Fort Heiman and Paris Landing with instructions to aid Buford in blockading the Tennessee River at those points. This effort quickly produced results. The unsuspecting Federal steamboat *Mazeppa* appeared at Fort Heiman towing two barges on October 29, and Morton's artillerymen disabled them, forcing the *Mazeppa* to the eastern bank, where crew and passengers took to the woods. Her cargo—of such military necessities as "blankets, shoes, clothing, hard bread, &c."—was still being unloaded by the Confederates when three Union gunboats arrived. The Southerners were driven off, and Buford burned the *Mazeppa* to keep her from falling back into Federal hands.[23]

The next day, the Confederates struck again. When the Federal steamboat *Anna*, leading the transports *J. W. Cheeseman* and *Venus* as well as two barges and the gunboat *Undine*, came downriver past the Confederate batteries, she was so disabled that she had to limp into Paducah, and she was comparatively fortunate. The rest were so damaged by both artillery and rifle fire in a six-hour battle that they landed on the river's east shore and their crews fled, leaving dead and wounded. Kelley and two of his companies were sent across to recover these vessels and bring them to Paris Landing; the disabled *Cheeseman* and two barges were burned. The gleeful Confederates then boarded the *Undine* and the *Venus* and raised the Stars and Bars. On the morning of October 31, after assigning officers to command the two craft, Forrest took a short run with them to Fort Heiman to try out his new navy. As they headed out into the river, his troops—who hadn't seen a Confederate flag afloat since the sinking of Confederate gunboats at Memphis two years earlier—"made the air ring with cheer upon cheer. . . ."[24]

At Fort Heiman, the *Venus* was loaded with goods captured from the *Mazeppa*, and by noon of November 1 both boats and Forrest's other troops were in concerted motion toward Johnsonville; the vessels had been instructed to stay where troops toiling along the banks could cover them. It began to rain, making the roads and riverbanks harder to travel, and the *Venus* had gotten ahead of its marching guard on November 2 when it rounded a bend above Davidson's Ferry and met two Federal gunboats.

In the fight that quickly followed, the *Venus,* its steering damaged, was run into a bank, where boat and cargo were abandoned to recapture by the Federals. Chalmers got artillery to Davidson's Ferry in time to help the *Undine* escape, allowing Forrest's navy to continue to exist until the next morning. Then nine Federal gunboats appeared, challenged the Confederate batteries, and hit the *Undine* with three shots. With her cavalry crewmen "demoralized" by water warfare, she was run to shore, set afire, and abandoned.[25]

All this, however, was but prelude to Forrest's chief aim in visiting this part of the Tennessee River. On the afternoon of November 3, he made a personal reconnaissance of the environs of Johnsonville, a Union supply depot named after Andrew Johnson, Tennessee's Federal military governor. Its "wharf . . . was lined with transports and gunboats," and "[a]n immense warehouse presented itself and was represented as being stored with the most valuable supplies, while several acres of the shore were covered with every description of army stores." A fort overlooking these riches, though, "was situated on a high hill and in a commanding position . . . defended by strong works," and the Federal side of the Tennessee was some twenty feet higher than Forrest's side. With the Union fort and guns thus commanding the positions Forrest's would occupy, great care had to be exercised to get the Confederate artillery into place undetected; too, these guns had to be placed where they not only could fire on Johnsonville, its landing, and the overlooking stronghold, but also could hold off gunboats from up- and downriver.[26]

Union colonel Charles R. Thompson, commanding Johnsonville, had been informed almost a week earlier of Forrest's presence near him, and he had pledged to fight to the death if attacked. He seems, however, to have given little thought to the sort of assault Forrest contemplated; the Federals behaved as if heedless of danger. Artillerist Morton, who played a large role in placing the guns where they could fire with most damaging effect, recalled that shortly before the attack, "[t]wo gunboats with steam up were moored at the landing," while a third "plied almost directly beneath the bluff." There were also a "number of barges clustered around; negroes were loading them, officers and men were coming and going, and passengers could be seen strolling down to the wharf. The river banks for some distance back were lined with quantities of stores, and two freight trains were being made up. It was an animated scene, and one which wore an air of complete security."[27]

This "air" lasted until 2 P.M., when the ten guns Forrest had leveled at Johnsonville—including one he aimed himself—opened fire. These shots struck "several gunboats . . . just beginning to swing out into the stream. . . . [S]team and smoke poured forth from the boats and at every aperture from one of them, while her crew were seen jumping into the river nearest the shore and swimming for the landing." One of the other gunboats "turned toward the landing; and the ladies [among the passengers] just approaching the transports rushed wildly up the hillside toward the fort. Only one of the gunboats returned the fire." The third volley from the Confederate batteries struck the boiler of a gunboat "not in action," and "the agonizing screams of the wounded and scalded were plainly heard across the broad river; but the Confederates plied their artillery with unabated energy. . . ."[28]

The bombardment continued without pause for forty minutes and, as its success became apparent, the glee on the Confederate bank penetrated even the highest echelons. Morton later recalled finding Forrest at one of the guns along with Colonel Bell and General Buford, with Forrest acting as gunner. He humorously and incompetently commented on his shots — "A rickety-shay! A rickety-shay! I'll hit her next time!" — and issued what Morton understatedly termed "amateur" orders regarding a change of range: "Elevate the breech of that gun lower!" He then laughed at the howls these comments prompted, while after the recoil of every shot Bell and Buford personally pushed the gun back up the bank into position.[29]

The effect on the river and landing below as well as on the hill above was devastating. Confederate fire was so intense and accurate that it seems to have unnerved Federal officers. Disabled gunboats were burned by the Federals themselves. So were steamboats, in unreasonable fear that the Confederates, who were almost totally without vessels, might cross the river and capture them; these fires, a Union assistant inspector general claimed, then ignited supplies piled on the levee — after which "the rebels concentrated their fire upon the levee and warehouses to prevent the flames from being extinguished." With all river craft in sight afire by 4 P.M., the Confederates turned their guns onto the mountains of supplies intended for Sherman's army. Some barrels of whisky were hit and set afire, causing "burning liquor" to run "in torrents of livid flame down the hillside . . . and filling the air with the blended yet distinct fumes of burning spirits, sugar, coffee, and meat." Forrest reported that by dark "the wharf for nearly one mile up and down the river presented one solid sheet of flame." He finally pulled most of his force out to six miles southward, traveling "by the light of the enemy's burning property."[30]

The next morning, he rode back to inspect damage and found "[n]othing" had been "left unconsumed." Satisfied, he began withdrawing his artillery, taking a parting shot at a "regiment of negroes" who had thrown off their coats "and shaking their clenched fists at the hated Confederates . . . hurled across the stream upon the morning air their whole arsenal of explosive, offensive epithets, oaths, and maledictions." Confederate gunners were halted and ordered to turn their pieces around and fire on the blacks, which "howling, capering crowd . . . scampered away in the wildest confusion," leaving "a number . . . dead or wounded upon the riverbank."[31]

Forrest said that a total of $6.7 million in Federal property had been destroyed, while U.S. Army assistant inspector general William Sinclair estimated the loss "of the property destroyed and captured during the operations of the rebels on the Tennessee River, including steamboats and barges"—but apparently not including the value of the four gunboats lost—at $2.2 million. Forrest claimed to have captured and destroyed four gunboats, fourteen transports, twenty barges, and twenty-six pieces of artillery, as well as taking 150 prisoners. He reported suffering a total Confederate loss of two killed and nine wounded throughout the campaign.[32]

He had no time, though, to savor his triumph. Taylor informed him in the third week of October that Hood had crossed into Alabama from Georgia and was heading for Middle Tennessee in a movement Taylor thought Forrest's Johnsonville operations would enhance. On October 26, however, Taylor wrote him again, ordering that as soon as he had "accomplished the objects of your present movement," he must go to Middle Tennessee to "put yourself in communication with General Hood and be governed by his orders." Feeling pressure to terminate the Johnsonville campaign, Forrest remarked to Chalmers in a dispatch on October 30, "We must be prompt." He wasn't prompt enough to suit Hood. While he was incommunicado in the midst of his gunboat captures on the Tennessee River, Hood impatiently wrote him on November 2 from Tuscumbia: "When can I expect you here or when can I hear from you? I am waiting for you."[33]

Hood waited another dozen days. After the destruction of Johnsonville, Forrest's withdrawal to northern Alabama was hampered by muddy roads, rising rivers, and worn-out horses. As he contended with these obstacles, the Confederacy's last best hope of survival as a nation was strangled in the U.S. presidential election of November 8. By a fifty-five percent popular vote and a landslide in the electoral college, Abraham Lincoln defeated George B. McClellan and remained in the White House. In a November 12 letter to Taylor, perhaps the only superior for whom he ever voiced unqualified admiration, Forrest said he "deplore[d]" being separated from Taylor to go with Hood, adding:

I know not how long we are to labor for that independence for which we have thus far struggled in vain, but this I do know, that I will never weary in defending our cause, which must ultimately succeed. Faith is the duty of the hour. We will succeed. We have only to "work and wait."[34]

23

WITH LEE'S ARMY of Northern Virginia holding grimly on in the face of Grant's bludgeoning attacks around Richmond, the Army of Tennessee now began a headlong rush to suicide. Its seeming death wish dated from July 17, when Jefferson Davis, alarmed by Johnston's continual withdrawal from Sherman across northern Georgia, replaced the self-possessed Johnston with the volatile Hood.

More a fighter than a thinker (having graduated forty-fourth in a West Point class of fifty-two) and weakened by incapacitation of an arm at Gettysburg and amputation of a leg at Chickamauga, Hood by early September had lost Atlanta, single-handedly transforming the North's political climate from gloom to euphoria and handing Lincoln the reelection that doomed Southern hopes of a negotiated peace. Hood's frontal attacks during the Atlanta battles also cost Confederate casualties of more than 13,000 (compared to Sherman's 6,000), leaving him with insufficient troops to effectively oppose Sherman's large army any longer. Hoping to lure his adversary away from Atlanta and into a division of the overpowering Federal force, Hood set out across northwestern Georgia with some 30,000 men. Sherman refused the bait; deeming it foolish to give up Atlanta to fight the campaign of North Georgia all over again, he left Hood to his own devices. Hood then concocted an all-but-fantastic plan: to reclaim Tennessee, possibly Kentucky, then perhaps even move east to Virginia and join Lee, the commander under whom he had made his pugnacious reputation.

The several days Hood spent awaiting Forrest's 3,500 cavalrymen, as well as twenty days' rations that had to be brought by rail to Cherokee and then overland by wagon to Tuscumbia, saw the Federal commander in central Tennessee, George Thomas, frantically begin gathering another 25,000 men to add to the 17,500 he had at his immediate disposal. By the time Forrest arrived in mid-November, Hood had moved across the Tennessee River to Florence, and Forrest was given command of the army's cavalry units. At least one trooper, the gentleman–enlisted man Harry St. John Dixon, was unimpressed with the Wizard of the Saddle, confiding to his diary on November 18 that the "dog's dead: finally we are under N. Bedford Forrest." It was a circumstance Dixon said he had "dreaded since the death of the noble Van Dorn." Acidly terming his unlettered commander "The Wizzard," he expressed his "distaste [at] being commanded by a man having no pretension to gentility—a negro trader, gambler,—an ambitious man, careless of the lives of his men so long as preferment be *en prospectu.* Forrest may be & no doubt is, the best Cav[alry] officer in the West, but I object to a tyrannical, hotheaded vulgarian's commanding me."[1]

Hood's opinion may have coincided with Dixon's. Had departmental commander P. G. T. Beauregard not directed that Hood's previous cavalry chief be left in Georgia to harass Sherman, Hood doubtless would have retained Wheeler in that position, and he quickly found Forrest a different breed of soldier. Soon after the new cavalry commander arrived, Hood's headquarters sent him an order reducing the army's number of mules per wagon and ordering that all surplus animals be turned over to Hood's transportation quartermaster. Forrest ignored the directive, and when Major A. L. Landis arrived the next day to inquire why no mules had been sent, he was given a tongue-lashing certain to cause talk at headquarters. According to John Morton:

The atmosphere was blue for a while. Stripped of General Forrest's bad words, he said to Major Landis: "Go back to your quarters, and don't you come here again or send anybody here again about mules. The order will not be obeyed; and, moreover, if [the quartermaster] bothers me any further about this matter, I'll come down to his office, tie his long legs into a double bowknot around his neck, and choke him to death with his own shins. It's a fool order, anyway. General Hood had better send his inspectors to overhaul [his] wagons, rid them of all surplus baggage, tents, adjutant desks, and everything that can be spared. Reduce the number of his wagons instead of reducing the strength of his teams. . . . [I]f he knew the road from here to Pulaski [Tennessee], this order would be countermanded. I whipped the enemy and captured every mule wagon and ambulance in my command; have not made a requisition on the

*government for anything of the kind for two years, and . . . my
teams will go as they are or not at all.*[2]

Ironically, Forrest was accorded a joyous reception by Hood's troops,
"serenaded by the Tennesseans [among them] in the evening," Hood's
chief of staff noted in his journal. Perhaps fired by their confidence in him,
and certainly by his coup at Johnsonville, he delivered what the chief of
staff described as "a very encouraging speech." It probably was the same
interesting oration reported on November 26 by the Montgomery *Daily
Mail.*

> *Well, soldiers, I came here to jine you. I'm gwine to show you the
> way into Tennessee. My conscripts are going, and I know Hood's
> veterans can go. I come down here with 350 men. I got 3,500
> conscripts. Since May I have fought in every county in West
> Tennessee. I fought in the streets of Memphis, and the women run
> out in their night clothes to see us, and they will do it again in
> Nashville. I have fought a battle every 25 days. I have seen the
> Mississippi run with blood for 200 yards, and I'm gwine to see it
> again. I've captured 78 pieces of artillery and 16,000 Yankees, and
> buried 2,500 of them!*[3]

The Memphis *Appeal*, by then also being published in Montgomery,
protested on November 27 the *Daily Mail*'s attribution to Forrest of
braggadocio and misstatement of facts. The *Daily Mail* editor, Henry
Watterson, warmly defended his reporter and characterized the printed
speech as an authentic expression of his ex-commander's "brusque, eccen-
tric eloquence." Watterson also later disclosed that a cavalry officer present at the scene vouched for the accuracy of the *Daily Mail* report.[4]

By the time these newspaper accounts appeared, the subject of them was
gone to Tennessee with Hood's thin legions. Forrest was moving rapidly
through snow and bad roads at the head of a Hood drive to slip behind
28,000 Federals retreating to the safety of heavily fortified Nashville.
Major General John M. Schofield's Union troops had been headquartered
at Pulaski, some thirty miles south of Columbia, when Hood's forces
finally left Florence heading for Columbia and Schofield's rear. Ordered
to oppose their northward progress, Schofield on November 28 found his
own northward course imperiled.

The head of the Confederate column had been moving fast for a week
by then. Forrest later reported that his men were in combat every day,

virtually driving Federal detachments along. At Henryville, Chalmers captured forty-five prisoners. At Fouche Springs, after directing Chalmers to skirmish with the Federal front, Forrest charged the rear with just his escort and "produc[ed] a perfect stampede, capturing about 50 prisoners, 20 horses, and 1 ambulance." At nightfall after this exploit, he placed his escort in ambush and, as Chalmers's men "pressed" the Federals, "they rushed into the ambuscade [and] my escort fired into them, producing the wildest confusion." He then rested Chalmers's men until 1 A.M. before starting them northward again and capturing "35,000 rounds of small-arm ammunition and the guard left in charge of it" at Mount Pleasant.

Reaching Columbia, his force crossed Duck River under Hood's orders and moved on northward toward Spring Hill. Two miles from that hamlet, Forrest gathered his command and ordered Chalmers on an exploratory charge of a patch of woods thought to contain only cavalry; when Union infantry roughly repelled the probe, Forrest laconically remarked to his subordinate, "They was in there sure enough, wasn't they, Chalmers?" He then ascended a hill to study the situation more carefully and discovered part of Schofield's army "hurriedly moving his wagon train up the Franklin Pike." Recognizing this as an attempt to flee, Forrest charged repeatedly. He eventually received orders from Hood to "hold my position at all hazards, as the advance of his [Hood's] infantry column was only two miles distant and rapidly advancing." Complying, Forrest sent Bell's brigade into a charge with just four cartridges per man, but Hood fortunately positioned Patrick Cleburne's arriving infantry brigade on Bell's left, and the combined movement struck the Federals front and flank, routing them from their fortifications and sending them running backward to a battery of at least eight guns. The battery halted the attackers with shrapnel near nightfall.[5]

Cleburne massed his men for a final push to gain control of the critical highway, but was stopped by an order from his superior, Major General B. F. Cheatham. Cheatham told him to await subsequent instructions, which never came; apparently a Hood order to Cheatham to block the Columbia-Franklin turnpike never reached Cheatham. The Army of Tennessee's crippled commander had been painfully thrown by a horse that day, and his muddled orders and counterorders in the evening suggest weariness and pain. After a concerted dusk attack by Cheatham's divisions failed to materialize, Hood seems to have allowed his infantry subordinates to rest and await daylight short of the crucial turnpike. He did so because, he said, Forrest was blocking this Federal escape route, but Forrest had hardly assured him of that. His troops were all but out of ammunition;

their ordnance wagons had been delayed in Columbia, bringing up the rear of the supply train of Hood's entire army. Asked for help by his commander, Forrest told Hood he would "do the best he could in the emergency" by sending Brigadier General W. H. Jackson's division, which had captured some Federal ammunition that day.[6]

It was hardly the sort of declaration that should have prompted Hood to let the rest of his men sleep, but he apparently did, while Forrest ordered Jackson to make an end run northward to Thompson's Station to attempt to cut off the Federal vanguard. He later reported that Jackson attacked on the Columbia-Franklin turnpike four miles above Spring Hill "just as the front of the enemy's column had passed," and the attack "produc[ed] much panic and confusion. . . . Jackson had possession of the pike and fought the enemy until near daylight, but receiving no support, he was compelled to retire, after killing a large number of horses and mules and burning several wagons." Jackson apparently did "fight all night," but he managed to block the highway only about half an hour, a Confederate on the scene later reported.[7]

By daybreak next morning Schofield's men and wagons were safely beyond Spring Hill, having hurried silently past the campfires of Confederate infantry bivouacked just off the turnpike. By noon, the whole army had reached Franklin and was frantically throwing up earthworks. Forrest, at the head of Confederate pursuit, made a thorough personal reconnaissance before Hood reached the field about 1 P.M. He advised Hood the Federal position was so strong it couldn't be taken by frontal assault without fearful and needless loss of life.

"I do not think the Federals will stand strong pressure from the front," Hood contradicted him, apparently believing Schofield had posted only a rear guard in the Franklin fortifications to cover a continuing withdrawal to Nashville. "The show of force they are making is a feint . . . to hold me back from a more vigorous pursuit."

Possibly recalling Harrisburg and the tragic consequences of similar Confederate thinking there, Forrest disagreed. "General Hood," he countered, "if you will give me one strong division of infantry with my cavalry, I will . . . flank the Federals from their works within two hours' time."

Thus were confronted two implacable fighters who had had little time to get to know each other, and the acquaintance they had had was not calculated to incline Hood toward Forrest's position. His dispatches displayed perceptible annoyance at being kept waiting in northern Alabama by Forrest's Johnsonville exploit, and there was also the incident in which

Forrest defied Hood's quartermaster in the matter of the mules. Too, the very night before this critical afternoon, the Forrest cavalry unit under Jackson had been unable to block the turnpike above Spring Hill, and Hood's rage at having Schofield slip past him was great.

Perhaps also wary of Forrest's sometime tendency to exceed his authority and orders, Hood now gave short shrift to the suggestion of a Forrest-led flank movement. He ordered Forrest instead to take command of the cavalry—only—for the unimaginative assault already ordered. He then compounded his error by sending Forrest, among the most intrepid fighters in the entire Confederate service, to the far right side, ordering him to be ready to pursue the Federals once they broke and fled toward Nashville under pressure of the frontal stroke. In issuing this questionable order, he probably also saved Forrest's life.[8]

From Winstead Hill two miles south of Franklin, Hood could see most of the Federal line, which extended a mile and a half. Its flanks rested on the Harpeth River southeast and northwest of the town and protected two bridges across it. The Union center intersected the Columbia-Franklin turnpike; the Federal line also covered the approach of Carter's Creek Pike on its right and Lewisburg Pike on its left. Four hundred yards out front of the center, a single Federal division—the Second—had been left behind a barricade of rails with orders "not to retire to the main line until forced to do so by the fighting of the enemy." Otherwise, for two miles in front of the Federal lines extended a fairly open, rolling plain, and behind those lines waited foot-weary Federals as numerically strong as their attackers. They were so well fortified that Major General D. S. Stanley, a Union corps commander, later reported that "nothing appeared so improbable as that they [the Confederates] would assault." Hood's whole army "was in sight and forming for attack" from 1 P.M. to 4 P.M., but Stanley was "so confident" no attack would be launched that he remained at Schofield's Franklin headquarters until he heard the Confederates assailing the Second Division. The assault was made with no prior artillery barrage—because, as Hood afterward reported, he "was restrained from using my artillery on account of the women and children remaining in the town."[9]

Stanley reported that the Confederate attack began about four o'clock and that the two Federal brigades out front of the center "stood their ground until the charging rebels were almost crossing bayonets with them, but the line then broke—Conrad's brigade first, then Lane's—and men and officers made the quickest time they could to our main lines. . . . A large proportion of Lane's men came back with loaded muskets, and turning at the breastworks, they fired a volley into the pressing rebels now not ten steps from them."[10]

The 15,000 charging Confederates—eager to fight, knowing the Federals must not be allowed to reach the entrenchments of Nashville—were by then enduring what may have been the most devastating fire of the war. Brigadier General George W. Gordon, leading six Tennessee regiments into the hottest of it in pursuit of Lane's men west of the pike, later remembered that the advance Federal units fired a volley and fled backward, and that among the Confederates "[t]he shout was raised, 'Go into the works with them!'" Gordon's men "rushed on" after the routed advance unit, killing some and capturing some others who couldn't run fast enough, meanwhile losing a comparative few of their own men "until we arrived within one hundred paces of their main line and stronghold. . . ." There, Gordon said, it seemed to him that "Hell itself had exploded in our faces! The enemy had thus long reserved their fire for the safety of their routed comrades who were flying to them for protection, and who were just in front of and mingled with the pursuing Confederates." When the main Union line could no longer safely hold its fire, "they opened upon us (regardless of their own men who were mingled with us) such a hailstorm of shot and shell, musketry and canister, that the very atmosphere was hideous with the shrieks and messengers of death . . . all made a scene of surpassing terror. . . ."[11]

Federals were as aghast as Confederates. Stanley later reported that the portion of the Twenty-third Corps "stationed in the works for a distance of about three or four [hundred] yards to the right of the Columbia pike . . . broke and ran to the rear with the fugitives from Conrad's Brigade." The Confederates then "appeared on the breastworks and in possession of . . . two batteries, which they commenced to turn upon us." At this moment Stanley "arrived at the scene of the disorder, coming from . . . town on the Columbia pike; the moment was critical beyond any I have known in any battle—could the enemy hold that part of the line, he was nearer to our two bridges than the extremities of our line." He saw Opdycke's brigade "lying down about 100 yards in rear of the works," and he galloped to its nearest regiment and ordered it to charge as he "saw Colonel Opdycke near the center of the line urging his men forward."[12]

Emerson Opdycke, a thirty-four-year-old Ohioan, had commanded the Federal rear guard in the retreat through Spring Hill and had skillfully kept some 500 newly conscripted Union stragglers from capture by cutting their large, heavy, new knapsacks off them and herding them, thus lightened, "at the point of the bayonet" on to Franklin. A prewar mercantile dealer and fervent abolitionist who displayed great military talent, he found himself and his brigade in reserve just to the Federal right of the turnpike. He was about 100 yards behind not only the main line but a rise on which sat a home afterward known as the Carter House. He later reported that he "knew that Carter's hill was the key to it all . . . and I commenced moving the command to the left of the pike for greater security to the men and for easier maneuvering in case of need." As he was making this move, "a most horrible stampede of our front troops came surging and rushing back past Carter's house . . . to the right and left of the pike." He "gave the order, 'First Brigade, forward to the works,' [and] bayonets came down to a charge, the yell was raised, and the regiments rushed most grandly forward, carrying many stragglers back with them." The Confederates, "following our troops with great celerity and force," were "met this side of Carter's house by our charge, and at once put to rout with a loss of 394 prisoners, 19 of whom were officers, 1 a colonel, and 9 battle-flags. . . . Our lines were now restored, and the battle raged with indescribable fury. The enemy hurled his masses against us with seeming desperation. . . . I never saw the dead lay near so thick."

In this area of the fighting, George Gordon was captured and his commander, Major General John C. Brown, badly wounded, and they were the lucky ones. Within a couple of hundred yards of them, Cleburne and Brigadier Generals John Adams, States Rights Gist, Hiram Granbury, and Otto Strahl were killed, and six more generals wounded.[13]

As this slaughter occurred, Forrest's much-feared cavalry, relegated to a minor role, was giving an unimpressive account of itself. On the extreme left, Chalmers's division "drove back double its number of the enemy, who were strongly posted behind a stone wall, and pushed them back rapidly for one mile until they reached their . . . [main] fortifications at Franklin," Chalmers later reported. "My line was pressed forward until the skirmishers were within sixty yards of the fortifications," he added, but there he stopped; " . . . my force was too small to justify an attempt to storm them, and I could only hold my position." This position and the action getting to it occurred so far to the left that it prompted implied criticism in the report of Major General William B. Bate, who had command of an infantry division that was supposed to be located immediately to Chalmers's right. Bate didn't reach a position to hit the main Federal line until well after Brown's and Cleburne's units struck the center, and he said that when his own charge began his left moved "steadily on, not waiting for the cavalry. . . . The cavalry (dismounted) not touching my left, nor being on a line with it, exposed that flank to a furious fire." Bate eventually moved a Florida brigade to the left side of Carter's Creek Pike, where Chalmers's cavalrymen apparently should have been. The next morning, Bate learned that the "works on the left of the Carter Creek turnpike were not strong, and with a vigorous assault should have been carried." Chalmers's division lost 116 killed and wounded, compared to Bate's division's 319.[14]

Forrest himself was operating on the extreme right of the Confederate line with Buford's and Jackson's divisions. Finding a Federal force positioned atop a hill across the Harpeth firing on Confederates advancing along the Lewisburg pike, he ordered Jackson's men to cross the river and drive the Federals off the hill. Buford's force, meanwhile, was sent forward dismounted on the right of Lieutenant General Alexander P. Stewart's infantry corps between Lewisburg pike and the river. According to Forrest's subsequent report, Buford's men "rapidly advancing drove the enemy across the river, where he joined the cavalry." On the other side of the river, Jackson then was faced with both Federal infantry and Federal cavalry, but "held [them] in check until night, when he . . . retired across Harpeth for the purpose of replenishing his ammunition." Stewart put it more succinctly: "A body of the enemy's cavalry in front of [Major General William W.] Loring and the [cavalry] division on his right was soon routed, and the [Confederate] cavalry division [Buford's] ceased to operate with us."[15]

Forrest initially may have had in mind attempting what he had suggested to Hood, except without the requested infantry division; he instinctively knew that the easiest—perhaps only—victory here lay in reaching the Federal rear, and the only way to get to it was on the north side of the Harpeth. The Federals were expecting him there, though, and in much greater force than Hood's orders made him able to muster. Had he had his entire cavalry reinforced by an infantry division—say Bate's, which didn't attack in time to be of assistance on the left, anyway—and had he been able to attack the bridges, covered only by Federal cavalry, in his accustomed slashing manner at the time of or just before Brown and Cleburne broke the center of the main Federal line, he might well have handed Hood a victory that day. Instead, Hood suffered an appalling loss of 6,252 men, including 12 generals. The official Federal casualty total was 2,326.

The next day, the Federals continued their retreat toward Nashville, and the Confederate Press Association, misinformed on the extent of Hood's casualties, reported the result of the Franklin carnage as a victory. Forrest's comparatively unbloodied cavalry pushed rapidly around the town and galloped north to Brentwood, seeking to catch Schofield's men en route to Nashville. All they could do was skirmish with the Union rear guard, which ultimately reached the heavily fortified Tennessee capital by noon. Forrest's troops bivouacked that night in sight of the State Capitol building. Hood, whose judgment may have been impaired by use of laudanum to treat the continuing pain of his war wounds, arrived with the rest of his shaken army the next day. Besieging some 60,000 Federals with troops half their number, he then detached Bate's infantry division and Forrest's cavalry—except for Chalmers's division—to deal with 8,000 dug-in Federals thirty miles south in Murfreesboro. That left Hood about 23,000 men in his lines around Nashville.[16]

At Murfreesboro, Forrest was as active as he could prudently be, eventually reporting to Hood (in Hood's words) that "nothing could be done with the place by assault." Declining to make the mistake made by Stephen Lee at Harrisburg and Hood at so many other places, he contented himself with capturing railroad blockhouses and similarly isolated pockets of Federals while trying to coax the Union commander at Murfreesboro, Major General R. H. Milroy, from Fortress Rosecrans. On December 7 he managed to do it, but with dismaying results. Awaiting Milroy in a well-fortified position southwest of town and a couple of miles from the Federal works, he saw Milroy refuse to take the bait, retire into some woods, and move northeastwardly off to the right; Milroy's report said he was reluctant to give battle with the Confederates between him and Fortress Rosecrans, and he was moving around to put the fort behind him. When he finally did attack, it was from the Confederate left, which forced Forrest to hurriedly change his alignment, pulling some of Bate's infantry-men from behind their cover and facing them leftward about the time the assault struck. With the Federals advancing, Forrest addressed the infantry-men, telling them they were as numerically strong as their attackers and that if they would hold the enemy just fifteen minutes, his cavalry could get behind Milroy and capture the entire 1,326-man force. Suddenly, however—"from some cause which I cannot explain," Forrest's report said—two of the four brigades of infantry "made a shameful retreat, losing two pieces of our artillery. I seized the colors of the retreating troops and endeavored to rally them, but they could not be moved by any entreaty or appeal to their patriotism. Major-General Bate did the same thing, but was equally as unsuccessful as myself."[17]

To Bate, the unordered retreat doesn't appear to have been so inexplica-ble. His report, sounding as disdainful of Forrest's and the cavalry's contributions as he was of Chalmers's at Franklin, said that when Milroy moved into the woods, the Confederate infantrymen supposed the Federals were on their way back to Murfreesboro and the cavalry provided no information to the contrary. The report implied that the stampede began because Forrest was moving the infantry units around when the Federals struck them, and that this movement caused a "space of perhaps 75 or 100 yards" between two of the brigades. Cavalrymen supposedly protecting the left from attack had "fallen back with slight resistance," Bate reported, and after the retreat began, he himself remained with the two brigades that didn't run. "I did not again see the Florida and Palmer's nor Sears' brigade until night, they being under the immediate conduct of General Forrest."[18]

Forrest hardly encouraged their behavior, though. According to two men who claimed well after the war to have been eyewitnesses, he did more than just "seize the colors" to stop the flying Confederate retreat. One of these purported eyewitnesses, an artillerist serving nearby that day, said that "[d]uring the stampede or retreat, which almost amounted to a panic, Forrest rode in among the infantry, ordering the men to rally, and doing all in his power to stop the retreat." The troops disregarded him, and Forrest rushed at a color-bearer who was "running for dear life" and "ordered him to halt." When the color-bearer kept running, Forrest "drew his pistol and shot the retreating soldier down." He then dismounted, snatched up the colors, remounted, "and, riding in front of the soldiers, waved the colors at them and finally succeeded in rallying them to their duty." This story was disputed by one of Forrest's soldiers and postwar associates, who said a cursing Forrest merely grabbed a flag from a color-bearer and used it to hit at fleeing infantrymen "beyond the reach of his sword. Finally, in his exasperated fury, he hurled the flag, staff and all, at a man running by just beyond his reach."[19]

Whatever he did to the color-bearer, it apparently wasn't all he tried to avert disaster. He "hurriedly sent Major Strange, of my staff, to Brigadier-Generals Armstrong and [Lawrence S.] Ross of Jackson's division, with orders to say to them that everything depended on their cavalry. They proved themselves equal to the emergency by charging on the enemy, thereby checking his farther advance." Milroy's report, by contrast, indicated his "farther advance" was halted of its own accord, to replenish the ammunition of some of his men. Whatever the truth was, Forrest's attempt to deal a crushing defeat to an important part of the Murfreesboro garrison had been itself crushed. According to Forrest, Milroy "return[ed]" to the Federal stronghold, but Bate's account makes it plain that the Confederates were the ones who retreated; Bate says he placed one of the infantry brigades that hadn't run "in position to resist in case of pursuit," and it "brought up the rear in good order to the bivouac on the Nashville turnpike [north of Murfreesboro]." Two wintry days later, Bate was ordered to leave Forrest and return to Hood's Nashville line, and he found the march a climatic nightmare. "The sleet and severe freezes had made the surface of the earth a sheet of ice. Nearly one-fourth of the men were still barefooted, yet plodded . . . under these adverse circumstances (many with bleeding feet). . . ."[20]

Forrest was sent a smaller infantry force and on December 12 got back to the work of destroying railroad tracks "from LaVergne to Murfreesboro, which was most effectually done." On the southern side of Murfreesboro the next day, Jackson's cavalry division captured a seventeen-car train loaded with 200 soldiers and 60,000 rations en route from Stevenson, Alabama, to Murfreesboro; the supplies were "consumed by fire," Forrest reported, and the prisoners sent to the rear. Forrest led two of the three small infantry brigades east of Murfreesboro on December 14 on an abortive attempt to capture a Federal forage train operating there; the next day he "received notice from General Hood that a general engagement was then going on at Nashville, and to hold myself in readiness to move at any moment." On the evening of December 16 "one of General Hood's staff officers arrived, informing me of the disaster. . . ."[21]

Hood had had no chance at Nashville. Outnumbered three-to-one by December 15, he seems to have stayed in his lines there because he could think of nothing else to do; he later lamely claimed to have been awaiting reinforcements from across the Mississippi River and disdaining withdrawal because "our army was in that condition which rendered it more judicious the men should face a decisive issue rather than retreat." The issue proved to be decisive in the extreme. George Thomas attacked Hood's long thin line with his left to hold the Confederates in position, then sent 40,000 men—almost twice as many as Hood's total force—against and around the Confederate left. Early in the day, Chalmers's cavalry was so quickly and unceremoniously ejected from its position on the far Confederate left that Chalmers himself lost "some 20 wagons, with teams, &c., complete, some 40 prisoners, and a large amount of plunder belonging to [his] headquarters." Soon after nightfall, the Confederates had retreated nearly two miles and formed a new line that shrank their earlier six-mile front by nearly half.[22]

The next day, Thomas repeated his successful maneuver, striking with his left to hold the Confederate right and then slamming an overpowering force against Hood's left while a horde of cavalry poured around it and into the Confederate rear. About 4:30 P.M., under pressure from the front, flank, and rear, the Confederates on the left broke and fled, and the rest of the line followed, streaming southward in a bone-chilling rain along the Hillsboro, Granny White, and Franklin pikes. Chalmers dug in eight miles south of Nashville and tried to stem the Federal onrush at twilight "behind rail breast-works," reported Major General James H. Wilson, the Federal cavalry commander. Brigadier General Edward Hatch, whose men led the assault on Chalmers, later reported "[t]hrowing some dismounted men upon the flanks of the road" before the Twelfth Tennessee Cavalry (U.S.) charged Chalmers's "center, capturing the division colors and Brigadier-General Rucker. The enemy were thrown into confusion, and only the darkness saved him from a thorough rout."[23]

Forrest by this time was retreating through sleet and rain with 400 prisoners and a drove of several hundred hogs and cattle, precious supplies for the survivors of Hood's shattered army. He had been ordered to fall back through Shelbyville and Pulaski, but, because his wagons were already west of Murfreesboro at Triune when he received the directive, he ignored it and moved more sharply westward toward Columbia. There he would be of more use than Hood so far had permitted; in the meantime, he sent Armstrong's cavalry brigade directly to Hood and pushed on into Columbia, where he arrived on December 18 after an "unavoidably slow" march "along the almost impassable roads." Tension and despair were so pronounced that at the Duck crossing at Columbia, at which Forrest arrived simultaneously with Cheatham's infantry, he was told by Cheatham to move out of the way and took it personally. Drawing his pistol, he rode to Cheatham and extended a challenge: "If you are a better man than I am, General Cheatham, your troops can cross ahead of mine." Only mediation by Stephen Lee, who arrived on the scene in the nick of time, prevented threatened battle not only between two Confederate commanders but two Confederate units. Which of them ultimately crossed first later became a matter of dispute.[24]

Hood's rear guard—commanded skillfully by Stephen Lee and then, after Lee was wounded in the foot, by Major General Carter Stevenson— meanwhile had fallen back through Brentwood, Thompson's Station, Spring Hill, and across rain-swollen Rutherford's Creek. By December 19 Hood's army had crossed the Duck and destroyed the bridges. Hood's plan had been to retreat into a winter camp beyond the Duck, but "after arriving at Columbia I became convinced that the condition of the army made it necessary" to fall back another eighty miles to the southern banks of the Tennessee River; the defeat at Nashville had been so overwhelming, and the Federal pursuit under Thomas and Wilson so dogged, that he felt he could not hold a line at the Duck. In fact, by then Hood may have been wondering whether his remnant could survive at all. In a meeting with Forrest on the night of December 19, Hood "expressed the belief that he could not escape in such weather, with unfavorable roads and broken-down teams." Forrest responded "that to remain there would certainly result in the capture of the whole force, but that, if reinforced with 4,000 infantry, he would undertake to secure time and opportunity for the escape of all across the Tennessee." This time Hood took his recommendation and, on December 20, departed, leaving Forrest with eight small infantry brigades and the unenviable designation of rearguard commander.[25]

He now had just 3,000 cavalrymen, eight pieces of Morton's artillery, and 1,900 infantrymen under Major General Edward C. Walthall—less than half the infantry force he had requested from Hood. Of the 1,900, "400 were unserviceable for want of shoes," Forrest later reported, and by the evening of December 20 Hatch's Federal cavalry had begun shelling Columbia from across the Duck. Forrest rode under a flag of truce to the riverbank and informed Hatch "by verbal communication across the river that there were no Confederate troops in town, and that his shelling would result in injury to the women and children and his own wounded." He also offered to exchange 2,000 prisoners taken by the Confederates in the campaign, saying they were without means to endure the severe cold and in many cases would likely die from exposure if not exchanged. After two hours, an answer came from Thomas himself, refusing to make an exchange or even to receive Forrest's prisoners on parole—no doubt to encumber the Confederate retreat as much as possible. Hatch, however, stopped the shelling.[26]

The Federals forced their way across the river on the night of December 21, and the following day Forrest began falling back. Pursued by Federal infantry, the Confederates held them "in check for some time in a gap made by two high hills on each side of the road" five miles south of Columbia on December 23; by nightfall, though, they had fallen back past Lynnville, where they halted again "to hold the enemy . . . and prevent any pressure upon my wagon train and the stock then being driven out." The next day, Wilson's cavalry took the lead of Federal pursuit, but Forrest stopped them at Richland Creek by skillful employment of Morton's artillery. Supported by Buford's, Chalmers's and Ross's cavalrymen, Morton's guns delayed the Federals long enough to permit repair of a bridge heavily damaged by the passing of Hood's troops. Morton's cannons then were carried across by hand, the horses led over, and the planks pulled up and thrown into the creek, further hindering Wilson.[27]

When the Federals finally crossed, Forrest retreated again, heading toward Pulaski with his pursuers so close that the fighting was "largely hand-to-hand." In this struggle, Buford was wounded, and Forrest told Chalmers to take command of Buford's as well as his own division. Both armies passed the night of December 24 near Pulaski, but Forrest slipped off early, leaving a small rear guard under Jackson and burning all supplies that couldn't be moved. Seven miles south at Anthony's Hill, Forrest stopped and positioned Morton's guns on the crest. On each side of the road leading toward them he posted most of his troopers and infantrymen, except for a small force assigned to draw the Federals in. The ambush worked to near perfection. The Confederates out front fired and rapidly retreated as the Federals came charging in and then, sensing danger, recalled the pursuit and sent forward a cannon supported by a regiment. Morton waited until gun and regiment were close, then opened with double-shotted canister as the rest of the Confederates loosed a volley with rifles and pistols. A Georgia soldier in an infantry regiment supporting Morton's guns later recalled that before the engagement opened, Forrest passed his position bent over on foot to watch the Federals move up the winding road toward him. Then he hurried back to the rear—from which, "[i]n a moment we hear the clatter of a horse's feet," the soldier continued, "and Forrest dashes by at half speed, riding magnificently, his martial figure as straight as an arrow and looking six inches taller than was his wont . . . yelling as he reaches the waiting ranks: 'Charge! CHARGE! CH-A-A-A-RGE!'"[28]

His men killed or wounded some 150 Federals and captured several prisoners and a cannon before the Union horde finally flanked them and drove them backward again. Before they did, Forrest ordered Armstrong to hold his men in line even though they were running out of ammunition. Armstrong did, but only after making three separate protests. The third time, he rode up to where Forrest and Walthall were sitting horses and, angrily weeping this time, shouted to the latter: "General Walthall, won't you please make that damned man there on the horse see that my men are forced to retreat?" Forrest replied with unusual quietude that he only had been trying to gain time for the rest of Hood's army to cross Sugar Creek less than ten miles farther southwest and that Armstrong's men had played a great role in making that possible. Then he looked at his watch and added: "It is about time for us all to get out of here."[29]

Flanked by the Federals, he now had to race them via a parallel road—

through darkness, heavily falling "rain and sleet," and "a bitter wind"— to the Sugar Creek crossings. The road had been "reduced . . . to a terrible state" by "[a]lternate rain, snow and thaw." Perhaps fearing another ambush, the Federals moved more slowly, and Forrest's shivering Confederates reached the crossings first, at about 11 P.M. There they found "a large part of the army ordnance train, which had been delayed at this point, as we were informed, that the mules which belonged to it might be used to aid in moving the pontoon train to the [Tennessee] river." Horses and mules now were at a premium. Union general Wilson later recalled that "thousands [of horses], exhausted by overwork, famished with hunger or crippled so that death was a mercy, with hoofs dropping off from frost and mud, fell by the roadside, never to rise again."[30]

Forrest's rear guard sent the pontoon train on toward the Tennessee as soon as the mules returned, then hastily threw up a fortification of logs and rails with which to buy the train some time. The day after Christmas dawned with Hood's main force moving across the Tennessee sixteen miles southwest at Bainbridge, Alabama, while Forrest's troops laid another ambush. Part of the infantry was placed just in front of Sugar Creek between the two crossings, the rest of it behind the creek "to guard," as Walthall put it, "against disaster." The ordnance train had hardly gotten out of sight when Walthall received notice from Forrest that the Federals were still pressing the Confederate cavalry and were less than a mile away. A dense fog concealed all of the Confederates except "a small force purposely exposed in advance," which by design turned and retreated as soon as it encountered the Federals. The Federals again fell into the trap; they were facing in the opposite direction when the fire of the main Confederate line hit them, "causing the wildest confusion." Two regiments of Confederates then charged, "producing a complete rout" and driving many of the Federals into the creek. In all, Forrest reported killing or wounding some 150 Union troops, capturing "many prisoners and horses" and destroying "about 400 horses" at Sugar Creek. Fearing another Federal flanking movement in the fog, he moved on after two hours, but was bothered no further. He finally crossed the Tennessee at Bainbridge on the evening of December 27.[31]

Morton later recalled that the mules over which Forrest had been so insubordinate to Hood's officers at the outset of the campaign proved to be "a Godsend . . . to Hood's retreating army."

From Richland Creek to the Tennessee River the road was strewn with his [Hood's] abandoned wagons, and but for the help afforded the pontoon train by General Forrest's fine six-mule teams, great delay and probable disaster to the army would have occurred before a passage of the river was effected.[32]

24

HOURS AFTER GETTING the last of his men across the Tennessee, Forrest reported to Hood at Tuscumbia that his horses had been thoroughly "broken-down" during the retreat and that there was little forage on which to rehabilitate them. Hood authorized him to take his cavalry, except Roddey's detachment, westward to the comparatively lush prairies of eastern Mississippi, and he left for Corinth on December 29. A scare from Federals who crossed the Tennessee and struck Roddey around Decatur caused Armstrong's brigade to be returned to guard Hood's rear, and the surviving remnant of the Army of Tennessee followed Forrest's path to Corinth. Forrest arrived on December 30 two days in advance of the infantry, which was shuttled by rail another forty miles southward to Tupelo.[1]

There on January 10, 1865, Hood's army officially reported its ranks thinned to an effective strength of 18,742, and three days later its commander was relieved of duty. Richard Taylor was named Hood's successor, but there was no replacing Hood's army. Its killed, wounded, and captured in the butchery around Atlanta, Franklin, and Nashville rendered it all but nonexistent. Part of it soon was rushed to Mobile to meet a Federal threat there; most of it eventually was marched to North Carolina to make its last fight under a reactivated Joseph E. Johnston; but a significant portion dissolved through desertion into the rural hinterlands within or beyond Confederate lines, where women and children long left at home were being preyed upon by straggling vandals from both sides or none.

In late January, Taylor placed Forrest in command of every Confederate cavalryman in Alabama, Mississippi, and East Louisiana. It was an impressive jurisdiction, but it encompassed a paltry total of some 10,000 widely scattered troops, and their new commander went about his duties with appropriate gravity. Moving his headquarters southward to the more central point of Verona, Mississippi, he issued a circular from "Headquarters Cavalry Department of Alabama, Mississippi, and East Louisiana" announcing he would brook no trifling. He demanded "strict obedience to all orders" and "prompt punishment . . . for all violations of law and of orders." Calling for the "respect and protect[ion]" of the "rights and property of citizens," he added that "illegal organizations of cavalry prowling through the country must be placed regularly and properly in the service or driven from the country." He termed such elements "in many instances . . . nothing more or less than roving bands of deserters, absentees, stragglers, horse thieves, and robbers, who consume the substance and appropriate the property of citizens without remuneration." He said their "acts of lawlessness and crime demand a remedy, which I shall not hesitate to apply even to extermination. . . ."[2]

"Extermination" had never been something Forrest shrank from, and it still wasn't. With the South's cause looking irretrievable after the stampede from Nashville, more and more barefoot Confederates went absent without leave, and he resorted to firing squads. Perhaps to forestall some of the attrition and simultaneously avoid some of the executions, he began granting twenty-day furloughs as soon as his troops reached Corinth, sending his Mississippians and Tennesseans home—often beyond enemy lines—for fresh horses, clothes, absent friends, etc.; during this time, he kept only Ross's Texans on guard duty in camp, because their homes were too distant to be reached and returned from in twenty days. Forrest organized his troops, as far as possible, into divisions by state. Bell's and Rucker's brigades of Tennesseans (the latter commanded by Brigadier General A. W. Campbell because of Rucker's capture at Nashville) were combined with Ross's Texans in a division under W. H. Jackson. Chalmers was given charge of Mississippi brigades under Armstrong, Wirt Adams, and Peter B. Starke. Buford, accompanied by his Kentucky detachment, was put in charge of cavalry in Alabama, while McCulloch's Second Missouri, now a remnant, became part of Forrest's personal troops.[3]

During all this rest and reorganization, there was contact with the Federals. In mid-February, George Thomas sent to Forrest some Union officers to discuss a Forrest proposal to exchange prisoners—or at least to have the Federals supply clothes, shoes, and blankets for some 7,000 Union troops Forrest was guarding in Mississippi. Included in the party were Colonel John G. Parkhurst, himself a captive of Forrest at Murfreesboro in 1862, and Captain Lewis M. Hosea, a young West Pointer ordered to pay close attention to any indications of Confederate supplies and of Forrest's apparent inclinations. After several delays because of heavy rains, the Federal party finally saw Forrest on February 23–24 at Rienzi, Mississippi. Hosea's flattering description of the Confederate cavalryman in a letter home indicates that Forrest was regarded with admiration and deference by many of his opponents—and also that he was doing his best to impress them. His hair seems to have been white enough by then to remind Hosea of the powdered wigs of Revolutionary War heroes, and, never one to forgo any possible show of strength, he wore the "rich gray uniform" and the new three-star collar of a lieutenant general five days before he was officially entitled to it. Hosea found that this enemy's "habitual expression seemed rather subdued and thoughtful, but when his face lighted up with a smile, which ripples all over his features, the effect is really charming. . . . His language indicates a very limited education, but his impressive manner conceals many otherwise notable defects." The latter, Hosea specified, included "invariabl[e]" omission of "the final 'g' in the termination 'ing.' " Forrest also "inexcusably mispronounced" a lot of words, as well as "always" using "the past participle in place of the past tense in such words as 'see' (as 'I seen' instead of 'I saw' and 'holp tote' meaning to 'help carry') etc. . . . In a very short time, however, these pass unnoticed. He speaks of his success with a soldierly vanity, and expresses the kindliest feelings toward prisoners and wounded."[4]

He also told the Union officers a little of his unorthodox military philosophy, specifically that he knew nothing of tactics except what he had absorbed in almost four years of war. What he had learned he summed up in two laconic lessons: (1) "I always make it a rule to get there first with the most men." (2) He preferred pistols to sabers for sidearms and "would give more for fifteen minutes of bulge on [an opponent] than for three days of tactics." The then hopeless character of the Confederate cause is reflected in a strange prediction he made that Lee would "have to get out of Richmond" and "would move his army into Kentucky" and the next summer "would march with 200,000 men into Illinois. . . . The rebel authorities are enrolling the negroes in Mississippi preparatory to putting them into the service." He also told Parkhurst "he was as anxious to rid the country of . . . [guerrillas] as was any officer in the U.S. Army, and that he would esteem it a favor if General Thomas would hang every one he caught." As to the matter at hand, he informed Parkhurst he didn't have the authority to make an agreement regarding prisoners without consulting Taylor; he said he would go to Meridian to see his superior while Parkhurst waited at Rienzi. Torrential rains then washed out railroad tracks and delayed the prisoner exchange for weeks.[5]

Forrest continued preparing for the next, inevitable Federal offensive and meanwhile tried to maintain a semblance of military order amid the gathering pall of defeat. Morton on February 25 led members of his battery to meet as a democratic body and pass flowery resolutions supporting the Confederate government, Jefferson Davis, and "our great and indomitable chieftain, under whose banner we have ever been victorious." While the "chieftain" labored over reorganization and recruiting, however, his bivouacked troops became bored, and finally one evening many "rebelled" against camp rules prohibiting the squandering of ammunition and the jading of horseflesh by needlessly firing guns and racing horses. "That night they wasted hundreds of pounds of ammunition," Captain Harvey Mathes later wrote. "The next day, growing bolder, a party of daredevils rode up in front of his tent and, staking off a quarter-course, began racing their horses." Mathes noted that Forrest often joined his men in their sports and games, and that during such moments allowed them personal latitude in their "mischievous chatter" with him. When they began racing their horses in front of his tent this day, the general and some members of his staff watched the races and even bet on some of the horses. Afterward, the racers "drew up in front of his quarters and gave three cheers for General Forrest . . . then rode off in triumph" — only to be apprehended a few yards farther on "by a strong [provost] guard, arrested, and carried before the general, who at once had them court-martialed and severely punished. His own son suffered the same penalty as the rest, and carried fence-rails until his shoulders were sore."[6]

On March 22 the weather put an abrupt end to his troops' leisure. It moderated sufficiently for Union general Wilson to put three cavalry divisions — a mammoth raiding force of 14,000 troopers, the largest mounted army ever assembled in North America — across the Tennessee River in the northwest corner of Alabama. Streaming southeastward on three roads to confuse the Confederates and make the most of scant forage, they moved first to Jasper. There Wilson, hearing Chalmers's division was approaching Tuscaloosa from the west, divested himself of his wagons on March 27 and, retaining just his artillery, began racing to reach his goal ahead of Forrest. Forrest didn't know for certain what the goal was, but he and Taylor, also watching other aggressive Federal activity in Memphis and in front of Mobile, suspected the target was Selma, a major Confederate munitions and manufacturing center.

The Union raiders hurried on to Elyton (later Birmingham) on March 29. That day Forrest, struggling to concentrate his widely dispersed troops in front of Selma, saw his own advance units reach the Sipsey River a little to the south and well west of Elyton. Near the banks of the Sipsey, a summary court-martial condemned to death two Kentuckians, a man and boy charged with desertion after being arrested without papers on their way home. Despite protestations of innocence, later found to be true, the two were put before a firing squad and their bodies left by the road under a large sign: SHOT FOR DESERTION. The corpses were ordered to be left that way for two days in sight of all of Forrest's passing men, after which their commander ordered Jackson to have the pair buried—by a party whose officer-in-charge was empowered also to execute any other deserters who might be discovered by then.[7]

The next night, Forrest reached Scottsville, within five miles of the important Cahaba River bridge at Centreville. Chalmers, minus a brigade left behind in Mississippi to guard the railroad, was assumed to be approaching the Federal flank near Plantersville, and Jackson was at Tuscaloosa. At 6 P.M. on March 31 Forrest sent a dispatch return-addressed "Six Miles from Montevallo" to Jackson, thought to be behind the Federals, ordering him to "follow down after them" from Montevallo but not to bring "on a general engagement . . . unless you find the balance of our forces in supporting distance of you." Less than three hours later, Jackson sent Forrest a note giving his location as "James Hill's" and saying he planned to attack the Federals "at daylight." At 2 A.M., Forrest aide-de-camp Charles Anderson wrote a note to his general return-addressed Centreville saying the Federals—in reality, a detachment sent by Wilson to burn Tuscaloosa—appeared to have gotten between Jackson and Jackson's artillery. To Chalmers, whose location was unclear, Anderson reported sending an order to "move to or between the enemy and Selma."[8]

These dispatches never reached their intended destinations. The courier carrying them was captured by Federals before morning, by which time Wilson, even without the men sent west to Tuscaloosa, was thus in possession not only of imposing odds of about 12,000 to 6,000 in potential available manpower but also of the knowledge of where most of Forrest's units were and that Forrest planned to use them to attack from front, flank, and rear. Putting this windfall of information to immediate use, the Federal commander sent a brigade to Centreville to take the Cahaba River bridge Forrest's troops were holding for Jackson and Chalmers, thus effectively cutting off nearly 5,000 of Forrest's converging forces. Wilson himself pushed furiously forward toward Selma. Armed with new seven-shot Spencer repeating rifles, he gobbled up a few hundred Kentucky and Alabama cavalry and a detachment of some 300 infantry just arrived from Selma. From then on, in a forty-eight-hour, fifty-mile, running fight from Six Mile Creek below Montevallo through Randolph, Maplesville, and Ebenezer Church finally to the outskirts of Selma itself, Wilson's Federals—although they later reported otherwise—were opposed by a total of perhaps only 2,000 hastily gathered Confederates.[9]

Some of the best of these, Forrest and his escort, reached the scene of battle after the initial fight at Six Mile Creek. Riding from Centreville toward the sound of firing on the afternoon of March 31, Forrest hit the Federal column in the flank, severed it, drove its rear backward, turned and attacked its forward units, and then, from prisoners, learned that the few Confederates in Wilson's front were being driven pell-mell southward. Forrest then pulled his men out east of the Federal path, rode hard to the south, and finally at 10 P.M. reached the Confederate camp in Wilson's front sixteen miles south of Montevallo.[10]

Expecting Chalmers to arrive momentarily from Plantersville and Jackson from Tuscaloosa, he devised a delaying action. Putting his men into line the next morning at Ebenezer Church six miles north of Plantersville, Forrest waited in vain for the arrival of Chalmers. Only some 200 men of Armstrong's advance brigade materialized, and when he received a note from Chalmers saying he would be unable to reach Plantersville that day, Forrest became enraged—to no avail. The overwhelming Federal force and its Spencers "completely routed" the small band of Confederates as Forrest himself once again fought hand to hand. He managed to kill an Indiana captain named J. D. Taylor, who was officially reported to have died after being "engaged in a running fight of 200 yards with Forrest in person." Confederate accounts are even more vivid. Captain John Eaton of Forrest's escort later recalled that "[e]ach of us was armed with a pair of six-shooters, and I emptied the twelve chambers of my two army-pistols . . . not . . . more than five paces from the Federal trooper at whom it was aimed. It seemed as if these fellows were bent upon killing the general, whom they recognized as an officer of high rank. I saw five or six slashing away at him with their sabres at one time." Lieutenant George Cowan said he saw "six Federals . . . all slashing at" Forrest, one of whom "struck one of his pistols and knocked it from his hand. Private Phil Dodd . . . spurred his horse to the general's rescue, and shot the Federal soldier who was so close upon him, thus enabling General Forrest to draw his other pistol, with which he killed another of the group." Forrest himself later would recall to Wilson that the Hoosier captain had hacked his arm with the saber, and "if that boy had known enough to give me the point of his saber instead of the edge, I should not have been here to tell you about it."[11]

Fighting all the way, Forrest and his escort were pushed backward twenty-four miles that day. At midmorning on April 2, he rode into Selma, where the streets and river landing were full of vehicles being loaded hastily for departure. The sight of him took aback Richard Taylor, who said Forrest suddenly "appeared, horse and man covered with blood, and announced the enemy at his heels, and that I must move at once to escape capture. I felt anxious for him, but he said he was unhurt and would cut his way through, as most of his men had done, whom he had ordered to meet him west of the Cahaba." Taylor's train barely got out of Selma past the encircling Federals, and its departure left Forrest in command of a fortress boasting parapets three miles long rising six feet high and eight feet thick above a ditch five feet deep and fifteen feet wide. It was designed for defense by 10,000 men, and Forrest was able to muster less than one-third that number.[12]

The end came three hours later. Having captured the engineer who had designed the facility, Wilson knew the Selma fortifications better than Forrest did, and he readied an assault against the Confederate left by 1,500 men under Brigadier General Eli Long. Long was told to await a signal to synchronize his advance with another by 300 Federals on the other wing, and as he waited, Chalmers finally arrived on the field and attacked a parked Union wagon train in the Federal rear. Realizing the Union assault would have to be scrubbed if he turned to face Chalmers, Long sent back a few men to help defend the train and then, refusing to await the signal any longer and aided greatly by a Forrest deficiency in artillery ammunition, charged 600 yards straight at the Selma works. Long's men overlapped Armstrong's veterans, who were standing as much as ten feet apart on the left side of the thin Confederate defense line, and some raw militiamen manning the area between Armstrong on the left and Roddey on the right suddenly turned and fled. Forrest tried to move Roddey leftward in time to close the gap, but couldn't, and the Confederate line snapped. Federals poured through to victory, the whole thing taking "less than 15 minutes." By the end of the evening the Federals reported taking 2,700 prisoners.[13]

The Confederates reeled backward to a second line nearer the city itself, and after that line had been flanked under vigorous assault from in front, Forrest told his men to mount their horses and get out any way they could. Some simply waited in hiding in the homes of citizens and came out later, after the Federals had gone, but their commander, at the head of his escort and some other troopers who had gathered around him, cut his way out northward along the same road on which the Federals had attacked. Around nightfall, he personally killed yet another Union cavalryman, his thirtieth and final Federal victim of the war.[14]

His men continued fighting most of that night. Picking their way along unfamiliar roads, reproached by the flames of unaccustomed and bitter defeat in the night sky over Selma, they were in a desperate state of mind. They happened past a home where booty-seeking Federal foragers, having already looted the place of its valuables, were attempting to "outrage" the women who lived there. Hearing female screams, the Confederates became "greatly excited and provoked . . . , and . . . did not hesitate to slay them [the Federal looters] on the spot." Soon afterward, they encountered and captured pickets of a scouting squad of Federal regulars who had taken over the home of an absent resident named Godwin. As they readied a surprise attack against the squad itself, Forrest's troopers—either divining that this might be their last fight, perhaps, or having something in mind they didn't want their commander to see—prevailed on him to remain in the rear this time, vowing not to obey his orders if he didn't accede to their wish. He therefore waited a quarter mile away as they ended his military career by providing a basis, however questionable, of one last charge of atrocity. Rushing the Federal squad from front and rear, in "an animated fight" of "a few minutes" they killed or wounded thirty-five and captured five. The sole Confederate casualty was one man wounded.[15]

Once again, Federals charged massacre. Wilson's report said Forrest found the Union detachment "asleep in a neighboring field. . . . He charged on them in their sleep, and refusing to listen to their cries of surrender, killed or wounded the entire party, numbering 25 men." A later account in a biography of George Thomas says: "Forrest fell upon the party with the ferocity of a wild Indian, and killed every man of it." Forrest biographers eventually countered with reminiscences of participants swearing that the Union detachment wasn't sleeping—that, in fact, the first shot fired was by a Federal—and that the outcome was in doubt until decided by a charge at the Union rear by a Confederate detachment detailed for that purpose. By design or otherwise, Forrest was not directly accountable for any excesses there may have been. The Federals obviously believed there were some; they burned the Godwin house in reprisal.[16]

Moving northward the next day, April 3, Forrest's remnant arrived at Plantersville in the morning—where, Wilson's Federal report remarks, Forrest "captured the hospital, which had been left without a guard . . . paroled all the nurses and slightly wounded men, and left the surgeons and patients unmolested"—then turned westward. Almost immediately, his troops met Federals under Brigadier General McCook coming in from the bridge at Centreville that had so disrupted Forrest's Selma plans. Forrest ordered a charge, after which he pulled his men back into some woods and, while the Federals deployed to meet an attack, slipped off westward. On April 4 he crossed the Cahaba and, at Marion, found Chalmers with one brigade and Jackson, who after being unable to penetrate McCook at the Centreville bridge had come down the river's west bank. Forrest's wagon train and artillery also were there, having arrived from Mississippi, and he and his escort virtually fell from their horses here, having "now been in their saddles, with little intermission, for seven days and nights, with the scantiest fare for men and horses. . . . [A]ll were so greatly worn down that rest and sleep were essential."[17]

They were still in the Cahaba area when, a couple of days later, Wilson asked Forrest for a meeting to consider paroling and exchanging prisoners, and Forrest agreed to talk in the town of Cahaba April 8. On this, the day before Lee rode to meet Grant at Appomattox, it was decided at Cahaba that officers and men paroled were declared exchanged and returned to duty. After dinner at the house of a Colonel Matthews, Wilson conferred alone with Forrest, who still had an arm in a sling. Wilson found him a little despondent but continuing to show the "great firmness, excellent judgment, inflexible will" Wilson expected of him. Captain Hosea also was present at Cahaba, and he thought the second meeting with Forrest much less agreeably impressive than the first. Having heard the Union story of the clash at the Godwin house, Hosea later wrote that in the Forrest he saw at Cahaba "all the brutal instincts of the slave driver stood out unconcealed; and to these was added a sulky and guilty consciousness that we regarded him as the murderer of [Captain] Royce [the Federal detachment's commanding officer] and his party."[18]

Two days later, after destroying the munitions works in Selma and shooting 500 surplus horses to keep them from bearing Confederate saddles, Wilson moved eastward toward Montgomery. Forrest did not follow. His force was too small and surely too demoralized to have much effect on Wilson now; with Selma fallen, there was little left in the Deep South to defend, anyway. Remaining in the Cahaba area a week, long enough to gather up his escapees from Selma, he moved further westward, then north to Gainesville. Although there is no record of it, he probably first heard of Lee's surrender soon after Wilson left Selma; some telegraph service was still intact, and Richard Taylor seems to have learned of it April 10.[19]

At Gainesville, Forrest tried—despite rivers and streams at spring-flood stage—to gather what men he could, remount them, get them into a semblance of fighting shape, and cover various reconnaissance assignments ordered every two or three days by Taylor as rumor and desperation ran rampant. He meanwhile began to learn "the particulars" of Lee's surrender through Northern newspapers; news soon came of the fall of Mobile, as well as telegraphic notification of Johnston's surrender negotiations with Sherman near Durham, North Carolina. By then, other wild and unsubstantiated talk was sweeping the South. Jefferson Davis had fled Richmond and was on his way southward and westward to try to continue the war wherever another stand could be made. Abraham Lincoln had been assassinated April 15 in a Washington theater by a crazed Southernborn actor. Some of the few Southern newspapers still publishing reported that the war remained viable; the Augusta *Constitutionalist* editorialized April 18 under the headline "The End Is Not In Sight" that Confederate victory and the "glorious independence of the South" remained possible while the Trans-Mississippi Confederacy was unconquered; but two days earlier, the long-homeless Memphis *Appeal*, which had left Montgomery ahead of Wilson's raiders, had to cease operations when Federals caught up with one of its proprietors in Columbus, Georgia.[20]

As Wilson rattled around inside its skeleton, the Confederacy fell apart. There was no one left for the Federals to fight; on March 18, too late, the Confederate Congress finally had bowed to pleas by Lee and Davis to pass legislation allowing slaves to become soldiers for the South (although refusing to grant them freedom for doing so), and the first blacks were mustered into gray uniforms in Richmond only days before the Confederate capital fell. Homeward-heading, long-unpaid (white) Confederates from Lee's once proud Army of Northern Virginia now could be seen meandering through the lines of Johnston's still intact army in North Carolina stealing mules, horses, and even clothes hung out to dry. Within weeks, they would be breaking into Confederate arsenals and, when these were exhausted, into civilian stores. On April 19 Forrest was notified by Taylor that perhaps some of his own troops, men identifying themselves as members of Jackson's cavalry, were "going through this country [near Demopolis, Alabama] forcibly dismounting citizens on the road, taking horses, mares, and colts; in some instances . . . firing on them." Forrest issued a general order to his troops on April 25:

> *SOLDIERS: The enemy have originated and sent through our lines various and conflicting dispatches indicating the surrender of General Robert E. Lee and the Army of Northern Virginia. A morbid appetite for news and sensation rumors has magnified a simple flag of truce from Lieutenant General Taylor to General Canby at Mobile into a mission for negotiating the terms of surrender of the troops of his department. Your commanding general desires to say to you that*

no credence should be given to such reports. . . . On the contrary, from Southern sources and now published in our papers, it is reported that General Lee has not surrendered; that a cessation of hostilities has been agreed upon between Generals Johnston and Sherman for the purpose of adjusting the difficulties and differences between the Confederate and the United States of America. Also that since the evacuation of Richmond and the death of Abraham Lincoln, Grant has lost in battle and by desertion 100,000 men. As your commander, he further assures you that at this time, above all others, it is the duty of every man to stand firm at his post and true to his colors. . . . A few days more will determine the truth or falsity of all the reports now in circulation. . . .[21]

Forrest's private mood was growing less sanguine. He always had been at bottom a realist, and it took no genius to assess the Southern situation now. On April 29 Taylor met Union major general E. R. S. Canby twelve miles north of Mobile and agreed to surrender. The concord was rendered slightly premature by notification from the Federals that highly generous terms Sherman had given Johnston—which could even be construed as allowing slave owners to retain their slaves—had been repudiated by Grant, who insisted on the same terms he had given Lee at Appomattox. On May 3 in response to Grant's repudiation of the Sherman terms, Mississippi governor Charles Clark and Isham G. Harris, who since Nashville's fall had spent many days traveling with Forrest's staff, came to Forrest's headquarters. Their intention was to plan a retreat into the Trans-Mississippi to join unsurrendered Confederates in Texas. For Forrest, the pipe dreams of the politicians were too much. Rising to interrupt them, he minced no words. "Men," he said, "you may all do as you damn please, but I'm a-going home." Harris insisted that Forrest lead his men back into battle; Forrest replied that his troops soon would be outnumbered ten to one.

"To make men fight under such circumstances would be nothing but murder," he added. "Any man who is in favor of a further prosecution of this war is a fit subject for a lunatic asylum."[22]

The following day Taylor surrendered to Canby, and both Taylor and Forrest made speeches to the troops at Meridian, Mississippi. Forrest had gone there to confer with Taylor and meet Federal major general E. S. Dennis, who had been assigned to parole him and his men. Four decades later Samuel Donelson recalled that while the deliberations proceeded, a throng of soldiers from both sides assembled in the yard, clamoring for speeches from Taylor and Forrest. The polished Taylor "made a beautiful and earnest talk," and at its close "a perfect storm of yells arose for 'Forrest,' many of those present having never seen him, but knowing of his oft-repeated deeds of valor." Forty years later, Donelson would claim to be able to remember Forrest's words verbatim:

> Men, we have surrendered. We have made our last fight. I came here tonight to meet the Federal general who will go with me tomorrow to Gainesville, Ala., to be paroled and to lay down our arms. Men, you have been good soldiers; a man who has been a good soldier can be a good citizen. I shall go back to my home upon the Mississippi River, there to begin life anew, and to you good old Confederates, I want to say that the latchstring of Bedford Forrest will always be on the outside of the door.[23]

Apparently, though, he still wasn't fully decided about going home. The thought of his surrender was so foreign to his "good old Confederates" that when they learned he intended to do it, they "were bowed down with unutterable grief," one later wrote in a history of the Seventh Tennessee Cavalry, C.S.A. They wanted to "go to the Trans-Mississippi Department and continue the struggle for Southern independence. But Gen. Forrest said: 'No.' What could not be accomplished here could never be done in the thinly settled West." He himself seemingly had no thought of continuing the Confederate fight in Texas—even though Jefferson Davis was at that moment trying to get to him with just that object, fleeing through Georgia with a remnant of cavalry under a longtime Forrest subordinate, Brigadier General George Dibrell; but Forrest seems to have been very affected by the talk of his diehards. They were mostly such younger men as J. P. Young, who wrote the Seventh Cavalry history, and the fearless artillery captain John Morton, who was finally turning twenty-one.[24]

Too practical to continue a senseless fight, Forrest did consider fleeing the odium of surrender in favor of another struggle offering brighter possibilities: the Mexican Revolution, where the French had installed Maximilian of Austria as head of state opposing the popular uprising of Juarez. Many of Forrest's men begged him to lead them there, and among these men he was widely reported to be "organizing" a Mexican "colony." Morton's use of the third person in his memoirs hides any direct knowledge he, as a Forrest intimate, may have had of such matters, but he adds: "That General Forrest had at one time entertained the idea of leaving without surrendering is believed, but there is no conclusive evidence that he had formulated a definite plan to found a colony. . . ." At daybreak of May 9, the day the paroles were to be signed by Dennis, Forrest called Charles Anderson out for a horseback ride. They rode into the country without talking, Forrest with his chin down, brooding. Anderson deferred to his melancholy and kept silent until there was no alternative. Coming to a crossroads, Anderson asked which fork they should take. "It makes no difference," Forrest replied. "If one of them led to hell and the other to Mexico, I wouldn't care which one I took." He went on to express "his bitter distaste for surrender," saying that "the idea of going to Mexico was alluring to him." Anderson replied that if Forrest did go to Mexico "the majority of his men would have to suffer the humiliation of surrender," and that these men, " 'who have by their unflinching devotion to your fortunes made your reputation as a commander,' " would suffer " 'added humiliation to be compelled to bear the bitterness of surrender without your example and inspiration.' "[25]

There were other considerations, too. At nearly forty-four he was tired, utterly debilitated by four years of constant exposure to weather, four bullet wounds, continual personal combat, and the persistent and rapidly expanding responsibilities of command. If he did indeed intend returning to his plantation on the Mississippi, he needed to husband the strength he had left and get there as soon as possible; the spring planting season was already well along. He also probably knew by now that back in Nashville, George Thomas had heard the widespread speculation that he intended cutting his way across the Mississippi to Texas. On May 3 Thomas had directed his source for the rumor, Brigadier General Edward Hatch, to send Forrest a "summons to surrender" under a flag of truce, adding to Hatch: "Inform him . . . of the rumors which have reached you, and that . . . if he attempts such a reckless and bloodthirsty adventure he will be treated thereafter as an outlaw, and the States of Mississippi and Alabama will be so destroyed that they will not recover for fifty years."[26]

Apparently Anderson's reasoning, added to the other factors, tipped the scale. "That settles it," Forrest replied to Anderson. "I will share the fate of my men." He then asked Anderson to prepare an address to the troops and apparently suggested incorporating the "good soldiers/good citizens" idea from his Meridian speech plus others Anderson had voiced. Anderson complied, writing the document atop a cracker box. As soon as Forrest read it, it was set in type and uncharacteristically run off on an old printing press in sufficient number that each soldier could have a personal copy. This "farewell address," under the inspired pen of Anderson, turned out to be perhaps the most conciliatory Confederate message of its kind.

Asserting the reality "that we are beaten is a self-evident fact," it went on to note they were the last of the Confederate armies east of the Mississippi to quit the fight, and that the Lost Cause was "to-day hopeless." In part, it added:

Civil war, such as you have just passed through, naturally engenders feelings of animosity, hatred, and revenge. It is our duty to divest ourselves of all such feelings, and, as far as in our power to do so, to cultivate friendly feelings toward those with whom we have so long contended. . . . Neighborhood feuds, personal animosities, and private differences should be blotted out; and, when you return home, a manly, straightforward course of conduct will secure the respect even of your enemies. Whatever your responsibilities may be to the government, to society, or to individuals, meet them like men.

. . . I have never, on the field of battle, sent you where I was unwilling to go myself; nor would I now advise you to a course which I felt myself unwilling to pursue. You have been good soldiers; you can be good citizens. Obey the laws, preserve your honor, and the government to which you have surrendered can afford to be, and will be, magnanimous.

N. B. Forrest, Lieutenant General.[27]

After the formal surrender later that day, the bulk of his troops headed for home clutching these sheets of paper, which Morton says would become "faded," "flimsy," and all the more treasured by any man entitled, as a rider with Forrest, to possess one. Some carried home something else as well. The remnant of the Seventh Tennessee Cavalry, one of the most feared and celebrated of Forrest units, gathered on the eve of the surrender rites and swore that their bullet-riddled flag—sewn from the dress of a young woman from Aberdeen, Mississippi—never would become property of the victors. Under cover of darkness, they surrounded their officers in front of the regiment's headquarters and ripped the tattered silk pennant to shreds. Then each took a swatch, hiding within his clothes that token of their dark and bloody glory.[28]

Part IV

KLANSMAN

25

THOSE IN CHARGE of the paroling process hung around the Gainesville camps a few days duplicating muster rolls. Forrest and his officer corps then "remained some days" further in the Gainesville area after the paroling work was done, perhaps out of reluctance to leave military friends and move on to cope with peace. John Morton later recalled that his commander's farewells to his lieutenants "were sad in the extreme." Morton's memoirs do not include the words he spoke to Forrest, but the latter's reply indicates they expressed bitter regret at the outcome of the long struggle. "You are young, John, and you will soon get over it all," he remembered Forrest responding. "Go home and study medicine with your father. It is a noble and grand profession, and I shall love to think of you as being of service to your fellow men in that way." His feelings for Morton obviously ran deep. He gave the young captain a letter to his father, a prominent Nashville physician, attesting that the son was as genuine a war hero as Forrest's small but deeply scarred legions had produced. This letter, possibly written for Forrest by Major Anderson along with other such commendatory correspondence, suggests he was proudly reviewing his military record.[1]

Four days following the surrender, though, he was prevailed on to recall a scene of which he may have been less proud, one whose legend still horrified the North and prompted questions that would last for decades, perhaps forever. In Meridian in a roomful of surrendered Southern officers, he was approached by Northern writer Bryan McAlister, who was in civilian clothes and didn't immediately disclose his recent position on the staff of a Federal general. McAlister later recalled that he met the controversial Confederate on the hearth of a small "cabin-room . . . dimly lighted by a small tallow candle," and that one other person and he were the only Unionists present. He saw Forrest as "a man of fine appearance, about six feet in height, having dark, piercing hazel eyes, carefully trimmed moustache, and chin-whiskers, dark as night, finely cut features, and iron-gray hair." His "lithe" figure connoted "great physical power and activity," and McAlister said he would "have marked him as a prominent man had I seen him on Broadway; and when I was told that he was the 'Forrest of Fort Pillow,' I devoted my whole attention to him. . . ." His "first impression," he went on, "was rather favorable," despite the infamy of Fort Pillow and the fact of having "spoken to numbers of Confederate officers" who "speak of him with disgust, though all admit his bravery and fitness for the cavalry service."

Opening a conversation, the writer remarked that he never expected to be seated by a fire with such a personage. "Why so?" Forrest asked. Because his name was on nearly everyone's lips, McAlister said. "Yes," Forrest said, showing "the finest set of teeth" McAlister had ever seen, "I have waked up the Yankees everywhere, lately." McAlister asked if Forrest would write "the true account" of the storming of Fort Pillow. "Well," Forrest answered, "the Yankees ought to know [it]; they sent down their best men to investigate the affair." But was their report to be believed? "Yes, if we are to believe any thing a nigger says," Forrest replied, and repeated one of his favorite maxims. "When I went into the war, I meant to fight," he said. "Fighting means killing." He proceeded to his prodigious personal combat record and what seems to have been a brief account of his final fight: "I have lost 29 horses in the war, and have killed a man each time. The other day I was a horse ahead, but at Selma they surrounded me, and I killed two, jumped my horse over a one-horse wagon, and got away." He talked on, telling McAlister that giving no quarter wasn't his usual practice; to the contrary, he said, his "Provost-Marshal's book will show that I have taken 31,000 prisoners during the war." Fort Pillow, he told McAlister, was full of "niggers and deserters from our army" who "were all drunk" and "kept . . . firing" as they ran down the hill to the river with their flag "still flying." He himself had "cut the halyards, and let it down, and stopped the fight," and if any Union soldiers were burned to death, as was charged, it happened in some tents out front of the Federal position which the Federals themselves set afire because they were obstructing the fort's view of the advancing Confederates.

McAlister drew him into similarly garrulous accounts of his defeats of Sturgis and Streight and a Federal blockhouse commander at Athens, Alabama. Then the observer came to telling conclusions, with the comment that "the heart sickens at the conduct of this infamous butcher."

He is one of the few men that are general "blowers," and yet will fight. Forrest is a thorough bravo — a desperate man in every respect. He was a negro-trader before the war, and in "personal affairs," as he calls them, had killed several men. . . . He has two brothers living, one of whom is spoken of as being a greater butcher than the Lieutenant-General. He [the lieutenant general] *is a man without education or refinement, married, I believe, to a very pretty wife. Any one would call him handsome. Any one hearing him talk, would call him a braggadocio. As for myself, I would believe one half he said, and only dispute with him with one finger on the trigger of my pistol.*

Closing his account of the interview with a brief mention of what seem to have been the innocent Kentucky man and boy ordered executed at the Sipsey River bridge on the way to Selma, McAlister added that the "fathers of these youths are upon Forrest's track, sworn to kill him," and that "poetic justice" dictated that he should die violently; he "probably" had killed a hundred men with his own hands. Forrest informed McAlister that since the war was "played [out]," he intended to take a tent on a long fishing trip on which he hoped not "to see any one for twelve months. What a charming hero he would make," McAlister concluded, "for a sensational 'King of the Cannibal Islands.' "[2]

Word of the enmity between him and friends of the Kentuckians shot at the Sipsey bridge soon reached Memphis, where the Unionist-sympathizing *Bulletin* ran a story at the top of its front page on May 18 headlined GENERAL FORREST KILLED, informing Memphians he had been shot to death by four of his troops after one of his courts-martial had slain six of their comrades for celebrating news of Johnston's surrender. The next day the *Bulletin* recanted its hasty information, explaining that people had "seen and conversed with" Forrest in Mississippi. The false report, it added, "seems to have been founded on the fact that his life was threatened by an old gentleman from Kentucky whose sons, it is alleged, Forrest had caused to be shot without trial. Their offense was absence from their command without leave."[3]

Alive but possibly looking over his shoulder, Forrest headed homeward aboard a train. One of the few such Southern conveyances still able to move, it transported him across a new world. Long-unpaid and half-starved ex-Confederate soldiers were breaking into their late government's quartermaster stores and, soon, even civilian ones on their journeys homeward, and guerrillas who had stolen from both sides during the war continued their depredations even more ferociously, unfettered by legal restraint. Most of the South, in which Federal decree had outlawed existing local order, had become a land without law, as the U.S. military authority—never to become very pervasive—was still aborning. Thousands upon thousands of refugees, who had wandered across a shrinking Confederacy since their homes had fallen beneath the inexorable Federal advance, were joined by other tens of thousands of newly freed slaves, who wonderingly initiated their first legal treks across the boundaries of their home communities, some seeking relatives sold away from them, some the rumored succor of Federal authorities, and some presumably just a feel of their lives' first freedom to go where they pleased.

The South had become a melting pot of misery. In Memphis the week Forrest arrived home at his plantation in northern Mississippi, daily publication of the *Bulletin* belied the anarchy threatening the region; the newspaper's columns, though, often reflected it. On May 25 the *Bulletin* printed a long account of an assault on a black Union soldier by four white men, two in Confederate uniform and two in civilian clothes, at a Memphis parade. Three days later, a patrol of the 113th Illinois was fired on "by some person unknown" at the corner of Eleventh and Union. A black reported to Memphis authorities that when he declared his intention to avail himself of his rights as a free man "and his determination to have pay for his work if he continued to labor, he was seized and had the sinews of his legs cut and part of his toes cut off." Every few days there appeared the headline SHALL [Jefferson] DAVIS BE HUNG?[4]

The homeward-bound general could have been little cheered, either, by the fact that in Washington the president of the now forcibly re-United States was Andrew Johnson, a fellow prewar Southern Democrat, who on May 9 had announced that Lincoln's assassination had been plotted by Jefferson Davis and thereupon authorized $335,000 in rewards for the capture of Davis and a number of other men labeled co-conspirators. Ruling the statehouse at Nashville, as the result of a March 4 election from which all men of Confederate leanings were excluded, was William G. "Parson" Brownlow, a Knoxville preacher-newspaperman whose son was lieutenant colonel of the Ninth Tennessee Cavalry (U.S.) and who himself on May 10 used the authorization of a new Unionist legislature to offer a $5,000 reward for the capture of Isham G. Harris. In his Knoxville *Whig* of May 10, Brownlow—who remained a sometime correspondent of his journal while the state's chief executive—wrote that "[i]f captured the fugitive must be delivered to me alive, to the end that justice may be done upon him here, upon the theatre of his former villainous deeds!"[5]

The homeward ride was a wrenching affair in many more ways than one. On the first leg of it, from Meridian to Jackson, Mississippi, the train was crowded with soldiers and other refugees, and the tracks were in such poor condition that at one point the rails spread, causing the train to run off them. C. B. Kilgore, later a judge and a congressman, was a passenger that day, and he recalled that Forrest quickly took command of the situation, ordering "every one of us out of the cars." The erstwhile general "soon had us at work with levers placed in position to lift the . . . coach so that the displaced rails could be pushed back in proper line." After a first effort was unsuccessful, someone said: "General, there are some men in the car, and if they would get out we could lift it more readily." Outraged that his initial command to leave the cars had not been fully obeyed, he sprang up the locomotive's steps and onto its platform shouting: "If you damned rascals don't get out of here and help get this car on the track, I will throw every one of you through the windows." In "rapid fashion," Kilgore said, the offenders "tumbled out," and the train was made mobile again.[6]

26

> . . . *General Forrest is said to be at his home in Co[a]homa,*
> *Mississippi. His last address to his soldiers, in which he frankly*
> *admitted the condition of affairs, has placed him higher in the*
> *estimation of the mass of people than he ever was before; but it is*
> *denounced in severe terms by that class of malignant but*
> *pusillanimous traitors, who prated and plotted treason while under*
> *federal protection, to keep out of the rebel army.*
>
> —*Memphis* Bulletin, *May 26, 1865*[1]

AT SUNFLOWER LANDING in Coahoma County, Forrest must have looked around himself with an unaccustomed sigh of foreboding. He would not have the luxury of resting and recuperating from the long war's wounds and weariness. During the conflict, notes due on his 3,400-acre plantation had gone unpaid, and to retain ownership he had to move quickly. Employing some of his ex-slaves, who had returned from flight to Georgia during his years of combat, he put in a crop of corn that, he said in a letter written about a month later, promised a bumper harvest.[2]

The letter, to General Stephen Lee, was written from Jackson, where Forrest seems to have gone almost as soon as President Johnson appointed a Mississippi governor through whom he could apply for a pardon. The new governor was William L. Sharkey, an aging prewar Whig who had taken no known part in aiding the Confederacy and thus was qualified to hold public office under guidelines Johnson laid down in his first major proclamations on "reconstruction" of the ex-Confederate states. One such granted amnesty and pardon, including all former rights to own property (except slaves), to all Southerners except those in fourteen categories. Among the latter were high Confederate officials and officers as well as owners of property worth more than $20,000; these were required to apply directly and individually to Johnson himself—which, Forrest explained to Lee, was what he was doing.

> *General: I am here for the pirpos of making application to the Pres for a pardon. I find it necessary to first take the amnesty oath and took the oath to the application . . . and strove[?] to have[?] the governors approval . . . for sending to Washington. . . . Governor Sharky thinks the applications Should be made and forwarded as Early as posable. I have aranged withe the Governor to forward my application for me. I wold advise if you will allow me to do So that you arange and Send yours forward as Early as practable.*
>
> *I have Setled for the present at my plantation in Coahoma Co Miss have gone to hard work have a fine crop of corn if the Seasons hit wil make a fine crop Mrs F is making Buter and Rasing chickens so come to See us and Bring Mrs Lee if you go to planting the Miss River is the place to do So Give my kindeste Regardes to Mrs Lee and allow me to Remain as Ever*
>
> *Your friend*
> *N. B. Forrest*[3]

As evidence of a wish to be assimilated into the postbellum age, Forrest had brought seven Federal officers to his area of Mississippi and taken one of them, Major B. E. Diffenbacher from Minnesota, into partnership in some of his farming operations; he also helped find plantations and similar situations for the other officers. The Unionists seem to have found him as singular as had his fellow Confederates. One party of them still in the service rode up to his place one day soon after his homecoming and were attacked by his old warhorse, King Philip, who rushed at their blue uniforms and tried to bite them; then, as they were defending themselves from the horse, Forrest's body servant, Jerry, ran out to protect the animal. One of the officers subsequently told Forrest he now understood how he had achieved his remarkable war record: "Your negroes fight for you, and your horses fight for you."[4]

By now, he must have been thoroughly confused about his status and prospects. The *Bulletin* of May 27 had quoted a New York newspaper as saying it was "understood that all the rebel officers concerned in the atrocious starvation of our prisoners . . . and also the Fort Pillow murder" would "be excluded from the benefit of the amnesty proclamation." On June 17 the *Bulletin* reported that a Kentucky Brigadier General Grigsby formerly "attached to Forrest's command," whose wife was a granddaughter of a former Kentucky governor, had been hanged by Federal soldiers at Danville upon his return home from the war. In the face of such alarming news, Forrest probably wouldn't have rushed to seek a pardon had he felt he had no chance of being granted one, and a feeling that he did have seems well founded.[5]

Johnson, whose wartime rhetoric had demanded heavy retribution from the Confederates, now held the formerly abolitionist so-called Radicals at bay with actions at first ostensibly in sympathy with them—such as initial denial of pardons to high-ranking and/or rich Confederates—while quietly building the foundations of a political base on which to run for reelection. A Southern Democrat who once had owned slaves himself, the President appeared to care little about the condition of freedmen and was uncomfortable with the Radicals, and he apparently thought that naming men of his Southern Unionist stamp as governors in the postwar South would gain him their states' votes. Requiring influential Southerners to apply to him individually and personally for their pardons, which at first pleased the Radicals, seems to have been a ploy by which he planned to build or rebuild political relationships with the most influential men of the South. Abandonment of his hatred of wealthy Southern planters and acceptance of them as prospective supporters was recommended to the President by the family of Major General Frank Blair of Missouri, a dedicated Unionist. Forrest, who wasn't without political acumen, possibly discerned all this, thereby causing him to rush his pardon request to Sharkey. It also may be, however, that by now he was getting to know Blair, who was his own age and around this time—like himself—was trying to rebuild a war-shattered fortune by investing in a Mississippi cotton plantation; twelve months later, he and Blair were warm friends.[6]

If Forrest did meet Blair this early, he must have known not only of Johnson's changing feelings toward influential Confederates but also of other powerful Northern forces dictating a lenient policy toward the

South. One was the wealth of Wall Street, where the interest of Northern manufacturers lay in seeing Southern cotton plantations begin producing again. Another was Northern public opinion on race matters, emphasized in three referenda (in Connecticut, Ohio, and Wisconsin) where voters rejected black suffrage inside their own borders; only five Northern states, all in formerly abolitionist New England, permitted blacks to vote on the same basis as whites.

As summer wore on, political activity quickened across the South, particularly in Forrest's corner of it. The Mississippi Reconstruction Convention, meeting in Jackson under intense scrutiny from the North, declared the state's secession ordinance of 1861 null and void, abolished slavery within its borders, and accorded blacks the rights to sue in the courts and to buy and own real estate—but refused them the right to vote. The last-mentioned, all-important action caused Radical senator Charles Sumner of Massachusetts on September 16 to dismiss the gathering as not much more than a "rebel conspiracy to obtain political power." With U.S. Army courts-martial empowered to decide many civilian cases, but lacking sufficient force to maintain order, Sharkey tried to organize a militia, thereby outraging the Northern Republican press; Northern Republicans saw it as an attempt to reconstitute the Confederate Army.[7]

In Tennessee, Governor Brownlow possessed strongly partisan leanings bordering on intolerance thanks to his personal ill treatment at the hands of Confederate occupation troops. He now began to declare publicly that he could not blame Tennessee's victorious loyalists for exacting an eye for an eye from the Confederate traitors who had oppressed them so long. Beseeched by ex-Confederates for protection from their Unionist neighbors, Brownlow offered little sympathy and less protection.[8]

In Memphis, where the black population was mushrooming from 3,000 in 1860 toward 15,000 in 1870, a formerly white-ruled city was being crowded with ex-slaves looking for urban jobs and lives removed from the rural domain of their former masters. As in many other cities across the South, reports of clashes between white Memphians and black Federal occupation troops mounted. Even most Unionist whites appear to have despised the rifle-carrying ex-slaves, regarding them as political pawns-to-be of the rich Confederates who had owned them; like President Johnson (and Frank Blair), Brownlow had owned slaves and during the war had been reluctantly converted to abolitionism—although not to any notable sympathy for blacks. To most white Southerners, meanwhile, the black ex-soldiers represented de facto accomplishment of the racial Armageddon that had given the white South nightmares for generations.

In Coahoma County, things weren't going well for Forrest. On September 16, as Sumner was deploring the Mississippi Reconstruction Convention, Forrest and his wife sold back 1,445 acres of their 3,400-acre holdings to Henry C. Chambers because of the unpaid wartime notes. Chambers gave the Forrests $16,605 in cash and promised notes of $6,678.96 per annum for each of the next five years. Perhaps to acquire funds with which to try to pay off and operate the plantation's other 1,900 acres, Forrest advertised locally that his "Steam Saw Mill" could "now furnish the public with lumber of every description," and he soon was reduced to commission work reminiscent of that with which he had opened his business career two decades earlier. Advertisements such as the following began appearing in Memphis newspapers:

Sam. Tate   Geo. E. Gill

N. B. Forrest   Dan. Able

Tate, Gill, Able & Co.

Wholesale Grocers,

Cotton Factors,

COMMISSION MERCHANTS

and Dealers in

Plantation Supplies, Wines, Liquors,

Cigars, Etc.

No. 278 Front Street, Memphis, Tenn.[9]

In Memphis, the news must have been alternately dismaying and reassuring. On December 1 the *Appeal* printed on its front page an account of a speech in Brooklyn, New York, by Major General Judson Kilpatrick in which that notoriously glib Union cavalry officer was reported to have said of Jefferson Davis: "The man must die because he was at the head of the rebellion. He must die upon the scaffold! Let England protest! Let Italy remonstrate! Let the Southern States send in their petitions! But that man MUST DIE!" The same day, on its second page, the *Appeal* reported a speech in Jackson, Mississippi, by Major General O. O. Howard, chief of the newly formed Freedmen's Bureau, in which Howard said that contrary to reports, the federal government wasn't going to give the land of Confederate Southern planters to freed blacks. Two days later, the *Appeal* noted that the Mississippi legislature had authorized the apprenticing of orphaned black minors and had provided stiff penalties for apprentices leaving their masters or for people enticing them away, provisions remarkably like ones that had been on the books to protect slavery. On December 14 the *Appeal* reported that a Negro Union soldier shot a white

"Mr. Roland" in the hip from behind after first stopping Roland and then ordering him to go on. The next day the newspaper disclosed that four of the city's policemen had been arrested for violence within the past three weeks, one charged with "shooting and killing a negro on Jefferson street"; all four were Irish-American, and the slain black recently had been discharged from the U.S. Navy.[10]

The day after Christmas, the *Appeal* acknowledged a report from the New Orleans *Crescent* "that Admiral Raphael Semmes, late of the Confederates States navy . . . was arrested at his home in Mobile on Friday night, by order of the Secretary of the Navy. He was paroled at the time of the surrender of Johnston to Sherman . . . [but] is to be carried north." Semmes was taken from Mobile to New Orleans on a steamer on which ex-Confederate major general Dabney Maury—now employed with an express company—happened to be a passenger. A couple of days later, visiting Memphis on his business rounds, Maury tried to warn Forrest that a fate similar to Semmes's might well lie in store for the "butcher of Fort Pillow." Not finding Forrest in the city at the time, he went to Sam Tate, who asked him to write Forrest about it and to add that a letter of credit would be forwarded to him to pay his way to Europe until affairs settled. Maury left Memphis the next day, but learned later from Tate that Forrest had politely refused the letter of credit.[11]

Forrest's decision in this matter wasn't known in Memphis for some time, however. On January 30, 1866, Matthew Gallaway's newly reactivated *Avalanche* printed a brief extract from the New York *Tribune* asking why Semmes, "who shed no blood," should be "on trial for his life for a violation of the rules of civilized warfare" while "Major General Forrest, of the Confederate army, is peacefully running a sawmill in Mississippi. Where are our soldiers who perished at Fort Pillow?" The *Avalanche,* noting that its senior editor had served on Forrest's staff from the Streight chase until the war's end, went on to defend editorially "one of the greatest military chieftains of the age" and his action at Fort Pillow, and to report sadly that he "is now, in all probability, an exile." Three weeks later, though, the *Avalanche* published a somewhat testy letter from the supposed exile. Explaining that he recently had returned from his plantation and been shown the *Avalanche* report of his emigration, he added:

> *I regret that you should suppose for a moment that I could be induced to leave the country. Certainly no act or expression of mine could have furnished ground for such a supposition. . . . [S]ince the*

*surrender, I have been silent and unobtrusive, laboring upon my
farm, and I regret my seclusion is so often disturbed by reports in
the newspapers, which are as unjust to the Government as they are
to my own character. I have never committed an act, uttered a word,
or entertained a sentiment not in strict accordance with the most
humanizing military usages, and fear no investigation into my
conduct. I certainly do not intend to leave the country, for my
destiny is now with the great American Union, and I shall contribute
all of my influence toward strengthening the Government, sustaining
its credit, and uniting the people once more in the indissoluble bonds
of peace and affection. As ever,*

> *Truly your friend,*
> *N. B. Forrest*[12]

Obviously, Forrest didn't write this letter himself, but he had plenty of
former military subordinates around Memphis who could have done it for
him. His adjutant, J. P. Strange, was in business there. Chalmers had just
moved his law office to the city. The recipient himself may even have been
induced to write it; Gallaway, coproprietor of the *Avalanche*, surely had
composed other Forrest communications in wartime. This letter, however,
may not have conveyed Forrest's initial reaction to Maury's warning of his
possible arrest. One story has it that when the report first reached him, his
remarks were not nearly so considerate of the feelings of the "Government" in the matter. "I am hard at work upon my plantation and carefully
observing the obligations of my parole," he is reported to have said. "If
the Federal government does not regard it, they will be sorry."[13]

His temper was shortening, probably for several reasons. For one, his
farming in Coahoma County wasn't proving profitable enough. On February 17, acknowledging a $20,000 debt to an L. F. Beech of Nashville,
he promised to pay Beech eight $2,500 notes—made through Tate, Gill
& Able—by January of 1867; if he proved unable to do so, he stipulated,
the remaining 1,900 acres of his plantation were to be auctioned off under
arrangements to be made by J. P. Strange. Then on March 13 he had to
put up a bond of $10,000 at his arraignment in Memphis on a treason
charge brought against him during the war; his bond was guaranteed by
prominent Memphians R. C. Brinkley and Frazer Titus.[14]

The South had been turned upside down, and, as the ex-slaves were
fond of proclaiming, "the bottom rail" had been put "on top now."
Tensions rose accordingly. On March 6 the *Avalanche* printed a warning
letter from Marshall County, Mississippi, where Forrest had spent his later

youth, ordering a former colonel in the Sixth Tennessee Cavalry (U.S.) who had become a store owner in nearby La Grange, Tennessee, to leave La Grange. Also demanding the departure of other named "negro-wor-shipers" in the area, it added: "You have all fought us for four years and now think to make your fortunes by selling arms and ammunition to our former slaves to murder ourselves, women and children. But you will be foiled in your schemes. . . . We have given you all fair warning in time."[15]

That the times had changed must have occurred to many readers of the *Avalanche* on April 3. That day the newspaper printed a letter reacting to an article in the Republican-leaning Memphis *Post* a day or so earlier:

> *Plantation, Miss. River,*
> *April 1, 1866.*

> *The following version of the tragedy which occurred on the plan-tation of General N. B. Forrest, yesterday evening, comes to me from the most authentic sources. From this it appears the General was standing near the gateway of one Thomas Edwards, a freedman, employed as a field hand on the plantation.*

> *The General himself had given a holiday that evening to all hands, and had himself just returned from the river with a recent Memphis newspaper, in which was detailed a case of Asiatic cholera, occurring recently in Mobile. At this time, all the hands were engaged in play in and about their cabins, when the General went among them and told them of this case of cholera, and advised them to drain some stagnant pools of water in the rear of their quarters, and that it was best to do it immediately. All parties went to work immediately. . . . At this juncture, Thomas Edwards approached, and, as he was not present when the other hands were obliged to do the work, the General explained the importance of drainage, and advised him to drain at once some nasty pools near his quarters. To this he made no reply, but passing into his cabin, he immediately commenced abusing his wife, and in loud language threatening instant punishment. His wife was recovering from an attack of illness, brought on by injury inflicted upon her by her husband's brutality, and she had been a constant victim to these outrages at his hands since he had been employed on the place.*

> *On hearing him commence his abuse, the General stepped into the cabin and told him that he should not beat his wife anymore; that he had, on several occasions, beaten her most cruelly; that these outrages should and must cease, and that he (the General) would*

hereafter protect the wife. To this, Thomas Edwards replied that "he would be d——d if he would not thrash his wife whenever he pleased; that he did not care a d——n for General Forrest, and would do as he pleased," at the same time assuming a threatening attitude and insulting language. The General remarked to him that he would not permit him or anybody else to insult him, and that if he persisted in using such language he would strike him. Edwards did continue to use insulting language, whereupon the General struck him over the head with a broom or its handle. Edwards immediately assaulted the General with a knife, wounding him slightly in the hand. Unfortunately for Edwards there was an axe in the cabin which the General seized, and as Edwards was rushing upon him he received a blow upon the head which was instantly fatal. . . .

The General immediately sent for the deputy sheriff, who was in the neighborhood, and surrendered himself into his hands, at the same time he despatched messengers for the surrounding citizens — taking particular pains to have summoned every Northern planter within reach to sit on the coroner's inquest, so that the affair should be properly and fairly investigated. . . .

Respectfully, &c.,
A. M. Henderson.[16]

More details emerged shortly. Forrest's partner Diffenbacher wrote his own account of the killing, which differed little from Henderson's and asked for "a suspension of opinion on this case, both North and South, until the facts are elicited by judicial proceedings." The ex-Union officer added that he himself arrived on the scene about 8 P.M., some four hours after Edwards's death, and found "about a hundred of the freedmen greatly excited and disposed to mob violence," but that Forrest came out onto his porch and made them a speech explaining how it had occurred and, prevailed on by "some of the better of the freedmen, they finally dispersed to await the future." Appended to this story was a statement from the coroner's jury in the case declaring that Edwards died "from a blow on the back of the head delivered by N. B. Forrest, with an axe . . . arising from the interference of said Forrest to prevent the deceased from abusing his (the deceased's) wife."[17]

Yet another account, in the *Avalanche* of April 10, said that Forrest had given all the freedmen the opportunity to leave the contracts with which he had bound them, and all but 18 — out of some 200 — had refused to leave. It also said that the widow of the man Forrest had killed blamed her purported rescuer, saying her husband had never hurt her. Forrest, however, soon was exonerated by both the Circuit Court of Coahoma County, meeting at Friar's Point, and Captain Collis of the Freedmen's Bureau at Vicksburg. In the Bureau's investigation, Mrs. Sarah Jane Edwards continued to maintain that her husband had never hurt her and that Forrest had killed him without provocation. Witness Hannah Powell, who lived with the Edwardses, generally supported Forrest's version of the story, although she said Forrest was between her and Edwards during the fight and thus prevented her from seeing Edwards draw a knife. The investigation also disclosed labor problems on the plantation: Employees of Forrest's partner, Diffenbacher, had provoked insubordination from the black laborers by threatening physical punishment of those refusing to work the number of daily hours specified by their contracts, and Edwards, a cruel man who had whipped a mule to death a month earlier, was a leader of the resentful blacks.

According to the *Avalanche,* Collis, a career Army officer from Connecticut, "expressed himself highly pleased with General Forrest's management of the freedmen, saying that his plantation, in all its details of comfort, hours of labor, recreation, &c., excelled any plantation in advantage to the freedmen, he had seen." Collis's only objection was Forrest's "indulgence" of his black employees, which Collis regarded as "productive of the demoralization" which had resulted in the death of Edwards. The Federal official said his investigation showed that Forrest had made financial "advances of too liberal a character" to the employees and allowed them "to purchase and carry firearms," habits which Collis "as an officer of the Freedmen's Bureau" ordered Forrest no longer to "tolerate." Collis was quoted as saying in summary that "in view of the new and novel condition of this people," Forrest had granted them "indulgences injurious to a fair test of the new system, prejudicial to their best interests and hurtful to your own as the compensating employer of their labor."[18]

Several of the accounts mentioned that a number of the freedmen— "about a hundred," according to Diffenbacher—gathered before Forrest's house and that he emerged and made them a speech "deploring the affair and stating the particulars, and promising to await a legal examination. While some of the negroes exhibited the audacity that not two in a thousand white men would show, the others were controlled by the efforts of some of the most intelligent and better of the freedmen, and they finally dispersed to await the future." Such appears to be the basis still extant for biographers' anecdotes concerning a dramatic confrontation in which Forrest, with drawn pistols, gave the angry black ex-soldiers military orders to "halt" and "ground arms," then dispersed them by threatening to "shoot the heads off every one of you" if they didn't return to their quarters. The reality seems to have been that a deputy sent to arrest Forrest arrived about midnight, a few hours after the killing, and found Forrest heavily armed and having barricaded himself inside his house, which was surrounded by fires lit by the freedmen to prevent his escape. When the deputy went to the door and announced his purpose, Forrest replied with words that sound relieved: "It's all right. You've got me. Come in."[19]

Little more than six weeks later, on April 6, Forrest began sharecropping on land that formerly had been his, pledging half the crops and goods from 1,500 of his acres that year to satisfy a debt of $30,000 to Tate, Gill & Able—and to obtain another $3,750 in so-called "rent money" from the firm. His efforts seemed doomed to fail, however. On April 21, the *Appeal* reported the Coahoma County cotton crop endangered by high water from the Mississippi River flooding through "the large number of breaks in the levees," presumably owing to wartime damage and disrepair.[20]

Other matters may have given Forrest concern. While Andrew Johnson's attitude toward his fellow Democrats, the prominent ex-Confederates, was perceptibly warming, that of Governor Brownlow was growing colder; it appeared to encourage more and more threatening behavior on the part of the state's wartime Unionists as well as such black troops as had yet to be mustered out of the peacetime army. For a year, Memphis had been tense as armed black soldiers refused to brook antebellum-style racial slurs—and used their newfound power to do some slurring of their own; meanwhile, frightened whites, accustomed to the old order and its long-held terror of black insurrection, became increasingly fearful and angry. Three weeks after Forrest descended to the status of glorified sharecropper on his own plantation, his home city exploded.

On the afternoon of May 1 a crowd of black ex-soldiers who had just been paid and mustered out of the service at Fort Pickering were drinking in a saloon when, a block away, two Memphis policemen arrested a black involved in a civil disturbance with a white man. A crowd gathered, and shots were fired on both sides, killing one policeman and one ex-soldier and wounding several more of each. More discharged black soldiers, along with some fifty policemen and many poor white Memphians of the same Irish-American heritage as the police, joined the fray, and the clash escalated quickly into what the *Avalanche* branded a "war." By the time peace was temporarily restored three hours later, seven blacks and the one white were counted dead, and a few whites and thirteen or fourteen more blacks were wounded.[21]

That, though, was just the beginning. Later that night, with the city's Irish-American mayor widely reported to be too drunk to do anything constructive, violence erupted again on a far wider scale. Whites decided to protect themselves from the blacks by attacking. This time the white victory was even more emphatic, an outcome hardly surprising since the discharged black soldiers must have had to leave their military weapons inside the fort. Although they obviously had some guns, the blacks could not have had access to the sort of firepower available to the police and a 100-man posse deputized by the Shelby County sheriff. The result of this imbalance of arms was hellish. The white mob moved into black-dominated South Memphis shooting down blacks whether they had been soldiers or not and burning ninety-one black dwellings, four black churches, and twelve black schools. The scene was savage enough to prompt even such a conservative local journal as the *Avalanche* to plead for an end to the killing of innocent blacks—and to elicit sickening reports in Northern newspapers. A Chicago *Tribune* "special correspondent" a few days later, in a long account of cruel behavior by "the Rebel mob," claimed to have seen with his own eyes an aging black man accosted, thrown down, and shot in the street by a band of rioters who then cut out his tongue.[22]

The uneven battle—which most of the local press irresponsibly dubbed "the negro riot"—continued until May 3 when, two days after being requested to do so by Mayor John Park, General Stoneman finally consented to throw his 150 Army regulars into the city to, as he put it, "interfere with the civil affairs of the city of Memphis." By then, a policeman, a fireman and forty-six blacks—including two children and three women—had perished.[23]

27

FOR THE CAUSE of conservative Democrats, the Memphis riot couldn't have been more ill timed. On the national level, it played directly into the plans of Radical senators and congressmen opposing Andrew Johnson's conciliatory policy toward the South; thanks in part to the Northern press (which seemed to forget that the New York Draft Riots saw Manhattan Irish-Americans kill 105 blacks and abolitionists in 1863), the Memphis melee spawned a congressional investigation reminiscent of that of Fort

Pillow. In Tennessee, it strengthened Governor Brownlow, who recently had shrunk the franchise for a second time, paring it to some 50,000 wartime loyalists predominantly located in the state's eastern third. The Memphis bloodbath furnished Brownlow convincing evidence of need for legislative passage of a measure removing local control of police in Nashville, Chattanooga, and Memphis; it placed this authority instead in the hands of a board of commissioners nominated by Brownlow and confirmed by the state Senate. The law was passed within a week after the riot.[1]

Brownlow's acts, widely decried then and later as the worst sort of vengefulness, were required to keep his minority Republican regime in existence and give it a chance to accomplish its goal of safeguarding wartime loyalists as well as the freedmen whose destinies lay in its charge. Although aged and feeble, Brownlow was a potent political figure nationally, having made much-noted wartime speeches across the North after being freed from a Confederate jail, and much was expected of him in circumstances growing increasingly dire. His wartime alliance with Andrew Johnson had dissolved as the President backed away from vengeance-seeking and became increasingly accommodating toward influential ex-Confederates; in all, out of 15,000 applications for pardon received from the latter, Johnson ultimately granted 13,500. Brownlow, now on his own in a region rife with animosity toward his Radical Republicanism, had to enact stringent legislation to try to protect his constituency, the franchised white part of which appeared to despise blacks as much as the ex-Confederates. "The buzzards can't eat up the niggers as fast as we'll kill them," one of his fellow eastern Tennessee Unionists said, making a personal forecast of what would happen if federal troops were removed. Needing votes to keep his administration in office, the governor moved reluctantly toward black suffrage.[2]

Ex-Confederates, who had been encouraged by Johnson during the first postsurrender months to expect a quick return to citizenship, regarded the actions of the Brownlow government—as well as real and imagined militance by the armed blacks—with not only anger but growing desperation. Disfranchisement and loss of control of their local police left them with one political alternative to abject submission to seeming anarchy: stepping outside the law. Many now proceeded to make that not very lengthy stride. In the antebellum South, men of substance long had taken turns riding night patrols to keep slaves on their home plantations; any blacks discovered off their owners' properties without permits had been legally whipped. With postwar racial paranoia running high and plantation owners desperately trying to force blacks to work the land and restart the region's economy, white Southerners returned to this system of nocturnal patrolling.

In Tennessee, these patrols were just more manifestations of a cataclysmic collision between the past and various prospective futures. With militant Loyal Leagues organizing in association with the Freedmen's Bureau to encourage ex-slaves to seek their rights, Memphis ex-Confederates founded a social and benevolent organization called the Confederate Relief and Historical Association, devoted to remembering the South's wartime sacrifices and aiding its battle-widowed and -orphaned. Two hundred or so miles to the east, ex-Confederates in Columbia formed a less public association known as the Pale Faces, apparently dedicated to white supremacy. One county line still further eastward, a few young ex-soldiers in Pulaski began making their night rides in ghostly garments.[3]

According to the most accepted stories, the Pulaski club started innocently in late 1865 or early 1866 in the law office of Judge Thomas M. Jones. Six locally prominent young ex-Confederate soldiers—Captains John C. Lester, John B. Kennedy, and James R. Crowe, along with Frank O. McCord, Richard R. Reed, and J. Calvin Jones—were seated around a fireplace complaining about the boredom of postwar existence when one of them, exactly *who* is lost to history, suggested they form a secret fraternity. The idea was attractive enough that they agreed to meet and discuss the matter further the next evening, at which time officers were elected and committees designated to choose a name, adopt a set of rules, and make up a ritual of initiation. For the name, the group decided on an imitation of the Greek-letter societies then just gaining popularity in Southern colleges; the name they chose, suggested by the name of the Kappa Alpha (or "Kuklos Adelphon") fraternity, corrupted the Greek word *kuklos*, meaning "circle," into the weirder-sounding "Kuklux." Because another name that had been suggested was "Lost Clan of the Cocletz" after an obscure Indian legend, Captain Kennedy went on to suggest they emphasize "Kuklux's" alliterative sounds by adding the redundant word "Klan."[4]

Eager to gain a public presence and still preserve their secrecy, members of this "Kuklux Klan" donned Halloween-style sheets one evening and galloped down Pulaski's streets. The sensation they made—particularly among superstitious blacks, who are reported to have fled inside their homes in panic—was so gratifying that they began to augment their eerie aura with an appropriate organizational lexicon. The meeting place became the den, the den leader the grand cyclops, the grand cyclops's deputy the grand magi (*sic*), the secretary the grand scribe, the messengers night-hawks, and the rank-and-file members ghouls. At first, their primary activities consisted mostly of riding around in sheets frightening people and inducting new members in prankish initiations; in these, blindfolded inductees wearing hats festooned with donkey ears were placed in front of a large mirror where their blindfolds were removed.[5]

There was a constant search for new prospects to provide the entertainment of such initiation, but members were strictly forbidden to approach them directly; the leaders felt a mysterious aloofness would make candidates for membership all the more eager—and that any who became dissatisfied following initiation could be reminded that they had sought, rather than been recruited for, their places in the organization. Because of this obtuseness, a member would approach a nonmember, bring up the subject of the Klan, and pretend he had decided to join it. Then, if the nonmember appeared interested, the incognito member would inform him that he had discovered how to join and suggest they do so together. Finally he would conduct his unsuspecting prey to initiation ceremonies.[6]

During the Klan's early nocturnal emergences onto roads and streets, scaring blacks quickly became its most noted activity. Because a sheet-cloaked guard in front of the Pulaski meeting place had started telling passersby he was the spirit of a Confederate soldier slain at Chickamauga, the Kuklux began being described as "ghosts of the Confederate dead," and they soon played on this public perception. Beneath their robes they donned elaborate paraphernalia that made them appear able to drink whole buckets of water at a time; one would "drink" such a bucket in front of a black, smack his lips and say something such as: "That's the first drink I've had since I was killed at the battle of Shiloh, and you get mighty thirsty in Hell." This line and trick became standard. Another trick was to sport a false head—usually made of a large gourd wrapped in a headdress—above a member's Klan robe, remove it in the presence of a black, and request that he "hold my head a minute." Because of the effect of such ruses—their tendency, for instance, to cause blacks to stay home at night instead of wandering the countryside or attending meetings of the Loyal League—the Klan grew fairly quickly, aided by local publicity supplied by cofounder and grand cyclops Frank O. McCord, editor of the Pulaski *Citizen*.[7]

By fall and winter of 1866, the organization had gained such local fame as a sub-rosa racial regulatory body in sparsely populated Giles County, and so many visitors from surrounding counties had had to be inducted to keep its entertaining initiations going, that it began spreading. It also began attracting much more prominent people. One of the first important converts is reported to have been Pulaski attorney George W. Gordon, the Confederate brigadier captured in the center of Hood's 1864 charge at Franklin. Thirty years old, an antebellum college graduate who immediately after the war began studying law at Cumberland University in Lebanon, Gordon may have seen the Klan's explosive political possibilities in a Brownlow-governed Tennessee.

Back in Memphis, Forrest was enduring minor annoyances and major reverses. In August he sold back to Henry C. Chambers 2,620 acres of his Coahoma County plantation for $85,000 in notes—which couldn't have been a lot more than he had invested in the place; the same day he sold the remaining 725 acres to Memphis attorney Charles Kortrecht, his fellow antebellum Third Ward alderman, for $15,000. His dream of accession to the landed gentry thus died, and he may have felt that his devoted wartime service entitled him to more leniency than he had been accorded by his creditors; seven years later, in a Memphis speech, he would remark that when he "left here in 1861, I left with as good credit as any man in the city," but when he "returned, after four years absence, I was met by men who tried to crush me." In September he had to return to the Memphis courthouse to renew his bond in the annoying treason case and to concern himself with Fort Pillow, the victory that was proving all too memorable. From Memphis on September 13, he wrote a friend that he was "making out a full statement of the so-called Fort Pillow massacre, and as soon as completed I will send it forward to the President as Commander-in-chief of the Army and Navy of the United States, in which I mention that if my explanation is not satisfactory, I demand an investigation by a board of officers." He added that he was, "as well as yourself, ruined by the war, and am opening a commission business in this city."[8]

On September 21 he entered the Memphis Odd Fellows Hall arm in arm with Frank Blair of Missouri ("an earnest advocate of the President's policy and the recognition of the rights which ample justice demands for the South," the *Avalanche* would explain the next day) and introduced a Blair speech to which the newspaper devoted four columns. Still in Memphis the next day, the well-connected Blair wrote and gave to Forrest a letter to Blair's brother, ex-cabinet member Montgomery Blair, seeking the latter's intercession with President Johnson in behalf of a Forrest pardon. Saying he had met Forrest in the fall of 1865, Blair noted "all the prejudice that has existed against him" and said he had "felt it myself," but had "discarded" it and not only had come "to esteem and admire" but had formed "a very great personal attachment" to him. He said Forrest had "impressed me as a man perfectly sincere in the desire to accept the condition of affairs as determined by the results of the war. His influence, more powerful than that of any man in Western Tennessee, has been wielded invariably in the maintenance of peace and the retention of amicable feelings between the people of the States." The "prejudice" against pardoning him had to do with "the clamor raised against him on account of . . . Fort Pillow," Blair said, but, after reviewing Forrest's version of that story, he had concluded that "[h]is courage, in more than a hundred battlefields, ought to convince any man that he is incapable of the dastardly outrage alleged against him." He said Forrest's "noble bearing . . . in accepting without complaint the results of a disastrous war, and using his powerful influence to make others accept it in the same spirit, ha[s] inspired me with a respect and admiration that I have not felt for any other man." Blair closed the letter by telling his brother that Forrest "will probably write to you . . . and I hope you will aid him . . . to obtain his objects."[9]

On September 25 an uncharacteristically humble-sounding one-column advertisement began running at the top of the front page of the *Avalanche*:

N. B. FORREST
Cotton Factor
and
Commission Merchant
No. 272 Front Street (Up stairs.)

Liberal cash advances made on Cotton and other produce consigned to me. Bagging, Rope and other supplies furnished at the lowest market rates.

The disastrous results of the late war having forced me to dispose of the most of my property, I have concluded to undertake this business, here in the midst of my old friends, for the purpose of making an honest living for myself and family, by my own labor, and to retrieve, as far as may be possible, the losses entailed by the late war.

To my old friends, and to all who may feel disposed to give me their business, I pledge my personal attention to its efficient transaction.[10]

This notice disappeared on November 23, indicating that the cotton factoring firm wasn't prospering. Now its scrambling proprietor moved on to new interests which at that time were attracting other penniless ex-Confederate officers. He apparently took steps toward establishing a fire-insurance firm, meanwhile plunging into a without-portfolio role in a railroad project headed by Sam Tate, R. C. Brinkley, and others. In a December 6 letter he professed himself to be "devoting my whole energy to the construction of the Memphis and Little Rock Railroad, with the expectation of extending it to Fort Smith subsequently." Asserting that quick completion of such railroads was crucial to "the prosperity of this city and the development of an immense scope of unsurpassed cotton lands," he said he had "recently, by my personal attention to the matter, assisted in raising as much as five hundred thousand dollars on the mortgage bonds of the company. . . ." A day earlier, he had written O. O. Howard seeking the general's help in employing 1,000 freedmen as construction workers for the Memphis & Little Rock. Howard replied cautiously: "You are a stranger to me personally, therefore I depend upon your reputation for my opinions. Yet I do not wish to act with a view to your personal injury. . . ." By December 29, however, Howard had had "a personal interview" with Forrest at New Orleans and wrote the Arkansas Freedmen's Bureau commissioner that he believed Forrest "is disposed to do everything that is fair and right for the negroes which may be employed." Howard did, however, recommend that the commissioner "select a capable, discreet officer" to personally watch the progress of the project from close at hand.[11]

The railroad work required that Forrest travel further afield, which induced him to use the letter Frank Blair had written to his brother ten weeks earlier. Enclosing it along with one of his own to President Johnson, he wrote to Montgomery Blair describing his railroad work and adding that the Memphis & Little Rock had "about eight hundred thousand acres of excellent lands which, if sold," could finance the construction of the railroad. He said he would like to be able to visit Washington or New York to see if he could interest "some foreign emigration company" in the property, "but I do not feel warranted in doing so under the terms of my parole. I have therefore to ask your good services in procuring me the permission, or such extension of my parole, as would clearly give me the unquestionable right to make this visit. . . ." He added that he was "not an officer of either of the two roads just mentioned, but have been induced to give personal influence in aid of the work of construction and in soliciting money, and otherwise raising means for that purpose, as a matter of general public concern."

His enclosed letter to Johnson showed great sensitivity to the President's political problems, recognizing that his own personal infamy could complicate them. Saying he had made and kept a pledge to "submit to the constituted authority of the United States," he added that he had counseled "patience and forbearance" by ex-Confederates. Then he got to the meat of the matter:

> *I am . . . aware that I am at this moment regarded in large communities at the north with abhorrence, as a detestable monster, ruthless and swift to take life, and guilty of unpardonable crimes in connection with the capture of Fort Pillow, on the twelfth of April, 1864. Perhaps, at a time of political excitement so fierce and high as at present, this misjudgement of my conduct and character should not surprise me; nevertheless, it pains and mortifies me greatly; yet, if any good can be wrought from it, I am still willing to rest for a time longer under this heavy wounding weight of undeserved obloquy, without any attempt at that perfect justification before the world, of my course as a soldier and commander in the storming of Fort Pillow, which I am satisfied I can make to the conviction of all fair minded people, and in complete refutation, of the ex parte proceedings of the congressional committee, with their manifestly leading questions and willing witnesses whose prompted evidence should, thenceforward, mislead no one. I have, however, to appeal to the judgement of your excellency, in this regard, and to invoke your advice as to my present course, and especially, whether the time is propitious or inauspicious, for an attempt on my part to throw off the load of these widely believed and injurious calumnies; and I have presumed to make this appeal from a sincere desire to do nothing that shall in the least contribute to those sectional animosities which now rend the country. . . . Struggling as you are, with an appalling army of forces hostile to constitutional, regulated liberty, I have been unwilling to ask you for that amnesty which I felt your own sense of right had disposed you to grant me, much as it was desirable for the proper conduct of my greatly involved private fortunes. I have preferred to endure those private embarrassments rather than to give your vindictive enemies an opportunity to misrepresent your motives were you to grant my amnesty. In conclusion, I . . . shall continue to do all that I can to assuage ill-feeling and promote a spirit of moderation and accommodation. . . . I will say further that should your excellency deem it as likely to subserve the purposes of*

pacification, I would even waive all immunity from investigation into my conduct at Fort Pillow that might attach to my parole. I have the honor to remain your excellency's obedient servant,

N. B. Forrest

Johnson is reported to have "kept" this letter, to have "more than once . . . commended" its writer as "a model example of what the true 'restorationist' of the South should have been," and to have quickly granted the requested parole extension. Whether Forrest really sought the extension only for business travel, though, is open to question. His letter to Johnson was written around, if not indeed amid, the time in which he was learning of the Ku Klux Klan.[12]

By the autumn of 1866 the Klan apparently had started to outgrow Pulaski. Some of its out-of-county inductees began forming their own dens in sporadic and uncontrolled fashion, with only the most tenuous affiliation to the original one. Meanwhile, the first den drifted toward involvement in more serious concerns as a Pulaski political struggle pitted Giles County's black population (which in the 1870 census would amount to thirty-nine percent), along with a few wartime-loyalist whites, against a white ex-Confederate majority probably as edgy and prone to violence as the rioters in Memphis. Pulaski had become a reactionary mecca for the lawless where robbery and assault were common, where for tax purposes the local sheriff still listed his ex-slaves as property, and where a white youth described as obviously guilty of murdering a black was acquitted — because, the local Freedmen's Bureau agent complained, "the jury presumed a justification, none being shown."[13]

This local tension may have encouraged Gordon and his onetime division commander, General John C. Brown — a fellow Pulaskian who was the brother of antebellum Tennessee governor Neill S. Brown and himself an elector on the Bell-Everett Constitutional Union ticket of 1860 — to envision far-reaching political potential in the night riders whom Gordon had joined. One story has it that between late 1866 and early 1867 Gordon, who soon would establish a law practice in Memphis, journeyed there to bring the Klan and its regulatory possibilities to the attention of Forrest. This version of the Klan's initial overture came from an unidentified Klan associate of John Morton, and it holds that Forrest accepted Gordon's news emphatically, saying: "That's a good thing; that's a damned good thing. We can use that to keep the niggers in their place." The story purports to have come to its unidentified teller through Morton himself, and adds that Forrest quickly went to Nashville, sought out

Morton, and asked him about the Klan and how to join. It continues that he was driven by Morton out into the countryside, where Morton offered to administer him the oath; at which point, the story concludes, Forrest laughed loudly, slapped Morton on the back, and said: "Why, you damned little fool, don't you know I'm head of the whole damned thing?"[14]

Morton's own version of Forrest's preliminary induction into the Klan, a sidling gift to posterity in the form of a magazine article reprinted in the appendix of his memoirs, doesn't mention Gordon, saying only that Forrest came to Nashville "when rumors of the Kuklux Klan first spread over Tennessee." Arriving there, he found Morton and told him he knew the Klan was "organized in Nashville, and I know you are in it. I want to join." The magazine article, whose details writer Thomas Dixon Jr. later disclosed came from Morton himself, says Morton then drove Forrest to a wooded area out of town, administered him a preliminary Klan oath, and told him to go to a room at the Maxwell House Hotel later that evening to learn the rest of the Klan's secrets. The conclusion of this story has Morton then driving Forrest back into town to meet his fiancée, whom Forrest advised: "Miss Annie, if you can get John Morton, you take him. I know him. He'll take care of you."[15]

The truth may lie in a combination of these accounts. Forrest may well have been apprised of the Klan initially by Gordon, and it would have been in keeping with the Klan's recruitment policy for Gordon to conceal his own affiliation, mentioning only that he had heard something about the organization but understood that Forrest's former artillery chief in Nashville might know more. It seems more than coincidental that Forrest arrived in Nashville the very day of a Klan meeting at the Maxwell House; he more likely was encouraged to arrive there then by Gordon, who may also have alerted Morton, grand cyclops of a Nashville den and organizer of another in nearby Clarksville. Forrest apparently was lured to the Tennessee capital to take over the organization. "After the order grew to large numbers, we found it necessary to have someone of large experience to command us," Klan cofounder James R. Crowe has been quoted. "So we chose General N. B. Forrest. . . . He was made a member and took the oath in Room No. 10 at the Maxwell House . . . in the fall of 1866. The oath was administered to him by Captain J. W. Morton. . . ."[16]

Men such as Gordon and Brown would have realized the need to centralize the loose collection of proliferating dens if any political use was to be made of them; Gordon and Brown also would have known that the only way to get the dens to agree to centralization was to offer them a prominent and exciting leader — the more prominent and exciting, the better. Klan lore has it that the leadership first was offered to Robert E. Lee, who replied that his health would not permit him to serve but wrote a letter approving of the Klan and saying his support had to be "invisible." Lee also is supposed to have said, when asked his opinion of Forrest as a second choice: "There is no man in the South who can handle so large a body of men so successfully. Will you pay my respects to the General and tell him I hope he will accept." Lee scholars, as well as unsympathetic students of Klan history, dismiss such unsubstantiated rumor as myth, and it well may be; Lee's public stance was that quietude and submissiveness constituted the best course for the vanquished Confederates. On the other hand, when Lee was called to testify before Congress in February 1866 by Radical Republicans to show that the South was unready for self-government, he gave short shrift to his inquisitors and guardedly vented views very much in keeping with the emerging ones of the Klan. He seemed to feel, as the Klan soon began to proclaim, that the Constitution of the United States was being subverted by Radical Republicans for their political ends. On January 27, 1866, he wrote a friendly United States senator that pursuit of "a policy which will continue the prostration of one-half the country, alienate the affections of its inhabitants from the Government, and . . . eventually result in injury to the country and to the American people, appears to me so manifestly injudicious that I do not see how those responsible can tolerate it." To men of Lee's political views, to say nothing of Forrest's, opposing the Radical revolutionary subversion of the old Constitution would have been patriotism. Lee's opinions imparted privately to friends don't appear to have been nearly as scrupulously apolitical and submissive as he tried to make his public ones, and at this time there was occasion for delegations of Tennesseans to be in Virginia talking to Lee; the Memphis newspapers were full of appeals for gifts for the endowment fund of Washington College, the bankrupt Shenandoah Valley institution whose postwar president was Lee.[17]

Any supposed Ku Klux connection of Lee's could have been fabricated by the Klan to try to legitimize itself; Lee was the most popular man in the South, and the gentleness and forbearance of his public example had much impact in keeping it peaceful. That Lee was in sympathy with the Klan, however, was believed within the organization. J. P. Young, a Memphis judge and historian who was first a soldier in Forrest's cavalry and then an avowed Klansman, eventually recalled that in the Maxwell House Hotel's Room 10 a letter from Lee was read. When subsequent discussion centered on another name for the organization, somebody alluded to Lee's word "invisible" and suggested the Klan be otherwise called the Invisible Empire, and the meeting adopted the suggestion. The next order of business was the naming of a leader and the designation of his title. Nominations were solicited. "The Wizard of the Saddle, General Nathan Bedford Forrest," a voice from the back of the room called out. The nominee was elected quickly, and in keeping with the off-the-cuff impulsiveness of the early Klan, was designated grand wizard of the Invisible Empire.[18]

While there appears to be no evidence in hotel-guest columns of Nashville newspapers of the day that Forrest was in the capital in April, he could well have been Morton's houseguest. There definitely is evidence that other Klan-connected individuals were at the Maxwell House. These included Klan founders Crowe and Frank O. McCord, a couple of dozen other Pulaskians, and onetime Forrest military subordinate G. G. Dibrell of Sparta, who went on to become a Klan deputy grand titan. Another participant in the Maxwell House meeting, although his public presence seems to have been as unobtrusive as Forrest's, was Major General John B. Gordon of Georgia, one of Lee's most trusted subordinates in the Army of Northern Virginia. A writer who knew Gordon eventually wrote a Klan history in which she claimed Forrest named Gordon grand dragon of the Realm of Georgia at the April meeting.[19]

It is perhaps an indication of the all-pervasiveness of the South's perception of its need for a Klan that Gordon reportedly first learned of the Ku Klux on a visit to his brother at Athens, Alabama, just across the state line from Pulaski. His brother was pastor of Athens's First Baptist Church.[20]

28

Art. IV, Sec. 1 — It shall be the duty of the Grand Wizard, who is the Supreme Officer of the Empire, to communicate with and receive reports from the Grand Dragons of the Realms, as to the condition, strength, efficiency and progress of the *[Klan]s within their respective Realms. And he shall communicate from time to time, to all subordinate *s, through the Grand Dragon, the condition, strength, efficiency and progress of the *s throughout his vast Empire; and such other information as he may deem expedient to impart. And it shall further be his duty to keep by his G[rand] Scribe a list of the names (without any caption or explanation whatever) of the Grand Dragons of the different Realms of his

Empire, and shall number such Realms with the Arabic numerals, 1, 2, 3, &c, ad finem. And he shall instruct his Grand Exchequer as to the appropriation and disbursement which he shall make of the revenue of the * that comes to his hands. He shall have through his Subalterns and Deputies power for the organization and establishment of subordinate *s. And he shall have the further power to appoint his Genii; also a Grand Scribe and a Grand Exchequer for his Department, and to appoint and instruct Deputies, to organize and control Realms, Dominions, Provinces and Dens, until the same shall elect a Grand Dragon, a Grand Titan, a Grand Giant and a Grand Cyclops in the manner hereafter provided. And when a question of paramount importance to the interest or prosperity of the * arises, not provided for in this Prescript, he shall have power to determine such question, and his decision shall be final. . . .

— *From the original Prescript of the Ku Klux Klan*[1]

THE DEMOCRATIC-SOUNDING CONSTITUTION, or Prescript, of the Klan reads as if it was written by an attorney, and it was. George Gordon composed it in longhand in a Pulaski law office, then apparently employed less-than-straightforward means to get it printed next door at the local newspaper. The editor of the Pulaski *Citizen*, Frank McCord, was one of the Klan's six founders, and he and his fellow members apparently had devised a method of communicating about Klan business without running the risk of face-to-face meetings. Thus McCord claimed to have a habit of checking behind a loose brick in the *Citizen* wall — which, he said, served as the newspaper's informal Klan postbox — and one morning found there an unsigned letter. It inquired about the cost of printing some copies of a twenty-four-page pamphlet measuring three and one-half by five and one-half inches. McCord wrote a note quoting a price of $100 and placed his reply in the wall — and, next morning, found there a $100 bill attached to a longhand copy of the Prescript. He then ordered the printing, which is said to have been done at night by *Citizen* employees who were Klan members.[2]

This initial Prescript bore lingering evidences of the Klan's original playfulness. Its opening lines were poetic, mysterious, and full of vague but portentous warning, describing the resurrection of a "dead cor[p]se" whose return makes "night hideous," a "Ghoul" who is "rantin', drinkin' " and who, "some luckless night," will visit "your black pit" and "cheat you yet." The document ended with a valedictory: "To the lovers of Law and Order, Peace and Justice, we send greeting; and to the shades of the venerated Dead, we affectionately dedicate the * * [Ku Klux]."

The Prescript also, however, bore signs that its purpose was being amended to one less fun-loving. It expressly and somberly acknowledged the "supremacy" of the laws of the United States, and the authority it invested in its officers was divided according to conventional political boundaries; i.e., the Empire was the South, the realms were the individual states, the dominions were blocs of counties joined together the way they were grouped as U.S. congressional districts; the provinces were individual counties; and the provinces were divided into dens. Ranked beneath the grand wizard in order of importance were his ten genii; a grand dragon of each realm, assisted by eight hydras; a grand titan of each dominion, assisted by six furies; and a grand giant of each province, assisted by four nighthawks. Each den was headed by a grand cyclops, who presided over a grand magi, a grand monk, a grand exchequer, a grand turk, a grand scribe, a grand sentinel, and a grand ensign, all of which ruled a "body politic" of "ghouls."

The fact that the document never once mentioned the three words of the organization's name, instead designating them with asterisks, was another indication of how much the leadership prized secrecy. A provision that "any member who shall reveal or betray the secrets or purposes of this * shall suffer the extreme penalty of the law" — death — underscored the developing tone of grave political concern. The declaration of the supremacy of the U.S. Constitution notwithstanding, the Klan's new, politically oriented leaders actually were pledging fealty to the original, unamended, prewar Constitution — and surely realized they were embarking on a course that could be branded treason by Radical Republicans, a designation that well might get them hanged. The stringent requirements for silence in public possibly constituted an attempt to ensure from the outset that no Klansman would turn state's evidence against fellow members. It was doubtless concern over possible prosecution that prompted the story about the mysterious appearance of Klan messages in the niche in the *Citizen* wall; how else could McCord explain his knowledge of Klan business without disclosing his membership in it?

The sudden burst of Klan interest in politics in general and in that of states, congressional districts, and counties in particular seems to have arisen in the wake of the March 2, 1867, congressional passage of the Reconstruction Act — which, ironically, didn't affect Tennessee. This legislation laid down provisions by which the other seceded states might reenter the Union; Tennessee already had been readmitted following its

1866 ratification (by minority franchise) of the Fourteenth Amendment. Dividing the remaining ten ex-Confederate states into five military districts and declaring their governments provisional and subject to orders from Union soldiers stationed within them, the Reconstruction Act was enacted by a Radical-leaning Congress over the veto of Andrew Johnson. The Act's overtones and reverberations led Klan leaders to arm for battle; the entire South, they understandably felt, now could look forward to the woes ex-Confederate Tennesseans were suffering under Brownlow. In the spring of 1867, the governor vowed that he would enforce his Disfranchisement Law—and that "[i]f to do so it becomes necessary that there shall be violence and bloodshed, so be it."[3]

To the recent Confederates, Brownlow's domain had become a frightening place where the Union League and the Loyal Leagues were armed, militant, and seemingly near winning their long-published and muchfeared demands that plantations of once wealthy ex-Confederates be carved into farms of "forty acres and a mule" for freed blacks. Even ex-Confederates who owned no land apparently thought they faced a future in which the possibility of obtaining any was declining rapidly; the financial outlook was ruinous. A son of ex-Confederate major Minor Meriwether wrote of an evening in 1867 when "several of father's friends" came to the Meriwether home in Memphis "to discuss the Ku Klux Klan and how it might save Memphis and the South from bankruptcy." The "friends" in attendance that evening, Lee Meriwether wrote at different times, included Forrest, Isham G. Harris, "General Gordon of Georgia," and *Avalanche* editor Matthew Gallaway—who, along with Meriwether's father, "agreed the only hope of averting bankruptcy was in the Ku Klux Klan." The younger Meriwether later explained that the "ignorant ex-slaves, elected to City Councils and State Legislatures, and dominated by carpetbaggers who had come from the North to plunder the South, voted millions of dollars of bonds for which little or no value was received"—and then "federal courts ordered mayors of cities to levy taxes big enough to pay 100 cents on the dollar." This, he contended, would have necessitated "selling the city's parks, fire engines, and everything it possessed." Therefore, at the "party at my father's house in 1867 it was agreed that the Ku Klux Klan by midnight parades as 'Ghosts,' and by whipping and even by killing Negro voters," would render blacks "afraid to vote" and proscribe them from public office, thus keeping them from issuing "hundreds of millions of bonds. This [Klan strategy] was illegal, fantastic, but self-preservation is the first law of Nature. . . ."[4]

In a political hothouse of impending local elections, the Klan began proliferating soon after the April 1867 meeting in Nashville (and soon after the political "party" at the Meriwethers'). By early June, it appears to have established dens in at least the Tennessee towns of Columbia, Franklin, Shelbyville, and Nashville, and on the night of June 5 — purportedly to observe its first anniversary (and probably to court newspaper coverage that might spread its name further) — it held a public parade in its birthplace, Pulaski. Advertised by handbills printed by the *Citizen*, the march materialized about 10 P.M. in the ghostly and virtually silent forms of some seventy-five Klansmen. A reporter for the *Citizen*, which since March had lost no opportunity to publicize the Klan, wrote that its paraders were carrying "banners and transparenc[i]es, with all manner of mottoes and devices, speers [sic], sabres, &c." The *Citizen* account described the procession as "led by what we supposed to be the Grand Cyclops, who had on a flowing white robe, a white hat about eighteen inches high. . . . He had an escort on each side of him . . . and his 'toot, toot, toot,' on a very graveyard-ish sounding instrument, seemed to be perfectly understood by every ku kluxer." Responding to the "toot" of its leader's whistle, the strange parade marched up and down the town's streets, returned to the courthouse square, circled it several times, then left.[5]

In Memphis, there was during this period no similar public evidence of Klan organizing per se; there seems, however, to have been some activity by the Confederate Relief & Historical Association, which probably included many Klan members and apparently even shared some of the Klan's leadership. Founded in Memphis in 1866, the Association, like the Klan, appears to have retained no written records until a formal "reorganization" in 1869, the year several sources claim the Klan disbanded in Tennessee. One of the prominent members in regular attendance at the Association's early meetings, however, is known to have been George W. Gordon; so was Minor Meriwether, an Association secretary who eventually admitted to serving in the identical capacity — grand scribe — for the Klan. The fact of Meriwether's high-ranking Klansmanship is affirmed by his wife, who later became a published author. In her last book, written at ninety-two, Elizabeth Meriwether said she did "not know who first thought of the Ku Klux Klan, but I do know that General Nathan Bedford Forrest, the great cavalry soldier who lived near us on Union Street, was the Supreme Grand Wizard; and Minor was one of his counsellors and lieutenants."[6]

In 1867, things weren't going well for the Meriwethers' neighbor; it seems hardly surprising that, as Lee Meriwether's memory of the meeting in their home has it, Forrest was worried about the area's financial outlook. With his farming operations having floundered, he persisted in actuarial pursuits. Beginning on May 7, the *Appeal* started running daily front-page advertisements for the Planters' Insurance Company of Tennessee, which listed its offices as 272 Front Street, its capital assets as $200,000, and its president as N. B. Forrest. He didn't prosper at that, either, in an economic climate of gathering gloom. To a young ex-Confederate colonel in Yazoo City, Mississippi, who wrote him inquiring about job prospects in Memphis, Forrest wrote back that he had "no business nor do I no of any by which you could find employment in this City at any price." He said he had "sold out all the contracts I have had on hand and am now settling up my affairs as rapidly as possible, believing as I do that Every thing under the laws that will be inaugurated by the military authority will result in ruin to our people." His "affairs" continued on a descending course. After moving its offices from Front Street to upstairs at the southwest corner of Main and Madison, the Planters' Insurance Co. of Tennessee failed. On March 13, 1868, its president was adjudged bankrupt and agent William Y. Cirode of Memphis was assigned to dispose of his possessions. By now he had joined a Memphis street paving firm, Hopper & Montgomery, doing business with the city. Between the summer of 1867 and autumn 1868, the enterprise became Forrest, Montgomery & Co. and then Forrest, Mitchell & Co., with Forrest attempting to sell paving bonds in behalf of a municipality whose financial credit was so shaky that prospective investors in Louisville, St. Louis, and New York declined to buy. Undercapitalized, Forrest, Mitchell & Co. finally passed from sight after turning over its unfinished work to another firm.[7]

Between the day he filed for bankruptcy in United States District Court in Memphis, February 5, and the March date when the judgment was finalized, he had a revealing discussion with another Southerner in no very congenial state of mind. Brigadier General Thomas Benton Smith was a Nashvillian so gravely wounded by Federals after being captured in the Battle of Nashville that, although still functional in 1868, he would spend the last four decades of his life in an insane asylum. A third ex-officer who had fought under Smith and apparently was no huge admirer of Forrest was present when they talked, and he wrote his fiancée that Forrest "told us of a scheme of his for conquering Mexico, and asked Tom if he could raise a regiment, and wanted to know if I would go with him: Now I have no idea of trying such a desperate venture. . . . Smith, however seemed willing. . . ."

Forrest said that he had been promised 20,000 muskets and that he would want 30,000 men, he would conquer the country in six months; that he would then confiscate the mines and the church property; that is about ⅓ of all the real estate of the country; hold possession of each state, as he advanced, by leaving four or five thousand men in each; take possession of all the offices for himself and his men, among which, of course, N. B. would get the lion's share with the title of King or President; while the private would get his in bullets; and then he concluded: "I would open up the country to immigration, after I had given it a free government, and would get at least 200,000 people from the southern states, besides many from Europe and the north." He said there are at least 50,000 young men in the South who won't plow, but who would fight or dig for gold. I asked him if he did not think the United States would interfere with his little arrangement, but he said they would be glad to get rid of him.

The correspondent added that "[f]rom the appearance of things at Washington[,] if Mr. Forrest would just keep quiet a little while he can get enough fighting in this country." He was hardly a man for keeping quiet, however; his life had been a constant refusal to back off, especially in desperate times, and he may well have viewed these as his most desperate yet. His lifelong drive to stand above his peers always had had some financial overtones, and he now had lost the last of the mortgaged fortune he had amassed before the war. The dream of wealth suddenly recouped by adventurism south of the border was possibly fed by Isham G. Harris, who now pennilessly occupied a Memphis law office; he had come from Mexico via England, where he worked briefly as a commission buyer of Southern cotton in 1867 after the Mexican Revolution turned against Maximilian.[8]

The Mexican pipe dream contrasted gallingly with reality at home. To many, the Civil War seemed about to be formally resumed, and the state and national situation must have been another source of the grand wizard's ache to gallop off to brighter prospects. In the 1867 elections, the Klan laid low because politically conservative Southerners assumed freed blacks would vote the Conservative-Democratic ticket their ex-masters instructed them to; but they didn't. Instead, they voted overwhelmingly Republican, especially (and doubtless humiliatingly) in Giles County, cradle of the Klan. The Invisible Empire's initially peaceful, scare-only stance thus had failed spectacularly, and a bolder one seemed called for.

In late February 1868, after a white man named Bicknell was robbed and murdered by a black in Maury County, Klansmen attended the funeral in costume; the next day, a party of twenty of them entered the county jail in Columbia and took the black from it, and his body later was found hanging from a tree. Klan raiders in Maury and surrounding counties administered blacks hundreds of lashes with hickory sticks, confiscated guns from Union League and Loyal League members, and ordered teachers at black schools to shutter their institutions and evacuate the area. Many of these night riders worked with the stealth and canniness of Forrest's wartime cavalry, usually moving quickly in small bands. Various dens and provinces cooperated, swapping missions so as to minimize chances of recognition by the public at large.[9]

The grand wizard, his lurid Fort Pillow reputation notwithstanding, was intelligent enough to understand the practical perils of escalating violence in a hostile political environment. By the time of his discussion of Mexico with General Smith, he surely also had begun to realize the thorny problem of operating an organization whose hooded facelessness, while vital to avoiding Radical Republican prosecution, encouraged irresponsible excesses from within its own ranks and invited imitation by even more irresponsible pretenders. There is no evidence to suggest he personally advocated more than minimal "regulatory" violence perpetrated in self-defense, and that is perhaps true, especially early on; had the Klan's new activist role initially been intended to be one of simply mistreating blacks and their advocates, the organization doubtless would have played a more violent part in the 1867 campaign.[10]

On the other hand, throughout his life up to then, Forrest never shrank from violence when he felt it justified, and now, in the wake of the 1867 elections (and that evening meeting at the Meriwethers') he may well have thought it was. His Klan began proliferating across the South, and evidence indicates he played a considerable part in its spread. In early March of 1868 he was in Atlanta, nominally on insurance business and probably conferring with reputed Georgia grand dragon John B. Gordon about Klan matters and a new, Memphis-based actuarial venture. The Memphis-based Southern Life Insurance Company recently had employed Gordon as president of its Atlanta division at a salary of $5,000 or more a year; it later came to boast among its principals Lieutenant General Wade Hampton of South Carolina and Senator Benjamin H. Hill of Georgia. Six weeks earlier, Southern Life first was advertised in Memphis newspapers, claiming net assets of $256,917 and a board of directors that included Forrest's old friend and benefactor, Sam Tate; Forrest himself had a role advertised as "Gen'l Traveling Agent." Four months following Forrest's Georgia trip, Southern Life would begin proclaiming in bigger Memphis newspaper advertisements that it now boasted branches in Kentucky and Georgia, the latter headed by Gordon; in these new advertisements, however, Forrest's name no longer would be mentioned. Eventually, the presidency of the firm would be accepted by Jefferson Davis—after it, like the fabled leadership of the Klan, was declined by Robert E. Lee.[11]

During Forrest's Georgia stay, the Atlanta *Intelligencer* of March 14, 1868, disavowing any knowledge of its origin, published a notice from HEADQUARTERS MYSTIC ORDER OF THE KU KLUX KLAN, OFFICE GRAND CYCLOPS "RED LEGION," OFFICE OF GRAND CROSS OF MYSTERY. Possibly referring to the sort of upbeat organizational progress report a grand wizard might give his burgeoning flock, its militaristic-sounding message informed Klansmen that their organization was "prosperous," but exhorted them to continue to "do justice to the afflicted and oppressed! In the pride of our strength, fail not to defend the orphan and protect the weak!" It directed them to "[b]e wise, cool, calm, cautious, wary, and brave . . . and heed not the growling of the wolf; but if he follows you far, ring the signal, and award the doom of the hound upon the tiger's back!" Telling them of the passing of a "sentence of the Second Grand Division" upon an unnamed "Traitor," it said "flesh and bone" of the "cowardly slayer of the innocent" had "been offered up as a sacrifice upon the altar of the innocent and lost. Our wrath has been appeased; we have tasted and are satisfied. Homage is due and is rendered unto Him who alone can vouchsafe power to the weak and avenge the blood of murdered innocence. . . ."[12]

Less than a month later George W. Ashburn, a white Republican leader in Columbus, Georgia, was shot to death by a mob of thirty-five or so disguised men who broke into his room in a black-owned house, making headlines across the North. A major change of strategy was in the wind; Tennessee's Brownlow noticed it. On April 1 the governor's newspaper, the Knoxville *Whig*, used the headline "Terrorism In Tennessee" and reported that: "Within a few weeks a mysterious organization has spread over the whole State, and its strange operations have created no little alarm. This is the Kuklux Klan, a secret organization whose purposes are unknown but . . . intensely rebel."[13]

On May 13 from Nashville, where he possibly was attending another Maxwell House Klan meeting (and where, on May 12, the Nashville press reported a large Ku Klux parade in nearby Murfreesboro), Forrest wrote—or at least signed—a letter to the Memphis *Avalanche* urging a concerted political effort in the national elections. Written three days before President Johnson's narrow survival of the key impeachment vote and a week before Ulysses S. Grant's heavily favored nomination as the Republican Party's candidate for president, this letter announced a profound change in Forrest's public political stance:

> Editors *AVALANCHE*— Gents: *An influence is at work in this State, as I have discovered since my recent departure from Memphis, to preclude any participation by the late Confederate soldiers in the coming convention of the Democracy of Tennessee . . . and in the National Democratic Convention. . . .*
>
> *Upon consultation with many of my late associates in the war, I have concluded to advise against any further political emasculation of ourselves in the party movements of the State. We are already sufficiently proscribed in the constitution and statutes which now govern the State, against our consent, the proscription of which have, through the mendacious hostility of our legislative enemies, been added to time and time again, until now we barely live under the accumulated weight of disfranchisement and oppression. Shall we super-add, by our own action, to those proscriptions and exorcisms of ourselves from all participation in the assemblies of the State and National Democracy, and publish to the world a confession that we are too unworthy to intrude ourselves into the councils of the party?*
>
> *. . . The only hope of a restoration of a good government in this country is in the success of the National Democracy in the next Presidential campaign. I trust my late comrades will not, from expediency or other motives, absent themselves from a participation in the political exercises which are to result in the choice of standard bearers. . . .*[14]

Forrest's new public position approximated that of the clandestine one of the Klan: to enter the political fight, even without the right to vote, rather than abandoning the field to an otherwise-invincible Grant. It sounded like the indomitable fighter of old, and the about-face seems to have been accepted joyfully by Forrest's "late comrades." An *Avalanche* correspondent from Corinth, Mississippi, soon reported that the letter "is everywhere hailed with unqualified approbation."[15]

His declaration's closing lines had professed "personally" to have "no desire to take any part in politics, nor to occupy any political position whatever," saying he merely wanted not "to see my State represented by men whose only claim to public favor is the dexterity with which they took either side of the question in the late war, as interest dictated. . . ." This renunciation of political ambition was unnecessary; the recently passed Fourteenth Amendment, while not excluding him from party activities, prohibited high-ranking former Confederates from seeking political office. The *Avalanche,* however, felt he should have as much influence as the law allowed; Gallaway editorialized that he hoped Forrest's "suggestions will be adopted and carried out by people all over the State, and that the real people of Tennessee will be properly represented [at the convention] by such honest, constitutional, law-abiding men as FORREST . . . [George W.] GORDON and others of the same class." Gallaway went on to add notes of both encouragement and warning, saying: "Tennesseans, your hour is coming. We speak to the nobility of the State, now disfranchised and downtrodden. And, tyrants, your time is coming, as sure as justice rules above."[16]

On June 1 Forrest and a number of known or suspected Klansmen and/or men personally close to its grand wizard were included among a total of forty-nine delegates named to go to the Nashville state convention a week later. These included Minor Meriwether, ex-U.S. congressman (and Meriwether brother-in-law) W. T. Avery, *Avalanche* editor Gallaway, Memphis *Public Ledger* editor J. J. DuBose, Memphis merchant and former Forrest adjutant J. P. Strange, and eventual Forrest biographer J. Harvey Mathes. The meeting approved a resolution, read by resolutions committee chairman Meriwether, pledging its participants to "abide by the result" of "the late war" that "extinguished slavery in the Southern States" — but branding the investiture of freedmen with the rights to vote, hold office, and sit on juries a "political crime" tending to "destroy the peace, happiness and prosperity of both the white and black races." Calling for restoration of the Constitution to supremacy in the national government, along with a reenfranchisement of "more than seventy thousand white" disfranchised Tennesseans, the resolution went on to declare Memphis Democrats "emphatically in favor of a white man's government and opposed to military despotism and the negro supremacy of the Congressional plan of reconstruction."[17]

Eight days later, at the state convocation at Nashville, some Memphis representatives pushed for Forrest's election as a delegate-at-large to the upcoming National Democratic convention. Others, however, resisted the idea; in fact, the kindredly conservative Memphis *Appeal,* headed by Forrest's fellow ex-Confederate general Albert Pike, and Gallaway's *Avalanche* clashed over the question. The *Avalanche* representatives persisted, however, and when the Committee for Delegates nominated eight men who did not include Forrest (but did include high-ranking Klansman John C. Brown), Meriwether "moved that the name of General N. B. Forrest be inserted in the list of delegates at large." Judge P. T. Scruggs, a member of the Memphis delegation, "remarked that General Forrest had not been selected by the delegation from West Tennessee. They had already signified their choice to the convention, and that choice should be respected." Another delegate suggested it would cause "endless discussion" if the meeting departed from an agreed-upon procedure of having the committee name the delegates, and the meeting's chairman, Bedford County Unionist Edmund Cooper, pointed out that adding Forrest's name "would not be legitimate unless some name were taken off." Judge Scruggs then offered, in the interest of harmony, to withdraw the name of Judge Humphrey Bate, the West Tennessee nominee. Forrest, according to a Nashville account reprinted in the *Avalanche,* soon "addressed the convention as follows:"

> He regretted very much that any excitement should have been raised on the subject of his nomination as a delegate. He had come here to harmonize and for the purpose of defeating the Radical party. He was one of the first men who started out in the rebellion, though he had never voted for the State to go out of the Union. When the State did go out, he took up arms in the State's defense; believed he was right, and now believed that he was ready to help harmonize and bring conflicting elements together. He was still willing to make sacrifices and would abide by the convention. [He] did not mean to create any discord, but he had come there for the good of the whole people. But he would insist that those who went out and fought this thing (in the rebellion) were the representative men, and were entitled to a fair representation of the offices. (Cheers.) He was willing to withdraw his name. There was no position wherein he was not willing to work. He was willing to work in the saddle, in the lead, as the off horse, or at the wheels. (Laughter.) He had not come there for self-aggrandizement, but had come without any enemies to punish and no friends to reward. He had come to harmonize with the Federal soldier and the Union man. . . . (Cheers.)

These well-received remarks didn't end the wrangling. Soon Judge Bate's brother, General William B. Bate, made a considerable speech in which he finally withdrew his brother's name, saying "There must be harmony." After still more discussion, the matter again was referred to the committee, while Forrest "defined his position" for the benefit of the convention participants. He said his first choice for president was Ohio senator George H. Pendleton, who championed a looser fiscal policy that would benefit farmers and laborers. He added that he was for "Johnson second, but would heartily support any man through whom the Radical party could be defeated."

After a recess until evening, the Committee on Resolutions finally returned with Forrest's name substituted for that of Bate—and prompted a delegate from East Tennessee, a Colonel Edwards, to move Forrest's name be stricken from the list of delegates, citing a fear that "his appointment as a delegate [was] a bad stroke of policy, to be taken advantage of by the Radicals." A Middle Tennessean, Brigadier General William A. Quarles, retorted that national delegates should be selected from "both the rebel and Union elements" because "the help of all is needed, and no man more unflinchingly true and gallant is to be found than General N. B. Forrest." Following more discussion, Edwards finally withdrew his motion, and Judge Scruggs recalled that he "was in company with General Forrest a few days since, when a rebel, who had attended the decoration of . . . Federal soldiers' graves, was censured for his act." Scruggs said Forrest quickly "spoke up" in the man's defense, saying that "if he [himself] had been there he would have contributed his part in the work in decoration, as he, for one, wished to have the dead past bury its dead; we should not carry our prejudices and enmities beyond the grave."[18]

During a final consultation of local delegations before the naming of national delegates and alternates from each congressional district—who, incidentally, came to include alternates George W. Gordon, Matthew Gallaway and W. T. Avery—at-large representative Forrest made a few more remarks, perhaps in celebration of his hard-won victory. Notable among them was the promise that "he would not be driven from the great National party . . . and he thought the Conservative Tennesseans acted very strangely when they wished to proscribe him."[19]

Gallaway wrote in an *Avalanche* editorial that Edmund Cooper, the chairman of the Nashville convention, had said privately "that his [Forrest's] nomination as a delegate for the State at large would produce incalculable injury to the Democracy in the approaching struggle." The "struggle" against Grant, the Union's hero of heroes, promised to be Herculean; against such an opponent, with most ex-Confederates disfranchised, any controversy that could adversely affect the undecided should be avoided at all costs. Brownlow's Knoxville *Whig* was the first of many Radical newspapers that refused to let the Democrats' appointment of Forrest pass unnoted. It pointed to the appointment of "N. B. Forrest, the

Fort Pillow Butcher," as evidence that the "late Rebel-Conservative-White-Man's-Convention at Nashville" had proven "true to its rebel instincts."[20]

His ongoing controversiality, especially above the Mason-Dixon line, became quickly evident. A couple of weeks after the Nashville meeting, as he rode a train to New York in a car with a group of Democratic conventioneers, the bully of some now-forgotten Northern town assembled a crowd by threatening to manhandle Forrest. One of the other convention-goers, ex-general Basil W. Duke of Kentucky, later wrote that as the train stopped at a water tank on the outskirts of the town, the conductor, a former Federal soldier, informed him that the bully—a well-known fighter who never had been beaten—had threatened to remove Forrest from the train and "thrash" him; the conductor said he feared that in the excitement of such a challenge some of the townspeople might be moved to help him try it, and he suggested Duke ask Forrest to remain in his seat "and not go out on the platform, no matter what that fellow says or does." When Duke told him, Forrest agreed to stay in his seat, "being too much accustomed to affairs of that kind to become excited." Then, when the train stopped at the depot, the bully immediately leapt onto the platform and burst into the coach in which Forrest was riding, shouting: "Where's that d——d butcher Forrest? I want him." Duke said he "never in my life witnessed such an instantaneous and marvelous transformation in any one's appearance" as his traveling companion "bounded from his seat" and reverted to the Forrest so familiar to his troops in battle. His form was "erect and dilated, his face the colour of heated bronze, and his eyes flaming, blazing. He strode rapidly down the aisle toward the approaching champion, his gait and manner evincing perfect, invincible determination. 'I am Forrest,' he said. 'What do you want?' " Although smaller than his boisterous challenger, he had something in his aspect—the characteristic contemptuous and resentful lack of fear, perhaps—that stopped the man cold. The latter "gave one look," Duke recalled, and "his purpose evaporated." When Forrest got within a few feet of him, "he turned and rushed out of the coach," and Forrest followed him outside shouting for him to stop, to no avail. The lout "darted into and down the street with quarterhorse speed, losing his hat in his hurry, and vanished around a corner." Forrest then "burst into a great shout of laughter" in which "the entire crowd" soon joined. When the train departed five minutes later, Forrest "was standing on the platform receiving the cheers and plaudits of the multitude. . . ."[21]

The authorized participation of the Fort Pillow Butcher in the National

Democratic convention at New York was widely noted, but he wasn't the only prominent ex-Confederate there; in fact, he apparently wasn't the most noted. That questionable honor seems to have gone to Wade Hampton of South Carolina, cavalryman and lieutenant general who, unlike Forrest, had enjoyed the advantage of an aristocratic education and upbringing. Present also were the Georgians John B. Gordon and B. H. Hill, with whom Hampton was soon to become an associate in Southern Life Insurance Co.

Forrest "took little part" in the convention's "more public proceedings," Basil Duke later wrote. Having known Forrest hardly at all until after the war, Duke was unaware of his prewar political career, and he assumed that the Memphian's comparative reticence during the convention stemmed from "having had no practice as a speaker and unfamiliar[ity] with parliamentary methods." Perhaps, with his Fort Pillow reputation having so thunderously preceded him, he allowed other delegates to persuade him to be discreet. He does seem to have taken considerable part in the behind-the-scenes work of a convention that offered many opportunities for it. The nomination process droned on through a total of twenty-three ballots. Andrew Johnson, having barely survived impeachment less than three months earlier, was regarded generally as carrying too much heavy baggage, and he seriously contended only in the first couple of rounds; Tennessee's delegation, however, stood unanimously by him through the first six ballots. Forrest's preferred candidate, Pendleton, led through much of the convention-wide balloting—and received about half of Tennessee's ten delegate votes from the seventh through the seventeenth ballots—but he, too, was unable to attract enough support to be nominated. On the twenty-third ballot, the exhausted convention turned to ex-governor Horatio Seymour of New York, who had addressed the New York Draft Rioters of 1863 as "my friends." Forrest's friend Frank Blair of Missouri was nominated for vice president. In a speech six weeks later in Tennessee, Forrest would say he had "press[ed]" for the nomination of Johnson "and used all my influence with the Southern delegates— Gen. Hampton and others—and procured him fifty votes." It became obvious that the president "could not be nominated, and [that] we had, therefore, to change" because "the others would not continue voting for Mr. Johnson. . . . I did not think there was any hope of a nomination after several votes had been cast."[22]

One of the convocation's climactic moments came after Hampton rose in the wake of Blair's nomination and thanked "the Federal soldiers who have met us so cordially," adding that it was only fair "that they should have the second place on the ticket"; for that reason, Hampton said, he would "most heartily and cordially second the nomination of General Blair." When Hampton sat down amid cheers, ex-Federal general John A. McClernand, who a few minutes earlier had asked that his own name be withdrawn from consideration for the nomination, "crossed the hall and took Hampton's hand, amid vociferous cheers." When Tennessee's vote was called for, its chairman introduced Forrest, "who cast the vote of the State for Blair, amid prolonged cheers." He also "thanked the convention for the courtesy and kindness extended by its members to the soldiers of the South." Afterward, McClernand—a Kentucky-rooted Illinoisan who was an abolition-hating politician before and after the war and the most political of generals during it—"came to Forrest and embraced him." In the North as a whole, though, McClernand's attitude was probably the exception, not the rule. The New York *Tribune* referred sarcastically to Forrest as "the hero of the Massacre of Fort Pillow," and many Northern private citizens seem to have regarded him with horrified contempt— which he met with wry disgust.[23]

One morning, according to a story apparently handed down through the Forrest family, he was in his hotel room still in his nightshirt when a knock came at the door. He told Willie to answer it, and the opened door revealed an austerely dressed woman carrying a Bible and an umbrella. She moved past Willie into the room where the just-rising Forrest, hair still sleep-disheveled, was seated on his bed. "Are you the Rebel General Forrest?" she is reported to have abruptly inquired. "And is it true you murdered those dear colored people at Fort Pillow? Tell me, sir; I want no evasive answer." The answer she reportedly received was so direct that it was remembered to have sent her screaming down the hallway into the street. Rising from his bed to his full six feet one and a half, the Butcher replied:

"Yes, madam. I killed the men and women for my soldiers' dinner and ate the babies myself for breakfast."[24]

29

ON JULY 8 the *Appeal* published an intriguing article concerning a meeting of the local Democratic Club, an organization paralleling the regular Democratic Party. In the 1868 national election campaign, Democratic Clubs often were virtually indistinguishable from the Klan in many Southern towns, and this appears to have been true in Memphis. In the

Memphis meeting of July 7, public people long close to Forrest or linked with the Klan prominently figured; they included Meriwether, Gallaway, and ex-Memphis mayor (and possible Forrest relative) R. D. Baugh. The *Appeal* article featured a vigorous protest by Meriwether of a "statement disseminated by evil-minded persons, who were seeking to sow discord . . . , that the origin of the Democratic Club was a secret conclave on Front Street"—where, it may be remembered, Forrest's Planters' Insurance Co. had had its offices during the time of the Klan's early Tennessee proliferation. The *Appeal* indirectly quoted Meriwether as saying that there had been "no secrecy about it." He acknowledged being "one of the originators" and granted that "but few [were] concerned in its inception, but there were as many Democrats as Whigs, as many privates as officers, as many of those who had not been in the Confederate army present as of those who had." He "denounced as utterly false any statement to the contrary."[1]

Meriwether's was at least the second such denial that had been made in two days. In the July 7 *Appeal,* editor Albert Pike referred to a no-longer-extant letter printed by the *Avalanche* that apparently accused the Democratic Club of attempting to supplant regular party machinery. Pike, who had been named the club's president, breezily denied the charge and described the organization in terms that sound reminiscent of the Klan Prescript, saying that the Democratic Club "intended to organize" chapters "all over the state to act in concert with each other" and "to establish Ward Clubs in Memphis, and District Clubs in Shelby County." It also "intended to procure exact information of the number of Conservative and Radical voters in each county, and of the disfranchised who cannot vote. . . . When it is attempted to make the negro our equal[,] every white man opposed to that becomes our brother."[2]

Within days of the Democratic Club meeting, the Klan made its first public appearance in Memphis. Elizabeth Avery Meriwether wrote in her reminiscences that one evening—apparently ten days or so after the Democratic Club assembled—her husband, Minor, instructed her to "[p]ut out all the lights in the house early tonight, but do not go to bed before midnight if you wish to see a ghostly army." She said he already had "gotten me to make him certain curious, long white garments—as if for a mask ball"—and "had absented himself from home at night a great deal." Discerning that "something out of the ordinary was 'in the wind,' " Elizabeth and her two eldest children sat up until midnight, at which time "that ghostly procession began to file before our home. It seemed to be an army of horses, but the horses' feet did not make the usual noise and clatter." With hooves "wrapped in cloth" and bodies "covered with flowing white cloth," these silent mounts bore riders wearing "white hoods and white gowns which trailed almost to the ground." Seeming, "in the light of that midnight moon," like "an army of ghosts," the riders "disappeared into DeSoto Street, a street given over to negroes; and a few minutes later a lot of black men and women fled by our house running away from DeSoto Street as if they thought the Devil himself were pursuing them."[3]

If there was such a thing as a typical Klan family of the time, the Meriwethers weren't it. Elizabeth Avery Meriwether's father was from New York, and both she and her Kentucky-rooted husband grew up inculcated with strong antislavery convictions. These were so strong that before Elizabeth and Minor married, he is reported to have honored a request from his father not only to free the Meriwether slaves but also to pay their way back to Africa. Minor is said to have done so with Elizabeth's consent (despite the fact that they weren't wealthy); and he periodically corresponded with the ex-slaves after they left. He also, however, had purchased at least two or three slaves, including one from Forrest in 1853, apparently because his wife was averse to what she termed "household drudgery." For her part, Elizabeth practiced a highly vocal feminism a century before its time. She had lived in the South all her life, however, and she seems to have had no patience with the idea that uneducated ex-slaves were the political and social equals of their white former masters (nor, in fact, did either her husband or her father). Despite her coy protestation of innocence as to the purpose of the "curious, long white garments" her husband had asked her to make for him before that first midnight Klan raid in Memphis, her son Lee eventually recalled that she had served sandwiches and coffee at the 1867 meeting at which Forrest, Gallaway, Minor Meriwether and others had decided that Klan-perpetrated violence was the only financial savior for the South.[4]

Elizabeth Meriwether also is the source of an illuminating account of the effect of the initial appearance of the Klan—about fifty riders—on black Memphians. She wrote it within hours and gave it to Gallaway, who "thought it unwise to publish it at the time," she remembered; "the *Avalanche* was then pursuing the policy of making light of the story of the Ku Kluxes. . . ." The manuscript describes how she listened in as the Meriwethers' black cook, Sally Ann, was being apprised by her minister, Reverend Hodges, of his face-to-face meeting with "dem ghosts" the night before. Identifying themselves as "spirits from Hell," several of them demanded and drank two buckets of water each at the minister's well, and one told him it was the best drink he had had since he had been "sent ter hell" at Shiloh. Bidding Hodges farewell, the seeming spirit added that he would ask the devil to be good to Hodges when Hodges arrived in Hades. The minister told Sally Ann he was so frightened that he let the "ghosts" ride away without informing them he was "a Baptis preacher in good standin' and wuzn't no ways tinkin' ob goin' ter hell." When Sally Ann asked how many of the "ghosts" there were, Hodges seriously replied: " 'Bout a million. I neber took no count ob dem, but dey wuz comin' down DeSoto Street jes as far as I could see." He went on to confess that he didn't remain in his yard any longer than necessary, running into the house as soon as possible and not emerging again until "broad day. Ghosts can't hurt you in de day, Sally Ann, but at midnight dey sho' is dangrus."[5]

Indeed. Yet the Klan, even the Klan as apparently reorganized at the Maxwell House Hotel in the spring of 1867, did not begin as an avowedly racist organization; it was founded to play jokes and reorganized to oppose Radical proponents of what it perceived to be black domination, not to scourge blacks themselves. Although it has been written that Ku Klux ranks were open only to the more than 100,000 honorably discharged ex-Confederate veterans, the hierarchy in some areas and in some instances seems to have accepted and even recruited blacks, provided they went along with Conservative-Democratic political philosophy. So did the Democratic Party for which it worked. In Memphis in late July of 1868, sixty-five blacks organized a "Colored Democratic Club" under the watchful eye of Klansman-editor Gallaway — who, according to an account in the *Appeal*, "made a motion on behalf of the white men present, that they give employment and protection to colored Democrats." Gallaway presumably would not have advocated "protection" for friendly blacks had they not needed it. Organized but not very well controlled violence was spreading across the former Confederate states to the horror and revulsion of the rest of the nation. About this time New York attorney George Templeton Strong wryly confided to his diary that the Klan seemed at work throughout the South, going "about nocturnally in large parties, masked and disguised, shooting inconvenient niggers and uncomfortable Union men. Southern papers applaud and encourage them in a guarded and semi-ironical way."[6]

In March the Ashburn killing in Columbus shook Georgia and the nation. In April in Murfreesboro, Rutherford County Republican sheriff J. S. Webb was dragged from his house at midnight and ordered to vacate his office — which he refused to do, but slept in other houses to foil uninvited guests thereafter. In June in Abbeville County, South Carolina, night-riding Klansmen burned the house of a Negro delegate to the constitutional convention and whipped more than a dozen freedmen in one neighborhood alone, causing some of them to flee to Georgia. On June 29 some 100 robed Klansmen swept into Pulaski and lynched a black who had been jailed on a charge of attempted rape, afterward riddling the body with bullets and leaving it in the street. On July 4 in Jefferson, Texas, 300 whites alarmed by a shooting incident involving a lone Democrat at a Republican political outing took over the town with guns, arrested and shot blacks, and threatened to hang white Republicans, who summarily fled and hid. Later that month in Moulton, Alabama, Klansmen hanged one black, whipped another to death, drove out all Northern men in the area, and threatened to expel homegrown Republicans. The New York *Times* published a July letter from "A Veteran Observer" describing the South as "in a state of quasi rebellion, and down to the present moment, with the Ku-Klux Klan, are murdering and robbing every loyal man, white or black, they can lay hands on."[7]

In Tennessee Governor Brownlow tried to fight fire with fire. He requested that General Thomas at Louisville dispatch Federal troop units into Lincoln, Marshall, Dyer, Obion, Gibson, and Fayette counties, contending that without them "the civil laws cannot be enforced, or loyal men allowed to exercise their rights and liberties." Thomas quickly wrote back that since Tennessee was already reconstructed and "in full exercise of all the civil functions of a state, the military authority of the United States cannot legally aid and interfere. . . ."[8]

Brownlow's plea for Federal troops seems to have had a highly moderating effect on the Tennessee Klan about this time. On June 20 the principal newspaper in what was possibly the strongest Klan county in Tennessee—the Columbia *Herald* in Maury County—published what its headline proclaimed was a "Warning To Bogus Ku Klux." This so-called Ku Klux General Order both mandated and promised that the committing of "unlawful acts" by "parties in Ku Klux and . . . other disguises . . . SHALL BE STOPPED." It ordered "members of former Ku Klux Klans" to "destroy their disguises, say nothing and remain at home" or face being treated as "traitors, enemies, and perjurers." Anyone caught wearing a mask after that day would "be punished for their misdeeds, as an example to others, BY HANGING." Proclaiming that "hundreds of well-armed and determined men can in two hours be rallied to any point in the county," it protested against the Klan's developing image of violence by saying that these "hundreds" "are not banded together to whip negroes, Rebels or

Radicals, to molest or annoy the soldiers of the Union, nor to resist in any way the laws of the land. They are organized to preserve law and order. . . ."[9]

While the Democratic convention was meeting in New York, Brownlow called an "extraordinary session" of the legislature for July 27, saying he would disclose its object the day the legislators convened. On July 17 the Nashville *Banner* published another Ku Klux General Order, this one purporting to come from the grand dragon (presumably George W. Gordon) of Realm No. 1 (Tennessee), ordering blacks in Marshall, Maury, Giles, and Lawrence counties to disband "military companies" organized to "make war upon and exterminate the Ku Klux Klan." The order added that "this Klan" was not "lawless" or "aggressive" or "military" or "revolutionary"; rather, it was "a protective organization," proposing to execute law instead of resisting it; and to protect "all good men, whether white or black, from the outrages and atrocities of bad men of both colors, who have been for the past three years a terror to society and an injury to us all." It noted that "blacks seem to be impressed with the belief that the Klan is especially their enemy. We are not the enemy of the blacks, as long as they behave themselves, make no threats upon us, and do not attack or interfere with us." It promised that the Klan "will never use violence except in resisting violence," and while it acknowledged that "[o]utrages may be and doubtless have been perpetrated by irresponsible parties in the name of this Klan," it branded the doers of such deeds as "imposters, and if they should be discovered and apprehended by this Klan, they will be dealt with in a manner to insure us future exemption from such impositions, as well as protection to those who have been wronged and outraged." Noting reports that the "imposters have frightened and in some instances whipped negroes without any cause or provocation whatever," it stormed that "This is wrong! wrong! wrong! And it is denounced by this Klan, as it must be by all good and humane men." It said the Klan "now, as in the past, is prohibited from doing these things, and they are requested to prohibit others from doing them, and to protect all good, peaceful, well disposed and law abiding men, whether white or black."[10]

The protestations notwithstanding, a week later the Tennessee statehouse declared war on the Klan. When legislators arrived for Brownlow's session, they heard a message from the governor asking them to reassemble a state militia disbanded ten months earlier. At that time, Brownlow now told them, "you were assured by leading Conservatives in their respective counties, and doubly assured by the leading rebel journals of the

State, there would be no necessity for any troops whatsoever, and that law and order would be strictly observed." The reality, he charged, was that "the rebellious elements of the State were at that time secretly arming themselves and perfecting a military organization known as the Ku Klux Klan, composed of ex–rebel soldiers and those who were in sympathy with them." Their aim, he went on, was "the overthrow of the State Government, and, ultimately, to carry . . . the State in the Presidential election. They have known . . . that the President of the United States was bitterly hostile to the men and measures of the present State Government, and would readily favor a movement that would overthrow both." These insurgents, Brownlow said, had made it understood "that the President would give them, as revolutionists, such aid by the disposition of troops, and changes in this military department, as would insure them an easy victory; and some of them have been so indiscreet as to openly boast of this." Their ultimate object, he added, was "the abolition of colored suffrage, [and] the immediate enfranchisement, under the revolutionary constitution, of every rebel who fought to destroy the government. . . ."

Brownlow went on to say the Klan had spread to "almost every part of the eleven States that once constituted the Southern Confederacy" and had grown into a "powerful and aggressive" "political engine of oppression." He said Memphis police had gotten their hands on a "constitution" of one of the Klan dens and found it to contain a "declaration" proclaiming that if necessary it would resort to "assassination" to "protect . . . the people of the South from the band of murderers and robbers now preying upon them. . . ." Therefore, Brownlow told the gathered lawmakers, he recommended "that these organized bands of assassins and robbers be declared outlaws by special legislation, and punished with death wherever found."[11]

Around this time, Forrest arrived back from New York. In his pocket, apparently, was — finally — a pardon from Andrew Johnson, whose lame duck administration no longer had anything to lose from bestowing it. It accorded Forrest nothing but hope, however. Under one of Brownlow's state laws, even pardoned Confederates in Forrest's classification were ineligible to vote or hold office until 1880. His bent toward politics remained, however. In response to Brownlow's call for the arming of a new state militia, he took a prominent part in a lobbying effort to persuade the legislature that there was no need for the measure. On August 1 he and a dozen other ex–Confederate generals appeared in Nashville to promise the legislature's Joint Military Committee that, contrary to Brownlow's stated reasons for seeking a remobilization of the state militia, "that class in Tennessee who are regarded . . . as hostile to the present organization" did not "seek the overthrow of the State Government or to do any other act by revolutionary or lawless means."

Forrest was unanimously elected chairman of this delegation, which also included Major Generals William B. Bate, B. F. Cheatham, and Bushrod R. Johnson from Nashville, John Brown from Pulaski, Brigadier Generals Gideon Pillow and George W. Gordon of Memphis, S. R. Anderson, George Maney and Thomas Benton Smith of Nashville, George G. Dibrell of Sparta, Joseph B. Palmer of Murfreesboro, and William A. Quarles of Clarksville; of these twelve generals, three—Gordon, Brown, and Dibrell—were subsequently reported to have been high-ranking Klansmen, Pillow was an attorney who (with his law partner, Isham G. Harris) provided legal defense for Klansmen, and all of the other eight conceivably could have been Klansmen. They told the committee that they did not "contemplate any such rashness or folly, nor do we believe there is in Tennessee any organization, either public or secret, which has such a purpose; and if there be, we have neither sympathy nor affiliation therewith." They pledged themselves "to maintain the order and peace of the State with whatever of influence we possess; to uphold and support the laws and aid in their execution, trusting that a reciprocation of these sentences by your honorable body will produce the enactment of such laws as will remove all irritating causes now disturbing society." They suggested "prompt and efficient actions on the part of the proper authorities for a removal of the political disabilities resting upon so many of our people would heal all the wounds of our State and make us once more a prosperous, contented and united people."

After delivering their message, some of the generals amplified their individual views. Forrest eventually took a turn, saying he had "tried to discharge all the duties of a soldier as a soldier, and he intended to do so as a citizen." He said that during the last election he "had offered 1,000 disfranchised men to help the public preserve order," adding that the "idea which had gotten into the public mind that there was an organization in the State whose purpose was to overthrow the State Government was utterly without foundation. His name had been used in connection with violence, especially to the negro, which was also false. He would always endeavor to see justice done to all." Yet the Council of Peace, as the generals' Nashville mission came to be called, failed. Brownlow, doubtless realizing the Klan's practical motives for trying to head off the militia bill, was not mollified. His *Whig* quickly branded the generals' proposal insincere, and he continued to push his original measure—which eventually made its way through a legislature that, like the administration, probably heard threats in the generals' statements. It hardly could help hearing threats soon afterward. The *Whig* reported that three days after the generals' petition was presented, General Quarles made insulting remarks against Brownlow and General Thomas and hinted at reprisals against them.[12]

At an August 11 convention in Brownsville to nominate a western Tennessee Democratic candidate for congress, Forrest himself made some press-reported remarks that didn't sound markedly peaceful, either. In response to a motion by Gallaway that he be requested to address the convention (which "was received with great cheering, and carried by acclamation"), he began by reporting on the Council of Peace and went on:

> I believe that Gov. Brownlow thinks that all confederate soldiers, and in fact the whole democratic party in the south, belong to the kuklux klan. (Cheers and laughter.) All are declared outlaws, for the governor says that he has no doubt they belong to the klan, if there is such a klan. The legislature has passed some laws, I believe, on the subject, in which the militia are called upon to shoot down all kukluxes they may find, and they need fear no prosecution for doing so. That is, simply, that they may call a confederate soldier a kuklux, shoot him down and no harm should befall any of the militia who may commit such an outrageous act, for Gov. Brownlow has proclaimed that they were all outlaws. (Applause.) When this is done, I tell you, fellow citizens, that there will be civil war.
>
> It is not our policy to get into another civil war or a war of any kind at the present time, as it would be used against us and weaken our cause in the north, and I have advised every confederate soldier whom I have met lately to do all in his power to prevent war of any kind taking place in Tennessee.

The crowd wishing to hear him was so large that the convention adjourned and went out into the courthouse square where, cheered on by the throng, he reviewed the Brownlow militia threat and said ex–Confederate general S. R. Anderson had written him from Nashville that a Brownlow militia call-up would be "a declaration of war." He said he agreed with Anderson.

> I can assure you, fellow-citizens, that I for one do not want any more war. . . . nor do I want to see negroes armed to shoot down

white men. If they bring this war upon us, there is one thing I will tell you: that I shall not shoot any negroes so long as I can see a white radical to shoot, for it is the radicals who will be to blame for bringing on this war.

I can assure you, fellow-citizens, that I shall at all times be ready to go forward and assist the sheriff or any other officer in carrying out the laws of the state, and in order to assist him thoroughly, I will get as many of my old soldiers as possible to go with me. But if they send the black men to hunt those confederate soldiers whom they call kuklux, then I say to you, "Go out and shoot the radicals." If they do want to inaugurate civil war, the sooner it comes the better, that we may know what to do. (Applause.) I do not wish it understood that I am inciting you to war. . . . I wish you to exhaust all honorable means before you do anything, and I would prefer that you should suffer before I should see civil war inaugurated in this country.

. . . I wish you to do nothing that will give the radical party any pretence to bring on a war. They would like nothing better than a war, for through it they might carry the election, and by this means keep office and continue to rob and bleed us. If, however, the war should come, and I hope it never will, I want no drones in my drum of bees. (Applause.) . . . I can tell you that every man shall be compelled to do his duty. . . . We will have no neutrals. . . . If they are not for us then they will be against us. . . . if it does come, I will do all in my power to meet it, let the consequences be what they may. (Loud and prolonged cheering.)

I now want to say a few words to the black men who are here before me . . . to ask them to stand by the men who raised you, who nursed you when you were sick, and who took care of you when you were little children. I say stand by those who are your real friends, and leave your loyal leagues, where you are taught to refuse the franchise to those who have always proved your friends. I tell you that if you will only stand by us that we will always stand by you, and do as much for you as any white man can do for you. You can have no interest with any scalawags and carpet-baggers. . . . I feel to-day that Gov. Brownlow is one of that class. (Hisses.) He has escaped to this time because he has been shaking with sickness and weakness, and is considered crazy, but if he inaugurates civil war in this state, then I tell him he must suffer the consequences. (Cheers.)[13]

In Nashville, the state legislators and the Brownlow administration saw the Council of Peace as a ploy to delay the militia call until too late for mobilization by election day; on the other hand, nobody was anxious to see a formal shooting war break out again. Partly because of the financial cost to a government already running large deficits, the Brownlow administration ultimately allowed itself to be talked into accepting Federal troops rather than mobilizing its own militia. Within weeks, national soldiers were posted in more than twenty Tennessee locations, including Pulaski, Columbia, Murfreesboro, and Shelbyville—which was highly agreeable to the Klan, since Federal powers were nowhere near as broad as those Brownlow had intended to give his militia.[14]

Within the Klan, discontent over its new and unaccustomed olive-branch policy rose closer to the surface. Forrest had to send his own ex-troopers (now nominally retired) to quell Klan raiding in Madison County, suggesting that unmasked Klansmen were forced to war against their masked comrades. Intra-Klan disagreement also seems to have involved more than the policy against violence. Gallaway's idea that the best way to reclaim the franchise for ex-Confederates was to pledge not to try to remove it from blacks, appears to have shaken the Klan. It certainly split the Memphis Democratic newspapers, with the *Appeal* denouncing Gallaway's *Avalanche* for not owning up to the black disfranchisement the *Appeal* presumed it really favored. The Brownsville convention exacerbated a public rift between Klansman-editors J. J. DuBose of the *Public Ledger* and Gallaway of the *Avalanche*. Gallaway offered a resolution to the effect that if blacks supported the Democrats, they should receive assurance that their present rights would remain undisturbed and that the Democrats favored universal manhood suffrage. DuBose rose to say he would vote against this proposal and "would not be bound by it" if it passed.[15]

The Klan's carrots of peace were not without their companion sticks of threat. The Invisible Empire and Forrest's identification with it were being discussed so openly by this time that a traveling correspondent for the Cincinnati *Commercial* interviewed him about it for an article that was widely reprinted.

Memphis, Tenn., August 28, 1868

Today I have enjoyed "big talks" enough to have gratified any of the famous Indian chiefs who have been treating with General Sherman for the past two years. First I met General N. B. Forrest, then General Gideon A. Pillow, and Governor Isham G. Harris. My first visit was to General Forrest, whom I found at his office, at 8 o'clock this morning, hard at work, although complaining of an illness contracted at the New York convention. . . .

"What are your feelings towards the Federal Government, General?"

"I loved the old Government in 1861; I love the Constitution yet. I think it is the best government in the world if administered as it was before the war. I do not hate it; I am opposing now only the radical revolutionists who are trying to destroy it. I believe that party to be composed, as I know it is in Tennessee, of the worst men on God's earth — men who would hesitate at no crime, and who have only one object in view, to enrich themselves."

"In the event of Governor Brownlow's calling out the militia, do you think there will be any resistance offered to their acts?" I asked.

"That will depend upon circumstances. If the militia are simply called out, and do not interfere with or molest anyone, I do not think there will be any fight. If, on the contrary, they do what I believe they will do, commit outrages, or even one outrage, upon the people, they and Mr. Brownlow's government will be swept out of existence; not a radical will be left alive. If the militia are called out, we can not but look upon it as a declaration of war, because Mr. Brownlow has already issued his proclamation directing them to shoot down the Ku Klux wherever they find them; and he calls all southern men Ku Klux."

"Why, general, we people up north have regarded the Ku Klux as an organization which existed only in the frightened imaginations of a few politicians."

Having delivered a postbellum approximation of his wartime surrender-or-die ultimatums, he here began a controversial disclosure.

"Well, sir, there is such an organization, not only in Tennessee but all over the South, and its numbers have not been exaggerated."

"What are its numbers, general?"

"In Tennessee there are over forty thousand; in all the Southern states about five hundred and fifty thousand men."

"What is the character of the organization, may I inquire?"

"Yes, sir. It is a protective, political, military organization. I am willing to show any man the constitution of the society. The members are sworn to recognize the Government of the United States. It does not say anything at all about the government of the State of Tennessee. Its objects originally were protection against Loyal

Leagues and the Grand Army of the Republic; but after it became general it was found that political matters and interests could best be promoted within it, and it was then made a political organization, giving its support, of course, to the democratic party."

"But is the organization connected throughout the State?"

"Yes, it is. In each voting precinct there is a captain, who, in addition to his other duties, is required to make out a list of names of men in his precinct, giving all the radicals and all the democrats who are positively known, and showing also the doubtful on both sides and of both colors. This list of names is forwarded to the grand commander of the State, who is thus enabled to know who are our friends and who are not."

"Can you, or are you at liberty to, give me the name of the commanding officer of this state?"

"No; it would be impolitic."

"Then I suppose there would be no doubt of a conflict if the militia interfere with the people; is that your view?"

"Yes, sir; if they attempt to carry out Governor Brownlow's proclamation by shooting down Ku Klux—for he calls all southern men Ku Klux—if they go to hunting down and shooting these men, there will be war, and a bloodier one than we have ever witnessed. I have told these radicals here what they might expect in such an event. I have no powder to burn killing negroes. I intend to kill the radicals. I have told them this and more. There is not a radical leader in this town but is a marked man; and if trouble should break out, not one of them would be left alive. I have told them that they were trying to create a disturbance and then slip out and leave the consequences to fall upon the negro; but they can't do it. Their houses are picketed, and when the fight comes not one of them would get out of this town alive. We don't intend they shall ever get out of the country. But I want it distinctly understood that I am opposed to any war, and will only fight in self-defense. If the militia attack us, we will resist to the last; and, if necessary, I think I could raise 40,000 men in five days, ready for the field."

"Do you think, general, that the Ku Klux have been of any benefit to the State?"

"No doubt of it. Since its organization the leagues have quit killing and murdering our people. There were some foolish young men who put masks on their faces and rode over the country frightening negroes; but orders have been issued to stop that, and it has ceased. You may say further that three members of the Ku Klux have been court-martialed and shot for violations of orders not to disturb or molest people."

"Are you a member of the Ku Klux, general?"

"I am not; but am in sympathy and will cooperate with them. I know they are charged with many crimes they are not guilty of."

". . . What do you think of General Grant?"

"I regard him as a great military commander, a good man, honest and liberal, and if elected will, I hope and believe, execute the laws honestly and faithfully. . . . I am opposed to General Grant in everything, but I would do him justice."

The foregoing is the principal part of my conversation with the general. I give the conversation, and leave the reader to form his own opinion as to what General Forrest means to do. I think he has been so plain in his talk that it cannot be misunderstood.[16]

Sometime during this busy summer, Forrest suffered a large personal loss. Mariam Beck Forrest Luxton—to whose prayers, along with those of Mary Ann Forrest, he sometimes attributed his survival of the war—perished suddenly of blood poisoning after stepping on a rusty nail in Texas, where she had moved after the war with her Luxton sons. The old lady who had once refused to surrender a basket of baby chickens to an attacking panther is reported to have died deliriously summoning her famous eldest son to her bedside, calmed only by hopeless assurances that he was on his way. He couldn't have arrived in time.[17]

30

MEMPHIS, August 28, 1868.

Mr. J. T. Brown, Esq.
Humboldt, Tennessee

Dear Sir: Your favor of the 26th instant has been received. While I sympathize with your desire to bring those who were guilty of murdering your brother to justice, and would willingly do anything in my power to aid you in this, I cannot consent to become a party, either directly or indirectly, to any act of violence, or to the infringement of any law. On the contrary, all my efforts have been, and shall be, exerted to preserve peace and order, and to maintain the law as far as possible. . . .

You will excuse me, I hope, for saying that it was very imprudent to send your letter by mail. If it had fallen into the hands of others it might, without some explanations, have caused some trouble to both of us. . . .

N. B. FORREST

BROWN, FORREST LATER explained, was "an old soldier" whose brother had been killed by "some Union men, and he wanted to try to get revenge, and he wrote to me to assist him." The Grand Wizard's reaction, so unlike his image, illustrates his cautious mood at the time. That he kept his own letter advising forbearance but burned the one that prompted it suggests he was afraid he was under government surveillance. His reply was written as if with an eye toward public consumption, and it well might have been.[1]

He was under intense public scrutiny now, not only in Tennessee but nationally, and the interview with the Cincinnati reporter only magnified the lens of the microscope. As his opposition in the state Democratic convention had predicted, he was becoming a significant negative influence for the Democrats in the uphill national presidential campaign against Grant. On September 3 the New York *Times* reprinted in its entirety the Cincinnati *Commercial* interview. Three days later, the *Times* published a letter of correction Forrest sent to the *Commercial* after reading the initial interview. In part, he wrote:

> *I said it was reported, and I believed the report, that there are forty thousand Ku Klux in Tennessee; and I believe the organization stronger in other states. I meant to imply, when I said that the Ku Klux recognize the Federal Government, that they would obey all State laws. They recognize all laws, and will obey them, so I have been informed, in protecting peaceable citizens from oppression from any quarter. I did not say that any man's house was picketed. I did not mean to convey the idea that I would raise any troops; and, more than that, no man could do it in five days, even if they were organized.[2]*

On September 13 the *Times* published two side-by-side articles reexamining the evidence of a massacre at Fort Pillow, one purporting to have come from a Cincinnati *Commercial* correspondent who had accompanied Forrest on a revisit to the fort to obtain his personal recollections of the battle. The longer of the two, however, expressed the prevailing Radical view of the attack and said that Forrest "supports Seymour and Blair earnestly . . . and, with other ex-rebel Generals, has recently undertaken to dictate to the loyal Legislature of [Tennessee] what they should do to conciliate the Kuklux Klan and other Ex-Confederate marauders, who are ravaging and pillaging that State. But even his Democratic friends look upon the Fort Pillow massacre as a blot upon the escutcheon of its author and hence have recently endeavored to relieve Mr. FORREST of the responsibility." The "friends," the article went on, had published letters "asserting that he was not present on that occasion, but that another officer was in command of the rebel troops, while FORREST was many miles in the rear. . . . [T]he Congressional Committee on the Conduct of the War made a thorough investigation . . . which . . . fails to sustain the statements made by Mr. FORREST's friends. . . ."[3]

The article from the *Commercial* later was repudiated by Forrest, even though it was highly sympathetic to the Confederate version of the massacre. He said that he had not accompanied the reporter to the battle site. If he had, which seems questionable, he learned soon afterward that he had erred in discussing such matters with the press; he realized, as he would put it later, that the *Commercial*'s interest in him was politically motivated: "There were a great many things said in regard to myself that I looked upon as gotten up merely to affect the elections in the North." He never fully denied speaking to the *Commercial* about the Klan but claimed that the interview was brief, occurring mostly during a short walk from his office to his home, and that he was so ill while it was being conducted that he repeatedly vomited.[4]

The next day the *Times* offered readers more Forrest news. In an article purporting to provide historical perspective to the question "Is Forrest A Butcher?", it published the 1864 letter from Union major general D. S. Stanley saying that "a rebel citizen of Middle Tennessee, a man of high standing in his community, who had it from his nephew, an officer serving under FORREST," had reported that during the 1862 attack on Murfreesboro Forrest personally "blew out the . . . brains" of a free mulatto who had been a servant to a Union officer and who was brought to Forrest after being captured. Stanley's letter added that the "murdered man was not a soldier, and, indeed, the occurrence took place before the United States Government determined to arm negroes." On a different page, the *Times* devoted a third of a column to a letter from Forrest to a Nashville friend who apparently was worried about the national impact of the *Commercial* interview. Forrest's letter said the article put "statements in my mouth which I never made, and it colors others so as to change their meaning entirely."

For instance, I said to him that in regard to the Kuklux Klan.
. . . I knew nothing positively of its organization, strength or objects,
but that I was informed that its purpose was the protection of the
people from injury, and that I was, so far at least, in sympathy
with it. All the other assertions in regard to this organization which
he puts into my mouth were derived from some other person, or are
the fabrications of his own brain. . . . I said to him . . . that . . . if
the Governor should proclaim martial law in any part of the State,
and attempt to enforce it . . . that . . . I thought that 40,000 or
50,000 men in this State would rise up in defense of their rights.
. . . I cannot feel that I am responsible for the misrepresentations of
which he has been guilty. If all that I have said on political
questions was reported correctly, I should think there would be
nothing found in it which would injure the Democratic Party or the
interests of the South.[5]

Closer to home, the Tennessee legislature appeared finally to be rousing itself to action. On September 2, a month and a day following the Nashville appearance of the Confederate generals, the Joint Military Committee made public a thirty-eight-page "synopsis" of evidence of Ku Klux activity in several counties of central and western Tennessee. Within days the legislature passed the so-called Anti-Ku Klux Law, which provided a minimum penalty of five years' imprisonment and a $500 fine for any person convicted of joining, associating with, promoting, or encouraging "any secret organization which prowled through country or town, disguised or otherwise," and disturbed the peace. Newspapers were forbidden to print Klan pronouncements, any person in the state was empowered to arrest anybody else charged with violating the new law, and in cases of "injuries to individuals" informers were authorized to receive half the amount of damages assessed against anyone convicted. A second new law passed at the same time empowered Brownlow again to call up a state militia, this one to consist of one or more regiments of "loyal" men from each of Tennessee's eight congressional districts. The measure provided that if ten "unconditional Union men" or three justices of the peace in any county certified that law-abiding citizens in that county could not protect themselves without military help, the governor could send in troops.[6]

Understandably, these measures caused the Klan to further discourage activity by its Tennessee dens—in Tennessee, at least. Using the Klan's tactic of employing members from outside the affected areas to make their local raids, they may have been involving themselves—masked or otherwise—in other states on a large scale. Three years later Forrest would recall that in 1868, in an area of eastern Mississippi in which he had conducted some of his wartime operations, an incident at Crawfordsville (now Crawford) on the Mobile & Ohio Railroad drew large numbers of whites to oppose a black crowd after "the negroes threatened to burn the town." He said this threat eventuated after a group of blacks, angered that the horse of a young white man knocked down one of their number when they met in a roadway, followed him into Crawfordsville "to beat him, and then they gathered together." Forrest was on his way to Memphis when word of the problem was wired up the railroad to West Point and Columbus. Discovering that groups of whites "had got all the trains they could and started down," he accompanied them and arrived at Crawfordsville to find the blacks "about eight hundred strong . . . out at the edge of town; the people of the town had fortified themselves; the negroes had burned one house." Forrest said he quickly "got the white people together, organized them . . . made speeches to them," and "told them to be quiet. . . . I then got on a horse and rode over to the negroes and made a speech to them. The negroes dispersed and went home, and nothing was done; nobody was hurt, nobody molested."[7]

An incident on the Mississippi River between Memphis and Arkansas was less abortive. Radical Arkansas governor Powell Clayton, having called up a loyalist state militia on July 2, could obtain guns for it only by ordering them from New York. The Klan seems to have learned of the shipment before it reached Memphis on October 5, and in the *Avalanche* Gallaway editorialized that the guns were "to be placed in the hands of the negroes of Arkansas . . . for the purpose of shooting down inoffensive citizens." Denouncing the warehouse firm that was storing them, Gallaway went on to promise "our friends in Arkansas" to keep them informed of the destination of the arms and to try to keep the cargo in Memphis as long as possible, but added that if Arkansans "quietly" submitted "to their [the guns] being distributed among negroes for their own destruction, they are unworthy of the life which these implements of death are intended to take." Gallaway also denounced any steamboat that would carry them, and a few days later he seemed to suggest that someone should destroy them before they reached their destination.

Because of the outcry, no steamboat line would carry the controversial cargo, and an independent vessel named the *Hesper,* operated by the only Republican steamboatmen on the Arkansas River, finally had to be chartered. The *Hesper* picked up the guns in Memphis on October 15 and headed south toward the mouth of the Arkansas, but twenty-five miles south of Memphis it was overtaken by a tugboat, the *Netty Jones*. The latter, whose captain later claimed to have been overpowered by pirates, ran the *Hesper* aground, chased off its operators in a hail of gunfire from sixty or more masked Klansmen, and hauled the *Hesper* back to the middle of the Mississippi. There the guns apparently were thrown overboard, after which the *Hesper* was allowed to drift back to the Arkansas shore. Then skiffs from the Mississippi side came, picked up the Klansmen from the *Netty Jones*, and returned them to Memphis, whence they all apparently had come. The *Hesper* captain later told Governor Clayton the Klan had intercepted every word of every dispatch the governor had sent him, indicating that its membership included a lot of telegraphers; coincidentally or otherwise, Forrest's secretary at the time was one.[8]

The Arkansas guns episode seems to have been a community affair popularly regarded as the Memphis Reconstruction equivalent of the Boston Tea Party. On the evening of October 15 a society ball was held at the Overton Hotel, and a large number of young men scheduled to attend sent their dates last-minute notification that they would arrive late to pick them up. There did prove to be numerous late arrivals, and many of the tardy men were noticed to be wearing mud-stained boots. The incident created such a national stir that Horace Greeley's New York *Tribune* sent a correspondent to Memphis to investigate, and in its November 2 — election-eve — issue, the newspaper theorized that Forrest "in person" had led the novel naval operation, saying it had reached that conclusion for several reasons: (1) He "is recognized as the leader of the organization, proof sufficient of which is found in his admissions in his famous 'big talk' some time ago"; (2) "no man would be so likely to be called upon to lead so desperate a venture as General N. B. Forrest"; (3) the day before the *Hesper* hijack, Forrest was reported to have "wanted to find five hundred desperate men"; (4) the *Hesper* crew's description of the Ku Klux leader on the tug was one "any man in Memphis . . . will at once" identify as Forrest's. Land forces cooperating with the pirates, the newspaper said, were reported to be commanded by "J. J. DuBose, reputed adjutant general for the organization for West Tennessee. This gentleman will hardly deny that on the evening of the piracy he went from his room with two revolvers buckled about his waist and a revolving carbine wrapped up in a blanket. . . ."

The *Public Ledger*, DuBose's newspaper, quickly disputed the *Tribune* charge regarding Forrest, saying, "That General Forrest was at home during the night on which these arms were destroyed is known to over fifty persons." This alibi sounds flimsy, but it appears questionable that

Forrest, in the mood of caution that seems to have characterized him in this period, would have led the *Hesper* capture himself, and Klan lore has it that this role was accorded Luke E. Wright, a young ex-Confederate officer-turned-attorney who had married a daughter of Admiral Raphael Semmes.[9]

Forrest's combativeness was never far below the surface, however, and by the latter days of October it reemerged dramatically. The day after Grant's victory in the presidential race (by 214 to 80 electoral votes, but a skin-of-the-teeth national popular-vote margin of just 29,862), the New York *Times* published "Fort Pillow Forrest's Impudent Challenge to Gen. Kilpatrick." A Forrest letter dated October 28, it noted a Connecticut speech by the loquacious Union general in which Kilpatrick was quoted as saying that at Fort Pillow Forrest had "nailed negroes to the fences, set fire to the fences and burned the negroes to death." In fairness to Kilpatrick, such testimony was included among the more questionable evidence turned up by the politically pressured 1864 congressional committee that investigated the massacre, but Forrest refused to brook the charge this time. After a rather breezily denunciatory opening two-thirds, the letter's final portion said, in part:

> . . . *I think the public will justify me in denouncing, as I now do, Gen. JUDSON KILPATRICK as a blackguard, a liar, a scoundrel, and poltroon. If he is the heroic figure he would have the Northern people believe him, my friend, Gen. BASIL W. DUKE, at Louisville, Ky., is authorized to receive, on my behalf, any communication he may choose to make.*

> *Respectfully, N. B. Forrest*[10]

When the refined Duke read this letter in the Louisville *Courier-Journal*, he was both "flattered" and "struck with consternation," he would later recall, since the Kentucky constitution held that "any citizen who participated in such an affair in any capacity within the borders of the state would be virtually disfranchised, and if he were a lawyer should be disbarred from practicing his profession. . . . I had come out of the war with a ready-made family and no visible means of support, and had begun the practice of law in Louisville . . . and I was exceedingly loath to relinquish even a very small chance of making a living." Nevertheless, he was determined to have the duel fought in Kentucky, fearing that Forrest would be dealt with "harshly" by the Federal administrators who then had ultimate control of most ex-Confederate states and that he "would not get fair play anywhere north of the Ohio River." The day Duke read the letter in the *Courier-Journal,* he also received a personal one from Forrest. It notified him to expect to hear from Kilpatrick and requested him to arrange a meeting with the Northerner, Duke later remembered, "as soon as possible." The note "went on to say that he recognized Kilpatrick's right to name 'time, place, and weapons,' and that he was prepared, of course, to accede to any terms the latter might designate; but, inasmuch as they had both been cavalry men, he thought it would be highly appropriate to fight mounted and with sabres."[11]

No duel eventuated. Kilpatrick authorized a friend to write a letter ignoring the challenge and saying briefly that his charges, as well as "additional and more shocking details of FORREST's inhuman conduct at Fort Pillow," had been "confirmed" by U.S. Army officers, hundreds of witnesses, and a congressional committee and that he therefore had "nothing to communicate to either FORREST or BASIL DUKE, except to reiterate his denunciations of FORREST's unparalleled atrocities."[12]

In the election, Klan violence had managed to deliver two Southern states, Georgia and Louisiana, to the Democrats, but in Tennessee the pared-down franchise had turned out 56,628 votes for Grant compared to 26,129 for Seymour. The all-but-declared war between the Brownlow administration and the Klan and its fellow Democrats raged on. To the convening second session of the legislature of 1868, the governor sent a November 10 message noting "strenuous efforts . . . made . . . to induce you to extend the franchise" in the special session three months earlier — and declaring the administration emphatically against any renewed attempt to do so on a large scale. Brownlow told the legislators that voluntary "rebels" who had remained faithful to the Confederacy to the last "and who, since the surrender . . . have continued to work for the lost cause . . . foment[ing] violence and lawlessness" should not have their voting rights restored "until the last dollar of the national debt incurred in suppressing the rebellion has been paid, and . . . [until] these unrepentant, unreconstructed rebels had restored to the ballot-box the half-million loyal voters who now sleep in premature graves."[13]

Brownlow had good reason for withholding the franchise: the protection of his administration from a Klan that had reversed its Council of Peace position and begun to ride hard again in the last days before the election. In Pulaski disguised men had raided on election eve throughout Giles County, murdering a black and threatening both white and black men with death if they voted Republican. Similar terrorism had surfaced nearby in Lincoln and Franklin counties, as well as in western Tennessee in Weakley County and rural areas of Shelby County. Such tactics had an effect which must have heartened the Klan; although the Tennessee margin for Grant was a comfortable two to one, the President-elect's vote total was 18,000 fewer than Brownlow received in his race for governor in August 1867. Much of the decrease came in counties in which the Klan was active; in Giles County, the Republican tally dropped from 1,879 to 561.[14]

Brownlow's Democratic opponents now could espy a light, however dim, flickering at the end of the tunnel. More than a year earlier the physically failing governor had named himself U.S. senator from Tennessee beginning in March 1869. By law, the balance of his term was to be filled by the speaker of the state senate, a fellow East Tennessean named DeWitt Clinton Senter. The Klan thus had reason to continue its pressure-by-violence on the state government, thereby giving the governor-to-be more urgent reason to seek a franchise accommodation with ex-Confederates.

Forrest meanwhile was embarking on yet another business venture, one more befitting his antebellum entrepreneurial record. Whereas in 1866–67 he had served as a labor contractor for the building of a Sam Tate railroad, he now set out to construct one of his own. In early 1868 he and Isham G. Harris had been invited to a meeting seeking revival of an 1859 plan to run rails from Memphis through Holly Springs to Okolona across the fertile eastern Mississippi prairies. Holly Springs businessman A. Q. Withers, one of the project's originators, initially tried to interest Harris in the leadership role, but the ex-governor declined out of personal "financial embarrassments." Withers then vacated his elected position as the meeting's presiding officer and proposed it be assumed by Forrest. Forrest later recalled that the handful of Holly Springs businessmen got the charter of their enterprise revised and updated "and insisted that I should go to work and secure a subscription sufficient to organize the company, which required $300,000." He "consented . . . and traversed the country from [Memphis] to Columbus, Miss., several times . . . finally . . . securing sufficient amount of subscriptions." The firm thereupon was formed, "and I was elected president." As such, he "was directed by the board of directors to proceed to Alabama, and procure, if possible, a consolidation with the Cahaba, Marion and Greensboro road and the Northwestern railroad; two short roads, one twelve, the other fourteen miles long, in order to get a direct line from Selma to Memphis."[15]

In early November, the *Appeal* announced it had been notified that the new board of directors of the Memphis, Okolona & Selma Railroad had "completed the reorganization of their company by the election of Gen.

FORREST, President, and Mr. W. R. Moore, of this city, Vice-President." It went on to add a sentence that must have been noted with interest by Democrats in general and Klansmen in particular, saying that "in their persons" Forrest and Moore "unite the Democratic and Republican parties."[16]

On November 7 the *Appeal* printed a long letter from "Maj. Minor Meriwether, the Engineer," detailing the new firm's proposed route from Memphis to Holly Springs. Meriwether estimated at $1 million the cost of running the line the forty-four miles between those points and cited as business reasons for the undertaking the "vital importance to Memphis of constructing this road to Selma; the immense advantages to be derived from a connection with the cotton and grain regions of Eastern Mississippi, the iron and coal regions of Alabama and the Atlantic seaboard and the gulf at Savannah, Pensacola and Mobile." He added that the forty-mile radius of Memphis offered no area "more lovely or more inviting to the thrifty emigrant who desires a small farm with all the comforts of a nice home" than that between Memphis and Holly Springs. He asserted that a railroad, "with trains run to suit the convenience of the inhabitants, with moderate fares, would be a paying institution if never extended beyond Holly Springs."[17]

Across the South, however, such Edens as Meriwether described existed only in the dreams of ambitious businessmen. The influx of people necessary to work the myriad small farms he mentioned would have to come from the North or perhaps Europe, and neither of these sorts of immigrants was likely to be attracted by the bloody reality in Tennessee or along its borders. Klan violence continued after the election, some of it consisting of punishment for blacks and whites who had voted Republican. In Coffee County within days after the polls closed, a black was given 200 lashes for voting with the Radicals. In Overton County in December, blacks and the Klan engaged in running battles, and after the latter lost a member killed, the Klan returned, shot his slayer, and disemboweled him with knives. In Shelbyville in early January, Klansmen rode into town shouting they wanted "fried nigger meat" and a schoolteacher named Dunlap, whom they already had whipped the previous July 4; this time they were fired on by opponents, and Dunlap suffered no further. At Columbia on the night of January 11, Klansmen—aided by telegraphers and crewmen who must have been members or sympathizers—boarded a train bound from Pulaski to Nashville and kidnapped a Brownlow-hired detective named Seymour Barmore, who apparently had infiltrated the organization; they shot and hanged him before dumping his body in the Duck River.[18]

By December a public outcry against the Klan again began rising from the very Southern aristocracy whose interests the Ku Klux had been organized to protect; again, as during the summer before the Council of Peace, the Invisible Empire apparently overdid the job its leaders intended when they loosed it once more to discourage Republican voting. Now the aristocracy feared the result of its excesses. Ex-governor Neill S. Brown, brother of high Klansman John C. Brown, wrote a widely reprinted letter saying that although the Klan's original purposes seemed to have been noble and the publicity of its outrages probably overblown, its activities had outlived their usefulness and were frightening away prospective investors and immigrants whom the South badly needed. These activities also, he added, hurt efforts to expand the franchise to ex-Confederates.[19]

Forrest himself must have been learning firsthand the truth of such arguments. He was in the process of getting a Selma, Marion & Memphis Railroad chartered in Tennessee and Mississippi on the route of the old (but never constructed) Memphis, Holly Springs & Okolona Railroad. On December 31 he got another Selma, Marion & Memphis line chartered in Alabama, adopting part of the route and the few miles of existing track of the old Cahaba, Marion & Greensboro Railroad between Demopolis and Selma. At Selma the line was to connect with the southern Atlantic seacoast by way of another, unaffiliated railroad project then being planned between Selma and Brunswick, Georgia.[20]

By now, Republicans again were proposing a mobilization to exterminate the Klan. On January 16, 1869, the legislature removed all restrictions against sending militiamen into local areas, giving the governor complete power over such decisions. Brownlow called for enlistments in a state guard, adding that he soon would issue another proclamation designating the counties these troops would occupy. The Klan's response was swift. On January 25 a dramatic order purporting to come from the grand wizard directed that, because evil men had infiltrated the Empire and begun to use it for their own lower purposes, "the masks and costumes of this order" were to be "entirely abolished and destroyed," and there were to be no more "demonstrations" unless ordered by "a Grand Titan or higher authority." Blacks no longer were to be robbed of their guns unless they were arming themselves in groups for political purposes; whippings—for any reason—were to cease, as were breaking into jails to harm prisoners, writing threatening letters in the Klan's name, or using it for self-enrichment. This remarkable proclamation specifically added, however, that it was "not to be understood to dissolve the Order of the Ku Klux Klan." On the contrary, the Klan was "hereby held more firmly together and more faithfully bound to each other in any emergency that may come."[21]

Democratic newspapers, which had winked and chuckled at Kukluxism's earlier lawlessness, now inveighed against it, and local party leaders converged on Nashville carrying petitions against the use of martial law and pledging once more to do their utmost to end the Klan's activity. Brownlow replied that if the terrorism stopped and past fomenters of it were seriously sought for arrest and trial, no militiamen would be used. Violence did significantly decrease, but no past perpetrators were sought with vigor, let alone arrested, and the governor refused to be taken in again as he had been the previous summer, when the pledge of the Council of Peace had proved so transitory. On February 20, as soon as he had gathered some 1,600 militia recruits (mostly from Republican eastern Tennessee), Brownlow issued another proclamation placing nine counties — Overton, Jackson, Maury, Marshall, Giles, and Lawrence in central Tennessee and Gibson, Madison, and Haywood in the west — under martial law.[22]

It was, however, too little too late. Less than a fortnight after his proclamation, Brownlow was sworn into his new U.S. Senate seat, and the governorship passed to Speaker Senter. It was a passage from ruthless strength to inadvertent weakness. Although Senter had a considerable political résumé of his own, he was no Brownlow, whose courage was matched only by his popularity among the state's wartime Unionists. Senter entered office as a lame duck who had to stand for reelection just five months later, with formidable opposition within his own party. Indeed, when the state Republican convention met in Nashville in late May, Congressman William B. Stokes, claiming the support of 40,000 blacks as well as delegates from fifty-four counties, was so strong that the convention split and adjourned; afterward, its two factions met separately and nominated Senter and Stokes.

In the ensuing campaign, Democrats and Klansmen offered the electorate no candidate from their own party, confining themselves instead to what seems to have been a considerable role in the Republican race. To supplement his Republican support with that of Democrats, Senter shortsightedly renounced the policy that had put and kept Republicans in power in Tennessee: he declared himself for universal suffrage and opened the polls to thousands of ex-Confederates. Many Democratic newspapers quickly endorsed him, and Stokes went down to defeat in August by a margin of more than 65,000 votes. In Senter's defense, it should be noted that his policy appealed at the time to numbers of white Republicans inside and outside Tennessee. Grant had just been elected President on a slogan of "Let Us Have Peace," the national party leadership favored universal suffrage, and many Tennessee Republicans were being influenced by these views.

The Klan had everything to gain by Senter's election. By helping him to a full term as governor, it achieved immediate Democratic reenfranchisement and thus almost certain restoration of the Democrats to full statehouse control after his term of office. After the election, there was no further Democratic need for the Ku Klux in Tennessee, and soon after it, apparently, the Klan, at least in Tennessee, was disbanded.

Klansman J. P. Young would say in an interview sixty years later that the Memphis den, in a regular noon meeting ten days after Senter's election, received an order from Forrest, who at the time was in Nashville, that its members should disband and destroy all records and regalia. Minor Meriwether, the Klan's grand scribe under Forrest, would write in a letter in 1909 that Forrest had resigned his grand wizardship by that time and that a Nashville gathering of high Klan leaders sent out orders disbanding the Empire; Meriwether said it occurred because the Empire had been infiltrated by undisciplined elements and its mission had been accomplished. Meriwether's memory of it, however, was that this disbandment order came in February instead of the more logical August date. John Morton, reportedly grand cyclops of the Nashville den and one of the grand wizard's "genii," apparently remembered the order as occurring still later, after "the white race had redeemed six Southern states from negro rule in 1870"; at least, he gave a prominent place in his memoirs to a 1905 magazine article (for which he may well have been the informant) saying so. Another indication that the Forrest-led Klan could have lasted into 1870 occurs in the original Prescript, which declared that the grand wizard was elected to a three-year term dating from "the first Monday in May, 1867." No steps to reelect him or to choose a successor apparently ever were taken.[23]

Anyway, shrouded in the same secret "invisibility" in which it originated, the Klan began to disappear, although its death throes were violent, long-lived, and halting—partly, it would seem, because of the ban against newspapers reprinting Klan orders. Perhaps as one last gesture of defiance against the establishment—or against the leaders who had ordered the disbandment—men in Ku Klux costumes raided in the rural counties of

Sumner, Wilson, and Rutherford adjoining Nashville toward the end of August, whipping, raping, and stealing guns. Such acts would continue, on a generally more limited and sporadic basis, for a while. By this time, the ostensible pillars of Tennessee communities apparently had withdrawn from the dens, leaving them to the rabble. After they left, they seem to have tried to disclaim any future act of Klan lawlessness.

In early September 1869 in Lebanon, the Wilson County *Herald*— ignoring the earlier law against disseminating Klan messages—reprinted a Klan circular that reportedly had been passed around the area. In the same sort of eerie language with which the Invisible Empire had first captured public notice scarcely three years earlier, this portion of it offered a ghostly valedictory:

> *Our mission on earth, to some extent is ended. Quiet and peace must be cast abroad in your land. Wherever possible, we have protected you from outrage and wrong. We will still lend a helping hand, and the evil doers must remember that while we sleep we are not gone. . . . For the present, and we hope forever, we are done. When you see men, things or demons on your premises, claiming to be of me, shoot them down, for you may be certain that we are not there.*[24]

31

THE SKETCHY, CIRCUMSTANTIAL, and hearsay evidence of the Klan hierarchy's activities begins to disappear in 1869, fading into a mist of difficult questions. Did the grand wizard disband the Invisible Empire after achieving victory only in Tennessee, turning his back on the rest of the South? Or did he order it kept operational in states not yet on the threshold of redemption from Radical rule? Did he himself really withdraw from Klan leadership to play no role at all afterward?

Encouraged by its leaders or otherwise, the Klan unquestionably rode on across the rest of the South after its Tennessee disbandment. During the November 1868 elections, it had been most active in Tennessee, Arkansas, Georgia, Louisiana, and South Carolina, and its impact on those states was more than sufficient to suggest to Southern conservatives that violent intimidation was an easy and effective weapon in the continuing struggle to regain political privileges—as long, at least, as it did not bring on Federal intervention. Seymour had beaten Grant in Georgia (where

John B. Gordon had narrowly lost a race for governor the previous April) as well as in Louisiana, where Republican control of the statehouse had to be reinforced with Federal bayonets. He lost in Tennessee, Arkansas, and South Carolina, but the reduction of Republican vote totals in those states (or, in the case of South Carolina, in the upcountry counties where the Klan was active) had been so marked that the Democrats' future in those states looked highly promising.

The conservatives' desired end, however, required justifying ugly means that apparently began to repel more and more of the higher-minded, and for ample reason. In South Carolina, although the Klan appears to have been organized in only a dozen counties, its record included the assassinations of two state legislators, one white and one black. More than 200 murders, not to mention other violence, had been committed in Arkansas in the three months before the election, virtually all directed at Republicans. Over the three months before the election in Georgia, the Freedmen's Bureau there counted thirty-one killings, forty-three shootings, five stabbings, fifty-five beatings, and eight whippings of 300 or more lashes each. A later congressional report would break down the political mayhem in Louisiana in the six months before the election into 1,081 killings, 135 shootings and 507 other outrages. Many, if not most, of these South-wide crimes ultimately were attributed to the Klan or kindred organizations.[1]

In the trans-Mississippi states of Louisiana, Arkansas, and Texas, the Klan virtually passed out of existence after 1868, and in Tennessee and Georgia, where conservatives appeared to have regained control of the electorate if not yet the statehouses, more prudent Democrats — such as, apparently, Gordon in Georgia and John C. Brown in Tennessee — exited the organization; it would continue periodically vicious activities in both states, however. Virginia seems to have been "redeemed" by conservatives without the help of the Klan, but in Alabama, Mississippi, South Carolina, and North Carolina, it would function potently for years to come.

After 1868 the Klan's operations tended to be more scattered but more savage. The viciousness, while effective politically, hardly promoted the economic rebirth the South needed at the time; inconsistently, the region's conservative politicians tended to rail against carpetbaggers while simultaneously pleading for Northern capital and Northern immigrants to buy or work lands the South's shattered white male population either could not work or, as Forrest told General Smith in February 1868, would not. Having donned his Klan robes out of concern for the South's economic plight, he now surely felt himself impelled in the opposite direction by the same concern; Klan violence was injurious to his railroad building. At that business, by early 1869, he appears to have been very busy.

On March 3 Forrest made a speech to the Memphis Chamber of Commerce at the northern end of his proposed line, noting the scrambling among merchants of such cities as Mobile, St. Louis, Louisville, and Cincinnati for the agricultural and mineral riches of interior Mississippi and Alabama; the *Avalanche* quoted him as saying desire "for the success of Memphis" had helped cause him to "invest . . . all the money he had in the road he represented, and also a good deal more. . . ." Five days later, he took a large Memphis delegation to a railroad convention at Selma on the southern end of his line, telling the assemblage there that he needed "to raise a little money. . . . From $10,000 to $20,000 will enable the company to proceed"; he implied that prospects for capital were bright because postbellum "planters and others cannot buy any more negroes and will be compelled to invest in railroads and other improvements."[2]

In a chance March 9 interview with a reporter for the Louisville *Courier-Journal* aboard a train to Memphis from Jackson, Mississippi, his public remarks took a dramatic new tack. Passing "through beautiful tracts of country lying waste," the journalist wrote, "I asked General Forrest how it could ever be repopulated," and Forrest's reply exhibited characteristic independence of thought. "With negroes," he said. "They are the best laborers we have ever had in the South." Asked how he expected to repopulate the devastated South with blacks, he said they could be gotten "from Africa." He explained that they would "improve after getting here; are the most imitative creatures in the world, and if you put them in squads of ten, with one experienced leader in each squad, they will soon revive our country." He desired not only blacks but Northerners to help resettle the South, he added, "and would protect any man who comes to build up the country with my life; but they won't come; Europeans won't come; then, I say, let's get Africans. By pursuing a liberal policy to them we can benefit them and they us." He went on to inform the *Courier-Journal* correspondent that he had had "an interest" in *Wanderer,* a well-known antebellum slave-trading ship, and he said he and his associates had "brought over 400 [blacks]; only six percent died. They were very fond of grasshoppers and bugs, but I taught them to eat cooked meat, and they were as good niggers as any I ever had." He predicted that the Federal government, once "prejudice gets over, . . . will foster this scheme; there is no need of a war of races. I want to see the whole country prosper."[3]

By now Forrest must have learned how injurious to this desired prosperity the Klan's activities had been. Either to find a new, less traumatized Southern work force or to try to gain more leverage over the traditional black one, he participated in a so-called Chinese Labor Convention in Memphis in July, offering to hire 1,000 Oriental workers if they would immigrate. When another speaker suggested that blacks might feel "enmity" toward the Chinese laborers, Forrest proudly asserted that after he announced an intention to use such workers in Alabama, his railroad obtained a number of individual subscriptions from blacks. He added that he was winning stock subscription votes in some counties by wooing the black electorate. Having advocated in the Louisville newspaper interview a considerable increase in the South's black population (surely no goal of the Klan's paranoiac rank and file), he was currying the favor of county Republican leaders, as well as the Democratic ones, to sell subscriptions to his company's stock and thus get his track laid. He apparently even gave his personal protection to at least one prominent Republican threatened with retribution for having counseled assertiveness on the part of Alabama's blacks. By September the nationally noted Klansman Ryland Randolph, editor of the Tuscaloosa (Alabama) *Monitor,* was thundering that Forrest's "associating with persons with whom he does not agree politically is disgraceful and disgusting." Forrest replied publicly with a vehemence that suggests either that his own Klan ride was indeed over or, at least, that a division in this nonelection year was splitting the masked brotherhood. To the Marion (Alabama) *Journal* he wrote a defense of his railroading that included a scathing denunciation of Randolph personally and professionally:

> [A]s a private citizen and as President of the railroad company, I am assailed . . . by the editor of the Monitor, in the violent language which is characteristic of his paper, because of the personal associations attending my work. In my intercourse with those who have kindly aided me, I have taken no account of their opinions, political or religious. I am in no wise accountable for them, and have neither wish nor reason to controvert them.
>
> But for purposes best known to himself, Mr. Randolph, editor of the Monitor, sees fit to assail me for associating in this manner with a gentleman who happens to differ from him on politics. . . . Had he striven as hard in his paper to bring peace and prosperity to the country as he does to keep up strife and discord, it would have been more to his credit and better for the people of the State. His course as an editor has been constantly injurious, not to the Republicans,

but to the Democratic party, and the true interests of the people of Alabama. . . .[4]

A week after counterattacking Randolph, he made a brief but well-reported welcome of some unidentified residents of Massachusetts and Connecticut to a barbecue at Will's Valley near Gadsden, Alabama. Terming it "the proudest hour in my life, when I can stand here and extend the right hand of fellowship to these men from the North," he went on to add, in what must have alluded to the Klan's famed midnight brutalization of "carpetbaggers," that two years earlier these visitors "might not have dared come among us, but a change is being wrought, and we are becoming as one people, having a common interest. We must hereafter meet the Northern men liberally; and second all their efforts to develop the resources of our country. . . . A revolution has set in, and it cannot be stopped. A new era has dawned upon our people, and we must keep pace to the march of events."[5]

By this time, a wedge between the Klan's central officer corps and many of its lower-class followers must have been driven, not just by the leaders' commercial ambitions for the region but by continual controversy over whether Democratic conservatives should support the new right of blacks to vote. That principle, it will be remembered, had divided Memphis Klansmen-editors the year before, and, as impending constitutional conventions and state ratifications of the Fifteenth Amendment fanned these disputes into new flame, Gallaway's *Avalanche* remained staunchly in favor of black suffrage — because being otherwise would unnecessarily antagonize both friendly blacks who now held the franchise (and thus could help ex-Confederates regain it) and white Republicans in Washington who controlled Federal power.

In early 1869, soon after the announcement of the Memphis-to-Selma enterprise (and after the Senter victory that virtually ended Tennessee conservatives' need of the Ku Klux), the *Avalanche* no longer regarded the Klan as a reader amusement. Rather, it attacked as "prowling vagabonds" some Klansmen who whipped black railroad construction workers for taking the jobs of white men; its sympathy, however, was reserved not for the whipped workers but, rather, the distressed labor contractor, a Confederate veteran. Several months later, the *Avalanche* would indicate that much of the Klan's old leadership now backed the blacks' right to vote as a fait accompli. Gallaway editorialized that he knew "for a fact" that such ex-Confederate heroes as General John C. Brown favored it, along with

"Robert E. Lee . . . Forrest, Hampton, Wheeler, Kirby Smith, Stewart, Johnston, Hood, Beauregard," etc.[6]

The New England visitors probably were Boston executives of a new Chattanooga, Meridian, and New Orleans railroad interested in cooperating with Forrest's line; they wanted to ship Alabama coal into Memphis. Forrest's thinly capitalized firm, meanwhile, was progressing with impressive speed. The concept of the 280-mile venture was well chosen, calculated to reap huge profits if completed before a host of prospective competitors encroached on its territory. An editorial in the *Appeal* explained its great possibilities, noting that "merchants of Selma have bought bacon and flour, bagging and rope, and farming utensils in St. Louis and Cincinnati" and then shipped them "to New Orleans, transferred them to seagoing vessels," and then reloaded them again at Mobile onto steamers bound up the Alabama River to Selma. The completion of Forrest's railroad would mean "Memphis, instead of Cincinnati and St. Louis, will become the great depository of supplies for a vast cotton growing region. . . ."[7]

That wasn't all. A branch railroad then under construction from Elyton to connect with Forrest's tracks at Aberdeen, Mississippi, would help supply a fledgling Memphis manufacturing community with Alabama coal at drastically lower prices than were charged for coal from Pennsylvania. Forrest's line also would correct the longtime bypassing of Memphis by both the Mobile & Ohio and the Mississippi Central railroads, causing produce and manufactured goods that for years should have been bought and sold in Memphis to be hauled instead to St. Louis, Louisville, Cincinnati, Chicago, New Orleans, and Mobile. The Mobile & Ohio and Mississippi Central, with a monopoly over the interior of eastern Mississippi and western Alabama, had charged rates and enforced freight routes and schedules that both Memphis merchants and the area's agricultural producers considered discriminatory.

On September 17 Forrest wrote Gallaway a letter which the latter published, detailing progress so far. Including a subscription from Columbus, Mississippi, he said, "about $800,000" had been subscribed in addition to an Alabama State grant of $16,000 per mile, all of "which will nearly build the road to Columbus. . . . I propose to visit Memphis soon . . . to wake up the people to the importance of doing something." All the Mississippi counties "from Okolona to Memphis are waiting to see" what Memphis would do, he said. "If Memphis will aid this road to an extent of half a million dollars, Marshall, DeSoto, Pontotoc, Tippah, Lafayette,

Lee and Chickasaw [counties] will assist liberally." Everything, he said, depended on Memphis. "[S]he can build the road, or defeat it, as she chooses. . . ." On November 6 Monroe County, Mississippi, voted a $150,000 subscription to be added to $100,000 from its county seat, Aberdeen. A proposal for a subscription of $200,000 was being prepared for submission to the people of Pontotoc, who, the *Avalanche* soon reported, were expected to pass it "by an overwhelming majority." Soon Gallaway proclaimed that "[n]othing but a commercial and financial revolution which will prostrate every department of trade can prevent the consummation of this great enterprise."[8]

Soon afterward prospects of the Selma, Marion & Memphis gradually began to straiten. Forrest wrote a friend on February 12 that he had "just returned from North Carolina and brought with me eighty old railroad hands, and have arranged to secure 220 more . . . which I propose working this year [only] between the Alabama line and Okolona" because of "want of money to do the work with." He said that when he had "15 or 20 miles completed connecting with the Selma end our credit will be much better than to build 20 or 30 miles of detached line. . . . I am ready to put the whole line under contract from Okolona to the Alabama line, so soon as I can see the money to pay for the work as completed. . . ."[9]

On March 25, a writer for the *Appeal* bound for Mobile found Forrest a fellow-traveler from Meridian south, "on his way to receive and attend to the shipping of a thousand tons of rail . . . over the Mobile and Ohio road to Columbus." Forrest told the journalist he intended "to commence laying track . . . both ways [from Columbus toward Memphis and from Columbus toward Selma] simultaneously" and expected to have his entire line ready to operate by January 1, 1871. He added proudly that he had "commenced . . . two years ago without a dollar and . . . has raised over two millions of dollars toward it, not including State aid." He had "sold the State aid bonds at ninety-two cents on the dollar, and various county bonds at eighty-five cents on the dollar," which, the *Appeal* observed, showed "a great degree of confidence among capitalists in the undertaking. . . ." This "confidence," however, began to ebb. Less than a month later, he was quoted in the *Appeal* as saying "influential parties" were making it possible for him to "negotiate the first mortgage bonds of the Memphis and Selma Railroad for 85c. on the dollar, or hypothecate them for 80c." Upon endorsement of the firm's board of directors, he expected to start working on his track route "on the Memphis as well as the Selma end. . . ."[10]

The same day this was published Forrest was in Nashville denying much of the seemingly deathless 1868 interview with the Cincinnati *Commercial* regarding the Klan; since writing his correction letter the day he read the article, he appeared to remember less and less. The *Appeal* reported that he "denies having said that there are 40,000 Ku-Klux in Tennessee" or that he knew anything "positively of its organization, strength or objects." He said he had told the *Commercial* reporter only that he "was informed that its purpose was the protection of the people from injury and violence, and that I was so far, at least, in sympathy with it." All other statements he was reported to have made regarding the Klan, he claimed, were "derived from other persons, or are the fabrications of his own brain."[11]

The *Appeal* now began appearing better informed about the grand wizard. About this time Gallaway left the *Avalanche* in a dispute with its senior owner over editorial direction; soon afterward, he surfaced as a political editor of the *Appeal,* which reported on May 1 that Forrest, despite feeling "very unwell," addressed a crowd of Memphis "merchants and citizens" to ask for a $500,000 subscription. He was quoted as saying that he "had left here to build this road penniless, and felt that the people thought here that he would fail," but he presently was operating forty miles of road in Alabama on which "the profits are greater than on any [other] unfinished road in Alabama. The Commissioner of Alabama says that [Forrest's] road pays more than any in the State." He said he had spent $700,000 in the past year and presently was spending $75,000 a month, but the debt he was asking Memphis to incur in his behalf "will be nothing" in thirty years, when he predicted the Memphis & Selma would have helped swell the city's population of 40,000 to 300,000.[12]

The Chamber of Commerce quickly recommended that the Shelby County Court and the Memphis Board of Aldermen each subscribe $250,000, and, via the eloquent spokesmanship of Isham G. Harris, the question was brought before each; then matters slowed. The Franco-Prussian War broke out, unsettling Wall Street and devaluing bond issues. At length a Shelby County referendum was scheduled for late August, but on August 5 Forrest wrote a "notice to the people" postponing it because "important business in New York and Alabama has put it out of my power at an earlier day than the present to be here." The same issue of the *Appeal* quoted a Columbus, Mississippi, newspaper to the effect that he also was forced to suspend work on the Mississippi part of his route, owing partly to "the depression in the sale of his bonds brought about by the European war" and partly to a county injunction stemming from "opposition of a part of the county to the collection of the railroad tax."[13]

The Memphis referendum did not occur in November, as Forrest requested; in early January, he, Harris, and Meriwether still were pushing enabling ordinances through the city council and the county court. When a member of the latter told Forrest in an open meeting that he could not bring himself to vote to increase the tax burdens of the county's many war-widowed and -orphaned, Forrest replied that if he could build his railroad "through the very country whence my soldiers came, and where their wives and children live, manufactories and schoolhouses will spring into existence[,] [e]very woman and girl will have employment, and schools and churches will be accessible to the poorest, most helpless and unfortunate. . . . In building this road, I am complying with the most sacred obligations that I ever assumed to my fellow man."

The question of whether Shelby County wanted to help him build it, though, didn't reach the polls until March 25, 1871. The two evenings previous, Forrest, Harris, and Meriwether spoke to mass meetings of citizens. The task they had set themselves was large; such a referendum had to pass by a three-fourths majority, and at one of these meetings, at the Greenlaw Opera House, Forrest noted that the specter of Fort Pillow had been raised again "by a few speculative monied men, who think they see their interests in the defeat of the proposed subscription. Gentlemen, that is a shame. It is contrary to the just and proper way of arguing against this enterprise to . . . evoke a feeling of that sort for the purpose of defeating the interests of Memphis. . . ." Almost incredibly — given not only the above circumstance and but also that election day was muddy and rainy, and the referendum was the only question on the ballot — Forrest won in a landslide; the vote in the city of Memphis was 4,611 to 365. The "colored vote," though, was reported "not very heavy."[14]

Soon after the referendum, press references to his project began to disappear. Memphis — the nation's primary noncoastal cotton market, trailing only New Orleans and Savannah overall — preoccupied itself with trying to become a primary way station on a transcontinental route to the Pacific. Forrest's name and salary did come up in a public dispute between Minor Meriwether and an ex-president of the Mississippi River Railroad, with Meriwether disclosing that Forrest's modest compensation consisted of $4,000 per year, a 2½ percent commission on "bona-fide stock" (rather than borrowed money), and no expense account. On May 21 the *Appeal* reported that, by a margin of 356 to 7, Holly Springs finally voted $50,000 aid to the Memphis & Selma, to be added to $200,000 "certain to be voted by Marshall County." On June 10, however, Gallaway soberingly editorialized that the Memphis & Selma tracks should be reduced to a less expensive narrow gauge to ensure the project's completion.[15]

On May 9 Forrest joined twenty-one other ex-Confederate officers—including John B. Gordon, Wade Hampton, Raphael Semmes, Dabney H. Maury, Richard Taylor, and his old enemy Braxton Bragg—in signing a recommendation "to our friends in the United States" urging support for Washington & Lee University, the ambitiously renamed institution that still had been struggling as Washington College at the time of General Lee's death at its helm the preceding autumn. On June 14 the *Appeal* reported that Forrest "has been ordered to appear before the Ku-Klux investigating committee in Washington" and "will repair to the Federal capital within a few days." In a Memphis speech two days later, the future presidential candidate Horace Greeley "spoke in severe terms of the Ku-Klux, which he said the Government ought to extirpate at once, and forever." The *Appeal* added parenthetically that when Forrest "and other trustworthy citizens of the South are questioned by the Ku-Klux Committee, Mr. Greeley will learn that there is no such organization in the South."[16]

The *Appeal* obviously knew whereof it spoke. When Forrest arrived in Washington, he told the politically Democratic Cincinnati *Enquirer* that although he "was charged as being the organizer and leader" of the Klan, "as yet he had failed to ascertain that any such Klan exists, except in the imaginations of those who, for political purposes, probably would like to see such a body in the South. His opportunities for observation, he said, were very great, and if such a band as the Ku-Klux existed, he would know it." Regarding his reason for being in Washington, he said to the correspondent that he "believed he was charged with organizing bands of Ku-Klux among the men employed in the construction of a railroad from Selma, Alabama, to Memphis, Tennessee . . . 'but,' said the General, 'the charge is so absurd that I often wonder who could have furnished such information, or whose idle brain could have conceived it.' " He claimed that when he took his railroad position he "gave special instructions to those under me in authority, who are charged with obtaining mechanics, workmen, etc., under no consideration to allow politics to be a barrier to the employment of any man; on the contrary, to secure good workmen, be they white or black." The idea that he had been "forming . . . bands of Ku-Klux among them . . . is too ridiculous to entertain a moment. . . . I really believe that, were a vote taken to-day among those working under me in the construction of that enterprise, there would be found three

Republican votes to one Democratic." He said he had "willingly borne" the "vituperation" of being widely identified as the Klan's leader "because I did not desire to appear prominently before the public in print, and knowing my denial would entangle me in . . . a controversy which I did not court . . . I remained silent."[17]

Merely being a member of the Klan, let alone its national leader, was now a grave federal offense. The Ku Klux Act passed by Congress on April 20, 1871, put teeth in two other new laws to try to prevent one of the Klan's main aims, interference with voting rights. The Ku Klux Act authorized President Grant to use the Army to enforce its provisions, gave him the right to suspend the writ of habeas corpus wherever he deemed it necessary, and threatened the Klan's power over local judiciaries by giving courts a weapon with which to keep suspected Klansmen off juries: an oath backed with heavy penalties for perjury. For the first time, the federal government was given jurisdiction over the states in the punishment of such violent crimes as murder, assault, and arson. With the Democratic opposition charging oppression, Republican officials in some Southern states, backed by Federal troops, had begun to arrest and indict large numbers of Klansmen, and the purported Ku Klux menace had grown to such proportions that both houses of Congress, through the investigations of a joint committee, were trying to assess, for example, what part the Klan had played in the "redemption" of four ex-Confederate states — Virginia, Tennessee, North Carolina, and Alabama — by Conservative-Democrats by the end of 1870.

Forrest had a warm friend on the Ku Klux Committee in newly elected Senator Frank Blair of Missouri. As a whole, however, the body naturally contained more Republicans than Democrats, and the former included Radical general-turned-congressman Benjamin F. Butler of Massachusetts, whose deportment as Union commander of New Orleans had earned him the Southern sobriquet "Beast." In such company, Forrest needed to present himself in as nonpolitical, as favorable, and yet as formidable a light as possible, and when he took the witness stand June 27 he seems to have tried to do that. Recalling that at the end of the war he had called upon his surrendered troops to become good citizens, he stressed that he himself was now a wounded and sick ex-soldier attempting to continue to set a good example by rebuilding his lost fortune amid war's devastation and emancipation's anarchy. He said, with typical lack of false modesty, that he had "done more, probably, than any other man in the South to suppress these difficulties and keep them down," yet had been "vilified and abused in the papers, and accused of things I never did while in the army and since." Saying he had "no desire to hide anything" from the committee, he added that he wanted "this matter settled; I want our country quiet once more; and I want to see our people united and working together harmoniously."

He even, he said, had advocated "the fourteenth and fifteenth amendments before the people. . . . I told our people they were inevitable and should be accepted." From a man claiming to have nothing to hide, though, his testimony was sometimes very strange — sometimes halting, sometimes angry, sometimes clumsy, sometimes laconically humorous, and always deliberately obfuscatory when questioning turned specific about the Klan. After a few opening questions regarding his railroad (fifty miles of which, he said, now were completed and had trains running on them "every day"), he was asked if he knew of any Southern "combinations of men for the purpose of violating the law or preventing the execution of the law"; he emphatically answered in the negative. His primary interrogator — Senator John Scott of Pennsylvania, the committee's chairman — brought up two documents suggesting otherwise: the 1868 Cincinnati *Commercial* interview and his subsequent letter to the *Commercial* making only minor corrections in the article. At considerable length, he again denied his reported statements.

Forrest and the committee played a long game of cat and mouse. He told its members that any information he had on the Klan was purely information given him by others. Asked to identify these others, he claimed to be able to call to mind only a couple of former acquaintances, one now dead in North Carolina and the other an émigré to Brazil. Asked why, if the Cincinnati article had been so erroneous, he had corrected only a few of its mistakes in his subsequent letter to the newspaper, he replied in terms that seem lame coming from a man who had been in local politics for years before the war and had had at least three prominent journalists on his staff during it; he was "not accustomed," he said, "to writing letters or to be[ing] interrogated by reporters. That was something entirely new to me; I did not expect it." He claimed to have received later a letter from the Cincinnati reporter admitting misrepresentation of his views; he had neglected to carry that letter with him, however, although he had remembered to bring along his own carefully worded — and even notarized — one to J. T. Brown in 1868.

After being pressed several times to return to the subject of the *Commercial* interview, he decided he had been extreme in his initial statement that he did not pass more than twenty words with the reporter; a more accurate estimate, he said, might be twenty "minutes." His statement that he was unaccustomed to writing letters was followed closely by another to the effect that during the same period, with the aid of the secretary of his insurance company (whose services he needed, he said, because his right shoulder had been "shot all to pieces" during the war), he wrote "hundreds." At one point in a long discussion of the Klan's "constitution" (which he admitted having seen but said he could not remember details of), he significantly slipped and identified the document by the strange word "Prescript." Having maintained he knew of the Klan only by reports from others, he suddenly reversed himself when asked if he had tried to organize any Klan units under the terms laid out in the Prescript.

"I do not think I am compelled to answer any question that would implicate me in anything," he protested. "I believe the law does not require that I should do anything of the sort." Asked if that was the ground on which he placed his refusal to answer, he reversed himself yet again: "I do not." "I only wish to know your reasons for declining to answer," Senator Scott said, with seeming exasperation. "I will communicate to you the fact that there is an act of Congress which provides that such a reason shall not excuse a witness from answering." Scott read the congressional act aloud, then restated the original question: "Did you take any steps for organizing an association or society under that prescript . . . ?" Denied his Fifth Amendment rights, Forrest took the only other prudent course left. "I did not," he answered.

Over the course of his interrogation, he did profess to know—secondhand—a lot about the "organization" under discussion. Its purpose, he said, was self-defense, needed because of the rising of the Loyal League in Southern communities "and these rapes [that were] being committed, and the impudent colored people [who were] constantly toting about arms, firing in the night-time, creat[ing] a great deal of uneasiness." He contended that the Klan's object "was not to disobey the laws of the country, but to see them enforced" and "to prevent a wholesale slaughter of women and children." He explained that in the war's aftermath the blacks (who he did not explain were hungry) "left their homes, traveled all over the country, killed all the stock there was in the country to eat, were holding these night meetings, were carrying arms, and were making threats. . . . They were dissatisfied and disposed to fight and be abusive," and when they were arrested for offenses "large crowds of them would gather around the magistrates' offices. . . . [The ex-Confederate whites] had but one way to resist; they did not expect any assistance from the government of the State of Tennessee."

Well into his testimony, he admitted having joined one of several organizations formed to resist the Brownlow administration, but said he knew nothing "directly" of the Klan. From the information he could get, he said, it was organized according to county boundaries, although it did not necessarily cover entire states. Instead, he said, "I think this organization was more in the neighborhood of places where there was danger of persons being molested, or in large negro counties, where they were fearful that the negroes would rise up." He said he thought the organization was "started" in Middle Tennessee, although he did not know where. "It is said . . . that I started it," he added. "Is that true?" "No, sir; it is not."

As to its membership, he said he had been informed that the Klan "admitted no man who was not a gentleman, and a man who could be relied upon to act discreetly; not men who were in the habit of drinking, boisterous men, or men liable to commit error or wrong." He said he did not think those chosen "intended to go and violate or wrong any one"; their purpose, rather, was "to punish those men who were guilty, and who the law would not touch; and to defend themselves in case of an attack." He said he had "never heard it said it was to have anything to do with elections. . . . A large portion of the people in the State were disfranchised, and they did not attempt to make any effort to carry elections."

Asked which states the Klan had spread into, he said it was rumored to be in Mississippi, was "reported" to be in North Alabama, and "probably" was also "in North Carolina . . . about Asheville; those are the only States I recollect of." Hadn't he heard of it in Louisiana? he was asked. "No, sir." Had he heard of the Knights of the White Camellia, a Klan-like organization, in Louisiana? "Yes, they were reported to be there." Was he ever a member of that order? "I was." He was a member of the Knights of the White Camellia? "No, sir; I never was a member of the Knights of the White Camellia." What order, then, was it that he was a member of? "An order they called the Pale Faces; a different order from that." Asked where the Pale Faces were first organized, he said he didn't know. He said he had joined them in Memphis in 1867, but noted that they were "a different order from this [Ku Klux Klan]." What, then, was the Pale Face order like? "Something like Odd Fellowship, Masonry, orders of that sort, for the purpose of protecting the weak and defenseless, &c."

There followed a lengthy and generally unproductive inquisition concerning the time or two he admitted having attended Pale Face meetings. These occasions, he said, had been in Memphis and perhaps on Second Street, but he couldn't recall the building. Did he remember who were present? "No, sir." "You do not remember any of them?" No. "You do not remember the name of one of them?"

No, sir. I might, if I had time to think the matter over, recollect these things. In the last two years I have been very busily engaged. I came out of the war pretty well wrecked. I was in the army four years; was on the front all the time, and was in the saddle more than half my time; and when I came out of the army I was completely used up—shot all to pieces, crippled up, and found myself and my family entirely dependent. I went into the army worth a million and a half of dollars, and came out a beggar. I have given all my time since then, so far as was in my power, to try to recover.

Some of his evasions were almost humorous. Soon after his vain attempt to refuse to answer the request for names of Klan members he knew, he replied he did not "now . . . recollect the members." Asked if two or three years earlier he had known any Klan members (which, if he had and had not reported the fact, would have been a grave crime in Tennessee), he again replied that he did not remember. Chairman Scott, perhaps getting vexed, put the question to him a third time: "Can you now tell us who were the members, or any single member, of that organization?" He paused. "Well, that is a question I do not want to answer now," he finally said. He was declining to answer? Scott asked. Not exactly: "I would prefer to have a little time, if you will permit me." Representative Job E. Stevenson of Ohio broke in to inquire why he needed time. "I want to study up and find out who they were, if I have got to answer the question; that is the reason," he said. What length of time would he probably require? "Well, sir, I do not know that I could say now, as I am in the midst of this examination. I would like you to pass that over for the present and let me have some time to think over it." Given little choice, the committee moved on to other questions.

He continually maintained that the Klan as he had known about it had not existed since around the time he had gone into the railroad business— or, at least, since soon thereafter; he was very vague about the exact time. "I think it was disorganized in the early part of 1868," he said at first. Then he said the understanding "among the southern people" was that it had "disbanded about the time of the nomination of candidates for President of the United States," which would have been during the summer of 1868. Later, he said it "must have been in the latter part of 1868, I reckon." In an attempt to link it with a political event, he was asked when Senter was elected governor of Tennessee—"in 1868 or 1869?" and he disdainfully digressed: "I do not recollect; I have never voted, and not paid any attention to the elections." The only vote he had cast since the war had been nonpolitical, he said: "for a subscription to build a railroad."

He eventually was drawn into another significant slip. Evading questions as to the Klan's secret signals, he said he had known some of them but could "not give you one of them correctly now to save my life. . . . It was a matter I knew very little about. . . . All my efforts were addressed to stop it, disband it, and prevent it." He had gotten to know some of these Klan signals, he said, "in order that I might try and check the thing; I was trying to keep it down as much as possible." Asked which he was trying to suppress, the "organization" or the "outrages" he several times had mentioned, he said the "outrages." Outrages committed by blacks? "By all people," he replied. "[M]y object was to keep the peace." Did he, then, "want to suppress that organization?" "Yes, sir; I did suppress it." "How?" "Had it broken up and disbanded."

Understandably, the committee was interested to hear how he, who claimed to have not even been a member, was able to accomplish such a thing. "I talked with different people that I believed were connected with it, and urged its disbandment, that it should be broken up," he blandly replied. Later on, he amplified his reasons for doing this. "There was no further use for it; . . . the country was safe; . . . there was no further apprehension of any trouble," he said at one point. Another time, asked if, in addition to his myriad letters from Southerners, he ever had received letters from the North, he said he had "got letters from Northern citizens urging me to try and keep things quiet, and let it work itself off." So everybody, North and South, looked to him for the cessation of the Klan troubles? He warily retreated: "No, sir; not particularly so. I suppose they looked to other men as well as to me." Had he heard of other Southerners having that kind of correspondence? "I understood that a great many of our Southern men corresponded with their friends in the North, and that was the advice of the Northern people generally, to try and keep this thing down."

Senator Scott asked if he was saying, then, that he had received advice from Northerners in 1868 "to have the Ku Klux society suppressed?" "No, not the Ku Klux," Forrest replied; "I do not want to be understood that way." To say such, after all, would have been difficult to explain to Klansmen and their sympathizers. "I got letters from persons in the Northern States whom I knew," he said, "giving it as their opinion that we should try and restrain everybody there from difficulty and violence, to let this thing blow over, work itself off in that way."

While claiming not to know about such things directly, Forrest maintained that any crimes purportedly being committed by Klansmen since the disbandment were not being committed by true Ku Klux. These recent savage acts, then, were being committed by "more temporary organizations?" "I think it has been among wild young men and bad men," he replied. "I do not think they have had any such organization." Yet they have been "called by the same name of the original organization that once existed?" "Yes, sir." Near the end of his testimony, Scott returned to this subject again. The congressional committee's purpose, he noted, was "not merely to ascertain who are members of it for the purpose of prosecuting them for crime, but to ascertain whether it continues to exist, and who are responsible for the present commission of crimes of this character, wherever they occur in the Southern States." Forrest replied that he was "satisfied, from my knowledge . . . , that no such organization does exist; that it was broken up in 1868, and never has existed since that time as an organization." Was that true throughout the South? "So far as I know; that was the understanding, that it was to be broken up wherever it existed, and to be no longer countenanced." Asked if "other men who were in the organization, and who felt differently from you," could have "kept it alive for political purposes," he hinted that he believed that had happened, although not "as an organization; I think all this that has been done in the course of [the past] eighteen months has been done by parties who are not responsible to anybody."

Just before the end of Forrest's testimony, Representative Stevenson suddenly returned to the matter of the names the witness had said he needed to "study up on"; Stevenson told him he "did not understand you to say whether you would send us those names by mail or not." This time the witness's parry was short, with what seems to have been a steely undertone. "I did not say whether I would or not," he said with finality.[18]

32

WASHINGTON, June 27.—Gen. FORREST was before the Kuklux Committee today, and his examination lasted four hours. . . . [A]fter the examination, [he] remarked to friends that the Committee treated him with much courtesy and respect.

—New York *Times*, June 28, 1871

Forrest's testimony, often dismissed as lies and flights of fancy made under threat of Federal prosecution, probably contained more truth than fiction. Certainly, his public behavior and the little known of his private life during this period circumstantially affirm his statements that he tried to, at the very least, deactivate the Klan. If, as Minor Meriwether later recalled, he resigned the grand wizardship in 1869, it was possibly on an understanding that the Klan was to be phased out by the subordinates in whose hands he left it. With his railroad endeavors already having begun, he doubtless scaled down his Klan work in late 1868 and possibly resigned after Senter's election to a full term as Tennessee's governor. Not only was a considerable portion of the South beginning to take Tennessee's path toward political "redemption"; there was growing apprehension among the Klan's more genteel fellow-travelers that its time had passed, that its bloody excesses now jeopardized further Conservative-Democratic political gains by threatening to precipitate return to martial law. Four months after Forrest's appearance before the congressional committee, Georgian B. H. Hill — who, as an associate of John B. Gordon in the Atlanta branch of the Southern Life Insurance Company, may have had inside knowledge of the Invisible Empire — told a reporter for the Cincinnati *Commercial* that "The Ku Klux business . . . is the greatest blunder our people ever committed."[1]

Forrest himself must have felt effects of that blunder as his business associations with Republicans, so necessary for the success of his new venture, tainted the image of the enterprise in the eyes of the majority of its prospective beneficiaries and patrons. Local Klans may well have renounced their leaders, as much as vice versa. Forrest's attempts to direct the Empire toward more prudent nonviolence and at least temporary political partnership with conservative blacks doubtless were never popular among rank-and-file Klansmen, and it seems likely that these orders were not always passed down below the leadership's intermediate levels. With the Klan's chain of command so secret and labyrinthine, the Empire may even have been continued under Forrest's name without his knowledge; one Mississippi den was founded by a man who went to Memphis to get the oath and ritual in 1870, and Captain Morton, it will be remembered, seems to suggest that disbandment occurred after the elections of that year. If the disbandment orders were deliberately ignored by some of Forrest's erstwhile lieutenants, he — busy with his railroading — may have taken for granted that the new violence was being instigated by imposters and pretenders. The former subordinates appear to have remained on good terms with him; that there was cohesion among the Klan's old leadership well after 1869 is suggested by a report from New York published by the *Appeal* just before Forrest's Washington testimony. It expressed surprise that there was "not a single instance where witnesses [called by the congressional committee] have been telegraphed for, that a favorable response has not been received on the same day." The universal readiness of Klansmen and/or ex-Klansmen to testify suggests that a policy may have been agreed on among them.[2]

Now, however, some of Forrest's Klan friendships began to dissolve under pressure of business. He and Minor Meriwether fell out over orders he gave Meriwether as straitening finances compounded the annoyance of an assistant engineer's strict adherence to regulations. The assistant, H. N. Pharr, had been hired by Meriwether, and Pharr later said the railroad's contractors grew "restive under the rigid execution of the orders of the chief-engineer [Meriwether]." The contractors, Pharr said, made complaints to Forrest, causing him to believe "their failure to push forward the work as fast as he expected was owing to me." Forrest ordered Meriwether to fire Pharr, but Meriwether refused, saying Pharr had "discharged his duty with strict fidelity to the company . . . and in my opinion was entirely competent for the work required." Forrest then went to the firm's board of directors with his demand that Pharr be terminated; again, he was refused. Learning of Forrest's dissatisfaction, Pharr tried to quit, but Meriwether declined to accept the resignation.[3]

Forrest always was a demanding superior, and his demands probably grew as funds for his enterprise dwindled. Around the time of the Pharr episode, he also upbraided an Alabama contractor named Shepherd in much the same way, apparently accepting without investigation others' reports that Shepherd wasn't doing his job. Stung by the injustice of his overbearing attack, Shepherd challenged Forrest to a duel, and Forrest quickly accepted. He set the terms as his favorite weapons, "navy six" pistols, from ten paces at sunrise the following morning. The night before the scheduled encounter, he occupied the same room with another contractor, Charles E. Waller of Greensboro, Alabama, and appeared restless. When he sat up on the side of his bed near morning, Waller asked what was the matter. Forrest said he had been unable to sleep "for thinking about the trouble with Shepherd." He went on to explain that he felt "sure I can kill him, and if I do I will never forgive myself. I am convinced that he was right in resenting the way I talked to him. I am in the wrong. . . ." Noting that Forrest's courage was no matter of conjecture, Waller suggested he apologize to Shepherd. "You are right," Forrest said.

"I will do it." He and Waller quickly dressed and went to find the prospective opponent, whom they discovered in a circle of friends. Forrest strode into the group, offered Shepherd his hand, and said: "Colonel, I am wrong in this affair, and I have come to say so." Shepherd appeared happy to let the matter drop.[4]

The Meriwether estrangement proved more difficult. Soon after persuading Pharr to stay on, Meriwether himself resigned from the Memphis & Selma, and Pharr left with him. The former's departure seems to have arisen out of his refusal to certify as finished any work along the line a moment before it was completed, even though Forrest desperately needed such certifications to obtain further funds promised by state and county governments. When, in a company board of directors meeting, Meriwether announced he intended to discuss the certifications before a public gathering that evening at the Greenlaw Opera House, Forrest bristled. Meriwether's son Lee wrote many years afterward that Forrest responded with a threat: If Meriwether made such a speech, "one of us will not leave the Greenlaw alive."

The next few hours in the Meriwether household constituted a maelstrom of preparations for battle involving not only the meticulous Meriwether but his wife, Elizabeth. Noting that "Forrest was four inches taller and forty pounds heavier than father," Lee Meriwether recalled that Elizabeth "tried to persuade father to stay at home." When he refused to consider it, she announced that she, too, was going to the Greenlaw that evening. In the interim, she "dashed off note after note to father's war comrades, begging them to come to our home at seven o'clock, and to come armed." Then she "sewed a pocket in the back of father's shirt . . . ten inches long and three inches wide" into which she "slipped a sharp dagger. 'When Forrest attacks you,' mother said to father, 'you can reach up behind your neck and grab this dagger.' " Friends arriving at the house admonished Meriwether to stay home; when he wouldn't, Matthew Gallaway suggested they take upon themselves the dangerous task of going to " 'see Forrest and tell him he must not interfere.' " They then sought out Forrest, who "listened courteously, but gave no sign what impression the appeal made upon him," and that evening he appeared at the Greenlaw and "took a seat . . . in a box separated from the stage only by a low railing. Mother, with several friends, occupied the opposite box; in orchestra seats below her were eight of father's friends."

Ever after, Lee Meriwether would remember "seeing mother take a pistol out of her handbag as she lifted me out of her lap and told me to lie down on the floor and go to sleep." Elizabeth later told him she had "put you out of my lap because I wanted to be free to step over the railing onto the stage. While Gen. Forrest assaulted your father I meant to jab my pistol in his back and shoot him dead." When the elder Meriwether moved to the podium, "he looked in Forrest's direction [and] drew from his pocket a pistol and laid it on the table. 'I understand,' he began, 'that some persons object to my speaking here tonight. If that is true, let the objections be made now. I do not wish to be interrupted after I begin my speech.' " The subsequent silence was "intense," Lee Meriwether recalled, and the audience "waited breathlessly to see what Forrest would do." Forrest did nothing, continuing to sit "silent while father talked about roadbeds, tunnels and bridges, and told the audience that the subsidies were not yet due." Forrest's behavior thus conformed with that which he displayed at his killing of Lieutenant Gould, his aborted duel with Shepherd, and apparently the last stages of the battle at Fort Pillow; with time to get past the heat of the moment and reflect, he did the moral thing.[5]

Oddly, no hint of the Greenlaw incident seems to have been published by the Memphis newspapers, but plenty of other news of the Memphis & Selma did. Long-awaited construction crews for the firm finally appeared in Shelby County in the late summer of 1871, and a September 11 *Appeal* editorial noted that "about 100 laborers are employed in the southwestern suburbs in grading the Memphis, Holly Springs and Selma road. The first five miles will soon be finished by the contractors having the work in charge, and others have agreed to finish the road to Holly Springs within 12 months." On December 30, residents of Holly Springs voted a $75,000 subscription to the Memphis & Selma. The company was reported on March 22, 1872, to have finished twenty miles of the distance between Memphis and Holly Springs—but needed to complete another twenty-five miles by September 1 to qualify for a promised and desperately needed $4,000-per-mile subsidy from the state of Mississippi. A week later, Forrest was at the St. Nicholas Hotel in New York City, doubtless on a money-hunting mission. The trip was unsuccessful, apparently, because on April 7 he and Memphis & Selma director Jacob Thompson were reported proposing to go to Europe to try to negotiate sales of their firm's bonds.[6]

The financial climate had grown terrible for railroad construction. The Franco-Prussian War had pushed the United States into a deep recession; a May item in the *Appeal* reported that "Iron is 50 percent higher than it was 12 months ago" and added that its price rise "will tell heavily against all the feebler new railroad undertakings, of which there are many in the country." Matters weren't helped by the fact that, as Grant's scandal-scarred administration neared the end of its first term, railroads were acquiring an unsavory national reputation; in the South, once-vaunted J. C. Stanton of the Chattanooga & Alabama line had been charged with corruption and his railroad confiscated by the state of Alabama. Some counties that had voted subsidies to the Memphis & Selma—Pontotoc, Mississippi, for one—began to scale down their pledges.[7]

The line's president plunged on. A large Memphis & Selma work crew was reported on June 3 to have arrived at Okolona, "from which point the work will be rapidly pushed forward to Aberdeen." Forrest and other Memphis & Selma representatives met with the Memphis Chamber of Commerce on July 11 to appeal to Shelby County businessmen for an investment of $150,000. That sum, they said, was required to buy and transport from New Orleans the iron with which to complete the twenty-five miles they had to finish by September 1 to qualify for Mississippi's subsidy. Jacob Thompson, they added, had been sent to Europe to negotiate sale of their bonds but "these treaties, involving vast sums, were necessarily tedious." The *Appeal* reported that Forrest "has already expended four hundred thousand dollars on the road between Memphis and Holly Springs, and has executed a preliminary contract with Englishmen to take his assets and complete the road from Selma to Memphis by the first of January, 1873." Both the Memphis and the European aid missions were unsuccessful. When the *Appeal* published a September article of several pages reviewing Memphis business progress—including railroad development—over the preceding year, it accorded not a word to the Memphis & Selma.[8]

Forrest's gambler's instinct in the face of adversity was to raise the stakes. In January 1873 he surfaced in Detroit, where a waggish local reporter requested and got a hotel-room interview with "the hero of Fort Pillow" and found his hair "as white as seventy, but his face and figure look no more than forty." In response to questions, he said he was in Detroit "to see if I cannot interest your capitalists" in the Memphis & Selma "and in another railroad project of much larger dimensions." He said the Memphis & Selma was "a section of an air line" stretching from the Atlantic coastal city of Brunswick, Georgia, "through Georgia, Alabama, Mississippi, Tennessee, Arkansas, [and] Missouri." He described Kansas City as this air line's "western terminus, and our plan is to extend this string of railroads to the line of the Northern Pacific, which will make the shortest route from the Atlantic to the Pacific." From Detroit, he added, he planned to proceed to New York in furtherance of his aims.[9]

Nothing came of that, either. A Memphis & Selma stockholders' meeting in Memphis on March 5–6 elected his old friend Sam Tate to the board and voted to publish a resolution acknowledging that the firm's "administration of affairs . . . has not come fully up to the expectations of the stockholders," although "we feel it our duty to say that, in our judgment, General Forrest and the other officers . . . have displayed great zeal, energy and ability under the embarrassing circumstances by which they have been surrounded." Two and a half weeks later, Forrest and Jacob Thompson went before the Memphis Chamber of Commerce to say their line could not be finished to Holly Springs without more monetary subscriptions by prosperous Memphians. Forrest said he had "spent three dollars and fifty cents for every dollar they had collected" and thus had "done his utmost to get the road through to Holly Springs by September in order that he might take advantage of the $4,000 per mile bonds, but he had not succeeded." The Chamber named a committee to try to raise money sufficient to lay track to Holly Springs "during the present season."[10]

In a Chamber committee meeting April 25, Forrest opposed a member's suggestion that a cheaper, narrow-gauge line be built because "nothing more or better could be done"; Forrest said the narrow-gauge idea had been considered and abandoned because $2 million already had been spent building the road as a broad-gauge line in Alabama. This dismissal of the narrow-gauge, long a pet project of Gallaway, prompted an *Appeal* editorial suggesting that a narrow-gauge line to Holly Springs would be profitable, and that the profits could be used to build a broad-gauge line on the same route later on. The *Appeal* chastisement of Forrest's rejection of the narrow-gauge indicates that a rift between him and Gallaway had developed, perhaps during the one with Meriwether. The tenor of the *Appeal* account suggests that Forrest was losing his self-control, reporting that he "says he is willing to get out of the way if anyone else will build the road." Gallaway added that there was "no need for this if he will build it. He does not think the county court intends to issue the scrip and [does think] that a mandamus may be required to enforce the company's rights."[11]

Opposition in the county court grew. On May 5 its members dawdled, voting to have a committee inspect the work done by the Memphis & Selma in Shelby County and make a detailed report that could not be submitted until the court's July meeting. Forrest warned that he recently had borrowed another $75,000 "on individual security" in New York, and although the company had spent $2.25 million and still had $4 million in subscriptions and county bonds, it "might lose all of this unless the [promised annual] installment be made" by the court. A Justice Walker countered that errors of $2,500, $3,000, and $20 or $30 had been made in a previous company report to the court in one item alone, and the court postponed further action until July.

At a stockholders meeting, Forrest grew testier. Saying that "if he were in the way of the enterprise he would no longer retain" the presidency, he added that he resented "people along the road who would not tell him to his face what they had said behind his back, to injure him personally." The nature of the charges being whispered is suggested by another sentence in the *Appeal* report of the meeting: "He [said he] had never received any money from the company but, on the contrary, the books show that he has given instead of taking." He was forced to await the July meeting of the court amid newspaper reports that were increasingly disheartening. The *Public Ledger* and the *Appeal* proposed that the line be split in two, with each end assuming its own debt and the northern portion being finished as a narrow-gauge; the *Appeal* said the court "prefers to invest in a narrow-gauge and will expend money in behalf of no other scheme if the necessity may be evaded." The Holly Springs *Reporter* noted that although $400,000 worth of grading, bridge building, tunnel construction, and crosstie buying had been done, "for ten months now . . . there . . . [has been] no sign of the work's being advanced to completion. The winter rains, snows and freezes, and the floods of spring all have beat upon the work, until, in many places, it is destroyed, and the process of destruction continues."[12]

In July the county court's inspection committee reported two explosive facts: (1) that an inspecting engineer was able to find only $76,521.99 worth of construction that had been done on the Memphis & Selma in Shelby County, whereas Forrest had reported spending $142,830.91 on construction there, and (2) that the engineer the committee had hired to make the inspection was H. N. Pharr. The $66,308.92 discrepancy made it "obvious," the committee concluded, "that the company has not complied with the terms and conditions of the subscription of $500,000 by this county, and until there is a full compliance on the part of the company with said terms and conditions, it is evident that this court cannot, without gross dereliction to the interests of the people of Shelby County, assess any more taxes or issue any more certificates for the purpose of the subscription of the county to said railroad company. Your committee would, therefore, recommend that the railroad company be required to make up from other sources of stock subscription . . . $95,478 in cash, and expend the same on the work to be done within the county of Shelby . . . before any more tax be levied or certificates be issued."[13]

The committee's parochial interpretation of the "said terms and conditions" was small-minded, even in a county mired in debt; strapped for funds, Forrest had been employing his military tactic of throwing thin resources where they would do the most good at the time, trusting that progress along any part of the line was progress for the entire project. The committee's choice of an inspector understandably enraged him. In a stormy July 14 meeting of the court, in which Memphis & Selma counsel Gideon Pillow presented many affidavits and other documents disputing parts of Pharr's report, Forrest finally rose and said that when he learned Pharr had been chosen to make the inspection he took it as "a direct thrust at me" because after separating from the Memphis & Selma Pharr had told one of the firm's contractors "that he would someday get revenge." Forrest then proceeded to an uglier subject.

Frequently remarks have been made that I was getting rich off the railroad, and that I had bought a fine house. Now, gentlemen, what have I done that I should not be able to own a home without exciting comment? When I left here in 1861, I left with as good credit as any man in the city. . . . I understand it has been hinted that money given to the road has been used by me for private purposes. No man dare[s] say that to my face.

He offered a history of the firm's financial bad luck. He recalled finishing twenty miles of track-laying one day before expiration of time to qualify for Alabama bonds that at the time were selling at 97.5 cents on the dollar, then had seen these and other Alabama bonds devalued almost immediately by the Franco-Prussian conflict; ultimately they were rendered unsalable by "political troubles" in the state. He pushed to build and equip twenty-five miles of track in Mississippi to get that state's $4,000-per-mile subsidy, working simultaneously from both Holly Springs and Memphis to do it, but then was unable to acquire iron in time to lay track and qualify. He amplified some admissions made earlier by Pillow. Some of the Shelby County money had indeed been spent in Mississippi and Alabama, he said, but only on work necessary to make the Shelby County end of the line more profitable when it was finished. In Mississippi, he said, some of the firm's contractors had gotten into such financial difficulty while working for it that he "could not see them suffer or allow their property to be sacrificed, when the company owed them and had money in its hands. . . ."

I used a part of the county scrip to prevent their utter destruction, financially. At the same time, having accepted their drafts for money due them, and having deposited the road's county securities from Alabama and Mississippi, and the acceptances having fallen due, and having been unable to sell any of the first-mortgage bonds, I was again forced to use Shelby county scrip. I have done three hundred and fifty thousand dollars' worth of work between Memphis and Holly Springs, and all the money I have had [on hand] to pay for that work has been seventy-five thousand dollars of Holly Springs bonds, which I was able to use at about seventy-five cents on the dollar[;] two hundred thousand dollars of Shelby county scrip at about eighty-seven cents[;] and ten thousand dollars in money collected from individuals, with such amounts as I was able to furnish myself. . . .

If this enterprise fails, it will not be my fault, but the fault of those along the line of the road. If the road is sold out to some foreign company, who feel no interest in the people except for the money they can get out of them, then it is the fault of the people, and not mine.[14]

When the question was put to a vote, the court ruled against him sixteen to five. The stone wall he had met in his home county was never explained in any newspaper account, but reading between the lines offers hints. For one thing, the county's debt was oppressive, and elected representatives were getting increasingly nervous about it. For another, there probably were, as Forrest charged, some Memphis businessmen who had financial reasons for wishing to see the Memphis & Selma fail; they either owned stock in competing lines or wished to see the price of Memphis & Selma stock fall so that it might be bought up cheaply.

Other reasons, though, must have had to do with Forrest himself. Surely he had made powerful Shelby County enemies with his commandeering of a seat in Tennessee's delegation to the 1868 Democratic national convention. It also is possible that some of his Klan subordinates became embittered and vengeful after he seemed to reverse himself and began associating with Republicans and advocating black retention of the ballot. He certainly picked an impolitic time to try to buy an impressive house, and there also was his gambling, another factor hardly calculated to inspire confidence in any discussion of his railroad's financial troubles. John Morton later recalled he "liked occasionally to play cards for money," and Morton's recollection of an example of this habit makes it sound less occasional than obsessive. Morton remembered that during the postwar period, "when very needy, he won $3,000 gambling although his wife, to whom he was very devoted, tried to persuade him to live on half rations rather than play cards." Morton said one evening in Nashville Forrest asked him if he knew where he might "find a gambling saloon." Morton replied that he didn't, but inquired why Forrest had asked. "Well," Forrest replied, "I found one tonight, broke the bank and have $2,500 of their money. I thought I had time to tackle another before I went to bed."[15]

Whatever the cause, Memphis — or at least the Shelby County court — plainly was unsympathetic toward his project. In what had to have been a demeaning display, he went again before the court on July 21 to reiterate his demand for its pledged third $100,000 annual installment; again he was defeated, although by the closer margin of thirteen to eleven. That, however, was the last chance; the court then quickly adjourned until October (after voting to pay Pharr $1,148.05 for his services).[16]

Having characteristically thrown every resource he had behind the Memphis & Selma, he now saw his personal financial situation grow precarious. In September he was in New York again trying to borrow money for the railroad from which he might also draw his own salary, or at least enough of it to make overdue payments on the "fine" house he had been criticized for attempting to purchase. To cotton merchant J. M. Farrington, who owned the house with his mother, Forrest wrote from New York a note obviously penned personally:

> St. Nicholas Hotel
> Sept. 8 1873

> Mr J M Farrington
> Memphis Tenn
>   Dear Sir yours of 2 from Memphis with your Ma[']s from Brookesville of the 1 Inst reached me on my arivl her this morning[.] I have note had time to Se what I can do in the way of Rasing Money but from all I can Se and learn to day I fear thair will be but little chance to rase Money her in Rail Road Securetes[.] I will promis to do my Best to comply with Mrs Bradford wishes[.] I am Sorry I have bin compeld to disappoint you as I hav don but it is imposabl for Me to pay unles I can collect from the R R[.] I have amassed more than twist the amt I owe you and your Ma and wil do all I can to pay[.] If I rase any Money I will place it to your credit and advise you by Telleygraph.

> Yours Truly
> N B Forrest[17]

No more seems to have been heard of the Memphis & Selma in Memphis newspapers until January 8, 1874, when a group of prominent local businessmen pushed to revive it, reasoning that although the county's terms had not been "literally followed" regarding use of the funds in Shelby County, the remaining installments would be "far more than adequate" to finish the Shelby County work. A day later, however, Minor Meriwether attacked the Memphis & Selma in print, recapitulating the financial discrepancy in the committee's and the company's reports of the work and saying the court's duty was to "compel" the company to replace the funds it had misused before granting any more installments. On January 12 the court met yet again, and a Justice Wallace sought to "kill" the Memphis & Selma and recover the $200,000 already given Forrest by the court; that measure lost twelve to ten, the votes in Forrest's favor including the court's single black member. In subsequent January 13 and January 21 meetings, proposals to continue the Memphis & Selma project were killed by votes of eleven to eight and fourteen to eight. Each time, the black member voted for Forrest.[18]

A remarkable Forrest letter appeared in the *Appeal* of February 20. Angrily reciting the history of his Memphis & Selma difficulties, from the Franco-Prussian War to the tendency of municipalities and counties to vote him money only to be used within their borders, it went on to recount two successes. The fifty miles of line finished in Alabama already had earned profits such that all but some $14,000 of a $75,000 floating debt had been retired, "although the cotton crop has been almost a failure for the last two years in that section of the country"; and the operating expenses of the Alabama end of the line were "less than fifty per cent of the receipts, which is less than any [other] railroad in the State of Alabama." He chided the Holly Springs *Reporter* for calling for a new Memphis & Selma stockholders election, a new president, and new Shelby County directors. He said no man in Shelby County not already on the board had bought enough Memphis & Selma stock to qualify for membership on it.

> *I will further state that I have paid more money for the building of this road than all the citizens of Shelby County, except the amounts paid on the Shelby County subscription. . . . I hold for myself and friends $130,000 [in] . . . bonds which have cost us seventyfive cents on the dollar. I also hold $30,000 of the stock, and am indorser on the company's paper for $20,000, and will make the following proposition to the Holly Springs Reporter, and all others*

who seem anxious for a change in the management of the road. To wit: Pay me interest on the bonds I hold; take $30,000 of the bonds I hold at what they cost me; pay me the company's indebtedness on open account, which is between $7000 and $8000; give me a guarantee against the indorsements I have made to the company, and I will hold $100,000 of the bonds and take my chances with the other bondholders; and I will further agree to give the parties the $30,000 of stock I hold and what good will and influence I have, if any, as I assure you, Mr. Editor, that I am heartily sick and tired of so much croaking from men who attempt to speculate on finances and financiering, who never had one thousand dollars at any one time in their lives. . . . I am weary of a community that has no appreciation of services rendered in their behalf.[19]

At a March 5 stockholders meeting Forrest was reelected to the board of directors in proceedings which the Shelby County court plainly tried to bully; the court demanded, unsuccessfully, that it be allowed to vote on the basis of its original $500,000 subscription even though it had paid but $200,000 of it and exhibited little intention of paying more.

Three weeks later, Forrest finally admitted defeat in this fight that had lasted half again as long as his wartime service. In a letter to the Memphis & Selma board of directors, he said he had come to believe the Shelby County court was "withholding the third installment of their subscription upon personal grounds to me, arising from their violent opposition to the subscription, notwithstanding the same was carried through my influence." He also cited the dissatisfaction of "many counties and towns along the road" because of his inability to negotiate the company's bonds in the nervous national financial atmosphere. For those reasons, he said, he believed "the interest of the company demands that I should retire from the position I have held as president and director since November 9, 1868."[20]

The Forrests had to vacate the Farrington house. A few weeks before they did, the Farrington family moved in.[21]

Part V

PENITENT

33

THE FARRINGTONS MAY have moved in as a last resort to encourage the Forrests to move out; no other explanation for the house's brief dual occupancy suggests itself. Later, though, the Farringtons recalled the interlude as a seemingly pleasurable glimpse into the domestic life-style of a famous man.

A relative eventually remembered hearing Mrs. Farrington say "what a gentle, lovely man General Forrest was. She said he . . . always helped Mrs. Forrest in things like setting the table." Mrs. Farrington also was quoted as saying Forrest "often would pitch right in and help with the family washing, and his spoken English was very correct — not at all like his written English." His lifelong affection for youngsters continued; the same relative said Mrs. Farrington had remarked on his particular kindness "to the children." In the evening, he would sit and talk with the Farringtons and, when asked about the war, would answer in characteristically direct style. The Farringtons' small son would pull his chair up next to Forrest's to listen to the stories, and when one was finished, the boy would reach up, put his hands on the bearded face, and beg to hear it again.[1]

If the Forrests were reluctant to leave the house, it is little wonder. The end of the railroad dream devastated the entire family; Willie had served as an assistant superintendent of the Memphis & Selma, listing that as his occupation in the 1870 census. When that census was taken (and the general was listing his own occupation as "R.R. President"), Willie, Willie's wife, and their ten-month-old daughter, Mary, were living under the same roof with the elder Forrests. Willie's family must have made other arrangements by late 1873; at least, no mention of them is made in connection with the Farrington place. After the collapse of the Memphis & Selma, Willie apparently took a job with the police department, because soon afterward he is randomly mentioned in a newspaper article as keeper of a station house in Memphis. His mother and father moved into a structure far different from the Farrington address. The next residence they occupied, so far as is known, was "a small but comfortable old-fashioned double log house, improvised from two cabins." Thus they finally came to occupy a house reminiscent of the one in which they set up housekeeping in Hernando in 1845, except that this one evidently had no clapboards covering the logs.[2]

Forrest's prospects now were bleak. Whereas in 1868 he had been one of the most influential among the ex-Confederate residents of Memphis, his unsuccessful rail venture and its accompanying moderation in his political views had now ravaged his popularity. Although he recently had become eligible to seek political office (because of post-Brownlow revisions in Tennessee law), he may have been doubtful of his capacity to be elected; there is no indication that he considered running. He sought instead to return to the theater of his glory. A few months before his resignation from the railroad, when the United States appeared on the verge of war in Cuba, he wrote a letter to an old adversary, Sherman, commander of the U.S. Army. Volunteering his services, he said he thought he could bring "1,000 to 5,000" of his former soldiers with him. Sherman replied a week later that he expected no war with Spain because "neither Government" wanted one, that if there was fighting most of it would be "afloat" with comparatively few land forces required for "the smaller task of occupation." He thus dashed any Forrest hope of galloping out of the Memphis & Selma morass onto a field where his military reputation, as well as the political influence it could engender, might be recouped. Sherman did treat his offer with a flattering respect, however. He informed Forrest that he had sent the letter on to the War Department with the endorsement that he regarded Forrest as "one of the most extraordinary men developed by our civil war, and were it left to me in the event of a war requiring cavalry, I would unhesitatingly accept his services and give him a prominent place. I believe now he would fight against our national enemies as vehemently as he did against us, and that is saying enough."[3]

A few days later the New York *Times* reprinted another Forrest letter, this one to the *Appeal*, saying that he had "received a large number of letters from men who were prominent Confederate officers and soldiers, volunteering to the Secretary of War, through me, their services to fight for the 'old flag,' in case of a war with Spain." To these volunteers, he said, he wished to say that "I hope and believe there will be no war, owing to the wise policy adopted by the distinguished soldier now at the head of the Government, but should it come, let us show our loyalty to the flag by standing ready to strike down any hand raised against it." With Grant being portrayed in Democratic Southern newspapers of the time as a Radical oppressor enslaving Southern whites in behalf of blacks, Forrest's reference to him as a "distinguished soldier," however true, may have raised eyebrows among ex-Confederates; it conformed, however, to his post-1868 course of political moderation.[4]

For at least five years now, he had condemned Klan-style violence, and six months following his resignation from the Memphis & Selma he took a strong and highly controversial public stand against the Klan itself. There had been a disturbance near the rural West Tennessee town of Trenton. Two white men reportedly attended a black barbecue, ate half of a barbecued pig, and then refused to pay for it. Blacks, insulted, armed themselves, formed a military-style company, fired on two whites (perhaps the two who ate the pig), and "manifested a strong desire to kill two or three citizens and fire and sack the town." Sixteen blacks were arrested and taken to the Trenton jail by a posse which had to defend itself from two attacks by masked whites en route. Later that night, around 1 A.M., "between fifty and one hundred masked men entered the town, rode up to the jail . . . and compelled the Sheriff" to hand over his keys. The masked party "then took the sixteen negroes from the jail," killing four and mortally wounding two others at the edge of town. "They then rode off with the other ten and are supposed to have killed them," one journalistic account reported. "Nothing has been heard from them since they left."[5]

Even the most conservative Memphis newspapers, although blaming the problem on the blacks, decried the crime and the national shame, with its specter of renewed Federal intervention, that had been brought on Tennessee. Editorialists once sympathetic to the Klan railed that the vigilantes should be caught and punished. In an August 28 Memphis "indignation meeting" attended by Jefferson Davis, Isham G. Harris, Forrest, and others, Forrest went a step beyond decrying the crime; he was quoted as saying that if he "were entrusted with proper authority he would capture and exterminate the white marauders who disgrace their race by this cowardly murder of negroes." A vitriolic response from the Trenton *Gazette* indicates how impossible it had become for him to distance himself from the grand-wizardship. A few days following publication of his remarks at the Memphis meeting, the *Gazette* defended the sheriff, jailer, and residents of Gibson County and attacked Forrest, the other speakers at the indignation meeting, and the *Appeal*.[6]

Two days later the *Gazette* bitterly denounced Forrest individually. Editorially inquiring "Why have none of the kuklux of Gibson County been arrested?," it then answered itself: "It is intimated around here that if there is a man in West Tennessee who knows how to ferret out the kuklux, that man lives in Memphis." The *Gazette* also published a reader's letter referring to Forrest by name and attacking his personal integrity, apparently in reference to the $66,000 Shelby County funds discrepancy in the affairs of the Memphis & Selma. The governor of Tennessee was now ex-Klansman John C. Brown, and the letter noted that the indignation meeting had called on Brown to "employ able counsel to repair at once to Trenton to investigate this outrage"; it went on to report that Brown had yet to send any of "these able lawyers who have had their carpetsacks packed for more than a week, awaiting orders from the governor for them to repair to Trenton, with General Forrest, to ride down the kuklux and bring them to justice." The *Gazette* editorialist purported to assume that "they want Forrest as a detective of the kuklux on the principle that 'it takes a thief to catch a thief,' " an idea "most heartily endorsed by our people, for they feel that if there is one man in all Tennessee who can ferret out the hiding-places of the kuklux, the general is that man."[7]

Any printed mention of his name in connection with the Klan was enough to get his previous reputation bandied around the North again. The Philadelphia *Bulletin* noted his remarks at the Memphis meeting and expressed doubt that "the black people of Tennessee will . . . readily accept General Forrest as their champion, or believe greatly in the sincerity of his expressions of detestation of the perpetrators of this fearful crime" because of his connection with Fort Pillow. Privately, in a letter in which he exhibited continuing proprietary interest in the affairs of the Memphis & Selma and a belated conversion to the merit of narrow-gauge rails, he informed E. W. Rucker, his former subordinate in both the Confederate army and the railroad firm, that "our Election paste off quiet and for the Democratic party by 4,000 majority." He added that the "Civil Rights Bil" had "Setled" the Republican Party in the South "if the white people will only do as we hav don all work together." By that he apparently meant remaining law-abiding, rather than following the Klan course he had repudiated. He seems to have felt that the South's future lay with the Democratic Party, particularly if the organization adopted his principle of the past five years and made itself a party of both races.[8]

Interestingly, soon after this latest round of ritualistic Northern condemnations, a Radical newspaper in Mississippi came to his defense.

Saying its proprietor had known Forrest since his earliest days as a Mississippi businessman, the editor of the Grenada *Republican* wrote that he had noticed "with regret" that Northern newspapers were being "very severe" in their reactions to his offer to help bring to justice the Gibson County "masked murderers." The *Republican* editor claimed to have known Forrest "almost from a beardless boy, when, as the keeper of a livery stable, he groomed his own horses, and developed even in that humble sphere some of those marked traits of character, which maturing in after years, made him one of the foremost men in the Confederate armies."

The newspaper regarded it as unfortunate that Northerners "cannot get over what they are pleased to term the atrocities of the Fort Pillow affair," presenting Forrest "to the world as a man of blood; without principle or honor. Here, we think, they are mistaken." While Forrest "may have committed acts, during his arduous campaigns, not strictly in accordance with military etiquette, or even compatible with the laws of justice . . . a man of his temperament would naturally overlook [such things] in pursuit of the one grand idea that absorbed all minor considerations—the success of the cause which he had espoused." Saying it believed "General Forrest is in full accord with the Democratic party," the Republican organ added that "notwithstanding, in the discharge of his duty, he would not be swayed in the least by party influences, but would exercise his official authority alike upon the Democrat and the Republican, looking wholly to his duty in the case as defined by the law"—and that he would have devoted his full energies to bringing the "Gibson County kuklux" to the bar of justice.[9]

In November Forrest possibly noted with a pang of envy the election to Congress of his old Confederate and Klan subordinate, George G. Dibrell; Dibrell had fought under him in 1862–63 and in June 1868 had been appointed by him, in an order written out in longhand by John W. Morton, to be assistant grand titan of a congressional district east of Nashville. Dibrell's mainstream political success may have caused his ex-commander to turn toward that arena once again himself. In January 1875 he was reported present in Nashville—along with such others as Isham G. Harris, Neill S. Brown, and Andrew Johnson—at the inauguration of Democratic governor James D. Porter. He apparently was taking a significant part in an election to replace retiring Senator Brownlow, whose political career finally was ending; in the race, Johnson was vying with Confederate generals Quarles and Bate, retiring governor Brown, and others. The Shelby County delegation was reported heavily for

Johnson, and Forrest was active in the interest of an *Appeal*-backed proposal to decide the issue in caucus to "avoid any apprehended disruption in the Democratic party." The caucus effort failed when Johnson and the other candidates refused to agree to it, and Johnson ultimately was elected after exhaustive balloting.[10]

An attempted reclamation of Forrest's local reputation appears to have begun in earnest about this time. In April 1875 he was named to the "Monumental collection committee" chaired by Harris in connection with the upcoming observance of Memorial Day, and two weeks later his name headed a published list of forty distinguished Memphians on the reception committee of a picnic to raise funds for "completing the monument over the Confederate dead at Elmwood Cemetery." Other members of that committee included Harvey Mathes, Gideon Pillow, and fellow reputed Klansmen Gallaway, George Gordon, J. J. DuBose and Luke E. Wright. On May 24 he led a 120-man escort in a huge Memphis Memorial Day parade, then sat on the speakers stand with forty others, including Jefferson Davis, Gallaway, Mathes, Pillow, Isham G. Harris, and Minor Meriwether. Meriwether's son Lee also was on the speakers stand, selected to recite a poem to the Confederate dead. He later remembered that Gallaway approached Forrest that day and suggested it was time to bury the hatchet raised so bitterly between him and his former grand scribe during their difficult days with the Memphis & Selma. Gallaway proposed that there "among the graves of our brothers . . . you and Col. Meriwether ought to shake hands. The boys here will sleep better in their graves if you two brave Confederates unite in peace as you did in war.' Another old Confederate approached father in the same spirit, and five minutes later the two men clasped hands over a Confederate grave. . . ."[11]

The handshake apparently prompted Minor Meriwether to write a note to Forrest the day after the celebration. That note, hand-delivered to Forrest by one of Meriwether's sons, prompted a reply dated May 26. It read:

> *Maj Miner Meriwether*
>   *Yours of yesterday by your son is to hand*[.] *I am glad that all diferances between us air satisfactory setled and I assure you that thair is no unkind feling towards you from me*[.] *I have all wase cherished a high reguard towards your Self and good lady and never felt unkindly towards your Self only when I felt you was using your*

influance against my Intrest[.] *hoping we may live and be as here to
fore good friends*[,]

*Yours Truly
N. B. Forrest*[12]

In a much less private letter three days later, Forrest accepted an
invitation from ex-Federals to attend and participate in another Elmwood
Cemetery ceremony: decoration of the graves of Union dead. The invitation came after former Federal soldiers had participated in an Elmwood
decoration of Confederate graves, and in the spirit of his surrender address
a decade earlier, he responded to this invitation by saying he "earnestly
request[ed] all ex-Confederate soldiers to join me in [the invitation's]
acceptance. . . ." The next day he led former Confederates in decorating
Elmwood's Federal headstones. The *Appeal* that morning carried a public
letter signed jointly by him and Gideon Pillow declaring that regardless
of their wartime differences with the Federals, "we must admit that they
fought gallantly for the preservation of the government which we fought
to destroy, which is now ours, was that of our fathers, and must be that
of our children. . . . Our love for free government, justly administered,
has not perished. . . ."[13]

Barely five weeks later, Forrest responded to a more striking gesture of
magnanimity by Shelby County blacks. Mathes, an eyewitness and fellow
honored guest, later would recall with smug contempt that "a number of
leading ex-Confederates" had been invited to attend a "grand barbecue"
at the fairgrounds some five miles east of Memphis, and that Forrest and
Gallaway [he doesn't mention himself] accepted in the wake of "many
overtures of peace and good-will between the races . . . from both sides."
The occasion, Mathes remembered, "was thought to be a good time to put
another plank in the bridge across the bloody chasm" as well as "incidentally to win the late serf and present colored brother over to the Democratic party." Nevertheless, Mathes wrote, the event's white visitors found
themselves "ill at ease, for they were aware that their [own] roasting was
near at hand." When his turn came, Forrest "made a strong commonsense
talk . . . and evoked some applause." When he sat down and, in apparent
relief, "began wiping his face with a big handkerchief, a beaming colored
damsel stepped forward to present him with a magnificent bouquet." In
response, Forrest rose and, "bowing very low, said that this unexpected
honor gave him great pleasure; that he had always admired the ladies, was
fond of flowers, and would accept these with many thanks. Yet he was

manifestly at a great disadvantage, and struggled through the ordeal with painful difficulty."[14]

Mathes wrote in 1902, after Southern blacks had been returned to a state of political vassalage, and his memory seems influenced by the casual arrogance with which blacks were taken for granted in the region by then. Even his version's facts are muddled, since he incorrectly dates the barbecue itself in 1868, when contemporary newspaper articles clearly show it to have occurred on July 5, 1875. According to the latter sources, Forrest, Gallaway, and Minor Meriwether—along with their sometime attorney, Pillow— accepted invitations to speak to a black gathering sponsored by the Independent Order of Pole-Bearers, and the tenor of these accounts seems decidedly different from Mathes's. The invitation's purpose, one of its leaders said, was to bring about "peace, joy, and union," and following a brief welcoming address a Miss Lou Lewis, daughter of an officer of the Pole-Bearers, brought forward flowers and assurances that she conveyed them "as a token of reconciliation and an offering of peace and good-will." The area's blacks must have been wearying of political, and all too often physical, warfare with their former masters. Across the state line southward, Mississippi was entering another bloody political campaign as Democrats violently prepared to reclaim the state government from Republicans.

The savvily Democratic Gallaway possibly had a hand in eliciting the invitations and roseate sentiments from the Memphis blacks; he had, after all, championed the formation of Democratic clubs by black leaders in 1868. Certainly he realized the potential political bonanza offered by the Pole-Bearers' overtures. The retirement of Grant from the presidency— with its bright chance for the first Democratic presidential victory since the war—was looming. Forrest, too, had plainly tired of the race struggle, as well as of his own reputation as Fort Pillow's Butcher and the Klan's grand wizard. Living in a city whose only barbers were blacks, he had made it a postbellum practice never to patronize the same one twice in succession, lest a plot be hatched to slit his throat.[15]

Now, after Miss Lewis handed him the flowers, he responded with a short speech that, in the contemporary pages of the *Appeal*, sounds more comfortable and less Democratically doctrinaire than the one of Mathes's memory. It evinces Forrest's familiar offhand vanity but also the racial open-mindedness that seemed to have been growing in him since 1868:

> *Ladies and Gentlemen—I accept the flowers as a memento of*
> *reconciliation between the white and colored races of the southern*
> *states. I accept it more particularly as it comes from a colored lady,*

for if there is any one on God's earth who loves the ladies I believe it is myself. (Immense applause and laughter.) . . . I came here with the jeers of some white people, who think that I am doing wrong. I believe I can exert some influence, and do much to assist the people in strengthening fraternal relations, and shall do all in my power to elevate every man—to depress none. (Applause.) I want to elevate you to take positions in law offices, in stores, on farms, and wherever you are capable of going. I have not said anything about politics today. I don't propose to say anything about politics. You have a right to elect whom you please; vote for the man you think best, and I think, when that is done, you and I are freemen. Do as you consider right and honest in electing men for office. I did not come here to make you a long speech, although invited to do so by you. I am not much of a speaker, and my business prevented me from preparing myself. I came to meet you as friends, and welcome you to the white people. I want you to come nearer to us. When I can serve you I will do so. We have but one flag, one country; let us stand together. We may differ in color, but not in sentiment. . . . Many things have been said about me which are wrong, and which white and black persons here, who stood by me through the war, can contradict. I have been in the heat of battle when colored men asked me to protect them. I have placed myself between them and the bullets of my men, and told them they should be kept unharmed. Go to work, be industrious, live honestly and act truly, and when you are oppressed I'll come to your relief. I thank you, ladies and gentlemen, for this opportunity you have afforded me to be with you, and to assure you that I am with you in heart and in hand. (Prolonged applause.)[16]

Seven weeks after the barbecue speech he replied jocularly to a letter from Aberdeen, Mississippi, a notorious center of past Klan activity, that requested assistance in acquiring a cannon with which to help Democrats prepare for the election the following November. On old Selma, Marion & Memphis Rail Road Co. stationery, apparently via the pen of a secretary (or perhaps Mary or Willie), he responded to prominent Aberdeen attorney Reuben Davis:

Dear Sir.

Your favor asking me to find you a cannon has been received, and have been looking around the city this morning, but am unable to procure one. Am promised one by a friend in Cincinnati.

*I will ship it on arrival. Would it not be as well to employ a
brass band to accompany the cannon: If so, I can order it from the
same place.*

*If you had applied 12 or 14 years ago, I could have furnished
you with almost any sort of a cannon. Go in—there is nothing like
fighting at the front. Wishing you all the success you may desire I
am Yours Very Truly,*

N. B. Forrest[17]

It may be that he took Davis's request as whimsical; the uncharacteristic
and undiluted tone of humor in his reply suggests as much. The request
was no joke, though. Soon afterward, a member of the Monroe County
Democratic Executive Committee purchased a cannon in Mobile and had
it transported to Aberdeen for service in the election campaign. Loaded
with blank charges, it was fired at Republicans on several occasions, and
on election day, November 3, was placed on the courthouse lawn to
prevent Radicals from voting. Apparently loaded more damagingly this
time, it reportedly drove Republicans into and across the Tombigbee
River, effectively ending Reconstruction in Monroe County. Aberdeen's
cannon apparently wasn't the only one used by Mississippi Democrats in
the 1875 election. On October 28 Democrats in Holmes County ordered
one from New Orleans for use in Lexington, Mississippi; they were told
by the prudent seller, however, that they themselves would have to
"provide ammunition." Forrest's own Democratic status was becoming
prominent enough again that by the next year (perhaps to appeal to some
blacks as well as ex-Confederates) he would be chairman of the party's
Shelby County Executive Committee, but a close reading of his letter
indicates no real intention on his part to conspire in any militaristic sense
with the Mississippians. The most serious-sounding portion of it recom-
mends that Davis "Go in" and fight "at the front," which may only have
been encouraging him to take an active part in the political fray; the humor
that goes before that recommendation, by contrast, indicates Forrest
didn't take the request for the cannon seriously. And he apparently didn't
send Davis a cannon.[18]

A major element in the 1875 waning of his warlike tendencies appears
to have been, finally, a recognition that his intelligence and industry had
only mired him in a morass of debt and litigation. The double log cabin
into which he had moved from the Farrington house sat on President's
Island in the Mississippi River, where he leased 1,300 acres and made
arrangements to work them with convicts; thus his last home was an

operating prison workhouse. The sole baronial feature of the place seems to have been a porch view of the Memphis waterfront four miles upstream. What was left of his energy he threw into yet another new start, setting his laborers the task of clearing fields for the growing season and cutting timber to supply the Memphis winter firewood market. On Memphis streets, he sometimes was sighted now in the plain clothes of a farmer; once he was observed buying a pair of boots for his grandson. His temper, however, had not mellowed. Under the stress of prolonged economic desperation, it may even have grown worse. He is reported to have drawn a pistol and threatened to "shoot . . . like a rat" a Memphis tailor who let moths damage a suit of his clothes. The next day, though, he returned to offer a shamefaced apology.[19]

Probably in late summer, he encountered on a street corner an old subordinate he had not seen in years: Raleigh R. White, onetime lieutenant colonel of the Fourteenth Tennessee Cavalry. The two greeted each other warmly, and Forrest asked White what he had been doing for a vocation in the postbellum years. "Preaching the Gospel of the Son of God," White stoutly replied. "What!" Forrest said in surprise. "I thought you were in South America or Europe. Tell me about yourself and your work."[20]

Years earlier, another officer-minister who served under him had met him in Memphis and reminded him of a war promise he had made to become a Christian when peace came; that time, his eyes flashing toward the uniforms of Federal occupation troops around them, he had growled a reply to the effect that there was too much un-Christian work still to do. This time he asked White to pray for him. The two stepped out of the street into a corner of the parlor of a bank and got on their knees. There White helped him perform for himself a rite that for five decades he had left mostly to his family's women.[21]

34

And every one that heareth these sayings of mine, and doeth them not, shall be likened unto a foolish man, which built his house upon the sand:

And the rain descended, and the floods came, and the winds blew, and beat upon that house; and it fell: and great was the fall of it.

—Matt. 7:26–27

ON THE EVENING of November 14, 1875, the Reverend George T. Stainback, minister of the Court Street Cumberland Presbyterian Church in Memphis, preached on the parable of the builders in Jesus Christ's Sermon on the Mount. Present as usual was Mary Ann Forrest, but beside her this night sat her husband. In those verses from the Book of Matthew, he saw all the withered fruit of his life's grand enterprises. At the service's end, he stopped at the church door and waited for Stainback to come out and bid a customary farewell to the flock. "He took my arm, and we passed [to] the pavement below," the clergyman, who had known Forrest for a quarter century, would remember two years later. At the sidewalk, Stainback said, Forrest suddenly leaned against a wall and his eyes filled with tears. "Sir, your sermon has removed the last prop from under me," he said. "I am the fool that built on sand; I am a poor miserable sinner." He looked "all shaken," recalled Stainback, who recommended that he study Psalm 51 to find spiritual relief. The next evening the minister visited him for a talk and a prayer, and after the latter, Forrest rose from his knees to say he felt "satisfied. All is right. I put my trust in my Redeemer."[1]

Not long afterward, when asked what had brought about his sudden abandonment of a lifetime of respectful nonacceptance of the faith, he replied with humor. "Why . . . it was perfectly simple," he said. "I was down on my plantation on the island and I took sick and I thought my last chance had come and I took it!" This explanation probably contained some grains of truth. The month before his confession to Stainback, he unexpectedly missed a reunion of his old Seventh Cavalry unit at Brownsville; Willie appeared instead, having apparently been sent as his father's substitute, and was chosen assistant grand marshal of the event.[2]

Forrest's health, which appears to have gradually worsened throughout the Memphis & Selma ordeal, became steadily more delicate as he faced a new growing season in the malarious fields of President's Island. Taking his strength for granted as always, he made characteristically large plans to recoup the appalling financial losses of his past decade. For one thing, he apparently sued the Memphis & Selma for the personal debts he had incurred on it, hiring Brigadier General John T. Morgan — a prominent Selma attorney who had fought under him and been connected with the railroad — to try to recover them. He also contracted with Shelby County for the use of some of its jail inmates in farming operations employing slave-style labor.

A glimpse into these enterprises was offered on May 5, 1876, by a newspaper whose reporter accompanied an inspection tour by representatives of the county grand jury. They were met by a shirtsleeved Forrest "at the landing in front of his door, where the steamboats dump off his freight when the water is up." He led the party first to his "small but very comfortable old-fashioned double log house" and then to "the quarters adjoining, occupied by the work-house prisoners when not at work in the fields." Inside a "strong fence" the visitors found a "main building . . . 120 × 24, divided off into five apartments" for (1) female prisoners, (2) white males, (3) the office and guardroom, (4) black males, and (5) a storeroom. There was also an L-shaped wing serving as a dining room and kitchen; behind that was a "bake-oven and laundry." East of this main building sat the stable, which contained forty-two stalls, "two cribs, a harness room, and a sleeping room for the guard. The stock is in excellent condition."

Forrest's contract with Shelby County for the labor of the prisoners dated from May 8, 1875, and was to run for five years. At the time of this inspection, he was employing seven guards and boarding "thirty-five white males and sixty black males, four white females and eighteen black females; total, 117." The reporter found that of the island's 6,000 acres, Forrest's operation covered nearly one-fourth, "of which 800 acres is cleared and in cultivation, or will be this summer, as follows: In cotton, 550 acres; corn, 150; millet, 30; Irish potatoes, 50; sweet potatoes, 10; garden, 3; promiscuous, 7. . . ." It was noted that Forrest thus far had "spent $20,000 in fixing up the place" and had realized no profit "except some wood he sold in the city. It will be remembered that he brought down the price from seven dollars to four dollars per cord last winter, and he will be in the market next season with 20,000 cords, which will keep the price down and be a public benefit." He was obligated to pay Shelby County "ten cents a day for all [prisoners] who are sent to him. This is a net gain, therefore, to the county of fifty cents a day, to say nothing of turnkeys, gas, guards and other expenses. . . ."[3]

Forrest continued to involve himself in civic and political events. On May 14 his name was atop a long list of those calling for a mass meeting of citizens in support of the proposed Robert E. Lee memorial statue in Richmond. As chairman, he called an August 2 meeting of the Shelby County Democratic Executive Committee. In September he was conspicuous at a reunion of the Seventh Tennessee Cavalry in Covington, constantly baring his head to a "scorching" sun in tribute to the occasion while getting around most of the time on horseback. Requested to make a speech, he complied from the saddle, sounding suddenly like a sentimental old man.[4]

Soldiers of the Seventh Tennessee Cavalry, Ladies and Gentlemen:
I name the soldiers first because I love them best. I am extremely
pleased to meet you here to-day. I love the gallant men with whom I
was so intimately connected during the war. You can hardly realize
what must pass through a commander's mind when called upon to
meet in reunion the brave spirits who, through four years of war and
bloodshed, fought fearlessly for a cause that they thought right, and
who, even when they foresaw as we did, that the war must soon close
in disaster, and that we must all surrender, yet did not quail, but
marched to victory in many battles, and fought as boldly and
persistently in their last battles as they did in their first. Nor do I
forget those many brave spirits who sleep coldly in death upon the
many bloody battle-fields of the late war. I love them, too, and honor
their memory. I have often been called to the side, on the battle-field,
of those who have been struck down, and they would put their arms
around my neck, draw me down to them, and kiss me, and say:
"General, I have fought my last battle and will soon be gone. I want
you to remember my wife and children and take care of them."
Comrades, I have remembered their wives and little ones, and have
taken care of them, and I want every one of you to remember them
too, and join with me in the labor of love.

Comrades, through the years of bloodshed and weary marches you
were tried and true soldiers. So through the years of peace you have
been good citizens, and now that we are again united under the old
flag, I love it as I did in the days of my youth, and I feel sure that
you love it also. . . . It has been thought by some that our social
reunions were wrong, and that they would be heralded to the North
as an evidence that we were again ready to break out into civil war.
But I think that they are right and proper, and we will show our
countrymen by our conduct and dignity that brave soldiers are
always good citizens and law-abiding and loyal people.

Soldiers, I was afraid that I could not be with you to-day, but I
could not bear the thought of not meeting with you, and I will
always try to meet with you in the future. And I hope that you will
continue to meet from year to year, and bring your wives and
children with you, and let them, and the children who may come
after them, enjoy with you the pleasure of your reunions.

The crowd gave him three cheers, and he seemed unable to tear himself
away. An *Avalanche* correspondent reported that after his remarks he

dismounted, mixed with the throng, and "listened to the remaining speeches with the greatest patience." Indulging in memories of the past must have been preferable to contemplating the present. The national political campaign of 1876 had turned out to be perhaps the bitterest in U.S. history, with Ohio Republican Rutherford B. Hayes pitted against New York Democrat Samuel J. Tilden in the battle to succeed Grant. The contest's high feeling—plus Klan-style Democratic intimidation that is estimated to have reduced Southern Republican vote totals by 250,000— resulted in a deadlock that threatened to precipitate a second civil war. The impasse continued for months as authorities tried to resolve critical, conflicting election totals in South Carolina, Louisiana, and Florida.[5]

Two of Forrest's closer associates, Isham G. Harris and John T. Morgan, had been elevated to the U.S. Senate in this election; Wade Hampton claimed victory in a disputed canvass for governor of South Carolina; and James Chalmers was elected to Congress from Mississippi. Chalmers, of course, had been second-in-command at Fort Pillow, a fact that raised bloody ghosts yet again. The New York *Times* proclaimed that if the votes in South Carolina, Florida, and Louisiana were certified in favor of Tilden, thus electing him over Hayes, the North—twelve years following Appomattox—would have lost the Civil War to the South: "it will be the sign of the subjugation of the nation by the rebels." The writer noted that a terroristic Democratic "shotgun policy" instituted in 1875 had transformed what shortly before had been the Radical Republican South into a conservative fiefdom where only the bravest Republicans reached the polls. Bloody campaigns were the norm in South Carolina, Florida, and Louisiana, and violent intimidation played a similar role in Mississippi, where the overwhelmingly black Sixth District ousted black congressman John Roy Lynch in favor of Chalmers. The *Times* correspondent took the opportunity to recount again at length some of the more sensational congressional testimony regarding Fort Pillow.[6]

The Hayes-Tilden deadlock and the fate of Radical Republican administrations in South Carolina, Florida, and Louisiana eventually were resolved in Washington with Senator John B. Gordon playing a large role. Gordon apparently helped forge a "bargain" under which the South agreed to certification of the election of Hayes on an understanding that the new President would evacuate the last Federal occupation troops from South Carolina, Florida, and Louisiana. This would remove Federal protection from those states' Reconstruction administrations, giving Gordon's friend Hampton the disputed South Carolina governorship and another Democrat, F. T. Nicholls, the governorship of Louisiana. This compromise completed the so-called "shotgun" political enterprise for which the Ku Klux Klan had been organized a decade before. The extended campaign of terror, led first by the Klan and then by myriad imitations or offshoots, swept the last troops of Federal occupation from the South, leaving the Southern Democratic power structure free to impose upon the region the white-supremacist program it desired. The New York *Times* had been proved essentially correct; even though Tilden had not been declared victorious over Hayes, the white South had nevertheless won its long struggle to begin the return of blacks to a status tantamount to their antebellum chains. In an economic sense, their new "freedom" would become worse than slavery, for with all Federal interference removed they soon would be allowed to vote only Democratic if at all—and this time there was no master charged with responsibility for providing them at least rudimentary shelter, food, and clothing.

The man who had had the ill-advised courage to become, however briefly, the regressive effort's supreme leader—"the last ruler of the South," as one biographer has chosen to term him—was to enjoy few of the victory's dubious fruits. For a brief period, as already noted, he chaired the local Democratic organization; subsequently he tried to remain involved in politics behind the scenes. But his strength was now ebbing badly. Although his fields on President's Island seem to have prospered, and thus to have promised eventual deliverance from debt, exposure to the elements there had greatly weakened him. The colds and other physical aggravations in recent years, possibly brought on by continual work in swampy terrain, turned into chronic diarrhea as he spent day after day supervising labor in President's Island's unhealthy atmosphere. By the spring of 1877 he was applying himself to farming and his other interests only intermittently, alternating these endeavors with stints at attempted rehabilitation. In April he appeared at Hot Springs, Arkansas, a fashionable site for restoration of health, in what the Hot Springs *Telegraph* described as an "apparently shattered condition." On May 5, a few days after the death of his old enemy Brownlow, the *Appeal* reported Forrest among such fellow Hot Springs guests as Congressman Chalmers and Jacob Thompson; it informed its readers he was "in very delicate health," confined to his rooms "mostly all day to-day . . . suffering . . . a general indisposition." In July he and his attorney, Senator John T. Morgan, were reported "among the distinguished guests" at a Fourth party near Nashville for an ex-Confederate unit, the Porter Rifles. Morgan "made an address, but, owing to ill health, General Forrest failed to respond to the call made by the Rifles and their friends."[7]

Around this time, if not before, Forrest instructed Morgan to drop the lawsuits he had instituted, saying he did not wish to leave Willie a legacy of legal warfare. He described himself as "broken in health and spirit," having "not long to live." His life, he reflected, had "been a battle from the start . . . a fight to achieve a livelihood for those dependent upon me in my younger days, and an independence for myself when I grew up to manhood, as well as in the terrible turmoil of the Civil War. I have seen too much of violence, and I want to close my days at peace with all the world, as I am now at peace with my Maker." Probably on this same trip to Middle Tennessee, he visited a onetime Confederate colonel Sevier who now was a professor at the University of the South at Sewanee. Sevier's son, then aged seven, remembered long afterward that the talk among his elders centered on the war and that Forrest appeared bored by the discussion. To escape it, he repeatedly went outside and spoke with the children. Informed that the seven-year-old had yet to learn to ride a horse, he called for one, along with a bridle and saddle, and several times, with great patience, reviewed the correct way to approach, bridle, saddle, mount, and sit the animal.[8]

A few days after the Fourth of July party of the Porter Rifles he arrived at Hurricane Springs near Tullahoma, where a reunion with some members of his wartime escort occurred — apparently to accommodate his wish to try the so-called "healing waters" of the place. He had written from Memphis to Charles W. Anderson, the aide who persuaded him to issue the eloquently conciliatory surrender address at Gainesville in 1865; he told Anderson that he was ill and contemplated "spending the hot summer months" at Hurricane Springs in "hope that the waters . . . would prove beneficial." If he did decide to go there, he added, he would enjoy seeing Anderson again, and upon arriving in early July he sent Anderson a note. Anderson left for Hurricane Springs the next day, and his stage was met there by a greatly changed Forrest. He had about him a new "mildness, a softness of expression, and a gentleness in his words that appeared to me strange and unnatural," Anderson later recalled. "At first I thought his bad health had brought about this change, but then I remembered that when sick or wounded he was the most restless and impatient man I ever saw":

Soon I told him . . . that he didn't appear to me to be the same man I used to know so well. He was silent for a moment, then . . .

halting suddenly, he took hold of the lapel of my coat and turned me squarely in front of him, and raising his right hand with that long index finger . . . extended, he said, "Major, I am not the man you were with so long and knew so well—I hope I am a better man. I've joined the Church and am trying to live a Christian life."

Anderson remained at Hurricane Springs several days, during which Forrest decided "that the water was not benefiting him, but he spoke hopefully of recovering his health." Mary Ann Forrest, however, was fearful. She told Anderson that her husband had "an unnatural appetite, and seemed always to crave food unsuited to him." As the three of them sat at the table awaiting breakfast one morning, Forrest, "with knife and fork in hand, started to help himself from one of the dishes brought in by the waiter." Mary Ann stopped him, saying, "Please don't eat that. Your breakfast has been prepared, and will be here in a few minutes." He put down his silverware, looked ruefully toward Anderson, and said, "Major, I know Mary is the best friend I have on earth, but sometimes it does seem that she is determined to starve me to death."[9]

He returned on July 27 to Memphis, where the *Appeal* claimed to find him "looking very much improved, we are happy to say, from his sojourn." If he indeed was improved, he didn't remain that way long. By August 10 some of the convicts who had been working on his farm were reported to have been moved to another one, and on August 14 he departed again, leaving Willie to attend a Seventh Cavalry reunion in Memphis. Two weeks later, the *Appeal* reported that "General Bedford Forrest is quite ill at Bailey Springs, Ala. He has been confined to his bed several days, and his condition is anything but encouraging." A physician, C. K. Caruthers, was called to consult with him there and later remembered the patient was "too feeble to mix with the crowd" or go to the dining area; he whiled away the hours, Caruthers said, playing cards on one of the galleries with Gallaway, Memphis congressman Casey Young, and "a steamboat captain." Once Caruthers was called to the Forrests' room, where he found Forrest in bed; a bedside table held "a Bible and a copy of 'The History of Forrest and His Men' by Lindsey."

The August 30 *Avalanche* carried a notice so grim that even the New York *Times* saw fit to reprint it. It noted that for months Forrest had "been afflicted with chronic diarrhea, and a malarial impregnation has brought on a combination of diseases which makes his case hopeless. . . . His life has been one wherein he became inured to exposure, and this gave him a confidence in his powers of physical endurance which perhaps was unfortunate." The item went on to report that on the President's Island plantation "he has given his farm work his strict attention. Often till 11 o'clock he would be out in the poisonous night air seeing to his stock" and giving "everything his personal supervision. The result is he lies now a shattered man on the verge of the grave. Beef tea is the only nourishment he can take, and he is gradually growing weaker and weaker."[10]

While he was at Bailey Springs, apparently, another prominent wartime associate arrived to pay his respects. General Joseph Wheeler, his graciously forgiving fellow cavalry commander, had not seen him for several years and could not help noticing the same "startling change" Anderson had observed. He looked "greatly emaciated . . . and the pale, thin face seemed to bring out in bolder relief than I had ever observed before the magnificent forehead and head." All the lines and "suggestion[s] of harshness had disappeared, and he seemed to possess . . . the gentleness of expression, the voice and manner of a woman." Once more, he tried to rally. On September 8 the *Appeal* quoted the Florence *Gazette* as reporting that he was "improving," and shortly afterward he wrote a letter to another old friend and ex–staff member, George W. Adair of Atlanta.

Bailey Springs, Sept. 15, 1877.

Capt. G. W. Adair:
  My Dear Sir: I have just persuaded my wife to write you a few lines. I have been lying here flat on my back for a month, unable to get up without help. I feel now that I am just passing out of a most terrible case of sickness, which has lasted me about 12 months. My disease has been inflammation of the stomach and bowels. I am too weak to walk about without help—only weigh about 120 pounds. My symptoms now are all gone, and the doctor thinks I will soon recover. My wife's health is unusually good. Willie has four fine children, and is planting with me just below Memphis. We have 800 acres in cotton, and 400 in corn. The crop looks very promising. I am endeavoring to raise all kinds of stock. My wife and myself send much love to Mrs. Adair, yourself, and all the children. Remember me kindly to . . . all the . . . escort who are with you, as well as any other friends that may inquire after me. Write soon, and direct your letter to this place. I am ever your true friend,

N. B. Forrest.[11]

Forrest may have been putting up a front to Adair. To an even closer friend, Gallaway, he seems to have been more frank, speaking "of his readiness to meet his God and his inward cravings for rest from the battle of life, which to him had been fierce and full of bitterness." He told Gallaway he was "extremely anxious to live for useful purposes and to make another fortune, which he saw in sight, for his wife and only son," but "to his confidential friends he invariably touched in the small hours the same Aeolian chord that murmured of failure, the nothingness of life, and death as a desire." The September 21 *Appeal* reported that he "is recovering and will soon be able to leave Bailey Springs," and a week later the newspaper described him as "rapidly recuperating" and soon to return home. On October 2 Forrest arrived back in Memphis and stayed at the home of his brother Jesse, who by now had become proprietor of what seems to have been Memphis's largest and finest livery stable. "General Forrest, though weak, is much improved and will rapidly recuperate," the *Appeal* said.[12]

Such lines were wishful thinking. Coming home from Bailey Springs on a train, he had had to "lean . . . upon the shoulders of friends as he dragged himself from the cars to the carriage," the *Avalanche* soon reported, and although he went from Jesse Forrest's house back to President's Island, it wasn't for long. His weight dropped to "scarcely more than 100 pounds," and the Reverend Stainback hurried to visit him. Stainback later recalled being brought from the river shore to the residence by two convicts, one of whom asked if he was "the preacher come to see the boss?" The minister said yes. "I hear he's very low, and that he may die," the convict said. "If he does, we will lose our best friend, sir." Inside the house Stainback found a man who knew his time was gone. Money and such stubborn lifelong vices as cursing and card playing seem to have been on his mind, and he talked about the debts he still owed on earth and elsewhere. "I've worked hard and may have killed myself," he told Stainback, "but in the providence of God I am in a way to discharge soon every obligation I owe to man." He "regretted" many things "said and done . . . in the presence of others" during his brief religious period that didn't look or sound very Christian, he told Stainback. Nevertheless, he said, " 'I want you to understand now that I feel that God has forgiven me for all'; and then, lifting up his emaciated hand, and pointing his finger to his breast, with a smile upon his face, said, 'Just here I have an indescribable peace. All is peace within. I want you to know that between me and . . . the face of my Heavenly Father, not a cloud intervenes. I have put my trust in my Lord and Saviour.' "[13]

Within days of Stainback's visit, the recent convert was returned to Jesse Forrest's house in Memphis, this time borne on a litter. Friends came to pay their respects. One was Minor Meriwether, with his son Lee. The ghostly appearance of the man who had loved children seemed to frighten the boy. "Don't be afraid, Lee," Forrest whispered. "Your father is my friend. Come closer. Let me look at you." The boy moved timidly to the bedside, and — decades afterward — remembered Forrest's hand running its thin fingers through his hair. "A fine boy, Colonel," the patient pronounced weakly. "I hope he will live to be a true son of the South." As they left Jesse Forrest's house that day, Lee Meriwether would remember later, his father's eyes suddenly brimmed with tears. "Lee," he said, "the man you just saw dying will never die. He will live in the memory of men who love patriotism, and who admire genius and daring."[14]

Jefferson Davis, a Memphian at the time, came by on the afternoon of October 29, but by then Forrest had slipped so far he seemed hardly to recognize the President of the tragically flawed nation whose labored and ultimately aborted birth had made his fame and ruined his life. Davis left, but Minor Meriwether returned to keep the death watch, and it was Meriwether who about 7 P.M. heard the patient speak his last coherent words. Unlike those of Lee, Jackson, and several other fellow Civil War titans, they did not concern a mind's fevered return to a scene of distant onslaught; his fantasy did not appear to have galloped back in time to the frustrations of Fort Donelson and Shiloh, the exhilaration of Brice's Cross Roads, the hounding of Abel Streight, or the maddened vaulting of the walls of Fort Pillow. Fighting had been so commonplace in his life that such military moments merely faded into the rest of the mosaic of struggle. All he sought in its final hour was succor in suffering his last defeat. Characteristically, though, the final words formed a command, a last assertion of his lifelong assumption of the right to tell others what to do.[15]

"Call my wife," he ordered. Then he died.[16]

Epilogue

THE *APPEAL* ANNOUNCED Nathan Bedford Forrest's death in front-page columns bordered in black. Shelby Countians whose elected representatives did so much to frustrate his postbellum dream arrived in mobs at his brother Jesse's door; admitted, they peered inside a casket at an "emaciated" corpse wearing the uniform of a Confederate lieutenant general. "Strange as it might appear to those ignorant of General Forrest's true character," the *Appeal* reported, the horde of visitants included "hundreds of colored men, women, and children [who] flocked to . . . ask . . . permission to view the remains. . . . [The blacks] manifested not only a deep interest in the proceedings, but evidenced a genuine sorrow in the death of the great soldier." On the morning of October 31 alone, the *Appeal* said, more than 500 blacks viewed the body; of that number, it felt constrained to add, "not a single one was heard to say anything . . . [not] in praise of General Forrest."[1]

The funeral procession was nearly two miles long. At the Court Street Cumberland Presbyterian Church "assembled thousands of persons, both white and black. The sidewalks, even the streets, were thronged and jammed with people and vehicles." Pallbearers included Jefferson Davis, Jacob Thompson, Governor James D. Porter, and Forrest military escort members Gallaway, J. B. Cowan, G. V. Rambaut, and Samuel Donelson, all of whom occupied carriages in the center of the procession. These followed a brass band, contingents of mounted ex-Confederates, and several lodges of the Independent Order of Odd Fellows. After the pallbearers came carriages of clergymen and a hearse drawn by four black horses, then the carriages of the family and of the mayor, city councilmen, and other city officials, details of policemen and firemen, and finally former soldiers on foot. At the grave in Elmwood Cemetery, the many floral arrangements reportedly included a clutch of wildflowers brought by a

Colonel John Donovan who had been handed them, he told someone, as his train stopped the day before at the platform of a little station in rural Alabama. "Take these to Memphis and place them on General Forrest's grave," said the thirteen-year-old girl who thrust them forward. "They are sent because General Joseph Wheeler's daughter loved him."[2]

Some others didn't. The New York *Times* published an obituary that was understatedly scathing. It noted, with some truth, that while Lee had been an example of the "gallant soldiers and dignified gentlemen" of refined Virginia, Forrest typified the "reckless ruffianism and cutthroat daring" of the Southwest's "rude border country." It reported that in the war's last days he was "considered by many to have been the most formidable cavalry commander then in the Armies of the South, but ... was ... essentially guerrilla-like in his methods of warfare" and hadn't the "scientific" daring of a Joe Wheeler. He was "so notoriously bloodthirsty and revengeful," the *Times* went on, that at the end of the war he had been expected to continue fighting guerrilla-fashion after the gentlemanly cavaliers surrendered. The *Times* chose not to mention his surrender address at Gainesville. It also did him what appears to have been a shameful injustice in a brief recapitulation of his 1868 challenge to Kilpatrick. The obituary inaccurately said Kilpatrick had "replied that he would not fight a duel, but if he ever met Forrest and the latter desired to do anything, he [Kilpatrick] would be ready." Then it added:

> *The outcome of this was that Forrest and Kilpatrick did meet somewhere in North Carolina, the latter going into the bar-room of the hotel where he was told Forrest was. Forrest was leaning against the bar. Kilpatrick brushed against him. Forrest looked up, recognized his enemy, turned and left the room, and that was the end of the matter.*

It seems noteworthy that this story appears not to have surfaced in time to be printed anywhere prior to Forrest's obituary—and that Kilpatrick, who must have been its source, never appears to have told it anywhere Forrest could have heard it. It is barely possible that Forrest, during his railroad associations with Kilpatrick's fellow Republicans, did encounter Kilpatrick in North Carolina and forwent the pleasure of killing him in the interest of business or national good feeling; given the preponderance of evidence over the span of his life (to say nothing of his 1868 inclination to fight Kilpatrick on horseback with sabers), the assumption that he feared Kilpatrick, which the *Times* clearly intended to imply, is ludicrous.

The obituary got to the meat of its message, though, by saying:

It is in connection with one of the most atrocious and cold-blooded massacres that ever disgraced civilized warfare that his name will forever be inseparably associated. "Fort Pillow Forrest" was the name which the deed conferred upon him, and by this he will be remembered by the present generation, and by it he will pass into history.

After giving considerable attention to that subject, it went on to observe:

Since the war, Forrest has lived at Memphis, and his principal occupation seems to have been to try and explain away the Fort Pillow affair. He wrote several letters about it, which were published, and always had something to say about it in any public speech he delivered. He seemed as if he were trying always to rub away the blood stains which marked him.[3]

Fort Pillow was indeed reprehensible, but possibly also unavoidable. To Americans who have lived through the ghetto riots of Watts and Newark, the assassinations of Martin Luther King and the Kennedys, and the brutality of Lieutenant Calley's Vietnam, the attitudes behind the excesses at Fort Pillow are all too familiar. It was neither the Civil War's first nor its last large-scale racial atrocity; but it was the only one studied by Congress — a Union Congress trying desperately and simultaneously to win both a civil war and a crucial presidential election conducted at that war's height — and it probably was chosen for national scrutiny because it occurred as that election was looming and because the officer in charge was the Confederacy's highest-ranking ex–slave trader. It is, however, the sort of thing that happens all too frequently in all wars, especially ones whose participants have different-colored skins; and its inevitability in 1864 was only heightened by the inherent pride of Southern whites reared in a slave society and the developing pride of freedom-tasting black slaves-turned-soldiers. In much less publicized and never investigated style (but publicly decried in July 1864 by black chaplain Henry M. Turner), black Union troops conducted massacres of their own that were just as horrible and just as understandable.[4]

For many who fought beside or against him, Fort Pillow could not dim the brilliance of his unschooled militarism, the intelligent obsession of his will to prevail. Sherman, who of all his enemies seemed to sense his essence best, proclaimed him "the most remarkable man" the war produced, with "a genius for strategy which was original and . . . to me incomprehensible.

... He seemed always to know what I was doing or intended to do, while I ... could never ... form any satisfactory idea of what he was trying to accomplish." Joseph E. Johnston, asked his opinion as to the greatest soldier of the war, quickly answered, "Forrest," adding that had the unlettered Memphian had the advantages of an education he would also have been the conflict's "great central figure." P. G. T. Beauregard remarked that Forrest's "capacity for war seemed only to be limited by the opportunities for its display."[5]

As years passed, the recognition of his genius grew. In 1892 General Viscount Wolseley, distinguished retired commander of Britain's armies, wrote a magazine profile of Forrest that prompted widespread Continental study of his amazing ability to win outnumbered. Wolseley pointed out that Forrest wasn't really a leader of cavalry but, rather, of mounted infantry: dragoons who used horses to reach their objectives and then generally dismounted to proffer pitched battle instead of riding away after a sally or two. "His mind was not narrowed by military apothegms learnt by rote," Viscount Wolseley wrote, adding that Forrest's "operations ... seem as if designed by a military professor, so thoroughly are the tactics ... in accordance with common sense and business principles." His method, Wolseley went on, was characterized by "invariable ... recklessness with which he dashed upon the enemy with his mounted men whenever and wherever he could do so, generally leading the mounted attack himself whilst his dismounted companies pressed the enemy's flanks and plied them with a storm of rifle bullets." The distinguished British officer noted that Forrest's "personal contempt [for] danger was remarkable," and his "practice" was "always to be in front of those he led." In that position "his acute judgment and power of perception" were usually able to "find out the enemy's weak point, and, having ascertained it, he forthwith went for it. ..."[6]

Today military thinkers consider Forrest not just, as the contemporary New York *Times* obituary said, the South's preeminent cavalryman at the end of the war but indeed the greatest American cavalryman of all time. His revolutionary fundamental philosophy was to attack even if severely outnumbered and, once the initiative had been thus seized, to pursue "with a brutal relentlessness that was extraordinary in military history"; this principle presaged the German blitzkrieg of 1940 and the airborne Allied behind-the-lines assaults of 1944. Revolutionary, too, was Forrest's frequent use of cannon as assault weapons accompanying his forward troops. His repeated division of forces in the presence of overpowering enemies, his cunning acumen for deceit and duplicity, his continual ability to make much of virtually nothing, his genius for employing whatever material was at hand, and his indomitable refusal to countenance effort less than total became lessons for later soldiers receiving the formal military education he never had the benefit of. His excellence as a raider was by no means all he left to military posterity, either. There were his incessant habit of assaulting from flanks and rear as well as head-on; his mastery of the psychology of the "skeer" and the intricate mechanics of inspiring it and keeping it operative; his instinctive grasp of the potentialities of terrain and weather; and such under-fire originality as the order to Morton's artillery to charge with neither cavalry nor infantry support at Brice's Cross Roads. The beating he administered to the Federals there was one of the worst ever suffered by a unit of the United States Army.[7]

The New York *Times* was also incorrect in forecasting that Fort Pillow would supply the infamy with which the subject of its obituary passed into history—or present-day history, at least. Fort Pillow, for better or worse, is all but forgotten. Forrest is more remembered for an even greater mistake: his brief leadership in galvanizing the terror of the Ku Klux Klan. Black students and their supporters in Tennessee periodically march to urge that statues of him be removed from public parks and college campuses, and, considering the information that history has provided them about him up to now, they are hardly to be blamed. When he was buried at Elmwood Cemetery on Hallowe'en day of 1877, both foes and friends had him where they wanted him. Racially responsible elements wished him to remain Fort Pillow Forrest and the grand wizard of the Ku Klux Klan as the quintessence of what can happen when Americans loose the worst features of their national character. Racial bigots likewise wished him to stand as a symbol of the same features, which they revered as sacred responses of patriotic Americans to unconstitutional tyranny.

Similar attitudes toward Forrest remain today. His relatively few biographers have focused mostly on his wartime courage and cunning, giving short shrift to the prewar world that formed his outlook and the postwar cataclysm during which it underwent a gradual but amazing change. Sometimes these biographers have labored to fit him into the classic and inappropriate mold of planter-aristocrat-cavalier. True, he did aspire, with some success, to the pretensions of that class before the war, but even then he had collisions with it, and during the war, serving under and alongside its representatives, he had many more. Much too individualistic to simply accept others' thinking in either war- or peacetime, he was an ex-frontiersman accustomed to dealing with whatever world he found, and after the war he pretty quickly evolved into a forward-looking businessman rather than a backward-looking slaveocrat. Unlike so many of his white Southern peers, after 1868 he seems to have become assured of the South's ability to survive and prosper in a nationally mandated New South in which whites and blacks mutually participated in the democratic process and society at large. Biographers have ignored the events and implications of his final eight years, the period during which he repeatedly heaped scorn upon the violent racial hatred and oppression epitomized by Fort Pillow and practiced by the Klan.

The reality is that over the length of his lifetime Nathan Bedford Forrest's racial attitudes probably developed more, and more in the direction of liberal enlightenment, than those of most other Americans in the nation's history. Born unprosperous and then made poorer by family financial misfortunes, he spent a deprived late youth and young manhood working a leased farm in an area where slave-owning plantation masters provided his sole models of wealth and attainment. Slave trading gave him a better opportunity than most to get to know blacks, from brand-new African importees to refined house servants. He became individually familiar with them by the thousands, and, because planters tended to sell their most troublesome slaves, he had to learn their traits well enough to see both the depth of their longing for liberty and the falsity of prevailing views that they were more animal than human. All available evidence, such as the bargain to free his wartime teamsters and the Klan's early adjurations against indiscriminate harming of blacks, indicates that even during his worst scourgings of them he personally regarded them as people, not simply the "property" of antebellum and Confederate law. The consummate realist, a man who seized upon whatever materials and conditions his world gave him, he embraced the Klan as a weapon in a savage fight for individual and sectional survival — and thrust it away soon after he saw that it injured, instead of aided, the best interests of the South and the nation.

It can be argued that these actions were closely entwined with his own economic self-interest during the railroading days, but that argument is harder to raise against his 1874 threat to exterminate the killers of the Trenton blacks and his similarly public assertion in 1875 that blacks should be allowed entry into the profession of law and anywhere else they were capable of going. Even the Great Emancipator, another Southerner born in a log cabin, never said that, and Forrest had to have been fully cognizant of the import of his words; he knew better than Lincoln and most other people of his time that, given a fair chance, blacks were capable of going anywhere anyone else could. He permitted no personal or political prejudice to keep him from advocating any measure he felt necessary to build up the whole South, white and black. Had more of his peers shared his vision and willingness to accept developing postbellum social reality on its own terms, the South might have achieved its present integration of free and equal blacks a century before the fact.

Both his admirers and his detractors, however, rushed to bury with his body all memory of his many postbellum departures from doctrinaire Southern Democratic–Conservatism. Brandishing his hallowed name and principles he had disowned, the Klan came back to life a half century or so after its initial demise, apparently inspired by a movie. *The Birth of a Nation*—D. W. Griffith's 1915 film canonizing the original Klan as a savior of constitutionalism battling Reconstruction's perversion—prompted the rise of another, and worse, Invisible Empire. Members of an Atlanta lynch mob styling itself the Knights of Mary Phagan, having recently hanged a Jew they mistakenly thought had murdered a young female factory worker, joined with a group led by ex-minister William J. Simmons in scaling Stone Mountain—where after nightfall, in sight of downtown Atlanta, they lit the first of the Klan's numberless crosses of fire. Thus rose the Knights of the Ku Klux Klan, which enlarged upon the bigotry of its predecessor by espousing hatred for not only blacks but Jews, Catholics, new waves of European immigrants pouring into the United States, and, in short, every nonwhite, non–Anglo-Saxon, or non-Protestant American. Spreading like wildfire, it reached an estimated membership of 4,000,000 in the 1920s, at which time its violence finally began to earn it the condemnation of responsible society. The Forrest name continued to be associated with it, and on more than an honorary basis.

Following the general's death, executors Jesse and Willie Forrest petitioned the Shelby County Court to permit his widow to continue operating the President's Island prison farm. The petition said the place's buildings had been destroyed by fire, the crops had incurred huge losses because of overflows of the Mississippi, and the estate of the deceased—who had held such high hopes of extricating himself from debt—was "insolvent," unable to pay the county several thousand dollars owed for using its convicts. The county court granted the petition, by terms of which Mary Ann Forrest agreed to repay the county the amount owed by her husband, a sum possibly supplied by the prosperous Jesse. Although the petition gives no indication of it, the farm probably was to be operated by Willie, while Mary retreated again into the background she had occupied most of her life. Dying in 1893, she was buried beside her husband.[8]

Willie Forrest eventually became a quietly successful railroad and levee contractor who, according to his daughter Mary, did not attend Confederate reunions or discuss the great conflict in which he had been wounded three times and shared the experiences of his famed father. Rather eerily, he is said to have died after a stroke suffered in 1908 as he sat in the Memphis audience of a stage adaptation of Thomas Dixon's *The Clansman,* the novel on which *The Birth of a Nation* was based. Reportedly, Willie was stricken with paralysis of his left side at the moment of the appearance onstage of an actor playing his father.[9]

One of Willie's children, a second Nathan Bedford Forrest, first worked with his father in the railroad and levee business, then sold insurance, and at some point spent five years in Alaska prospecting and mining for gold. Around 1919, after being highly active in the Sons of Confederate Veterans, he moved to Atlanta as aide to neo-Klan leader William J. Simmons; he went on to head Nathan Bedford Forrest Klan No. 1, which was to the new Invisible Empire what the first Pulaski den had been to the original one. Having served as grand dragon of Georgia and then as the organization's national secretary for five years, he died in Florida in 1931 of a paralytic stroke.[10]

The last Nathan Bedford Forrest was Army Air Corps Brigadier General Nathan Bedford Forrest III, the first American general to die in European combat during World War II. Son of the neo-Klansman and father of three daughters, the final male Forrest of his great-grandfather's direct line commanded twenty-six B17's in a 1943 bombing run over Kiel, Germany — where, with two of his aircraft's four engines disabled by German fire, he was its last man aboard to parachute into the Baltic Sea. His body, which washed ashore near the German town of Wiek, now lies in Arlington National Cemetery.[11]

NOTES

1. John A. Wyeth, *Life of General Nathan Bedford Forrest* (New York, 1899), p. 621.

2. Ibid., p. 623.

3. *War of the Rebellion: A Compilation of the Official Records of the Union and Confederate Armies* (Washington, D.C., 1890–91) [hereafter referred to as *O.R.*], ser. 1, vol. 39, pt. 2, pp. 121, 142; Robert S. Henry, *"First with the Most" Forrest* [hereafter referred to as Henry 1] (Indianapolis, 1944), pp. 536–37; Wyeth, p. 635.

4. Richard Taylor, *Destruction and Reconstruction* (New York, 1879), p. 200; Wyeth, p. 644.

5. Albert T. Goodloe, *Confederate Echoes* (Nashville, 1907), p. 179.

6. Robert S. Henry, *As They Saw Forrest* (Jackson, Tenn., 1956) [hereafter referred to as Henry 2], p. 93.

7. Henry 1, p. 350.

8. *O.R.*, ser. 1, vol. 32, pt. 1, p. 560.

9. Wyeth, p. 266.

10. Henry 1, p. 143.

11. Ibid., p. 21; Henry Watterson of the Chattanooga *Rebel*, the Atlanta *Daily Southern Confederacy*, and the Montgomery *Daily Mail*, George W. Adair of the Atlanta *Daily Southern Confederacy*, and M. C. Gallaway of the Memphis *Avalanche* were all Forrest staff members at various times.

12. Henry 2, pp. 292–93.

13. J. Harvey Mathes, *General Forrest* (New York, 1902) [hereafter referred to as Mathes 2], p. 383.

14. J. Cutler Andrews, *The South Reports the Civil War* (Princeton, N.J., 1970), p. 474, quoting Montgomery *Daily Mail*, November 26, 1864.

15. Wyeth, p. 628.

16. *Report of the Joint Select Committee to Inquire into the Condition of Affairs in the Late Insurrectionary States*, 2nd Session, 42nd Congress, 13 vols.

(Washington, D.C., 1872) [hereafter referred to as *Ku Klux Report*], vol. 13, p. 24; Lucy Leffingwell Cable Bikle, *George W. Cable, His Life and Letters* (New York, 1928), p. 20.

17. Henry 1, p. 26, quoting Lafcadio Hearn, *Occidental Gleanings* (New York, 1925), p. 148.

PART I: Frontiersman

I

1. Wyeth, pp. 19–20.
2. Henry 1, p. 25; *American Eagle*, Fort Pickering, Tennessee, March 21, 1845, p. 2.
3. General Thomas Jordan and J. P. Pryor, *The Campaigns of Lieutenant Gen. N. B. Forrest and of Forrest's Cavalry* (New Orleans and New York, 1868), pp. 23–24; Wyeth, p. 18; Mathes 2, pp. 11–12; Henry 1, p. 24.
4. Mathes 2, p. 14; Henry 1, p. 25; ibid.; *Confederate Veteran*, vol. 20, p. 210.
5. Elizabeth M. Curlee, "The *Phenix*: Hernando, Mississippi, 1841–46" (M.A. thesis, University of Mississippi, 1970), p. 103; Brian Steel Wills, *A Battle from the Start: The Life of Nathan Bedford Forrest* (New York, 1992), p. 23.
6. Henry 1, p. 25.

2

1. Jordan and Pryor, p. 25; Buelah Henry Anderson et al., comps. and publs., *John and Esther Houston Montgomery, 1719–1973* (Maryville, Tenn., 1974), pp. 73–74; Erick D. Montgomery, "The Montgomery Family of Franklin County," *Franklin County* (Tenn.) *Historical Review* (July 1978), pp. 96–97, 107.
2. DeSoto County Chancery Clerk's records, Book H, pp. 304–05; Montgomery, p. 107; DeSoto County Chancery Clerk's records, Book G, pp. 377–78; Book H, pp. 53–54, 423, 443–44.
3. Ibid., Book H, pp. 43–44.
4. Jordan and Pryor, p. 18; Bedford County Register's records, Book C, pp. 486–87, 488–89.
5. Wyeth, p. 4.
6. Jordan and Pryor, p. 19; Wyeth, p. 13.
7. Wyeth, p. 14; ibid., pp. 14–15; Andrew Lytle, *Bedford Forrest and His Critter Company* (New York, 1931), pp. 14–15.
8. Jordan and Pryor, p. 18; Wyeth, p. 2; Bedford County Register's records, Book W, pp. 34–35, Book BB, pp. 453, 175; Jordan and Pryor, p. 34; Beck Family Cemetery names and headstone inscriptions, Tippah County Library, Ripley, Miss.

9. Mathes 2, p. 10; Wyeth, pp. 11–12.
10. Wyeth, p. 5; Bedford County Register's records, Book W, p. 153, Book U, p. 58, Book BB, p. 19, Book DD, p. 109.
11. Wyeth, pp. 9–10.
12. Ibid., p. 15; Mathes 2, p. 4; Lytle, p. 14; Jordan and Pryor, p. 21.
13. Wyeth, pp. 15–16.
14. Jordan and Pryor, pp. 20–21.
15. Ibid., pp. 21–22.
16. Ibid., p. 22.
17. Lytle, p. 20.
18. Curlee, p. 94; Hernando *Phenix*, Dec. 31, 1842.
19. Lytle, p. 20.
20. Jordan and Pryor, p. 25.

3

1. Henry 1, p. 26.
2. DeSoto County Chancery Clerk's records, Book H, p. 49.
3. Ibid., pp. 43–44.
4. Jordan and Pryor, p. 23.
5. Montgomery, p. 98; DeSoto County Census of 1850, p. 368.
6. Lytle, p. 23; Jordan and Pryor, p. 25.
7. Curlee, p. 103; DeSoto County *Times*, August 14, 1986, Sect. D, p. 3; reprinted from North Mississippi *Times*, March 29, 1879.
8. Ibid.
9. Wyeth, p. 626.
10. Frederic Bancroft, *Slave Trading in the Old South* (Baltimore, 1931), p. 245; Kenneth M. Stampp, *The Peculiar Institution: Slavery in the Antebellum South* (New York, 1956), p. 268.
11. Bancroft, pp. 180–81, 141.
12. Jordan and Pryor, p. 25.

PART II: Slave Trader

4

1. Shelby County Register's records, Book 42, p. 163.
2. Jordan and Pryor, pp. 27–29.
3. Ibid., p. 27.
4. *Goodspeed's History of Shelby County, Tennessee,* reprinted from *Goodspeed's History, 1887* (Nashville, 1974), p. 872; Bancroft, p. 280.
5. *Goodspeed*, p. 865.
6. Gerald M. Capers, Jr., *The Biography of a River Town* (Memphis, 1966), p. 78; J. P. Young, *Standard History of Memphis* (Knoxville, Tenn., 1912),

p. 92; *Goodspeed*, p. 872; Capers, p. 108; U.S. Census, 1860, Introduction, pp. xxxii, 467; O. F. Vedder, *History of the City of Memphis and Shelby County, Tennessee* (Syracuse, N.Y., 1988), p. 193; Young, p. 89.

7. Ibid., pp. 75–76, 97; *Goodspeed*, p. 875.
8. Bancroft, p. 318; Stampp, p. 257; Daniel R. Hundley, *Social Relations in Our Southern States* (New York, 1860), pp. 139–42.
9. Stampp, p. 260.
10. Shelby County Register's records, Book 16, p. 468.

5

1. *Twyman's Memphis Directory & General Business Advertiser, for 1850* (Memphis, Tenn., 1849); Bancroft, pp. 250, 265.
2. Shelby County Register's records, Book 16, p. 125; Chicago *Tribune*, May 4, 1864, p. 3.
3. Shelby County Register's records, Book 15, p. 625.
4. Horatio J. Eden, *Diaries, Memoirs, Etc.*, Tennessee State Library and Archives, pp. 4–5.
5. Henry 1, p. 26.
6. Wyeth, pp. 20–21.
7. Ibid.
8. George P. Rawick, ed., *The American Slave: A Composite Autobiography* (Westport, Conn., 1972), vol. 7, p. 29.
9. Bancroft, p. 263.
10. Ibid., pp. 42, 208, 202.
11. Ibid., pp. 210, 321–22.
12. Stampp, pp. 266, 259.
13. Eden, pp. 4–5, 3–4.
14. Louis Hughes, *Thirty Years a Slave* (Milwaukee, 1897), pp. 92–93.
15. Bancroft, pp. 198–99.
16. Shelby County Register's records, Book 18, p. 249.
17. Memphis *Daily Appeal* [hereafter referred to as *Appeal*], July 4, 1854, p. 3.

6

1. *W. H. Rainey & Co.'s Memphis City Directory and General Business Advertiser for 1855–6.*
2. Shelby County Register's records, Book 17, p. 639, Book 18, p. 105.
3. Bancroft, pp. 77–78; Leslie Howard Owens, *This Species of Property: Slave Life and Culture in the Old South* (New York, 1976), pp. 37, 156, 160.
4. Ibid., p. 339; Bancroft, pp. 77, 340.
5. Eugene D. Genovese, *Roll Jordan, Roll: The World the Slaves Made* (New

York, 1974), pp. 462, 464; Frances A. Kemble, *Journal of Residence on a Georgian Plantation in 1838–1839* (reprint ed., New York, 1961), p. 122.

6. Bancroft, pp. 85–86, 87.
7. Ibid., pp. 80–81.
8. Nathan Bedford Forrest Collection, Memphis Public Library.
9. Shelby County Register's records, Book 21, p. 624.
10. Ibid., Book 23, pp. 45, 48, Book 39-1, p. 432.
11. Bancroft, pp. 317, 318–19.
12. *Goodspeed*, p. 1056; Shelby County Register's records, Book 26, p. 238; *Appeal*, Aug. 4, 1858, p. 2.
13. Shelby County Register's records, Book 29, p. 585, Book 27, p. 260, Book 28, pp. 57, 126, 470, and Book 30, pp. 247, 506.

7

1. *Appeal*, May 24, 1857, p. 2.
2. Ibid., May 26, 1857, p. 4.
3. Ibid., April 7, 1858, p. 2.
4. Bancroft, p. 256; *Appeal*, May 30, 1857, p. 2, and June 25, 1857, p. 3.
5. Ibid., June 26, 1857, p. 2, June 28, 1857, p. 2.
6. Ibid., June 27, 1857, p. 3.
7. Bedford County Register's records, Book DD, p. 204; Jordan and Pryor, p. 18.
8. *Appeal*, June 28, 1857, p. 3, June 27, 1857, p. 3.
9. Ibid., April 7, 1858, p. 3.
10. Bancroft, p. 255–56; Memphis *Eagle & Enquirer*, April 11, 1858.
11. Hughes, pp. 91–99.
12. *Appeal*, June 22, 1858, p. 2, June 27, 1858, p. 2.

8

1. *Appeal*, July 10, 1858, p. 2.
2. Ibid., July 2, 1858, p. 2, July 7, 1858, p. 2.
3. Ibid., July 21, 1858, p. 2.
4. Ibid., Sept. 8, 1858, p. 3; Capers, p. 128; *Appeal*, June 8, 1859, p. 3.
5. Ibid., August 4, 1858, p. 2.
6. Ibid., December 23, 1858, p. 3.
7. Ibid., March 23, 1859, p. 3.
8. Ibid., October 5, 1858, p. 3, October 7, 1858, p. 3, April 20, 1859, p. 3, August 8, 1860, p. 3; Jordan and Pryor, p. 34.
9. *Appeal*, September 8, 1858, p. 3; October 20, 1858, p. 3.
10. Ibid., March 23, 1858, p. 3.

11. Ibid., April 8, 1859, p. 3, June 11, 1859, p. 3, July 1, 1859, p. 3.

12. Ibid., August 2, 1859, p. 2.

13. Shelby County Register's records, Book 33, p. 623, Book, 34, pp. 97, 85, 442; Coahoma County, Miss., Chancery Clerk's records, Book G, p. 170; Phillips County, Ark., Chancery Clerk's records, Book G, pp. 494, 496; Shelby County Register's records, Book 35, p. 343, Book 40-1, pp. 581, 135.

14. *Memphis City Directory for 1859,* compiled by Tanner, Halpin & Co.; *Williams' Memphis Directory, City Guide, and Business Mirror,* vol. 1, 1860, Cleaves & Vaden.

15. Warren County, Miss., Register's records, Books AA and BB; Bancroft, p. 311.

16. Ibid., p. 264.

17. *Appeal,* September 9, 1859, p. 3, September 22, 1859, p. 3.

18. Ibid., September 28, 1859, p. 3, September 29, 1859, p. 3.

19. Ibid., October 30, 1859, p. 3.

9

1. *Appeal,* January 14, 1860, p. 3.

2. Ibid.; Bancroft, p. 263.

3. *Appeal,* February 8, 1860, p. 3.

4. Ibid., July 11, 1860, p. 3.

5. Ibid., August 3, 1860, p. 2, August 8, 1860, p. 3.

6. Ibid.

7. Ibid., August 11, 1860, p. 3.

8. Ibid., August 22, 1860, p. 3, September 11, 1860, p. 3.

9. Memphis *Daily Avalanche* [hereafter referred to as *Avalanche*] August 6, 1860, p. 3, August 15, 1860, p. 2.

10. Jordan and Pryor, p. 40; Coahoma County Chancery Clerk's records, Book G, p. 559; ibid., October 26, 1860, p. 1.

11. Shelby County Register's records, Book 39-1, p. 29, Book 36, p. 548, Book 39-2, p. 29; Warren County, Miss., Chancery Clerk's records, Book BB, p. 519.

12. Tennessee Census of 1860, mislabeled "W. B. Forrest"; Shelby County Register's records, Book 41-1, p. 96; Coahoma County Chancery Clerk's records, Book 6, p. 559.

13. Phillips County, Ark., Chancery Clerk's records, Book P, pp. 494, 496; Wyeth, p. 8; Henry I, p. 474.

14. Clarksdale (Miss.) *Press Register,* July 21, 1984.

15. Jordan and Pryor, p. 35; Wyeth, p. 22; Clarksdale *Press Register,* July 21, 1984.

10

1. *Avalanche,* January 21, 1861, p. 2.
2. Ibid., March 4, 1861, p. 3.
3. Thomas Harrison Baker, *The Memphis Commercial Appeal* (Baton Rouge, 1971), p. 75.
4. Coahoma County Chancery Clerk's records, Book G, p. 559; *Avalanche,* March 4, 1861, p. 3.
5. Ibid., April 28, 1861, p. 4.
6. Shelby County Register's records, Book 49, p. 596; Jordan and Pryor, p. 40.
7. Henry 1, p. 31.

PART III: Soldier

11

1. Henry 2, p. 143.
2. Wyeth, p. 23; *Southern Historical Society Papers,* vol. 7, p. 455; *Avalanche,* July 23, 1861, p. 2.
3. Ibid., p. 3; Gilbert R. Adkins, "Isham G. Harris: Faithful to the Truth As He Saw It," *Franklin County* (Tenn.) *Historical Review,* vol. 16, no. 2, 1985, p. 104.
4. *Avalanche,* July 25, 1861, p. 3, July 26, 1861, p. 3.
5. Jordan and Pryor, p. 41. These authorized biographers date this activity as mid-July, but either it occurred two or three weeks later or Forrest was engaging in it before he received his orders; Wyeth, p. 25; Jordan and Pryor, p. 42.
6. Ibid., pp. 42–43.
7. *Avalanche,* Aug. 26, 1861, p. 2.
8. Jordan and Pryor, p. 43; Henry 1, p. 34; Wyeth, pp. 26, 27.
9. *O.R.,* ser. 1, vol. 4, p. 513.

12

1. *O.R.,* ser. 1, vol. 4, p. 551.
2. Jordan and Pryor, p. 49.
3. *O.R.,* ser. 1, vol. 4, p. 549; Jordan and Pryor, pp. 44–45, 45–46.
4. Ibid., p. 49.
5. Henry 1, p. 43; Wyeth, p. 51; Jordan and Pryor, p. 47.
6. *O.R.,* ser. 1, vol. 7, pp. 65, 62–63.
7. Ibid., pp. 66, 62–63, 65–66; Jordan and Pryor, p. 53; *O.R.,* ser. 1, vol. 7, p. 64.
8. Jordan and Pryor, pp. 53–54.
9. Wyeth, p. 35.

10. Wills, p. 125; Wyeth, p. 47.
11. *O.R.*, ser. 1, vol. 7, pp. 384–85; Jordan and Pryor, p. 74.
12. *O.R.*, ser. 1, vol. 7, p. 385.
13. Jordan and Pryor, p. 83; Henry 1, p. 55; Jordan and Pryor, p. 83.
14. *O.R.*, ser. 1, vol. 7, p. 295.
15. Ibid., p. 386.
16. Ibid., pp. 296, 295.
17. Ibid., p. 386.

13

1. *O.R.*, ser. 1, vol. 7, pp. 386–87.
2. Jordan and Pryor, pp. 100, 101.
3. Ibid., p. 101.
4. Ibid., p. 102.
5. *O.R.*, ser. 1, vol. 7, p. 430; Jordan and Pryor, p. 103.
6. Ibid., p. 104; *O.R.*, ser. 1, vol. 7, p. 430; Jordan and Pryor, p. 104.
7. Wyeth, p. 74; Jordan and Pryor, p. 106.
8. Henry 2, pp. 56–57.
9. *O.R.*, ser. 1, vol. 10, pt. 1, p. 454.
10. Henry 2, p. 59.
11. Ibid., p. 60.
12. Jordan and Pryor, pp. 127–28; *O.R.*, ser. 1, vol. 10, pt. 1, pp. 437–43; Henry 2, p. 61.
13. Ibid.; Jordan and Pryor, pp. 133–35; *O.R.*, ser. 1, vol. 10, pt. 1, pp. 550–51.
14. Wyeth, p. 77.
15. Ibid., pp. 77–78; Jordan and Pryor, p. 137.
16. *O.R.*, ser. 1, vol. 10, pt. 1, p. 640.
17. Jordan and Pryor, pp. 146–48; Mathes 2, p. 60.
18. *O.R.*, ser. 1, vol. 10, pt. 1, pp. 923–24.
19. Jordan and Pryor, p. 148; Henry 1, p. 82; Jordan and Pryor, p. 149.
20. James A. Ramage, *Rebel Raider: The Life of General John Hunt Morgan* (Lexington, Ky., 1986), pp. 82–83.

14

1. Henry 1, p. 82.
2. Henry 2, pp. 287–88.
3. Jordan and Pryor, p. 159; Henry 1, p. 83; Alfred Roman, *Military Operations of General Beauregard* (New York, 1884), vol. 1, p. 402.
4. Jordan and Pryor, pp. 159, 173.
5. Ibid., p. 161; *O.R.*, ser. 1, vol. 16, pt. 1, p. 775.

6. Ibid., p. 810.
7. Jordan and Pryor, pp. 162–63, 173.
8. Wyeth, p. 85.
9. *O.R.*, ser. 1, vol. 16, pt. 1, p. 802.
10. Ibid., pp. 804, 803, 804.
11. Henry 1, p. 482; Wyeth, pp. 90, 91.
12. Ibid.
13. *O.R.*, ser. 1, vol. 16, pt. 1, pp. 802, 810.
14. Ibid., pp. 808–09, 810–11.
15. Jordan and Pryor, p. 171.
16. *O.R.*, ser. 1, vol. 16, pt. 1, p. 811.
17. Ibid.
18. Ibid., p. 796; Jordan and Pryor, p. 172.
19. *O.R.*, ser. 1, vol. 16, pt. 1, pp. 811, 809.
20. Ibid., pp. 806–07; Jordan and Pryor, p. 170.
21. New York *Times*, Sept. 14, 1868, p. 4, quoted in Wills, p. 77; quoted in Wills, p. 77.
22. Wyeth, pp. 91–92.

15

1. John Watson Morton, *The Artillery of Nathan Bedford Forrest* (Nashville, 1909), pp. 45, 46–47.
2. *O.R.*, ser. 1, vol. 20, pt. 2, p. 435.
3. Ibid., vol. 16, pt. 2, pp. 234, 759; Wills, p. 80; *O.R.*, ser. 1, vol. 16, pt. 2, p. 770.
4. Ibid., pp. 848–49, 856, 863–64, 868.
5. Ibid., p. 877; Jordan and Pryor, p. 185; *O.R.*, ser. 1, vol. 16, pt. 2, p. 876.
6. Ibid., pp. 918, 924, 931, 934, 931.
7. Ibid., vol. 17, pt. 1, p. 420; Wills, p. 84; *O.R.*, vol. 17, pt. 1, p. 420.
8. Ibid., pp. 404, 411.
9. Morton, pp. 45–46.
10. *O.R.*, ser. 1, vol. 17, pt. 1, p. 592; Morton, p. 47; Henry 1, p. 108; *O.R.*, ser. 1, vol. 17, pt. 1, pp. 598, 554–55.
11. Ibid., pp. 598, 594.
12. Jordan and Pryor, p. 201.
13. *O.R.*, ser. 1, vol. 17, pt. 1, pp. 594, 567–68; Jordan and Pryor, p. 205.
14. *O.R.*, ser. 1, vol. 17, pt. 1, p. 596, 599; Jordan and Pryor, p. 216; *O.R.*, ser. 1, vol. 17, pt. 1, p. 597; Jordan and Pryor, p. 216.
15. Ibid., pp. 217–18; Wyeth, pp. 137–38.
16. *O.R.*, ser. 1, vol. 23, pt. 1, p. 40; Jordan and Pryor, pp. 225–26; Wyeth, pp. 146–47.

17. *O.R.*, ser. 1, vol. 23, pt. 1, p. 40; Jordan and Pryor, pp. 227–28; *O.R.*, ser. 1, vol. 23, pt. 1, p. 40.
18. Wyeth, p. 151.
19. *O.R.*, ser. 1, vol. 23, pt. 1, pp. 88–90.
20. Henry 1, p. 130.
21. *O.R.*, ser. 1, vol. 23, pt. 1, p. 189; Henry 1, p. 135.
22. Ibid., p. 490.
23. Ibid., p. 137.
24. *O.R.*, ser. 1, vol. 23, pt. 1, p. 237.

16

1. Ezra J. Warner, *Generals in Gray* (Baton Rouge, La., and London, 1959), p. 315.
2. Streight's force consisted of troops from the Fifty-first and Seventy-third Indiana infantry regiments, the Third Ohio, the Eightieth Illinois, and the First Middle Tennessee Cavalry (U.S.); *O.R.*, ser. 1, vol. 23, pt. 1, p. 282.
3. Ibid., pp. 287–89.
4. Wyeth, p. 198; *O.R.*, ser. 1, vol. 23, pt. 1, p. 289; Jordan and Pryor, pp. 262–63; Wyeth, pp. 203–04.
5. Jordan and Pryor, p. 264; *O.R.*, ser. 1, vol. 23, pt. 1, p. 290.
6. Ibid.; Jordan and Pryor, p. 266; *O.R.*, ser. 1, vol. 23, pt. 1, p. 290.
7. Wyeth, pp. 211–12.
8. *O.R.*, ser. 1, vol. 23, pt. 1, pp. 290–92.
9. Henry 1, p. 157; Dabney H. Maury, *Recollections of a Virginian* (New York, 1894), p. 209.
10. Jordan and Pryor, pp. 275–76.
11. Henry 1, p. 151.
12. Wyeth, pp. 211–12.

17

1. Henry 1, p. 158.
2. Ibid.; Jordan and Pryor, p. 280.
3. Atlanta *Southern Confederacy*, May 16, 1863, p. 4, copied from Rome (Georgia) *Courier*, May 14, 1863; Wyeth, p. 20; Atlanta *Southern Confederacy*, May 8, 1863, p. 1.
4. Ibid.
5. Jordan and Pryor, p. 281; *O.R.*, ser. 1, vol. 23, pt. 2, p. 287.
6. Ibid., vol. 52, pt. 2, pp. 470, 472.
7. Frank H. Smith, account in Tennessee State Library and Archives, first printed in Nashville *Banner*, April 29, 1911. There are several widely

varying accounts of this encounter, but Smith's is by an eyewitness who became a local historian.

8. Lytle, p. 181; Smith, Tennessee State Library and Archives.
9. Ibid.
10. Wyeth, pp. 225–26; Wills, p. 127; Mathes 2, p. 132.
11. Morton, p. 110.
12. *O.R.*, ser. 1, vol. 30, pt. 4, pp. 507–09.
13. Ibid., pp. 509, 510.
14. Henry 1, p. 496.
15. *O.R.*, ser. 1, vol. 30, pt. 4, p. 588.
16. Jordan and Pryor, pp. 306–07.
17. Ibid., p. 308; Wills, p. 134; Wyeth, p. 240.
18. *O.R.*, ser. 1, vol. 30, pt. 2, p. 524.
19. Ibid., pp. 528–29, 248.
20. Wyeth, p. 250.
21. *O.R.*, ser. 1, vol. 30, pt. 2, pp. 524, 240, 524, 95.
22. Wyeth, p. 252.
23. Ibid., p. 259.
24. *O.R.*, ser. 1, vol. 30, pt. 4, p. 681.
25. Ibid., p. 675.
26. Ibid., pt. 2, pp. 525–26; Henry 1, p. 193, quoting ms. of Lieutenant Tully Brown of Morton's Battery, in Tennessee State Library and Archives; Jordan and Pryor, pp. 353–54.
27. Wills, p. 143; Jordan and Pryor, pp. 357–58.
28. Wyeth, pp. 265–66.

18

1. *O.R.*, ser. 1, vol. 31, pt. 3, p. 604.
2. *Southern Historical Society Papers*, vol. 7, p. 462.
3. *O.R.*, ser. 1, vol. 30, pt. 4, pp. 744–45; ibid., vol. 31, pt. 3, p. 603.
4. Ibid., p. 645.
5. Ibid., p. 646.
6. Ibid., pp. 789, 797, 817.
7. Ibid., pp. 844–45.
8. Ibid., pp. 428–29.
9. Ibid., p. 449.
10. Ibid., pp. 776, 816.
11. Wyeth, pp. 284–85; Henry 1, p. 209.
12. Jordan and Pryor, pp. 374, 375–76, 376–77.
13. *O.R.*, ser. 1, vol. 32, pt. 2, pp. 512–13, 614.

14. Ibid., pp. 616, 662–63, 673.

15. Ibid., p. 614.

16. R. R. Hancock, *Hancock's Diary, or a History of the Second Tennessee Cavalry* (Nashville, 1887), pp. 309–10; Henry 1, p. 215.

17. *O.R.*, ser. 1, vol. 32, pt. 1, pp. 181, 181–82.

18. Ibid., p. 257; Henry 1, p. 223.

19. *O.R.*, ser. 1, vol. 32, pt. 2, pp. 673, 703; ibid., vol. 32, pt. 1, p. 349.

20. Ibid., p. 252; ibid., pt. 2, p. 431; ibid., pt. 1, p. 257.

21. Ibid.

22. Wyeth, pp. 302–03.

23. *O.R.*, ser. 1, vol. 32, pt. 1, p. 353.

24. Ibid., pp. 350, 353; Jordan and Pryor, p. 392; *O.R.*, ser. 1, vol. 32, pt. 1, p. 353.

25. Ibid., pp. 283, 353; Hancock, 322–23.

26. *O.R.*, ser. 1, vol. 32, pt. 1, p. 353; Hancock, pp. 322–23; *O.R.*, ser. 1, vol. 32, pt. 1, p. 304.

27. Ibid., pp. 302, 304–05.

28. Ibid., p. 302.

29. Ibid., vol. 32, pt. 1, p. 268.

30. Morton, pp. 152–53.

31. Wyeth, pp. 314–15.

32. Ibid., pp. 316–17.

33. *O.R.*, ser. 1, vol. 32, pt. 1, p. 354.

34. Wyeth, p. 316; Jordan and Pryor, p. 398; Wyeth, p. 316.

35. *O.R.*, ser. 1, vol. 32, pt. 1, p. 354; Jordan and Pryor, p. 400.

36. Ibid., p. 398.

37. *O.R.*, ser. 1, vol. 32, pt. 1, p. 354.

19

1. *O.R.*, ser. 1, vol. 32, pt. 1, p. 356.

2. William T. Sherman, *Memoirs*, vol. 1, pp. 394–95; Ulysses Simpson Grant, *Memoirs*, vol. 2, p. 108; *Report No. 65, House of Representatives, 38th cong., 1st sess.* (Washington, D.C., 1864) [hereafter referred to as *Congressional Fort Pillow Report*], p. 64; *O.R.*, ser. 1, vol. 32, pt. 1, p. 367.

3. Ibid., p. 347.

4. Ibid., pt. 2, pp. 578–79.

5. Ibid., pp. 586, 594, 602.

6. *Southern Historical Society Papers*, vol. 7, p. 462.

7. *O.R.*, ser. 1, vol. 32, pt. 3, p. 609; ibid., p. 610.

8. Ibid., pp. 622, 644, 648.

9. Ibid., p. 664; Bob Womack, *Call Forth the Mighty Men* (Bessemer, Ala.,

1987), p. 326; Emma Inman Williams, "Historic Madison," *Madison County Historical Society* (Jackson, Tenn., 1946), pp. 178–79; O.R., ser. 1, vol. 32, pt. 3, pp. 664–65, 117; ibid., pp. 117, 118.

10. Ibid., pp. 119, 117.

11. Dudley Taylor Cornish, *The Sable Arm: Negro Troops in the Union Army 1861–65* (New York, 1966), pp. 161–62; O.R., ser. 1, vol. 52, pt. 2, pp. 592, 596, 598–99.

12. Ibid., vol. 32, pt. 3, p. 145.

13. J. P. Young, *The Seventh Tennessee Cavalry (Confederate): A History* (Nashville, Tenn., 1890), pp. 84–85.

14. O.R., ser. 1, vol. 32, pt. 1, p. 612; ibid., p. 547.

15. Chicago *Tribune*, April 3, 1864, p. 2; O.R., ser. 1, vol. 32, pt. 1, pp. 548, 612, 607.

16. Ibid., vol. 52, pt. 2, pp. 649–50.

17. Ibid., vol. 32, pt. 1, p. 548.

18. Cornish, p. 36; J. Harvey Mathes, *Old Guard in Gray* (Memphis, 1897) [hereafter referred to as Mathes 1], pt. 2, p. 98.

19. O.R., ser. 1, vol. 52, pt. 2, p. 653.

20. Ibid., vol. 32, pt. 2, pp. 585, 623.

21. Chicago *Tribune* (which copied the Louisville *Journal*), March 31, 1864, p. 1.

22. Ibid.; Jordan and Pryor, p. 413.

23. Ibid., p. 416; O.R., ser. 1, vol. 32, p. 609.

24. Womack, p. 345; Jordan and Pryor, pp. 422–23.

25. John Cimprich and Robert C. Mainfort Jr., eds., "Fort Pillow Revisited: New Evidence About an Old Controversy," *Civil War History*, December 1982, pp. 293–94; ibid.

26. O.R., ser. 1, vol. 32, pt. 2, p. 759.

27. Ibid., pt. 1, p. 538.

28. Jordan and Pryor, pp. 428–29; ibid, p. 429; Wyeth, p. 342.

29. Hancock, p. 355.

30. Wyeth, p. 344.

31. Jordan and Pryor, p. 431.

32. O.R., ser. 1, vol. 32, pt. 1, p. 573.

33. Jordan and Pryor, p. 434.

34. Cimprich and Mainfort, p. 299; ibid., p. 302; Jordan and Pryor, p. 435; O.R., ser. 1, vol. 32, pt. 1, p. 573; Wyeth, p. 349; *U.S. Serial Set No. 1178, 38th cong., 1st sess.* (Washington, D.C., 1864), p. 86.

35. Jordan and Pryor, p. 435; O.R., ser. 1, vol. 32, pt. 1, p. 561.

36. Ibid., p. 615.

37. Hancock, pp. 363–64; O.R., ser. 1, vol. 32, pt. 1, pp. 561, 535.

38. Ibid., pp. 566, 523.

39. Ibid., p. 531.

40. Womack, p. 347.

41. Chicago *Tribune*, April 16, 1864, p. 1; Cimprich and Mainfort, pp. 294–95.

42. Ibid., pp. 301–02.

43. Ibid., pp. 293, 295; *O.R.*, ser. 1, vol. 32, pt. 1, pp. 592, 557.

44. Hancock, p. 364.

45. Albert Castel, "The Fort Pillow Massacre: A Fresh Examination of the Evidence," *Civil War History*, March 1958, p. 48.

46. *O.R.*, ser. 1, vol. 32, pt. 1, pp. 610, 371.

47. Ibid., p. 558.

48. Ibid., p. 610; Dyer diary manuscript in Tennessee State Library and Archives; *Appeal*, April 18, 1864, p. 1.

49. Cimprich and Mainfort, p. 300; *Official Records of the Union and Confederate Navies*, ser. 1, vol. 26, pp. 224–25.

50. Wills, pp. 188–89.

51. *O.R.*, ser. 1, vol. 32, pt. 1, p. 553.

52. Wyeth, p. 47; *O.R.*, ser. 1, vol. 32, pt. 1, p. 622.

53. Ibid., p. 616.

20

1. *O.R.*, ser. 1, vol. 32, pt. 1, p. 619.

2. Archer H. Shaw, *The Lincoln Encyclopedia* (New York, 1950), p. 121; Chicago *Tribune*, May 4, 1864, p. 3.

3. Cimprich and Mainfort, p. 306; Castel, p. 49; *Congressional Fort Pillow Report*, pp. 13, 15, 20–21, 47, 51; *O.R.*, ser. 1, vol. 32, pt. 1, p. 537; Shaw, p. 121; Cornish, p. 176.

4. Ibid., pp. 168, 163–64.

5. *O.R.*, ser. 1, vol. 32, pt. 1, p. 586; Joseph T. Glatthaar, *Forged in Battle: The Civil War Alliance of Black Soldiers and White Officers* (New York, 1990), pp. 157–58.

6. *O.R.*, ser. 1, vol. 52, pt. 2, pp. 675–76; vol. 32, pt. 3, pp. 623, 782; pt. 1, p. 612.

7. Ibid., pt. 1, p. 613.

8. Ibid., pp. 167, 168.

9. *O.R.*, ser. 1, vol. 32, pt. 3, pp. 527, 536.

10. Ibid., vol. 38, pt. 4, p. 689; pt. 3, p. 625; vol. 39, pt. 2, pp. 627, 640–42.

11. Ibid., pp. 601, 608, 614.

12. Ibid., p. 606; vol. 38, pt. 4, pp. 294–95.

13. Ibid., vol. 39, pt. 1, p. 91.

14. Jordan and Pryor, p. 467; Wyeth, p. 399.

15. Henry 2, p. 124.
16. Wyeth, p. 409; *O.R.*, ser. 1, vol. 39, pt. 1, pp. 222–23.
17. Wyeth, p. 400.
18. Young, pp. 90–92.
19. *O.R.*, ser. 1, vol. 39, pt. 1, p. 132.
20. Henry 2, p. 164.
21. Ibid., pp. 119–21.
22. *O.R.*, ser. 1, vol. 39, pt. 1, p. 124.
23. Morton, p. 178.
24. Ibid., pp. 168–69.
25. Ibid., pp. 178–79; Henry 2, pp. 122, 164.
26. Ibid., pp. 124, 246, 164–65; Jordan and Pryor, p. 473; *O.R.*, ser. 1, vol. 32, pt. 1, p. 586.
27. *O.R.*, ser. 1, vol. 39, pt. 1, p. 215.
28. Ibid., vol. 39, pt. 1, pp. 125–26.
29. Henry 2, p. 127.
30. *O.R.*, ser. 1, vol. 39, pt. 1, p. 214.
31. Henry 2, pp. 128, 167; Morton, p. 181.
32. Henry 2, pp. 127–28.
33. *O.R.*, ser. 1, vol. 39, pt. 1, pp. 225, 95, 127, 230, 225.
34. Henry 1, pp. 299, 514; Jordan and Pryor, p. 481.
35. *O.R.*, ser. 1, vol. 32, pt. 1, pp. 586–91.
36. Ibid., p. 605.

21

1. *O.R.*, ser. 1, vol. 38, pt. 5, pp. 875–76.
2. Wyeth, p. 634; *O.R.*, ser. 1, vol. 39, pt. 2, p. 121.
3. Ibid., p. 142; vol. 38, pt. 5, pp. 16–17, 71, 123.
4. Ibid., vol. 39, pt. 2, p. 671.
5. Herman Hattaway, *General Stephen D. Lee* (Jackson, Miss., 1976), p. 110; Henry 1, p. 318, Stephen D. Lee, "Battle of Harrisburg, or Tupelo," *Publications of the Mississippi Historical Society*, vol. 6, pp. 38–52.
6. *O.R.*, ser. 1, vol. 39, pt. 2, p. 694; Henry 2, p. 171.
7. *O.R.*, ser. 1, vol. 52, pt. 2, pp. 679–80, 682.
8. Ibid., vol. 39, pt. 1, p. 250; Henry 1, p. 314.
9. *O.R.*, ser. 1, vol. 39, pt. 1, pp. 251, 326.
10. Morton, p. 207; ibid., pp. 204–05.
11. Henry 1, p. 317; *O.R.*, ser. 1, vol. 39, pt. 2, pp. 700, 697–98, 700.
12. Hattaway, p. 124; Mathes 2, p. 380; Edwin C. Bearss, *Forrest at Brice's Cross Roads and in North Mississippi in 1864* (repr. Dayton, Ohio, 1991), p. 200; *Southern Historical Society Papers*, vol. 7, pp. 476–77.

13. Ibid., p. 477.
14. *O.R.*, ser. 1, vol. 39, pt. 1, p. 322.
15. Ibid., pp. 330–31.
16. Morton, pp. 207–08; *O.R.*, ser. 1, vol. 39, pt. 1, pp. 336, 322.
17. Lee, p. 48.
18. *O.R.*, ser. 1., vol. 39, pt. 1, p. 326.
19. Mathes 2, pp. 380–81.
20. *O.R.*, ser. 1, vol. 39, pt. 1, p. 252.
21. Ibid., p. 320; Lytle, p. 315.
22. *O.R.*, ser. 1, vol. 39, pt. 1, pp. 252, 323.
23. Ibid.; Lytle, p. 315; *O.R.*, ser. 1, vol. 39, pt. 1, p. 327.
24. Wyeth, pp. 454–55.
25. Mathes 2, pp. 381–82.
26. Henry 2, pp. 178–79.
27. *Southern Historical Society Papers*, vol. 7, p. 477.
28. *O.R.*, ser. 1, vol. 39, pt. 2, pp. 184, 204, 219.
29. Ibid., p. 201; Henry 1, p. 329, quoting Joel Chandler Harris (who served as a clerk with Forrest about this time), "The Shadow Between His Shoulder Blades," p. 45.
30. *O.R.*, ser. 1, vol. 39, pt. 2, pp. 748–49.
31. Ibid., p. 756.
32. Ibid., p. 763.
33. Ibid., p. 765; pt. 1, pp. 397–98.
34. Morton, pp. 218–19.
35. Jordan and Pryor, pp. 535–36; Henry 2, p. 184.
36. Jordan and Pryor, p. 534.
37. Henry 2, p. 257.
38. *O.R.*, ser. 1, vol. 39, pt. 1, pp. 472–73.
39. Jordan and Pryor, pp. 540–43; *O.R.*, ser. 1, vol. 39, pt. 1, p. 472; Henry 1, p. 338.
40. *O.R.*, ser. 1, vol. 39, pt. 1, p. 473.
41. Jordan and Pryor, p. 542.
42. Mathes 2, p. 272.
43. *O.R.*, ser. 1, vol. 39, pt. 1, pp. 470, 471; pt. 2, p. 400.

22

1. Richard Taylor, *Destruction and Reconstruction* (New York, 1879), pp. 198–99.
2. Maury, p. 215.
3. *O.R.*, ser. 1, vol. 39, pt. 2, p. 859.
4. Ibid.

5. Ibid., pt. 1, pp. 519, 521.
6. Ibid., p. 543.
7. Ibid., p. 522; Morton, pp. 227–28.
8. Jordan and Pryor, pp. 564–65.
9. Morton, pp. 231–32.
10. *O.R.*, ser. 1, vol. 39, pt. 1, pp. 544, 533.
11. Jordan and Pryor, p. 566.
12. *O.R.*, ser. 1, vol. 39, pt. 1, pp. 544–45.
13. Ibid., pp. 506–07.
14. Ibid., p. 545.
15. Ibid., pp. 546–47; pt. 2, p. 533; pt. 1, pp. 516–17.
16. Ibid., pp. 547–48, 540.
17. Morton, pp. 239–40.
18. Wyeth, p. 508.
19. *O.R.*, ser. 1, vol. 39, pt. 2, p. 807.
20. Ibid., pp. 810, 815–16.
21. Ibid.
22. Ibid., pp. 816, 838, 859, 837–38.
23. *O.R.*, ser. 1, vol. 39, pt. 1, p. 870.
24. Jordan and Pryor, p. 597.
25. Ibid., p. 599.
26. *O.R.*, ser. 1, vol. 39, pt. 1, pp. 870–71.
27. Ibid., pt. 3, p. 548; Morton, p. 253 [Wills, p. 416, says Rucker later questioned whether Morton was present when the firing began].
28. Jordan and Pryor, 602–03.
29. Morton, pp. 255–56.
30. *O.R.*, ser. 1, vol. 39, pt. 1, p. 862; Jordan and Pryor, p. 604; *O.R.*, ser. 1, vol. 39, pt. 1, p. 871.
31. Jordan and Pryor, p. 605.
32. *O.R.*, ser. 1, vol. 39, pt. 1, pp. 871, 862, 871.
33. Ibid., pt. 3, pp. 853, 868, 879.
34. Ibid., p. 915.

23

1. Bell Irvin Wiley, *The Life of Johnny Reb* (Garden City, N.Y., 1943), p. 338.
2. Morton, p. 14.
3. *O.R.*, ser. 1, vol. 39, pt. 1, p. 808; Andrews, p. 474.
4. Ibid.; Montgomery *Daily Mail*, Nov. 26, 1864; *Appeal* as reprinted in the *Daily Mail*, Nov. 28, 1864.
5. Henry 1, p. 389; *Confederate Veteran*, vol. 16, p. 25; *O.R.*, ser. 1, vol. 45, pt. 1, p. 753; Henry 1, p. 391.

6. *Battles and Leaders of the Civil War* [hereafter referred to as *Battles and Leaders*], vol. 4, pp. 429–32; Henry 1, pp. 390–95; Jordan and Pryor, p. 623.

7. *O.R.*, ser. 1, vol. 45, pt. 1, pp. 753, 770.

8. Wyeth, p. 544.

9. *O.R.*, ser. 1, vol. 45, pt. 1, pp. 116, 115, 116, 653–54.

10. Ibid., p. 116.

11. William R. Scaife, *Hood's Campaign for Tennessee* (Atlanta, 1986), p. 32.

12. *O.R.*, ser. 1, vol. 45, pt. 1, p. 116.

13. Ibid., p. 240.

14. Ibid., pp. 765, 743.

15. Ibid., pp. 754, 708.

16. Andrews, p. 475.

17. *O.R.*, ser. 1, vol. 45, pt. 1, pp. 660, 617, 755.

18. Ibid., p. 746.

19. Wyeth, p. 552; Henry 1, pp. 404–05, 529.

20. *O.R.*, ser. 1, vol. 45, pt. 1, pp. 755, 618, 755, 747.

21. Ibid., p. 756.

22. *Battles and Leaders*, vol. 4, p. 436; *O.R.*, ser. 1, vol. 45, pt. 1, p. 589.

23. Ibid., pp. 552, 578.

24. Ibid., p. 756; Wills, p. 290.

25. *O.R.*, ser. 1, vol. 45, pt. 1, p. 655; Jordan and Pryor, p. 646; *O.R.*, ser. 1, vol. 45, pt. 1, pp. 655, 657.

26. Ibid., p. 757.

27. Ibid.; Morton, p. 294.

28. Henry 1, pp. 414–15.

29. Morton, p. 297.

30. Ibid., p. 298; *O.R.*, ser. 1, vol. 45, pt. 1, p. 727; *Battles and Leaders*, vol. 4, p. 472.

31. *O.R.*, ser. 1, vol. 45, pt. 1, pp. 727–28; Morton, p. 299; *O.R.*, ser. 1, vol. 45, pt. 1, p. 758.

32. Morton, p. 15.

24

1. Jordan and Pryor, pp. 655–56.

2. *O.R.*, ser. 1, vol. 49, pt. 1, p. 930.

3. Ibid., pp. 933, 952, 971–72, 1005; Jordan and Pryor, pp. 657–58.

4. Henry 1, pp. 423–24, quoting Captain Lewis M. Hosea, *Some Side Lights on the War for the Union* (Cleveland, 1912), p. 8.

5. *O.R.*, ser. 2, vol. 8, p. 324.

6. Morton, p. 302; Mathes 2, p. 364.

7. Wyeth, p. 589; *O.R.*, ser. 1, vol. 49, pt. 2, p. 1172.

8. Ibid., pp. 173, 1182, 174, 173.

9. *O.R.*, ser. 1, vol. 49, pt. 1, p. 359; Wyeth, pp. 587–88, 598–99.

10. Ibid., p. 597.

11. *O.R.*, ser. 1, vol. 49, pt. 1, p. 359; ibid., p. 601; Wyeth, pp. 601, 600; Henry 1, p. 431, quoting Major General James Harrison Wilson, *Under the Old Flag* (New York, 1912), vol. 2, pp. 214, 244.

12. Taylor, p. 219; *O.R.*, ser. 1, vol. 49, pt. 1, pp. 360–61; Jordan and Pryor, p. 673.

13. *O.R.*, ser. 1, vol. 49, pt. 1, pp. 360–61.

14. Wyeth, p. 605.

15. Jordan and Pryor, pp. 676–77.

16. *O.R.*, ser. 1, vol. 49, pt. 1, p. 406; Don Piatt and H. V. Boynton, *The Life of General George H. Thomas* (Cincinnati, 1893), p. 614; Wyeth, pp. 609, 610.

17. *O.R.*, ser. 1, vol. 49, pt. 1, p. 406; Jordan and Pryor, p. 678.

18. Henry 1, p. 434, quoting Wilson, vol. 2, pp. 240–45, and Hosea, pp. 17–18.

19. Taylor, pp. 221–22.

20. Jordan and Pryor, p. 679; Andrews, pp. 504–05.

21. Dan T. Carter, *When the War Was Over* (Baton Rouge, La., 1985), pp. 12–13; *O.R.*, ser. 1, vol. 49, pt. 1, pp. 1254, 1263–64.

22. Carter, p. 9, referring to Jason Niles Diary, *Southern Historical Collection*, May 6, 1865.

23. Morton, pp. 315–16.

24. Henry 1, p. 437; *Confederate Veteran*, vol. 23, p. 317.

25. Morton, pp. 316–17.

26. *O.R.*, ser. 1, vol. 49, pt. 2, pp. 552, 569.

27. Morton, pp. 316–19.

28. Ibid., p. 319; Young, *Seventh Tennessee Cavalry*, p. 138.

Part iv: Klansman

25

1. Morton, pp. 322–23.

2. Frank Moore, ed., *The Rebellion Record: A Diary of American Events* (New York, 1865), vol. 8, poetry, pp. 55–56.

3. Memphis *Bulletin* [hereafter referred to as *Bulletin*], May 18, 1865, p. 1; ibid., May 19, 1865, p. 1.

4. Ibid., May 25, 1865, p. 3; ibid., May 28, 1865, p. 3; ibid., June 17, 1865, p. 4.

5. Steve Humphrey, *That D——d Brownlow* (Boone, N.C., 1978), pp. 290–91.

6. Wyeth, pp. 615–16.

26

1. *Bulletin*, May 26, 1865, p. 3.
2. Mathes 2, p. 359; Forrest letter to S. D. Lee, July 1, 1865, reproduced in Mathes 2, p. 336.
3. Ibid.
4. *Joint Report of the Committee on Reconstruction, 1st sess., 39th cong.* (Washington, D.C., 1866), pt. 1, p. 106; Henry 1, p. 441.
5. *Bulletin*, May 27, 1865, p. 3; ibid., June 17, 1865, p. 3.
6. Eric Foner, *Reconstruction: America's Unfinished Revolution, 1865–1877* (New York, 1988), p. 184; ibid., p. 218; Henry 1, pp. 440–41; *Atlanta Constitution*, October 31, 1870, reprinted in *Appeal*, November 3, 1870.
7. James W. Garner, *Reconstruction in Mississippi* (Baton Rouge, La., 1901), p. 94.
8. Humphrey, pp. 298–99.
9. Coahoma County, Miss., land deeds, Book G, pp. 769–70; Wills, pp. 320–21; *Avalanche*, January 1, 1866, p. 1.
10. *Appeal*, December 3, 1865, p. 1; ibid., December 14, 1865, p. 3; ibid., December 15, 1865, p. 3.
11. Ibid., December 26, 1865, p. 2; ibid., December 28, 1865, p. 2; Wyeth, pp. 616–17.
12. *Avalanche*, January 30, 1866, p. 2; ibid., February 22, 1866, p. 2.
13. Wyeth, pp. 616–17.
14. Coahoma County land deeds, Book G, pp. 821–22; Henry 1, p. 442.
15. *Avalanche*, March 6, 1866, p. 3.
16. Ibid., April 3, 1866, p. 2.
17. *Appeal*, April 5, 1866, p. 2.
18. *Avalanche*, April 10, 1866, p. 2; Wills, pp. 327–28, 326, 325; *Avalanche*, April 10, 1866, p. 2.
19. *Appeal*, April 5, 1866, p. 2; Mathes 2, pp. 359–60; Henry 1, p. 442; Wills, pp. 328–29.
20. Coahoma County land deeds, Book H, pp. 7–8; *Appeal*, April 21, 1866, p. 1.
21. *Avalanche*, May 2, 1866, p. 3; *Appeal*, May 2, 1866, p. 3.
22. Capers, p. 178; Chicago *Tribune*, May 8, 1866, p. 3.
23. Ibid.; *Memphis Riots and Massacres, Report of the Select Committee, 39th cong., 1st sess., ser. 1274* (Washington, D.C., 1866), p. 35.

27

1. Iver Bernstein, *The New York City Draft Riots* (New York, 1990), p. 5; Robert H. White, *Messages of the Governors of Tennessee, 1857–1869*, vol. 5 (Nashville, 1955), pp. 504–05.

2. Carter, p. 58.

3. Mathes 1, p. 19.

4. Allen W. Trelease, *White Terror: The Ku Klux Klan Conspiracy and Southern Reconstruction* (New York, 1971), p. 4; J. E. Robuck, *My Own Personal Experience and Observation as a Soldier in the Confederate Army During the Civil War, 1861–65, Also During the Period of Reconstruction* (Memphis, n.d.) p. 105; Stanley F. Horn, *Invisible Empire: The Story of the Ku Klux Klan* (Boston, 1939), pp. 7–12.

5. Ibid., pp. 13, 10, 14–15.

6. Ibid., pp. 15–16.

7. Ibid., pp. 18–19; Robuck, p. 114.

8. Coahoma County land deeds, Book H, pp. 57–59; *Appeal*, July 15, 1873, p. 4; Henry 1, p. 442; Memphis *Commercial Appeal*, March 12, 1939, sect. 4, p. 1; Mathes 2, p. 383.

9. *Avalanche*, September 22, 1866, pp. 1–2; *Appeal*, November 3, 1877, p. 2.

10. Ibid., September 26, 1866, p. 1.

11. Ibid., November 3, 1877, p. 2; William S. McFeely, *Yankee Stepfather: General O. O. Howard and the Freedmen* (New York, 1870), pp. 263–64; National Archives, Record Group 105, Bureau of Refugees, Freedmen and Abandoned Lands for Howard to Forrest, December 15, 1866, and Howard to Maj. Gen. E. O. C Ord, December 29, 1866.

12. *Appeal*, November 3, 1877, p. 2.

13. Horn, p. 21; Trelease, p. 10.

14. Horn, pp. 314–15.

15. Morton, pp. 344–45.

16. Robuck, p. 118.

17. Lytle, p. 383; Horn, 312–13; Charles Bracelen Flood, *Lee: The Last Years* (New York, 1981), p. 122.

18. Lytle, p. 383.

19. Trelease, p. 14; Allen P. Tankersley, *John B. Gordon: A Study in Gallantry* (Atlanta, 1955), p. 248.

20. Ibid., p. 249.

28

1. Horn, pp. 34–35.

2. Ibid., p. 33.

3. Humphrey, p. 328.

4. Lee Meriwether, *My Yesteryears* (Webster Groves, Mo., 1942) p. v.

5. Trelease, p. 23.

6. Mathes 1, pp. 20–21; Elizabeth Meriwether, *Recollections of 92 Years, 1824–1916* (Nashville, 1958) p. 204.

7. *Appeal,* May 7, 1867, p. 1; Henry I, p. 452; *Appeal,* September 21, 1867, p. 1; Coahoma County land deeds, Book H, p. 547; Wills, pp. 339–41.

8. Henry I, pp. 452–53; *Appeal,* September 21, 1867, p. 2; *Avalanche,* February 7, 1868, p. 3.

9. Trelease, pp. 28–30.

10. Ibid., pp. 21–22.

11. *Appeal,* July 8, 1868, p. 1; ibid., July 25, 1868, p. 2.

12. Tankersley, pp. 247–48.

13. Trelease, pp. 50, 76–77; Knoxville *Whig,* April 1, 1868, p. 3.

14. *Avalanche,* May 20, 1868, p. 2.

15. Ibid., June 5, 1868, p. 1.

16. Ibid., May 20, 1868, p. 2; ibid., June 2, 1868, p. 3.

17. *Appeal,* June 2, 1868, p. 1.

18. *Avalanche,* June 10, 1868, p. 3.

19. Ibid.

20. Ibid., p. 2; Knoxville *Whig,* June 17, 1868, p. 2.

21. Basil W. Duke, *Reminiscences* (New York, 1911), pp. 348–49.

22. Ibid., pp. 349–50; New York *Times,* August 17, 1868, p. 8; *Bulletin,* August 28, 1868, p. 4.

23. Manly Wade Wellman, *Giant in Gray: Wade Hampton of South Carolina* (Dayton, Ohio, 1980), p. 223; *Appeal,* July 10, 1868, p. 2; ibid., July 19, 1868, p. 3; Wellman, p. 222.

24. Lytle, p. 381.

29

1. Trelease, pp. 92, 115, 245; *Appeal,* July 8, 1868, p. 2.

2. Ibid., July 7, 1868, p. 1.

3. Ibid., July 21, 1868, p. 2; Elizabeth Meriwether, p. 204.

4. Ibid., pp. 46–47, 49–50, 53–61; Lee Meriwether, in Elizabeth Meriwether, p. v.

5. Elizabeth Meriwether, pp. 204–05.

6. Lytle, p. 383; *Appeal,* August 1, 1868, p. 3; Trelease, p. 109.

7. Ibid., pp. 67, 76–77, 35, 72, 33, 108, 87; New York *Times,* July 6, 1868, p. 2.

8. White, pp. 608–11.

9. Trelease, p. 28; Horn, pp. 363–65.

10. White, p. 609; *Appeal,* July 18, 1868, p. 2.

11. White, pp. 609–13.

12. Ibid., p. 437; Trelease, pp. 169, 44; White, pp. 618–19; New York *Times,* August 6, 1868, p. 1; Humphrey, p. 333.

13. *Bulletin,* August 12, 1868, p. 4.

14. Trelease, p. 45.
15. Horn, p. 95; *Appeal*, August 11, 1868, p. 2.
16. Horn, pp. 410–15.
17. Henry 1, p. 456.

30

1. *Ku Klux Report*, vol. 13, p. 27.
2. Horn, pp. 415–16.
3. New York *Times*, September 13, 1868, p. 5.
4. *Ku Klux Report*, vol. 13, p. 5; ibid., p. 13; ibid., pp. 19, 21.
5. New York *Times*, September 14, 1868, pp. 2, 5.
6. White, p. 623.
7. *Ku Klux Report*, vol. 13, p. 31.
8. Trelease, pp. 156–57; *Ku Klux Report*, vol. 13, p. 27.
9. Horn, pp. 250–51; ibid., p. 252; Mathes 2, p. 230.
10. New York *Times*, November 3, 1868, p. 1.
11. Duke, pp. 351–55.
12. New York *Times*, November 12, 1868, p. 5.
13. Trelease, p. 185; White, pp. 627–28.
14. Trelease, pp. 175–77.
15. *Appeal*, June 16, 1871, p. 1; ibid., February 20, 1874, p. 4.
16. Ibid., November 11, 1868, p. 2.
17. Ibid., November 7, 1868, p. 3.
18. Trelease, pp. 177–78.
19. Ibid., p. 179.
20. Henry 1, pp. 456–57.
21. Horn, p. 357; Trelease, p. 180.
22. Ibid., pp. 179–81; White, p. 651.
23. Henry 1, p. 449; Trelease, p. 184; ibid., p. 183; Morton, p. 345; Horn, p. 359.
24. Trelease, pp. 184–85, 472.

31

1. Trelease, pp. 116, 154, 117, 135.
2. *Avalanche*, March 4, 1869, p. 2; ibid., March 14, 1869, p. 3.
3. New York *Times*, March 15, 1869, p. 5.
4. Wills, pp. 360–61; *Ku Klux Report*, vol. 13, pp. 17–18; New York *Times*, September 28, 1869, p. 3; *Avalanche*, September 23, 1869, p. 2.
5. Ibid., October 7, 1869, p. 2.
6. Trelease, p. 177; *Avalanche*, December 2, 1869, p. 2.
7. *Appeal*, June 6, 1870, p. 2.

8. *Avalanche,* September 23, 1869, p. 2; ibid., November 10, 1869, p. 2.
9. *Appeal,* February 23, 1870, p. 4.
10. Ibid., March 25, 1870, p. 4; ibid., April 14, 1870, p. 2.
11. Ibid., April 15, 1870, p. 1.
12. Ibid., May 11, 1870, p. 4.
13. Ibid., August 7, 1870, p. 4.
14. Ibid., January 5, 1871, p. 1; ibid., March 25, 1871, p. 1; ibid., March 26, 1871, p. 4.
15. Ibid., April 21, 1871, p. 4; ibid., May 21, 1871, p. 1; ibid., June 10, 1871, p. 2.
16. Ibid., May 9, 1871, p. 4; ibid., June 14, 1871, p. 4; ibid., June 16, 1871, p. 2.
17. Ibid., June 25, 1871, p. 1.
18. *Ku Klux Report,* vol. 13, pp. 3–32.

32

1. Horn, p. 375.
2. Ibid., p. 359; *Appeal,* June 18, 1871, p. 1.
3. Ibid., July 22, 1873, p. 4.
4. Wyeth, pp. 618–19.
5. Lee Meriwether, pp. 59–62.
6. *Appeal,* September 11, 1871, p. 2; ibid., December 31, 1871, p. 1; ibid., March 22, 1872, p. 2; ibid., April 7, 1872, p. 2.
7. Ibid., May 10, 1872, p. 2; ibid., April 18, 1872, p. 1.
8. Ibid., June 3, 1872, p. 1; ibid., July 12, 1872, pp. 1, 4; ibid., September 1, 1872, p. 1.
9. Ibid., January 28, 1873, p. 1.
10. Ibid., March 7, 1873, p. 4; ibid., March 25, 1873, p. 4.
11. Ibid., April 26, 1873, p. 4.
12. Ibid., May 6, 1873, p. 4; ibid., May 16, 1873, p. 4; ibid., May 23, 1873, p. 1; ibid., June 21, 1873, p. 2.
13. Ibid., July 9, 1873, p. 4.
14. Ibid., July 15, 1873, p. 4.
15. Henry 1, p. 474.
16. *Appeal,* July 22, 1873, p. 4.
17. Forrest File, Memphis Public Library, a clipping from the Memphis *Commercial Appeal* of January 23, 1954, pp. 1, 3.
18. *Appeal,* January 9, 1874, p. 4; ibid., January 10, 1874, p. 4; ibid., January 13, 1874, p. 4; ibid., January 14, 1874, p. 4; ibid., January 22, 1874, p. 4.
19. Ibid., February 20, 1874, p. 4.
20. Ibid., March 29, 1874, p. 4.
21. Forrest File, Memphis Public Library.

PART V: Penitent

33

1. Memphis *Commercial Appeal*, January 23, 1954, p. 3; Lytle, p. 386.
2. *Avalanche*, February 17, 1876, p. 3; Memphis *Public Ledger*, May 5, 1876, p. 3.
3. New York *Times*, December 9, 1873, p. 1.
4. Ibid., December 25, 1873, p. 4.
5. Memphis *Public Ledger*, August 26, 1874, p. 2; ibid., August 27, 1874, p. 2; Trenton (Tenn.) *Gazette* as quoted in *Appeal*, September 4, 1874, p. 1.
6. Philadelphia *Bulletin* quoted in *Appeal*, September 10, 1874, p. 1; *Appeal*, September 4, 1874, p. 1.
7. Ibid., September 6, 1874, p. 1.
8. Ibid., quoting from Philadelphia *Bulletin*, September 10, 1874, p. 1; Wills, p. 369.
9. *Appeal*, September 23, 1874, p. 1.
10. Morton, illustration facing p. 345; *Appeal*, January 19, 1875, p. 1.
11. Ibid., April 21, 1875, p. 4; ibid., May 5, 1874, p. 4; Lee Meriwether, pp. 63–64.
12. Henry 2, p. 292.
13. *Appeal*, May 29, 1875, p. 4; ibid., May 30, 1875, p. 4.
14. Mathes 2, pp. 366–67.
15. Shields McIlwaine, *Memphis Down in Dixie* (New York, 1948), p. 153.
16. *Appeal*, July 6, 1875, p. 1.
17. Memphis *Press-Scimitar*, February 27, 1954, sect. III, p. 7.
18. Ibid.; James W. Loewen and Charles Sallis, *Mississippi: Conflict & Change* (New York, 1974), p. 161; *Appeal*, August 2, 1876, p. 3.
19. Memphis *Public Ledger* May 5, 1876, p. 3; Lytle, p. 386; Wills, pp. 370–71.
20. Mathes 2, p. 374.
21. Memphis *Commercial Appeal*, clipping hand-dated "7-13-31?" in Forrest File, Memphis Public Library; Mathes 2, p. 374.

34

1. *Avalanche*, November 1, 1877, p. 4.
2. Memphis *Commercial Appeal*, clipping hand-dated "7-13-31?" in Forrest File, Memphis Public Library, Memphis *Appeal*, October 9, 1875, p. 4.
3. Undated petition to Shelby County Court by executors of Forrest estate obviously from late 1877 on file in Memphis Public Library (its official dating of the beginning of the contract as May 8, 1875, contradicts the newspaper report, which has it dated from January 1, 1876); clipping from Memphis *Public Ledger*, May 5, 1876, mislabeled "Memphis *Daily Appeal*" in Memphis Public Library.

4. Ibid., May 14, 1876, p. 1; ibid., August 2, 1876, p. 4.

5. Ibid., September 24, 1876, p. 1; James W. McPherson, *Ordeal by Fire: The Civil War and Reconstruction* (New York, 1982), p. 589.

6. New York *Times*, November 17, 1876, p. 4.

7. Lytle, p. 383; *Appeal*, April 28, 1877; Memphis *Public Ledger*, May 5, 1876, p. 2; *Appeal*, July 7, 1877, p. 4.

8. Wyeth, p. 622; Henry 1, p. 463.

9. *Confederate Veteran*, vol. 4, p. 387.

10. *Appeal*, July 28, 1877, p. 4; ibid., August 10, 1877, p. 4; *Avalanche*, September 2, 1877, p. 4; *Appeal*, August 28, 1877, p. 4; Memphis *Commercial Appeal*, March 28, 1954, p. 12; New York *Times*, September 3, 1877, p. 5.

11. Wyeth, p. 621; *Appeal*, September 8, 1877, p. 2; New York *Times*, September 23, 1877, p. 9.

12. *Appeal*, October 30, 1877, p. 1; ibid., September 21, 1877, p. 4; ibid., September 28, 1877, p. 4; ibid., October 3, 1877, p. 4.

13. *Avalanche*, October 30, 1877, p. 4; ibid., November 1, 1877, p. 4; *Appeal*, November 1, 1877, p. 4.

14. *Avalanche*, October 30, 1877, p. 4; Lee Meriwether, p. 64.

15. *Avalanche*, October 30, 1877, p. 4.

16. Henry 2, p. 292.

EPILOGUE

1. *Appeal*, November 1, 1877, p. 4.

2. Ibid.; *Avalanche*, November 1, 1877, p. 4.

3. New York *Times*, October 30, 1877, p. 5.

4. According to Glatthaar, p. 158, Turner wrote a June 30, 1864, letter to the editor of the *Christian Recorder* (which published it the following July 9) complaining about black atrocities, which were understandably numerous in the face of the official Confederate policy of refusing to treat black soldiers as prisoners of war. Glatthaar also says that at Fort Blakely, Alabama, blacks "charged without orders" and acted "not much different from the behavior of Forrest's command at Fort Pillow," giving no quarter to Confederates who tried to surrender to white Federals to, as Glatthaar quotes a lieutenant in the U.S. Colored Troops, "save being butchered by our niggers." By 1864, Confederates seem to have become desperate. Another Confederate atrocity occurred a few days after Fort Pillow at Poison Springs, Arkansas, where—according to Glatthaar, p. 156—wounded black troops falling into the hands of Confederates "were murdered on the spot."

5. Wyeth, pp. 635–36.

6. Henry 2, pp. 20–24, 31, 33, 35.

7. *Dictionary of American Military Biography*, Roger J. Spiller, ed., Joseph G. Dawson II, assoc. ed., T. Harry Williams, consult. ed. (Westport, Conn., 1984), pp. 337, 340, 339.

8. 1877 Shelby County Court petition filed by executors of Forrest estate, Forrest File, Memphis Public Library.

9. Memphis *Press-Scimitar*, February 9, 1908, p. 7.

10. Memphis *Commercial Appeal*, March 13, 1931, p. 7.

11. Forrest File, Memphis Public Library.

Index

About the Author

Jack Hurst was born in Maryville, Tennessee, in 1941 and graduated from Vanderbilt University in 1964. He was a staff reporter for the Nashville *Tennessean* for ten years, and for the Philadelphia *Inquirer* for three years, and is currently a syndicated columnist for the Chicago *Tribune*. Jack Hurst is descended from a Union cavalryman from Tennessee and related to a Confederate general from Georgia. He lives in Lancaster, Tennessee, with his wife, Donna.